Social Security Programs Throughout the World: Asia and the Pacific, 2006

Social Security Administration
Office of Policy
Office of Research, Evaluation, and Statistics

ISSA • AISS • IVSS

For sale by the Superintendent of Documents, U.S. Government Printing Office
Internet: bookstore.gpo.gov   Phone: toll free (866) 512-1800;   DC area (202) 512-1800
Fax: (202) 512-2104 Mail: Stop IDCC, Washington, DC 20402-0001

ISBN 978-0-16-078094-3

Preface

This second issue in the current four-volume series of *Social Security Programs Throughout the World* reports on the countries of Asia and the Pacific. The combined findings of this series, which also includes volumes on Europe, Africa, and the Americas, are published at 6-month intervals over a 2-year period. Each volume highlights features of social security programs in the particular region.

The information contained in these volumes is crucial to our efforts, and those of researchers in other countries, to review different ways of approaching social security challenges that will enable us to adapt our social security systems to the evolving needs of individuals, households, and families. These efforts are particularly important as each nation faces major demographic changes, especially the increasing number of aged persons, as well as economic and fiscal issues.

Social Security Programs Throughout the World is the product of a cooperative effort between the Social Security Administration (SSA) and the International Social Security Association (ISSA). Founded in 1927, the ISSA is a nonprofit organization bringing together institutions and administrative bodies from countries throughout the world. The ISSA deals with all forms of compulsory social protection that by legislation or national practice are an integral part of a country's social security system.

Previous editions of this report, which date back to 1937, were issued as one volume and were prepared by SSA staff. With the introduction of the four-volume format in 2002, however, the research and writing has been contracted out to the ISSA. The ISSA has conducted the research largely through its numerous country-based correspondents, as well as its Social Security World-wide Database and a myriad of other types of data that must be drawn together to update this report. Members of the ISSA's Information System and Databases Unit analyzed the information and revised the publication to reflect detailed changes to each social security program. *Social Security Programs Throughout the World* is based on information available to the ISSA and SSA with regard to legislation in effect in July 2006, or the last date for which information has been received.

Questions about the report should be sent to Barbara Kritzer at ssptw@ssa.gov. Corrections, updated information, and copies of relevant documentation and legislation are also welcome and may be sent to:

> International Social Security Association
> Information System and Databases Unit
> Case postale 1
> 4 route des Morillons
> CH-1211 Geneva 22
> Switzerland

This report is available at http://www.socialsecurity.gov/policy. For additional copies, please e-mail op.publications@ssa.gov or telephone 202-358-6274.

SSA staff members were responsible for technical and editorial assistance and production. Barbara Kritzer served as technical consultant and provided overall project management. Staff of the Division of Information Resources edited and produced the report and prepared the electronic versions for the Web.

Susan Grad
Acting Associate Commissioner
for Research, Evaluation, and Statistics

March 2007

Contents

Guide to Reading the Country Summaries

Sources of Information 1

Types of Programs
Employment-Related 2
Universal 3
Means-Tested 3
Other Types of Programs 3
Programs Delivered by Financial Services Providers...................................... 3

Format of Country Summaries
Old Age, Disability, and Survivors 4
Sickness and Maternity 8
Work Injury 11
Unemployment.. 13
Family Allowances... 15

Tables
1. Types of social security programs... 17
2. Types of mandatory systems for retirement income 19
3. Demographic and other statistics related to social security, 2006 21
4. Contribution rates for social security programs, 2006............................... 23

Country Summaries

Armenia............................	27	Malaysia..........................	139
Australia...........................	32	Marshall Islands..............	144
Azerbaijan........................	40	Micronesia.......................	146
Bahrain.............................	46	Nepal................................	148
Bangladesh.......................	50	New Zealand....................	151
Brunei...............................	52	Oman................................	158
Burma (Myanmar)	55	Pakistan...........................	160
China................................	58	Palau................................	163
Fiji....................................	63	Papua New Guinea...........	164
Georgia.............................	65	Philippines.......................	166
Hong Kong........................	69	Saudi Arabia....................	172
India.................................	75	Singapore	175
Indonesia..........................	81	Solomon Islands...............	180
Iran...................................	84	Sri Lanka.........................	182
Israel................................	89	Syria................................	185
Japan	98	Taiwan.............................	187
Jordan	106	Thailand	192
Kazakhstan.......................	109	Turkey.............................	197
Kiribati.............................	114	Turkmenistan	202
Korea, South	116	Uzbekistan.......................	207
Kuwait..............................	122	Vanuatu............................	212
Kyrgyzstan	125	Vietnam............................	214
Laos..................................	131	Western Samoa.................	218
Lebanon............................	136	Yemen	220

Guide to Reading the Country Summaries

This second issue in the current four-volume series of *Social Security Programs Throughout the World* reports on the countries of Asia and the Pacific. The combined findings of this series, which also includes volumes on Europe, Africa, and the Americas, are published at 6-month intervals over a 2-year period. Each volume highlights features of social security programs in the particular region.

This guide serves as an overview of programs in all regions. A few political jurisdictions have been excluded because they have no social security system or have issued no information regarding their social security legislation. In the absence of recent information, national programs reported in previous volumes may also be excluded.

In this volume on Asia and the Pacific, the data reported are based on laws and regulations in force in July 2006 or on the last date for which information has been received.[1] Information for each country on types of social security programs, types of mandatory systems for retirement income, contribution rates, and demographic and other statistics related to social security is shown in Tables 1–4 beginning on page 17.

The country summaries show each system's major features. Separate programs in the public sector and specialized funds for such groups as agricultural workers, collective farmers, or the self-employed have not been described in any detail. Benefit arrangements of private employers or individuals are not described in any detail, even though such arrangements may be mandatory in some countries or available as alternatives to statutory programs.

The country summaries also do not refer to international social security agreements that may be in force between two or more countries. Those agreements may modify coverage, contributions, and benefit provisions of national laws summarized in the country write-ups. Since the summary format requires brevity, technical terms have been developed that are concise as well as comparable and are applied to all programs.

The terminology may therefore differ from national concepts or usage.

Sources of Information

Most of the information in this report was collated from the Social Security Programs Throughout the World survey conducted by the International Social Security Association (ISSA) under the sponsorship of the U.S. Social Security Administration (SSA). This information was supplemented by data collected from the ISSA's Developments and Trends Annual Survey. Empirical data were also provided by numerous social security officials throughout the world. (For a listing of countries and jurisdictions that responded to the survey, see page 2.) Important sources of published information include the ISSA Documentation Center; the legislative database of the International Labour Office; and official publications, periodicals, and selected documents received from social security institutions. Information was also received from the Organisation for Economic Co-operation and Development, the World Bank, the International Monetary Fund, and the United Nations Development Programme. During the compilation process, international analysts at both SSA and the ISSA examined the material for factual errors, ambiguous statements, and contradictions in material from different sources.

Types of Programs

The term social security in this report refers to programs established by statute that insure individuals against interruption or loss of earning power and for certain special expenditures arising from marriage, birth, or death. This definition also includes allowances to families for the support of children.

Protection of the insured person and dependents usually is extended through cash payments to replace at least a portion of the income lost as the result of old age, disability, or death; sickness and maternity; work injury; unemployment; or through services, primarily hospitalization, medical care, and rehabilitation. Measures providing cash benefits to replace lost income are usually referred to as income maintenance programs; measures that finance or provide direct services are referred to as benefits in kind.

---

[1] The names of the countries in this report are those used by the U.S. Department of State. The term *country* has been used throughout the volume even though in some instances the term *jurisdiction* may be more appropriate.

Three broad approaches to coverage provide cash benefits under income-maintenance programs; namely, employment-related, universal, and means-tested systems. Under both the employment-related and the universal approaches, the insured, dependents, and survivors can claim benefits as a matter of right. Under means-tested approaches, benefits are based on a comparison of a person's income or resources against a standard measure. Some countries also provide other types of coverage.

Employment-Related

Employment-related systems, commonly referred to as social insurance systems, generally base eligibility for pensions and other periodic payments on length of employment or self-employment or, in the case of family allowances and work injuries, on the existence of the employment relationship itself. The amount of pensions (long-term payments, primarily) and of other periodic (short-term) payments in the event of unemployment, sickness, maternity, or work injury is usually related to the level of earnings before any of these contingencies caused earnings to cease. Such programs are financed entirely or largely from contributions (usually a percentage of earnings) made by employers, workers, or both and are in most instances compulsory for defined categories of workers and their employers.

The creation of notional defined contributions (NDC) is a relatively new method of calculating benefits. NDC schemes are a variant of contributory social insurance that seek to tie benefit entitlements more closely to contributions. A hypothetical account is created for each insured person that is made up of all contributions during his or her working life and, in some cases, credit for unpaid activity such as caregiving. A pension is calculated by dividing that amount by the average life expectancy at the time of retirement and indexing it to various economic factors. When benefits are due, the individual's notional account balance is converted into a periodic pension payment.

Some social insurance systems permit voluntary affiliation of workers, especially the self-employed. In some instances, the government subsidizes such programs to encourage voluntary participation.

The government is, pro forma, the ultimate guarantor of many benefits. In many countries, the national government participates in the financing of employment-related as well as other social security programs. The government may contribute through an appropriation from general revenues based on a percentage of total wages paid to insured workers, finance part or all of the cost of a program, or pay a subsidy to make up any deficit of an insurance fund. In some cases, the government pays the contributions for low-paid workers. These arrangements are separate from obligations the government may have as an employer under systems that cover government employees. Social security contributions and other earmarked income are kept in a dedicated fund and are shown as a separate item in government accounts. (For further details on the gov-

---

Countries in Asia and the Pacific that Responded to the Social Security Programs Throughout the World Survey

Armenia	Japan	Pakistan
Australia	Jordan	Palau
Azerbaijan	Kazakhstan	Philippines
Bahrain	Korea, South	Saudi Arabia
Bangladesh	Kuwait	Singapore
Brunei	Kyrgyzstan	Taiwan
China	Laos	Thailand
Fiji	Malaysia	Uzbekistan
Georgia	Marshall Islands	Vanuatu
Hong Kong	Micronesia	Vietnam
India	Nepal	Western Samoa
Iran	New Zealand	Yemen
Israel	Oman	

ernment's role in financing social security, see Source of Funds under Old Age, Disability, and Survivors.)

Universal

Universal programs provide flat-rate cash benefits to residents or citizens, without consideration of income, employment, or means. Typically financed from general revenues, these benefits may apply to all persons with sufficient residency. Universal programs may include old-age pensions for persons over a certain age; pensions for disabled workers, widow(er)s, and orphans; and family allowances. Most social security systems incorporating a universal program also have a second-tier earnings-related program. Some universal programs, although receiving substantial support from income taxes, are also financed in part by contributions from workers and employers.

Means-Tested

Means-tested programs establish eligibility for benefits by measuring individual or family resources against a calculated standard usually based on subsistence needs. Benefits are limited to applicants who satisfy a means test. The size and type of benefits awarded are determined in each case by administrative decision within the framework of the law.

The specific character of means, needs, or income tests, as well as the weight given to family resources, differ considerably from country to country. Such programs, commonly referred to as social pensions or equalization payments, traditionally are financed primarily from general revenues.

Means-tested systems constitute the sole or principal form of social security in only a few jurisdictions. In other jurisdictions, contributory programs operate in tandem with income-related benefits. In such instances, means- or income-tested programs may be administered by social insurance agencies. Means-tested programs apply to persons who are not in covered employment or whose benefits under employment-related programs, together with other individual or family resources, are inadequate to meet subsistence or special needs. Although means-tested programs can be administered at the national level, they are usually administered locally.

In this report, when national means-tested programs supplement an employment-related benefit, the existence of a means-tested program is generally noted, but no details concerning it are given. When a means-tested program represents the only or principal form of social security, however, further details are provided.

Other Types of Programs

Three other types of programs are those delivered, in the main, through financial services providers (mandatory individual accounts, mandatory occupational pensions, and mandatory private insurance), publicly operated provident funds, and employer-liability systems.

Programs Delivered by Financial Services Providers

Mandatory individual account. Applies to a program where covered persons and/or employers must contribute a certain percentage of earnings to the covered person's individual account managed by a contracted public or private fund manager. The mandate to establish membership in a scheme and the option to choose a fund manager lie with the individual. The accumulated capital in the individual account is normally intended as a source of income replacement for the contingencies of retirement, disability, ill health, or unemployment. It may also be possible for eligible survivors to access the accumulated capital in the case of the insured's death.

Contributions are assigned to an employee's individual account. The employee must pay administrative fees for the management of the individual account and usually purchase a separate policy for disability and survivors insurance.

Mandatory occupational pension. Applies to a program where employers are mandated by law to provide occupational pension schemes financed by employer, and in some cases, employee contributions. Benefits may be paid as a lump sum, annuity, or pension.

Mandatory private insurance. Applies to a program where individuals are mandated by law to purchase insurance directly from a private insurance company.

Provident Funds. These funds, which exist primarily in developing countries, are essentially compulsory savings programs in which regular contributions withheld from employees' wages are enhanced, and often matched, by employers' contributions. The contributions are set aside and invested for each employee in a single, publicly managed fund for later repayment to the worker when defined contingencies occur. Typically, benefits are paid out in the form of a lump sum with accrued interest, although in certain circumstances drawdown provisions enable partial access to savings prior to retirement or other defined contingencies. On retirement, some provident funds also permit beneficiaries to purchase an annuity or opt for a pension. Some provident funds provide pensions for survivors.

Employer-Liability Systems. Under these systems, workers are usually protected through labor codes that require employers, when liable, to provide specified payments or services directly to their employees. Specified payments or services can include the payment of lump-sum gratuities to the aged or disabled; the provision of medical care, paid sick leave, or both; the payment of maternity benefits or family allowances; the provision of temporary or long-term cash benefits and medical care in the case of a work injury; or the payment of severance indemnities in the case of dismissal. Employer-liability systems do not involve any direct pooling of risk, since the liability for payment is placed directly on each employer. Employers may insure themselves against liability, and in some jurisdictions such insurance is compulsory.

Format of Country Summaries

Each country summary discusses five types of programs:

- Old age, disability, and survivors;
- Sickness and maternity;
- Work injury;
- Unemployment; and
- Family allowances.

Old Age, Disability, and Survivors

Benefits under old age, disability, and survivor programs usually cover long-term risks, as distinct from short-term risks such as temporary incapacity resulting from sickness and maternity, work injury, or unemployment. The benefits are normally pensions payable for life or for a considerable number of years. Such benefits are usually provided as part of a single system with common financing and administration as well as interrelated qualifying conditions and benefit formulas.

The laws summarized under Old Age, Disability, and Survivors focus first on benefits providing pensions or lump-sum payments to compensate for loss of income resulting from old age or permanent retirement. Such benefits are usually payable after attaining a specified statutory age. Some countries require complete or substantial retirement in order to become eligible for a pension; other countries pay a retirement pension at a certain age regardless of whether workers retire or not.

The second type of long-term risk for which pensions are provided is disability (referred to in some countries as invalidity). Disability may be generally defined as long-term and more or less total work impairment resulting from a nonoccupational injury or disease. (Disability caused by a work injury or occupational disease is usually compensated under a separate program; see Work Injury, below.)

The third type of pension is payable to dependents of insured workers or pensioners who die. (Pensions for survivors of workers injured while working are usually provided under a separate Work Injury program.)

Coverage. The extent of social security coverage in any given country is determined by a number of diverse factors, including the kind of system, sometimes the age of the system, and the degree of economic development. A program may provide coverage for the entire country or some portion of the workforce.

In principle, universal systems cover the entire population for the contingencies of old age, disability, and survivorship. A person may have to meet certain conditions, such as long-term residence or citizenship. Many countries exclude aliens from benefits unless there is a reciprocal agreement with the country of which they are nationals.

The extent of employment-related benefits is usually determined by the age of the system. Historically, social security coverage was provided first to government employees and members of the armed forces, then to workers in industry and commerce, and eventually extended to the vast majority of wage earners and salaried employees through a general system. As a result, public employees (including military personnel and civil servants), teachers, and employees of public utilities, corporations, or monopolies are still covered by occupation-specific separate systems in many countries.

In many countries, special occupational systems have been set up for certain private-sector employees, such as miners, railway workers, and seamen. Qualifying conditions and benefits are often more liberal than under the general system. The risk involved in an occupation, its strategic importance for economic growth, and the economic and political strength of trade unions may have had a role in shaping the type and size of benefits offered by the particular program.

Groups that might be considered difficult to administer—family workers, domestics, day workers, agricultural workers, and the self-employed—were often initially excluded from coverage. The trend has been to extend coverage to these groups under separate funds or to bring them gradually under the general system. In some countries, noncovered workers become eligible for the right to an eventual pension if they make voluntary contributions at a specified level. Some systems also provide voluntary coverage for women who leave the labor force temporarily to have children or to raise a family, or for self-employed persons not covered by a mandatory program. Some developed countries with younger programs have constructed a unified national program, thus largely bypassing the need for developing separate industrial or agricultural funds.

Most developing countries have extended coverage gradually. Their first steps toward creating a social security system have commonly been to cover wage and salary workers against loss of income due to work injury, and then old age and, less commonly, disability.

In a number of developing countries, particularly in those that were once British colonies, this initial step has come via the institutional form of provident funds. Most provident funds provide coverage for wage and salary workers in the government and private sector. A few funds have exclusions based on the worker's earnings or the size of the firm. Funds that exclude employees with earnings above a certain level from compulsory coverage may in some cases give them the option to affiliate or continue to participate voluntarily.

Source of Funds. The financing of benefits for old-age, disability, and survivor programs can come from three possible sources:

- A percentage of covered wages or salaries paid by the worker,

- A percentage of covered payroll paid by the employer, and

- A government contribution.

Almost all pension programs under social insurance (as distinct from provident funds or universal systems) are financed at least in part by employer and employee contributions. Many derive their funds from all three sources. Contributions are determined by applying a percentage to salaries or wages up to a certain maximum. In many cases the employer pays a larger share.

The government's contribution may be derived from general revenues or, less commonly, from special earmarked or excise taxes (for example, a tax on tobacco, gasoline, or alcoholic beverages). Government contributions may be used in different ways to defray a portion of all expenditures (such as the cost of administration), to make up deficits, or even to finance the total cost of a program. Subsidies may be provided as a lump sum or an amount to make up the difference between employer/employee contributions and the total cost of the system. A number of countries reduce or, in some cases, eliminate contributions for the lowest-paid wage earners, financing their benefits entirely from general revenues or by the employer's contribution.

The contribution rate apportioned between the sources of financing may be identical or progressive, increasing with the size of the wage or changing according to wage class. Where universal and earnings-related systems exist side by side, and the universal benefit is not financed entirely by the government, separate rates may exist for each program. In other instances, flat-rate weekly contributions may finance basic pension programs. These amounts are uniform for all workers of the same age and sex, regardless of earnings level. However, the self-employed may have to contribute at a higher rate than wage and salary workers, thereby making up for the employer's share.

For administrative purposes, a number of countries assess a single overall social security contribution covering several contingencies. Benefits for sickness, work injury, unemployment, and family allowances as well as pensions may be financed from this single contribution. General revenue financing is the sole source of income in some universal systems. The contribution of the resident or citizen may be a percentage of taxable income under a national tax program. General revenues finance all or part of the means-tested supplementary benefits in many countries.

Contribution rates, as a rule, are applied to wages or salaries only up to a statutory ceiling. A portion of the wage of highly paid workers will escape taxation but will also not count in determining the benefit. In a few cases, an earnings ceiling applies for the determination of benefits but not for contribution purposes. In some countries, contribution rates are applied not to actual earnings but to a fixed amount that is set for all earnings falling within a specified range or wage class.

Qualifying Conditions. Qualifying to receive an old-age benefit is usually conditional on two requirements: attainment of a specified age and completion of a specified period of contributions or covered employment. Another common requirement is total or substantial withdrawal from the labor force. In some instances, eligibility is determined by resident status or citizenship.

Old-age benefits generally become payable between ages 60 and 65. In some countries, length-of-service benefits are payable at any age after a certain period of employment, most commonly between 30 and 40 years. In recent years, several countries have increased the age limit for entitlement, in part because of budgetary constraints arising as a consequence of demographic aging.

Many programs require the same pensionable age for women as for men. Others permit women to draw a full pension at an earlier age, even though women generally have a longer life expectancy. Although the norm has been for the differential to be about 5 years, there is now an emerging international trend toward equalizing the statutory retirement age.

Many programs offer optional retirement before the statutory retirement age is reached. A reduced pension, in some instances, may be claimed up to 5 years before the statutory retirement age. Some countries pay a full pension before the regular retirement age if the applicant meets one or more of the following conditions: work in an especially arduous, unhealthy, or hazardous occupation (for example, underground mining); involuntary unemployment for a period near retirement age; physical or mental exhaustion (as distinct from disability) near retirement age; or, occasionally, an especially long period of coverage. Some programs award old-age pensions to workers who are older than the statutory retirement age but who cannot satisfy the regular length-of-coverage requirement. Other programs provide increments to workers who have continued in employment beyond the normal retirement age.

Universal old-age pension systems usually do not require a minimum period of covered employment or contributions. However, most prescribe a minimum period of prior residence.

Some old-age pension systems credit periods during which persons, for reasons beyond their control, were not in covered employment. Credits can be awarded for reasons such as disability, involuntary unemployment, military service, education, child rearing, or training. Other systems disregard these periods and may proportionately reduce benefits for each year below the required minimum. Persons with only a few years of coverage may receive a refund of contributions or a settlement in which a proportion of the full benefit or earnings is paid for each year of contribution.

The majority of old-age pensions financed through social insurance systems require total or substantial withdrawal from covered employment. Under a retirement test, the benefit may be withheld or reduced for those who continue working, depending on the amount of earnings or, less often, the number of hours worked. Universal systems usually do not require retirement from work for receipt of a pension. Provident funds pay the benefit only when the worker leaves covered employment or emigrates.

Some countries provide a number of exemptions that act to eliminate the retirement condition for specified categories of pensioners. For instance, the retirement test may be eliminated for workers who reached a specified age above the minimum pensionable age or for pensioners with long working careers in covered employment. Occupations with manpower shortages may also be exempted from the retirement test.

The principal requirements for receiving a disability benefit are loss of productive capacity after completing a minimum period of work or having met the minimum contribution requirements. Many programs grant the full disability benefit for a two-thirds loss of working capacity in the worker's customary occupation, but this requirement may vary from one-third to 100 percent.

The qualifying period for a disability benefit is usually shorter than for an old-age benefit. Periods of 3 to 5 years of contributions or covered employment are most common. A few countries provide disability benefits in the form of an unlimited extension of ordinary cash sickness benefits.

Entitlement to disability benefits may have age limitations. The lower limit in most systems is in the teens, but it may be related to the lowest age for social insurance or employment or to the maximum age for a family allowance benefit. The upper age limit is frequently the statutory retirement age, when disability benefits may be converted to old-age benefits.

For survivors to be eligible for benefits, most programs require that the deceased worker was a pensioner, completed a minimum period of covered employment, or satisfied the minimum contribution conditions. The qualifying contribution period is often the same as that for the disability benefit. The surviving spouse and orphans may also have to meet certain conditions, such as age requirements.

Old-Age Benefits. The old-age benefit in most countries is a wage-related, periodic payment. However, some countries pay a universal fixed amount that bears no relationship to any prior earnings; others supplement their universal pension with an earnings-related pension.

Provident fund systems make a lump-sum payment, usually a refund of employer and employee contributions plus accrued interest. In programs that have mandatory individual accounts, options for retirement include purchasing an annuity, making withdrawals from an account regulated to guarantee income for an expected lifespan (programmed withdrawals), or a combination of the two (deferred annuity).

Benefits that are related to income are almost always based on average earnings. Some countries compute the average from gross earnings, including various fringe benefits; other countries compute the average from net earnings. Alternatively, some countries have opted to use wage classes rather than actual earnings. The wage classes may be based on occupations or, for administrative convenience, on earnings arranged by size using the midpoint in each step to compute the benefit.

Several methods are used to compensate for averages that may be reduced by low earnings early in a worker's career or by periods without any credited earnings due, for example, to unemployment or military service, and for the effects of price and wage increases due to inflation. One method is to exclude from consideration a number of periods with the lowest (including zero) earnings. In many systems the period over which earnings are averaged may be shortened to the last few years of coverage, or the average may be based on years when the worker had his or her highest earnings. Other systems revalue past earnings by applying an index that usually reflects changes in national average wages or the cost of living. Some assign hypothetical wages before a certain date. Alternatively, others have developed mechanisms for automatic adjustment of workers' wage records based on wage or price changes.

A variety of formulas are used in determining the benefit amount. Instead of a statutory minimum, some systems pay a percentage of average earnings—for instance, 35 percent or 50 percent—that is unchanged by length of coverage once the qualifying period is met. A more common practice is to provide a basic rate—for example, 30 percent of average earnings—plus an increment of 1 percent or 2 percent of earnings either for each year of coverage or for each year in excess of a minimum number of years. Several countries have a weighted benefit formula that returns a larger percentage of earnings to lower-paid workers than to higher-paid workers.

Most systems limit the size of the benefit. Many do so by establishing a ceiling on the earnings taken into account in the computation. Others establish a maximum cash amount or a maximum percentage of average earnings set, for example, at 80 percent. Some systems combine these and other, similar methods.

Most systems supplement the benefit for a wife or child. The wife's supplement may be 50 percent or more of the basic benefit, although in some countries the supplement is payable only for a wife who has reached a specified age, has children in her care, or is disabled. It may also be payable for a dependent husband.

Minimum benefits are intended to maintain a minimum standard of living in many countries, although that objective is not always achieved. A maximum that reduces the effect large families have on benefits is commonly used to limit total benefits, including those of survivors, in the interest of the financial stability of the program.

In some countries, benefits are automatically adjusted to reflect price or wage changes. In other countries, the process is semiautomatic—the adequacy of pensions is reviewed periodically by an advisory board or other administrative body that recommends a benefit adjustment to the government, usually requiring legislative approval.

Disability Benefits. Under most programs, provisions for disability benefits for persons who are permanently disabled as the result of nonoccupational causes are very similar to those for the aged. The same basic formula usually applies for total disability as for old age—a cash amount usually expressed as a percentage of average earnings. Increments and dependents' supplements are generally identical under the total disability and old-age programs. For the totally disabled, a constant-attendance supplement, usually 50 percent of the benefit, may be paid to those who need help on a daily basis. Partial disability benefits, if payable, are usually reduced, according to a fixed scale. The system may also provide rehabilitation and training. Some countries provide higher benefits for workers in arduous or dangerous employment.

Survivor Benefits. Most systems provide periodic benefits for survivors of covered persons or pensioners, although some pay only lump-sum benefits. Survivor benefits are generally a percentage of either the benefit paid to the deceased at death or the benefit to which the insured would have been entitled if he or she had attained pensionable age or become disabled at that time.

Survivor benefits are paid to some categories of widows under nearly all programs. The amount of a widow's benefit usually ranges from 50 percent to 75 percent of the deceased worker's benefit or, in some cases, 100 percent. In some countries, lifetime benefits are payable to every widow whose husband fulfills the necessary qualifying period. More commonly, the provision of widows' benefits is confined to widows who are caring for young children, are above a specified age, or are disabled.

Lifetime benefits are ordinarily payable to aged and disabled widows. Those awarded to younger mothers, however, are usually terminated when all children have passed a certain age, unless the widow has reached a specified age or is disabled. Most widows' benefits also terminate on remarriage, although a final lump-sum grant may be payable under this circumstance. Special provisions govern the rights of the divorced. Age limits for orphan's benefits are in many cases the same as for children's allowances. Many countries fix a somewhat higher age limit for orphans attending school or undergoing an apprenticeship or for those who are incapacitated. The age limit is usually removed for disabled orphans as long as their incapacity continues. Most survivor programs distinguish between half orphans (who have lost one parent) and full orphans (who have lost both parents), with the latter receiving benefits that are 50 percent to 100 percent larger than those for half orphans. Special payments are also made to orphans under the family allowance programs of some countries.

Benefits are payable under a number of programs to widowers of insured workers or pensioners. A widower usually must have been financially dependent on his wife and either disabled or old enough to receive an old-age benefit at her death. A widower's benefit is usually computed in the same way as a widow's benefit.

Many systems also pay benefits to other surviving close relatives, such as parents and grandparents, but only in the absence of qualifying widows, widowers, or children. The maximum total benefit to be split among survivors is usually between 80 percent and 100 percent of the benefit of the deceased.

Administrative Organization. Responsibility for administration generally rests with semiautonomous institutions or funds. These agencies are usually subject to general supervision by a ministry or government department but otherwise are largely self-governing, headed by a tripartite board that includes representatives of workers, employers, and the government. Some boards are bipartite with representatives of workers and employers only or of workers and the government. Where coverage is organized separately for different occupations, or for wage earners and salaried employees or self-employed workers, each program usually has a separate institution or fund. In a few cases, the administration of benefits is placed directly in the hands of a government ministry or department.

Sickness and Maternity

Sickness benefit programs are generally of two types: cash sickness benefits, which are paid when short-term illnesses prevent work, and health care benefits, which are provided in the form of medical, hospital, and pharmaceutical benefits. Some countries maintain a separate program for cash maternity benefits, which are paid to working mothers before and after childbirth. In most countries, however, maternity benefits are administered as part of the cash sickness program. (Benefits provided as a result of work injury or occupational disease are provided either under work injury or sickness programs. Details of the benefits are discussed under Work Injury.)

Cash sickness and maternity benefits as well as health care are usually administered under the same branch of social security. For this reason, these programs are grouped together in the country summaries.

An important reason for grouping these numerous benefits together is that each deals with the risk of temporary incapacity. Moreover, in most instances, such benefits are furnished as part of a single system with common financing and administration. Most countries provide medical care services for sickness and maternity as an integral part of the health insurance system and link those services directly with the provision of cash benefits. In some instances, however, maternity cash grants are covered under family allowance programs. Occasionally, medical care services are provided under a public health program, independent of the social insurance system. Where this dual approach is followed, it has been indicated in the summaries.

Where health care is dispensed directly by the government or its agencies and the principal source of funds is general revenue, the cash benefit program usually continues to be administered on an insurance basis, funded by payroll contributions, and merged in some instances with other aspects of the social insurance system such as old age and disability. However, countries that deliver health care primarily through private facilities and private funding are also likely to have developed separate programs. Where the social security program operates its own medical facilities, both types of benefits are usually administered jointly.

Benefits designed to assist in the provision of long-term care, often at home, are generally supported by a special tax. Benefit levels are normally set to the level of care required. These benefits may be payable in cash, as care services, or as a combination of the two.

Coverage. The proportion of the population covered by sickness programs varies considerably from country to country, in part because of the degree of economic development. Coverage for medical care and cash benefits is generally identical in countries where both types of benefits are provided through the same branch of social insurance. In a number of systems, particularly in developing countries, health care insurance extends only to employees in certain geographic areas. A common procedure is to start the program in major urban centers, then extend coverage gradually to other areas. Both cash sickness and health care programs may exclude agricultural workers, who, in some countries, account for a major proportion of the working population. Where a health insurance system (as distinguished from a national health service program) exists, most workers earning below a certain ceiling participate on a compulsory basis. Others, such as the self-employed, may be permitted to affiliate on a voluntary basis. In several countries, higher-paid employees are specifically excluded from one or both forms of sickness insurance, although some voluntary participation is usually permitted.

Many countries include pensioners as well as other social security beneficiaries under the medical care programs, in some cases without cost to the pensioner. Elsewhere, pensioners pay a percentage of their pension or a fixed premium for all or part of the medical care coverage. Special sickness insurance systems may be maintained for certain workers, such as railway employees, seamen, and public employees.

Where medical care coverage is provided through a national health service rather than social insurance, the program is usually open in principle to virtually all residents. However, restrictions on services to aliens may apply.

Source of Funds. Many countries have merged the financing of sickness programs with that of other social insurance benefits and collect only a single contribution from employees and employers. More commonly, however, a fixed percentage of wages, up to a ceiling, is contributed by employees and employers directly to a separate program that administers both health care and cash benefits for sickness and maternity. Some countries also provide a government contribution. Where medical care is available to residents, generally through some type of national health service, the government usually bears at least the major part of the cost from general revenues.

Qualifying Conditions. Generally, a person becoming ill must be gainfully employed, incapacitated for work, and not receiving regular wages or sick-leave payments from the employer to be eligible for cash sickness benefits. Most programs require claimants to meet a minimum period of contribution or to have some history of work attachment prior to the onset of illness to qualify. Some countries, however, have eliminated the qualifying period.

The length of the qualifying period for cash sickness benefits may range from less than 1 month to 6 months or more and is ordinarily somewhat longer for cash maternity benefits. Usually the period must be fairly recent, such as during the last 6 or 12 months. In the case of medical benefits, a qualifying period is usually not required. In instances where such a requirement does exist, it is generally of a short duration. Most programs providing medical services to dependents of workers, as well as to the workers themselves, do not distinguish in their qualifying conditions between the two types of beneficiaries. A few programs require a longer period of covered employment before medical services are provided to dependents.

Cash Benefits. The cash sickness benefit is usually 50 percent to 75 percent of current average earnings, frequently with supplements for dependents. Most programs, however, fix a maximum benefit amount or do so implicitly through a general earnings ceiling for contributions and benefits. Benefits may be reduced when beneficiaries are hospitalized at the expense of the social insurance system.

A waiting period of 2 to 7 days is imposed under most cash sickness programs. As a result, benefits may not be payable if an illness or injury lasts for only a few days. Similarly, in the case of a prolonged inability to work, benefits may not be payable for the first few days. Under some programs, however, benefits are retroactively paid for the waiting period when the disability continues beyond a specified time, commonly 2 to 3 weeks. A waiting period reduces administrative and benefit costs by excluding many claims for short illnesses or injuries during which relatively little income is lost and can also help reduce the potential for the inappropriate use of the system by workers.

The period during which a worker may receive benefits for a single illness or injury, or in a given 12-month period, is ordinarily limited to 26 weeks. In some instances, however, benefits may be drawn for considerably longer and even for an unlimited duration. A number of countries permit the agency to extend the maximum entitlement period to 39 or 52 weeks in specific cases. In most countries, when cash sickness benefits are exhausted, the recipient is paid a disability benefit if the incapacity continues.

Cash maternity benefits are usually payable for a specified period, both before and after childbirth. A woman is almost always required to stop working while receiving maternity benefits, and usually she must use the prenatal and postnatal medical services provided by the system. In some countries, cash maternity benefits are also payable to working men who stay home to care for a newborn child while the mother returns to work. Cash payments may also be available for a parent, usually the mother, who is absent from work to care for a sick child under a specified age.

The proportion of earnings payable as a cash maternity benefit differs considerably from country to country but, like cash sickness benefits, is usually between 50 percent and 75 percent of current earnings. However, in a number of countries, maternity benefits are set at 100 percent of wages. Benefit payments usually start approximately 6 weeks before the expected date of childbirth and end 6 to 8 weeks afterward.

A nursing allowance—usually 20 percent or 25 percent of the regular maternity benefit and payable for up to 6 months or longer—may be provided in addition to the basic cash maternity benefit. A grant for the purchase of a layette—clothes and other essentials for the new-born baby—or the provision of a layette itself is furnished under some programs. Finally, a lump-sum maternity grant may be paid on the birth of each child. The wives of insured men may be eligible for this grant. Similar benefits may be provided under the family allowance program.

Medical Benefits. Medical services usually include at least general practitioner care, some hospitalization, and essential drugs. Services of specialists, surgery, maternity care, some dental care, a wider range of medicines, and certain appliances are commonly added. Transportation of patients and home-nursing services may be included.

There are three principal methods of meeting the cost of health care: direct payment to providers by the public system or its agents, reimbursement of patients, and direct provision of medical care. These methods may be used in different combinations and may be varied for different kinds of services.

Under direct payment, the social security or public medical care system pays providers directly for services. Patients usually have little or no direct financial dealings with the care provider. Payments for care are commonly made on the basis of contracts with service providers or the professional groups representing them, such as practitioner or hospital associations. Remuneration may take the form of a specified fee for each service, a capitation payment in return for providing all necessary services to a given group of persons, or a salary.

Under the reimbursement method, the patient makes the initial payment and is reimbursed by social security for at least part of the cost. A maximum is sometimes placed on the refund, expressed as a percentage of the bill or a flat amount that can vary with the nature of the service as stipulated in a schedule of fees. The ceiling on medical bills can be placed on the provider when presenting the bill or on the patient when applying for reimbursement. In the latter case, the patient may be reimbursed for only a small portion of the bill.

Under the direct-provision method, the social security system or the government owns and operates its own medical facilities, largely manned by salaried staff. Countries using this method may contract for services of public or private providers. The patient normally pays no fee for most of these services, except insofar as part of the social security contribution may be allotted toward health care funding.

Regardless of the funding method used, all national health care programs provide for at least a small degree of cost-sharing by patients, usually on the assumption that such charges discourage overuse. Thus, the patient either pays part of the cost to the provider or social security agency or receives less than full reimbursement. Even under the direct-provision method, with its emphasis on basically free medical services to the whole population, patients are generally required to pay a small fixed fee per medical treatment or prescription or per day of hospitalization.

Some health care systems have no limit on how long medical care may be provided. Other systems fix a maximum, such as 26 weeks, for services provided for any given illness. Some set limits only on the duration of hospitalization paid for by social security. Where time limits are imposed, they may be extended.

Maternity Care. Prenatal, obstetric, and postnatal care for working women is provided in most countries under the medical services program. Obstetric care is sometimes limited to the services of a midwife, although a doctor is usually available in case of complications. Care in a maternity home or hospital, as well as essential drugs, are ordinarily furnished where necessary.

Medical Care for Dependents. When medical benefits for insured workers are provided through social insurance, similar services are typically furnished to their spouse and young children (and, in some cases, other adults or young relatives living with and dependent on the insured). Maternity care is generally provided to the wife of an insured man.

In some countries, however, medical services available to dependents are more limited than those provided to insured workers or heads of families. Dependents may be subject to a shorter maximum duration for hospital stays, for example, and may have to pay a larger percentage of the cost of certain services such as medicines.

Administrative Organization. The administrative organization for the sickness and maternity program is similar to that of the old-age, disability, and survivor program in many countries. Most commonly, such programs are administered by some form of national social security institution. Under some systems, social security agencies own and operate their own medical facilities, furnishing at least part of the services available under their programs.

In most countries with a national health insurance program, responsibility for detailed administration lies with semiautonomous, nongovernment health funds or associations. All workers covered by the program must join one of these funds.

Each health fund usually requires government approval and must satisfy certain requirements. Work-

ers and, in some countries, employers participate in the election of governing bodies. The funds normally collect contributions within minimum and maximum limits. Funds may also receive government subsidies related to their expenditures or to the number of affiliated members.

National law usually prescribes the minimum (and, in some cases, the maximum) cash benefits and medical services the health funds may provide. In a few countries, individual funds may determine what specific health care benefits and services to provide and arrange to furnish medical care to their members. This arrangement can involve delivery through contracts with care and service providers in the region.

Less commonly, government departments are responsible for the actual provision of medical services, usually through a national health service program. The administrative responsibility for delivering medical services in some countries is often separated from the administration of cash benefit programs, which tend to be linked with other types of social security benefits.

Work Injury

The oldest type of social security —the work injury program—provides compensation for work-connected injuries and occupational illnesses. Such programs usually furnish short- and long-term benefits, depending on both the duration of the incapacity and the age of survivors. Work injury benefits nearly always include cash benefits and medical services. Most countries attempt to maintain separate work injury programs that are not linked directly with other social security measures. In some countries, however, work injury benefits are paid under special provisions of the general social security programs. Both types of programs are dealt with under Work Injury.

Types of Systems. There are two basic types of work injury systems: social insurance systems that use a public fund, and various forms of private or semiprivate arrangements required by law. In most countries, work injury programs operate through a central public fund, which may or may not be part of the general social insurance system. All employers subject to the program must pay contributions to the public carrier, which in turn pays the benefits.

Countries that rely primarily on private arrangements require employers to insure their employees against the risk of employment injury. However, in some of these countries, only private insurance is available. In the remainder, a public fund does exist, but employers are allowed the option of insuring with either a private carrier or the public fund.

The premiums charged by private or mutual insurance companies for work injury protection usually vary according to the experience of work accidents in different undertakings or industries, and the cost of protection may vary widely. In some countries, however, experience rating has been eliminated, and all employers contribute to the program at one rate.

In other instances, workers' compensation laws simply impose on employers a liability to pay direct compensation to injured workers or their survivors. Employers covered under such laws may simply pay benefits from their own funds as injuries occur or may voluntarily purchase a private or mutual insurance contract to protect themselves against risk.

Coverage. Work injury programs commonly cover wage and salary workers and exclude the self-employed. The programs of some of the more highly industrialized nations cover practically all employees. However, many countries either exclude all agricultural employees or cover only those who operate power-driven machinery. Some programs also exclude employees of small enterprises.

Source of Funds. Work injury benefits are financed primarily by employer contributions, reflecting the traditional assumption that employers should be liable when their employees suffer work injuries. Where certain elements of the work injury program are meshed with one or more of the other branches of the social insurance system, however, financing usually involves contributions from employees, employers, and the government. Another exception occurs in countries that provide medical treatment for work-connected illnesses under their ordinary public medical care programs.

Work Injury Benefits. Work injury programs provide cash benefits and medical benefits. Cash benefits under work injury programs may be subdivided into three types: benefits for temporary disability, those for permanent total disability, and those for permanent partial disability. No qualifying period of coverage or employment is ordinarily required for entitlement to work injury benefits. The concept of work-connected injury has gradually been liberalized in a number of countries to cover injuries occurring while commuting to and from work.

Temporary disability benefits are usually payable from the start of an incapacity caused by a work injury, though some programs require a waiting period of 1 to 3 days. Benefits normally continue for a limited period, such as 26 to 52 weeks, depending on the duration of incapacity. If incapacity lasts longer, the temporary disability benefit may be replaced by a permanent disability benefit. In some systems, temporary benefits may continue for an extended period, particularly if the temporary and permanent benefit amounts are identical.

The temporary benefit is nearly always a fraction of the worker's average earnings during a period immediately before injury, usually at least one-third to one-half. A ceiling may be placed on the earnings considered in computing a benefit. Temporary benefits under work injury programs may be significantly higher than in the case of ordinary sickness. Benefits are reduced under some programs when a worker is hospitalized.

The second type of cash work injury benefit is provided in cases of permanent total disability. Generally, it becomes payable immediately after the temporary disability benefit ceases, based on a medical evaluation that the worker's incapacity is both permanent and total. The permanent total disability benefit is usually payable for life, unless the worker's condition changes. A minority of programs, however, pay only a single lump-sum grant equal to several years' wages.

The permanent total disability benefit usually amounts to two-thirds to three-fourths of the worker's average earnings before injury, somewhat higher than for ordinary disability benefits. In addition, unlike ordinary disability benefits, the rate usually does not vary based on the length of employment before the injury. Supplements may be added for dependents and for pensioners requiring the constant attendance of another person, in which case benefits may exceed former earnings. In some countries, the benefits of apprentices or new labor force entrants who become permanently disabled as a result of work-connected injury or disease are based on hypothetical lifetime wages or on the wage of an average worker in the particular industry. This mechanism overcomes the problem of establishing a lifetime benefit based on a very low starting wage.

The third type of cash work injury benefit is provided when permanent partial disability results in a worker's loss of partial working or earning capacity. It is usually equal to a portion of the full benefit corresponding to the percentage loss of capacity. Alternatively, permanent partial disability benefits may be paid in the form of a lump-sum grant. Partial disability payments are generally smaller and are usually stipulated in a schedule of payments for particular types of injuries. Some systems pay the benefit as a lump sum when the extent of disability is below a stated percentage, such as 20 percent.

Medical and hospital care and rehabilitation services are also provided to injured workers. Nearly always free, they may include a somewhat wider range of services than the general sickness program. Ordinarily, they are available until the worker recovers or the condition stabilizes. In some countries, however, free care is limited, the amount being based on the duration of services or their total cost.

Survivor Benefits. Most work injury programs also provide benefits to survivors. These benefits are customarily payable to a widow, regardless of her age, until her death or remarriage; to a disabled widower; and to orphans below specified age limits. If the benefit is not exhausted by the immediate survivors' claims, dependent parents or other relatives may be eligible for small benefits. No minimum period of coverage is required.

Survivor benefits are computed as a percentage of either the worker's average earnings immediately before death or the benefit payable (or potentially payable) at death. These percentages are typically larger than those for survivor benefits under the general program and do not normally vary with the length of covered employment. They are usually about one-third to one-half of the worker's average earnings for a widow, about half as much for each half orphan, and about two-thirds as much for each full orphan. A limit is commonly placed on the combined total of survivor benefits.

Not all countries, however, provide work injury benefits to survivors, and some do not differentiate between survivors in this category and survivors entitled to benefits under other social insurance programs. Some schemes pay only a lump sum equal to the worker's earnings over a specified number of years. Most systems also pay a funeral grant equivalent to a fixed sum or a percentage of the worker's earnings.

Administrative Organization. The functions involved in administering work injury programs differ widely between countries in which employers are not required to insure or can insure with private carriers and those in which a public agency or fund has sole responsibility for both collecting contributions and paying benefits.

Unemployment

Benefits in this category provide compensation for the loss of income resulting from involuntary unemployment. In some countries, these programs are independent of other social security measures and may be closely linked with employment services. In other countries, the unemployment programs are included with social security measures covering other short-term risks, although employment services may continue to verify unemployment and assist in a job search.

Unemployment programs, which exist mainly in industrialized countries, are compulsory and fairly broad in scope in many countries. Some countries restrict benefits to those who satisfy a means or income test. In addition to the programs offering scheduled payments, a number of countries provide lump-sum grants, payable by either a government agency or the employer; other countries provide mandatory individual severance accounts, providing total benefits equal to the value of accumulated capital in the individual account. In addition, employers in many instances are required to pay lump-sum severance indemnities to discharged workers.

Coverage. About half of the compulsory unemployment programs cover the majority of employed persons, regardless of the type of industry. Coverage under the remaining programs is limited to workers in industry and commerce. A few exclude salaried employees earning more than a specified amount. Some have special provisions covering temporary and seasonal employees. Several countries have special occupational unemployment programs, most typically for workers in the building trades, dockworkers, railway employees, and seafarers.

Voluntary insurance systems are limited to industries in which labor unions have established unemployment funds. Membership in these funds is usually compulsory for union members in a covered industry and may be open on a voluntary basis to nonunion employees. Noninsured workers, such as recent school graduates or the self-employed, for example, may be eligible for a government-subsidized assistance benefit when they become unemployed.

Source of Funds. The methods used to finance unemployment insurance are usually based on the same contributory principles as for other branches of social insurance—contributions amounting to a fixed percentage of covered wages are paid on a scheduled basis. In many cases, the government also grants a subsidy, particularly for extended benefits.

Unemployment insurance contributions are shared equally between employees and employers in many countries. Alternatively, the entire contribution may be made by the employer. However, government subsidies may be quite large, amounting to as much as two-thirds of the program's expenditures. Means-tested unemployment assistance programs are financed entirely by governments, with no employer or employee contribution.

Qualifying Conditions. To be entitled to unemployment benefits, a worker must be involuntarily unemployed and have completed a minimum period of contributions or covered employment. The most common qualifying period is 6 months of coverage within the year before employment ceased. In a number of industrialized countries, however, students recently out of school who are unable to find jobs may be eligible for unemployment benefits, even without a work record. This benefit provides a transition from school to work, particularly in periods of recession.

Nearly all unemployment insurance programs, as well as those providing unemployment assistance, require that applicants be capable of, and available for, work. An unemployed worker, therefore, is usually ineligible for unemployment benefits when incapacitated or otherwise unable to accept a job offer. Usually, the unemployed worker must register for work at an employment office and report regularly for as long as payments continue. This close linkage between unemployment benefits and placement services ensures that benefits will be paid only after the person has been informed of any current job opportunities and been found unsuitable.

An unemployed worker who refuses an offer of a suitable job without good cause usually will have benefits temporarily or permanently suspended. Most programs stipulate that the job offered must have been suitable for the worker. The definitions of suitable employment vary considerably. Generally, the criteria include the rate of pay for the job being offered in relation to previous earnings; distance from the worker's home; relationship to the worker's previous occupation, capabilities, and training; and the extent to which the job may involve dangerous or unhealthy work. In some countries, long-term unemployed workers may also be obliged to undertake employment retraining programs. Some countries also provide the unemployed with access to educational placements. If an unemployed worker refuses a place on a retrain-ing program or fails, without good cause, to attend an educational placement, benefits can be temporarily or permanently suspended.

An unemployed worker may satisfy all of the qualifying conditions for a benefit but still be temporarily or permanently disqualified. Nearly all unemployment systems disqualify a worker who left voluntarily without good cause, was dismissed because of misconduct, or participated in a labor dispute leading to a work stoppage that caused the unemployment. The period of disqualification varies considerably, from a few weeks to permanent disqualification.

Unemployment Benefits. Weekly benefits are usually a percentage of average wages during a recent period. A system of wage classes rather than a single fixed percentage is used in some countries. The basic rate of unemployment benefits is usually between 40 percent and 75 percent of average earnings. However, a ceiling on the wages used for benefit computations or maximum benefit provisions may considerably narrow the range within which the basic percentage of wages applies.

Flat-rate amounts are sometimes payable instead of graduated benefits that vary with past wages and customarily differ only according to the family status or, occasionally, the age of the worker. Supplements for a spouse and children are usually added to the basic benefit of unemployed workers who are heads of families. These supplements are either flat-rate amounts or an additional percentage of average earnings.

Most countries have a waiting period of several days before unemployment benefits become payable to reduce the administrative burden of dealing with a very large number of small claims. Most waiting periods are between 3 and 7 days. Some programs have a waiting period for each incident of unemployment, and others limit eligibility to once a year. Longer waiting periods may be prescribed for certain workers, such as the seasonally employed.

Most countries place a limit on the period during which unemployment benefits may be continuously drawn. Typically, this limit varies from 8 to 36 weeks but may be longer in certain cases.

Duration of benefits may also depend on the length of the preceding period of contribution or coverage under the program. That criterion may reduce the maximum duration of unemployment benefits for workers with brief work histories. However, workers with a long history of coverage may, under some programs, have their benefit period extended well beyond the ordinary maximum.

Many unemployed workers who exhaust the right to ordinary benefits continue to receive some assistance, provided their means or incomes are below specified levels. Recipients are usually required to continue registering and reporting at an employment exchange. Some countries that have unemployment assistance but no insurance program do not place any limit on the duration of payments. A number of countries require that insured workers approaching retirement age who have been out of work for a specified period be removed from the unemployment rolls and granted a regular old-age benefit.

Administrative Organization. Unemployment insurance systems may be administered by government departments or self-governing institutions that are usually managed by representatives of insured persons, employers, and the government.

Unemployment insurance and placement service programs usually maintain a close administrative relationship that ensures that benefits are paid only to workers who are registered for employment. At the same time, this liaison increases the effectiveness of the placement services by providing an incentive, through payment of benefits, for unemployed persons to register and report regularly.

Some countries have merged the administration of unemployment insurance and employment service programs, especially at the lower administrative levels where claims are received and benefits are paid by the local employment office. Other countries require persons to register with a local employment office, but the receipt of claims and payment of benefits are handled by a separate insurance office.

In addition to providing an income for the unemployed, many governments have elaborate measures to prevent or counteract unemployment. The typical procedure is for government employment services to work with industry to promote occupational and geographic mobility of labor and to minimize unemployment caused by economic or technological developments; they do that by subsidizing the retraining and relocation of workers in industries that are declining or being restructured. Governments may grant tax and other incentives to industry to locate in areas of high unemployment, or they may allocate funds to create jobs in anticipation of periods of seasonal unemployment.

Family Allowances

The general purpose of family allowance programs is to provide additional income for families with young children in order to meet at least part of the added costs of their support. These programs may either be integrated with other social security measures or kept entirely separate. In this report, family allowances primarily include regular cash payments to families with children. In some countries, they also include school grants, birth grants, maternal and child health services, and allowances for adult dependents.

Most industrialized countries have family allowance programs that originated in Europe in the 19th century when some large companies began paying premiums to workers with large families. The idea spread gradually, and several European countries enacted programs during the 1920s and 1930s. Most programs in operation today, however, have been in place since 1945.

Types of Systems and Coverage. Family allowance programs are of two types: universal and employment-related. The first category, in principle, provides allowances to all resident families with a specified number of children. The second category provides allowances to all wage and salary workers and, in some cases, the self-employed. A few systems cover some categories of nonemployed persons as well. Most employment-related programs continue to pay family allowances to insured persons with dependent children in their care when they retire or are temporarily off the job and receiving sickness, unemployment, work injury, disability, or other benefits. Employment-related family programs also pay allowances to widows of social security beneficiaries.

Source of Funds. The differences in family allowance programs are reflected in the methods used for financing. In universal systems, the entire cost is usually covered by general revenue. By contrast, countries linking eligibility with employment meet the cost of allowances entirely or in considerable part from employer contributions, usually at a uniform percentage-of-payroll rate. If employer contributions do not cover the entire cost, the remainder is usually met from a government subsidy. Few countries require an employee contribution toward family allowances, although some require self-employed persons to contribute.

Eligibility. Eligibility is commonly related to the size of the family and, in some cases, to family income. Many countries pay allowances beginning with the first child. In addition, some countries pay an allowance for a nonemployed wife or other adult dependent, even if there are no children.

In some countries, families with only one child are ineligible. Age requirements vary but are usually tied to the last year of school or the minimum working age, which are often the same and fall somewhere between ages 14 and 18. Under most programs, the continuation of schooling, apprenticeship, or vocational training qualifies a child for an extension of the age limit. In the case of disabled children, many countries extend the age limit beyond that for continued education or pay allowances indefinitely.

Benefits. Whether a program pays a uniform rate for all children or an increasing or decreasing amount for each additional child may reflect the history or the intent of the program. The allowance structure may vary, for example, depending on whether the primary intent is to provide assistance or stimulate population growth. The allowance in most countries is a uniform amount for every child, regardless of the number of children in a family. The allowance in most of the other countries increases for each additional child; the payment for a fifth child, for example, may be considerably larger than that for the first or second child. In a few countries, the allowance per child diminishes or ceases with the addition of children beyond a certain number. In some countries, family allowances (and tax exemptions for dependent family members) have been replaced or supplemented by credits or other forms of a negative income tax.

Administrative Organization. In countries where family allowances are available to all families and financed from general revenues, the program is usually administered by a government department. Where allowances are payable mainly to families of employed persons and financed primarily from employer contributions, the administration may be by a semiautonomous agency under public supervision. Equalization funds may handle the program's financial operations. Each employer pays family allowances to its employees with their wages. The firm then settles with the local fund only the surplus or deficit of contributions due, after deducting allowances the firm has paid. A similar procedure of settling only surpluses or deficits is followed by the local funds in relation to the regional equalization funds under whose supervision they operate. The equalization process makes it possible to fix a uniform contribution rate for all employers, regardless of the number of children in their employees' families. It also eliminates any effect allowances might have in inducing employers to discriminate in hiring workers with children.

Table 1.
Types of social security programs

| Country | Old age, disability, and survivors | Sickness and maternity | | Work injury | Unemploy-ment | Family allowances |
		Cash benefits for both	Cash benefits plus medical care [a]			
Armenia	X	X	X	X	X	X
Australia	X	X	X	X	X	X
Azerbaijan	X	X	X	X	X	X
Bahrain	X	b	b	X	b	b
Bangladesh	c	X	X	X	b	b
Brunei	X	b	d	X	b	b
Burma (Myanmar)	b	X	X	X	b	b
China	X	X	X	X	X	X
Fiji	X	b	b	X	b	b
Georgia	X	e	X	X	f	X
Hong Kong	X	X	X	X	X	X
India	X	X	X	X	X	b
Indonesia	X	b	d	X	b	b
Iran	X	X	X	X	X	X
Israel	X	X	X	X	X	X
Japan	X	X	X	X	X	X
Jordan	X	b	b	X	b	b
Kazakhstan	X	X	X	X	X	X
Kiribati	X	b	b	X	b	b
Korea, South	X	b	d	X	X	b
Kuwait	X	b	b	f	b	b
Kyrgyzstan	X	X	X	X	X	X
Laos	X	X	X	X	b	b
Lebanon	X	b	d	X	b	X
Malaysia	X	b	d	X	b	b
Marshall Islands	X	b	d	b	b	b
Micronesia	X	b	b	b	b	b
Nepal	X	b	d	X	b	b
New Zealand	X	X	X	X	X	X
Oman	X	b	b	X	b	b
Pakistan	X	X	X	X	b	b

(Continued)

Table 1.
Continued

Country	Old age, disability, and survivors	Sickness and maternity		Work injury	Unemploy-ment	Family allowances
		Cash benefits for both	Cash benefits plus medical care [a]			
Palau	X	b	b	b	b	b
Papua New Guinea	X	b	d	X	b	b
Philippines	X	X	X	X	b	b
Saudi Arabia	X	b	b	X	b	b
Singapore	X	X	X	X	b	b
Solomon Islands	X	b	b	X	f	b
Sri Lanka	X	b	d	X	f	X
Syria	X	b	b	X	b	b
Taiwan	X	X	X	X	X	b
Thailand	X	X	X	X	X	X
Turkey	X	X	X	X	X	b
Turkmenistan	X	X	X	X	X	f
Uzbekistan	X	X	X	X	X	X
Vanuatu	X	b	b	b	b	b
Vietnam	X	X	X	X	b	b
Western Samoa	X	b	d	X	b	b
Yemen	X	b	b	X	b	b

SOURCE: Based on information in the country summaries in this volume.

a. Coverage is provided for medical care, hospitalization, or both.
b. Has no program or information is not available.
c. Old-age benefits only.
d. Medical benefits only.
e. Maternity benefits only.
f. Coverage is provided under other programs or through social assistance.

Table 2.
Types of mandatory systems for retirement income

Country	Flat-rate	Earnings-related	Means-tested	Flat-rate universal	Provident funds	Occupational retirement schemes	Individual retirement schemes
Armenia	X [a]		X				
Australia			X			X	
Azerbaijan		X	X				
Bahrain		X					
Bangladesh			X				
Brunei				X	X		
Burma (Myanmar)	b						
China	X [a]						X
Fiji					X		
Georgia	X		X				
Hong Kong			X			X	
India		X	X		X		
Indonesia					X		
Iran		X					
Israel	X		X				
Japan	X	X					
Jordan		X					
Kazakhstan		X	X				X [c]
Kiribati					X		
Korea, South		X					
Kuwait		X					
Kyrgyzstan		X	X				
Laos		X					
Lebanon		X					
Malaysia					X		
Marshall Islands		X					
Micronesia		X					
Nepal				X	X		
New Zealand			X	X			
Oman		X					
Pakistan		X					

(Continued)

Table 2.
Continued

Country	Flat-rate	Earnings-related	Means-tested	Flat-rate universal	Provident funds	Occupational retirement schemes	Individual retirement schemes
Palau		X					
Papua New Guinea						X	
Philippines	X [a]						
Saudi Arabia		X					
Singapore					X		
Solomon Islands					X		
Sri Lanka					X		
Syria		X					
Taiwan		X					
Thailand		X					
Turkey		X					
Turkmenistan		X	X				
Uzbekistan		X	X				
Vanuatu					X		
Vietnam		X					
Western Samoa				X	X		
Yemen		X					

SOURCE: Based on information in the country summaries in this volume.

NOTE: The types of mandatory systems for retirement income are defined as follows:

Flat-rate pension: A pension of uniform amount or one based on years of service or residence but independent of earnings. It is financed by payroll tax contributions from employees, employers, or both.

Earnings-related pension: A pension based on earnings. It is financed by payroll tax contributions from employees, employers, or both.

Means-tested pension: A pension paid to eligible persons whose own or family income, assets, or both fall below designated levels. It is generally financed through government contributions, with no contributions from employers or

Flat-rate universal pension: A pension of uniform amount normally based on residence but independent of earnings. It is generally financed through government contributions, with no contributions from employers or employees.

Provident funds: Employee and employer contributions are set aside for each employee in publicly managed special funds. Benefits are generally paid as a lump sum with accrued interest.

Occupational retirement schemes: Employers are required by law to provide private occupational retirement schemes financed by employer and, in some cases, employee contributions. Benefits are paid as a lump sum, annuity, or pension.

Individual retirement schemes: Employees and, in some cases, employers must contribute a certain percentage of earnings to an individual account managed by a public or private fund manager chosen by the employee. The accumulated capital in the individual account is used to purchase an annuity, make programmed withdrawals, or a combination of the two and may be paid as a lump sum.

a. The benefit formula contains a flat-rate component as well as an element based on earnings or years of coverage.

b. No mandatory system for retirement income.

c. The government provides a guaranteed minimum pension.

Table 3.
Demographic and other statistics related to social security, 2006

Country	Total population (millions)	Percentage 65 or older	Dependency ratio [a]	Life expectancy at birth (years) Men	Women	Statutory pensionable age Men	Women	Early pensionable age [b] Men	Women	GDP per capita (US$)
Armenia	3	12.1	49	68.4	75.1	63	60.5	c	c	4,101
Australia	20.1	12.7	47.7	78.5	83.4	65	63	c	c	30,331
Azerbaijan	8.4	7.1	49	63.8	71.2	62	57	57	52	4,153
Bahrain	0.7	3	43	73.9	76.7	60	55	d	d	20,758
Bangladesh	141.8	3.6	64.2	63.8	65.8	62	62	c	c	1,870
Brunei	0.3	3.2	48.8	75	79.7	55	55	c	c	19,210
Burma (Myanmar)	50.5	4.9	52.4	58.9	64.8	e	e	e	e	1,027
China	1,315	7.6	40.8	70.8	74.6	60	60	c	c	5,896
Fiji	0.8	3.9	55.2	66.5	71	55	55	c	c	6,066
Georgia	4.4	14.3	49.7	67.1	74.8	65	60	c	c	2,844
Hong Kong	7	12	36	79.3	85.1	65	65	c	c	30,822
India	1,103	5.3	59.7	63.2	66.7	58	58	50	50	3,139
Indonesia	222.7	5.5	51	67	70.5	55	55	c	c	3,609
Iran	69.5	4.5	49.7	70.1	73.4	60	55	c	c	7,525
Israel	6.7	10.1	61	78.4	82.6	66	61	c	c	24,382
Japan	128	19.7	50.8	79.1	86.4	65	65	60	60	29,251
Jordan	5.7	3.2	67.5	71	74.2	60	55	45	45	4,688
Kazakhstan	14.8	8.5	46.4	58.7	69.8	63	58	55	55	7,440
Kiribati	0.1	3.4	72.4	59	65.2	50	50	c	c	1,900
Korea, South	47.8	9.4	38.6	74.5	81.9	60	60	55	55	20,499
Kuwait	2.6	1.8	35.5	75.8	80.2	50	50	c	c	19,384
Kyrgyzstan	5.2	6.1	60.2	63.6	71.9	62	57.8	c	c	1,935
Laos	5.9	3.7	80.1	55.3	57.8	60	60	55	55	1,954
Lebanon	3.5	7.3	56	70.9	75.3	64	64	d	d	5,837
Malaysia	25.3	4.6	58.7	71.9	76.5	55	55	c	c	10,276
Marshall Islands	0.06	2.7	68.9	68.3	72.3	60	60	55	55	2,900
Micronesia	0.1	3	65.5	68.2	71.9	60	60	c	c	2,300
Nepal	27.1	3.7	74.5	63	64.1	55	55	c	c	1,490
New Zealand	4	12.3	50.6	77.7	82	65	65	c	c	23,413
Oman	2.5	2.6	58.9	73.7	76.8	60	55	45	45	15,259
Pakistan	157.9	3.8	72.7	64.6	64.9	60	55	55	50	2,225

(Continued)

Table 3.
Continued

Country	Total population (millions)	Per-centage 65 or older	Depend-ency ratio [a]	Life expectancy at birth (years)		Statutory pensionable age		Early pensionable age [b]		GDP per capita (US$)
				Men	Women	Men	Women	Men	Women	
Palau	0.02	4.6	44.7	67.2	73.7	60	60	c	c	7,600
Papua New Guinea	5.8	2.4	74.2	56.6	57.8	55	55	c	c	2,543
Philippines	83	3.9	64.2	69.5	73.8	60	60	c	c	4,614
Saudi Arabia	24.5	2.9	67.2	71.1	75.1	60	55	d	d	13,825
Singapore	4.3	8.5	38.8	77.6	81.3	55	55	c	c	28,077
Solomon Islands	0.478	2.4	75.4	62.6	64.3	50	50	c	c	1,814
Sri Lanka	20.7	7.3	45.5	72.6	77.9	55	50	c	c	4,390
Syria	19	3.1	66.6	72.5	76.2	60	55	d	d	3,610
Taiwan	23	9.8	41.2	74.6	80.4	60	55	c	c	27,500
Thailand	64.2	7.1	44.7	68.5	75	55	55	c	c	8,090
Turkey	73.1	5.4	52.9	67.5	72.1	60	58	c	c	7,753
Turkmenistan	4.8	4.7	57.4	59	67.5	62	57	c	c	4,584
Uzbekistan	26.6	4.7	61	64	70.4	60	55	c	c	1,869
Vanuatu	0.211	3.4	76.6	68.3	72.1	55	55	c	c	3,051
Vietnam	84.2	5.4	53.8	69.9	73.9	60	55	d	d	2,745
Western Samoa	0.185	4.6	82.8	68.5	74.9	55	55	c	c	5,613
Yemen	20.9	2.3	94.9	61.3	64.1	60	55	50	46	879

SOURCES: United Nations Population Division, Department of Economic and Social Affairs. *World Population Prospects: The 2004 Revision Population Database*, available at http://esa.un.org/unpp (2005); *Human Development Report 2006*, prepared for the United Nations Development Programme (Gordonsville, VA: Palgrave Macmillan, 2006); U.S. Central Intelligence Agency. *The World Factbook, 2006* (Washington, DC: Central Intelligence Agency, 2006).

NOTES: Information on statutory and pensionable ages is taken from the country summaries in this volume.

GDP = gross domestic product.

a. Population aged 14 or younger plus population aged 65 or older, divided by population aged 15–64.
b. General early pensionable age only; excludes early pensionable ages for specific groups of employees.
c. The country has no early pensionable age, has one only for specific groups, or information is not available.
d. Regardless of age but subject to other requirements.
e. No mandatory old-age pension system.

Table 4.
Contribution rates for social security programs, 2006 (in percent)

Country	Old age, disability, and survivors			All social security programs [a]		
	Insured person	Employer	Total	Insured person	Employer	Total
Armenia	3 [b]	flat rate [b]	3 [b]	3	flat rate	3 [c]
Australia [d]	0	9	9 [e]	0	9 [f]	9 [e]
Azerbaijan	3 [b]	22 [b]	25 [b]	3	22	25
Bahrain	5	7	12	5	10	15
Bangladesh	0	0	0 [e]	0	0 [f,g]	0 [e]
Brunei	5	5	10 [h]	5	5 [f]	10
Burma (Myanmar) [i]	0	0	0	1.5	2.5	4
China [d]	8	20	28	11	29 [f]	40 [c]
Fiji [d]	8	8	16	8	8 [f]	16
Georgia	0	20	20	0	20	20 [c,j]
Hong Kong [d]	5	5	10	5	5 [f]	10 [c,j]
India [d]	12	17.61	29.61	13.75	22.36	36.11
Indonesia [i]	2	4	6	2	7 [f]	9
Iran	7 [b]	20 [b]	27 [b]	7	23	30 [k]
Israel [d]	0.34	2.76	3.1	3.85	5.4	9.25
Japan [d]	7.32	7.32	14.64	12.22	13.02	25.24 [c]
Jordan	5.5	9	14.5	5.5	11	16.5
Kazakhstan	10	20	30	10	20 [f,g]	30 [c]
Kiribati [i]	7.5	7.5	15	7.5	7.5 [f]	15
Korea, South [d]	4.5	4.5	9	7.19	7.94	15.13
Kuwait [d]	5	10	15	5	10	15
Kyrgyzstan	8 [b]	21 [b]	29 [b]	8	21	29 [c]
Laos [d]	4.5 [b]	5 [b]	9.5 [b]	4.5	5	9.5
Lebanon [d,i]	0	8.5	8.5	2	21.5 [f]	23.5
Malaysia [d]	11.5 [b]	12.5 [b]	24 [b]	11.5	13.75	25.25
Marshall Islands [d]	7	7	14	10.5	10.5	21
Micronesia [d]	6	6	12	6	6	12
Nepal	10	10	20	10	10 [f]	20
New Zealand	0	0	0 [e]	0	0	0 [e]
Oman [d]	6.5	9.5	16	6.5	10.5	17
Pakistan [d]	1	6	7	1 [l]	13	14 [l]

(Continued)

Table 4.
Continued

Country	Old age, disability, and survivors			All social security programs [a]		
	Insured person	Employer	Total	Insured person	Employer	Total
Palau [d]	6	6	12	6	6	12
Papua New Guinea [i]	5	7	12	5	7 [f]	12
Philippines [d]	3.33 [b]	6.07 [b]	9.4 [b]	4.58	8.32	12.9
Saudi Arabia [d]	9	9	18	9	11	20
Singapore [d]	20 [b]	13 [b]	33 [b]	20	13 [f]	33
Solomon Islands [i]	5	7.5	12.5	5	7.5 [f]	12.5
Sri Lanka [i]	8	12	20	8	12 [f]	20 [c]
Syria [i]	7	14	21	7	17	24
Taiwan [d]	1.1 [b]	3.85 [b]	4.95 [b]	2.665	8.005	10.67
Thailand [d]	3.44 [b]	3.44 [b]	6.88 [b]	5	5.2	10.2
Turkey [d,i]	9	11	20	15	16.5	31.5
Turkmenistan [i]	1 [b]	30 [b]	31 [b]	1	32	33
Uzbekistan	2.5 [b]	31.5 [b]	34 [b]	2.5	34.5	37
Vanuatu	4	6	10	4	6	10
Vietnam	5	10	15	6	17	23
Western Samoa	6	5	11 [m]	6	6	12 [m]
Yemen	6	9	15	6	13	19

SOURCE: Based on information in the country summaries in this volume.

a. Includes Old Age, Disability, and Survivors; Sickness and Maternity; Work Injury; Unemployment; and Family Allowances. In some countries, the rate may not cover all of these programs. In some cases, only certain groups, such as wage earners, are represented. When the contribution rate varies, either the average or the lowest rate in the range
b. Also includes the contribution rates for other programs.
c. Government pays the total or most of the cost of family allowances.
d. Contributions are submitted to a ceiling on some benefits.
e. Government pays the total cost of most programs from general revenues.
f. Employers pay the total or most of the cost of work injury benefits.
g. Employers pay the total cost of cash sickness and maternity benefits.
h. Government pays the total cost of the universal old-age and disability pensions.
i. Data are at least 2 years old.
j. Government pays the total cost of unemployment benefits.
k. Employers pay the total cost of family allowances.
l. Plus flat-rate contributions.
m. Government pays the total cost of the universal old-age pension.

Country
Summaries

Armenia

Exchange rate: US$1.00 equals 427 dram (dr.).

Old Age, Disability, and Survivors

Regulatory Framework

First laws: 1956 and 1964.

Current law: 2002 (state pensions), implemented in 2003, with 2005 amendment.

Type of program: Social insurance and social assistance system.

Coverage

Employed and self-employed persons.

Special systems for military personnel, the police, judges, public prosecutors, and their family members.

Source of Funds

Insured person: 3% of net monthly earnings.

The minimum monthly earnings for contribution purposes are 7,000 dr.

There are no maximum earnings for contribution purposes.

The insured's contributions also finance sickness and maternity, work injury, and unemployment benefits.

Self-employed person: 15% of annual income less than 1,200,000 dr. but not less than 60,000 dr. If annual income is greater than 1,200,000 dr., the contribution is a flat rate 180,000 dr., plus 5% of the amount greater than 1,200,000 dr. (Collective farmers are exempt from contributions.)

The self-employed person's contributions also finance sickness and maternity and unemployment benefits.

Employer: A flat-rate monthly contribution of 7,000 dr. is paid on behalf of employees with monthly income less than 20,000 dr.; if the employee's monthly income is between 20,000 dr. and 100,000 dr., a flat-rate monthly contribution of 7,000 dr., plus 15% of the amount greater than 20,000 dr.; if the employee's monthly income exceeds 100,000 dr., a flat-rate monthly contribution of 19,000 dr., plus 5% of the amount greater than 100,000 dr. (If collective farmers are employers, they contribute on behalf of employees.)

The employer's contributions also finance sickness and maternity, work injury, and unemployment benefits.

Government: The total cost of the social pension and subsidies as needed.

The government contributions also finance sickness and maternity, work injury, and unemployment benefits.

Qualifying Conditions

Old-age pension: Age 63 (men) or age 60.5 (women) with at least 25 years of covered employment. The retirement age for women is being raised gradually to age 63 by 2011.

Age 59 with at least 25 years of covered employment of which at least 20 years were in arduous or hazardous work; age 55 with at least 25 years of covered employment of which at least 15 years were in extremely arduous or hazardous work.

Covered employment includes years in university education, years of service in the armed forces, and periods receiving unemployment benefits.

Benefits are payable abroad under reciprocal agreement.

Social pension (old-age): Paid at age 65 (men and women) with less than 5 years of covered employment.

Benefits are payable abroad under reciprocal agreement.

Disability pension: Paid for a total or partial disability with at least 5 years of covered employment. The pension is paid according to three degrees of disability: total incapacity for work and requiring constant attendance (Group I); total incapacity for work but not requiring constant attendance (Group II); or partial incapacity for usual work (Group III).

Covered employment includes years in university education, years of service in the armed forces, and periods receiving unemployment benefits.

A specialized medical committee assesses the degree of disability.

Benefits are payable abroad under reciprocal agreement.

Social pension (disability): Must be assessed as disabled but with less than 5 years of covered employment.

Benefits are payable abroad under reciprocal agreement.

Survivor pension: The pension is paid to a surviving spouse; a person, not employed at the time of deceased's death and not receiving any pension, who cares for the deceased's children, brothers, sisters, or grandchildren younger than age 8; or full orphans younger than age 18 who are not receiving any other pension.

Covered employment includes years in university education, years of service in the armed forces, and periods receiving unemployment benefits.

Benefits are payable abroad under reciprocal agreement.

Old-Age Benefits

Old-age pension: The monthly pension is equal to 100% of the base pension, plus a bonus pension (180 dr. for each full calendar year of covered employment multiplied by a coefficient).

There is no legal minimum pension, but the base pension is 4,250 dr.

There is no maximum pension.

Benefit adjustment: Benefits are adjusted on an ad hoc basis according to available resources.

Social pension: 4,250 dr. a month is paid.

Benefit adjustment: Benefits are adjusted on an ad hoc basis according to available resources.

Permanent Disability Benefits

Disability pension: If assessed as totally incapable for work and requiring constant attendance (Group I), the monthly pension is equal to 140% of the base pension, plus a bonus pension (180 dr. for each full calendar year of covered employment); if assessed as totally incapable for work but not requiring constant attendance (Group II), the monthly pension is equal to 120% of the base pension, plus a bonus pension (180 dr. for each full calendar year of covered employment multiplied by a coefficient).

Partial disability: If assessed with a partial incapacity for usual work (Group III), the monthly pension is equal to 100% of the base pension, plus a bonus pension (180 dr. for each full calendar year of covered employment).

The base pension is 4,250 dr. a month.

There is no maximum pension.

Benefit adjustment: Benefits are adjusted on an ad hoc basis according to available resources.

Social pension: 4,250 dr. a month is paid.

Benefit adjustment: Benefits are adjusted on an ad hoc basis according to available resources.

Survivor Benefits

Survivor pension: 100% of the base pension is paid, plus 50% of the bonus pension (180 dr. for each year the deceased was in covered employment multiplied by a coefficient) for one eligible survivor; 90% for two eligible survivors; 120% for three; or 150% for four or more.

The base pension is 4,250 dr. a month.

The survivor pension paid to a spouse ceases on remarriage.

Full orphan's pension: The pension is equal to 500% of the base pension, plus 50% of the bonus pension (180 dr. for each full calendar year of covered employment of both deceased parents) for one eligible full orphan; 90% for two; 120% for three; or 150% for four or more.

The base pension is 4,250 dr. a month.

There is no maximum survivor pension.

Benefit adjustment: Benefits are adjusted on an ad hoc basis according to available resources.

Administrative Organization

Ministry of Labor and Social Affairs (http://www.mss.am) is responsible for policy.

Council of the State Fund of Social Insurance provides general coordination and oversight.

Regional and provincial branches of the State Fund of Social Insurance (http://www.sif.am) administer the program.

Sickness and Maternity

Regulatory Framework

First law: 1912.

Current laws: 2005 (insurance benefit) and 2005 (social benefits).

Type of program: Social insurance (cash benefits) and universal (medical benefits) system.

Coverage

Cash sickness and maternity benefits: All employed and self-employed persons.

Medical benefits: All persons residing in Armenia.

Source of Funds

Insured person

Cash benefits: See source of funds under Old Age, Disability, and Survivors, above.

Medical benefits: None.

Self-employed person

Cash benefits: See source of funds under Old Age, Disability, and Survivors, above.

Medical benefits: None.

Employer

Cash benefits: See source of funds under Old Age, Disability, and Survivors, above.

Medical benefits: None. (The total cost of optional employer-operated health care facilities.)

Government

Cash benefits: Subsidies as needed from central and local governments and the total cost of child-care leave benefit.

Medical benefits: The total cost of medical benefits is paid by central and local government budgets.

Qualifying Conditions

Cash sickness benefits: There is no minimum qualifying period.

Cash maternity benefits: Must be in insured employment.

Childbirth or adoption lump sum: There is no minimum qualifying period.

Medical benefits: Must reside in Armenia.

Sickness and Maternity Benefits

Sickness benefit: If the insured has been in covered employment for at least 8 years, the benefit is equal to 100% of average earnings in the last 3 months before the incapacity began; if in covered employment for less than 8 years, 80% of earnings is paid.

The benefit is also paid to an insured parent to provide care for a sick child.

Maternity benefit: The benefit is equal to 100% of average earnings regardless of the number of years of covered employment, divided by 30.4 (average number of days in a month) and multiplied by the number of temporary disability days. The benefit is paid for 140 days (70 days before and 70 days after the expected date of childbirth); 155 days if there are complications resulting from childbirth; 180 days for multiple births.

Child-care leave benefit: 2,300 dr. a month is paid until the child is age 2.

Childbirth or adoption lump sum: 35,000 dr. per child is paid during the 6 months after childbirth or adoption.

Benefit adjustment: Benefits are adjusted on an ad hoc basis according to available resources.

Workers' Medical Benefits

Medical services are provided directly to patients by government health providers. Medical benefits include preventive care, general and specialist curative care, hospitalization, laboratory services, dental care, maternity care, and transportation. Care in sanatoria and rest homes is provided, with preference being given to insured workers who may pay part of the cost.

Cost sharing: Patients pay part of the cost of appliances. Medicines, if provided with hospitalization, are free. Medicines are free for pensioners receiving only the base pension.

Dependents' Medical Benefits

Medical services are provided directly to patients by government health providers. Medical benefits include preventive care, general and specialist curative care, hospitalization, laboratory services, dental care, maternity care, and transportation. Care in sanatoria and rest homes is provided, with preference being given to insured workers who may pay part of the cost.

Cost sharing: Patients pay part of the cost of appliances. Medicines, if provided with hospitalization, are free. Medicines are free for disabled children younger than age 16, for all infants until age 1, and for pensioners receiving only the base pension.

Administrative Organization

Cash benefits: State Fund of Social Insurance (http://www.sif.am) provides general oversight of the program. The State Fund's regional and provincial departments within local governments administer benefits.

Medical benefits: Ministry of Health and health departments of local governments provide general supervision and coordination. Medical services are provided through clinics, hospitals, maternity homes, and other facilities administered by the Ministry of Health and local health departments.

Work Injury

Regulatory Framework

First laws: 1955 and 1974.

Current laws: 2002 (state pensions), implemented in 2003; 2005 (insurance benefit); and 2005 (social benefits).

Type of program: Social insurance system.

Coverage

All employed persons.

Exclusions: Self-employed persons.

Source of Funds

Insured person

Cash benefits: See source of funds under Old Age, Disability, and Survivors, above.

Medical benefits: None.

Self-employed person: Not applicable.

Employer

Cash benefits: See source of funds under Old Age, Disability, and Survivors, above.

Medical benefits: None. (The total cost of optional employer-operated health care facilities.)

Government

Cash benefits: Subsidies are provided by central and local governments as required.

Medical benefits: The total cost is paid by central and local governments.

Qualifying Conditions

Work injury benefits: There is no minimum qualifying period.

Temporary Disability Benefits

The daily benefit is calculated on the basis of 100% of the insured's average monthly earnings in the last 3 months.

The benefit is payable from the first day of incapacity until recovery or the award of a permanent disability pension.

A specialized medical committee assesses the degree of disability.

Benefit adjustment: Benefits are adjusted on an ad hoc basis according to available resources.

Permanent Disability Benefits

Permanent disability pension: If assessed with a total incapacity for any work (Group I), the monthly pension is equal to 140% of the base pension, plus a bonus pension (180 dr. for each full calendar year of covered employment); if assessed with a total incapacity for usual work (Group II), the monthly pension is equal to 120% of the base pension, plus a bonus pension (180 dr. for each full calendar year of covered employment multiplied by a coefficient).

Partial disability (Group III): The monthly pension is equal to 100% of the base pension, plus a bonus pension (180 dr. for each year of covered employment).

A specialized medical committee assesses the degree of disability.

The base pension is 4,250 dr. a month.

There is no maximum pension.

Benefit adjustment: Benefits are adjusted on an ad hoc basis according to available resources.

Survivor Benefits

Survivor pension (orphan's pension): 100% of the base pension is paid, plus 50% of the bonus pension (180 dr. for each year the deceased was in covered employment multiplied by a coefficient) for one eligible survivor; 90% for two eligible survivors; 120% for three; or 150% for four or more.

The base pension is 4,250 dr. a month.

Full orphan's pension: The pension is equal to 500% of the base pension, plus 50% of the bonus pension (180 dr. for each full calendar year of covered employment of both deceased parents), for one eligible full orphan; 90% for two; 120% for three; or 150% for four or more.

The base pension is 4,250 dr. a month.

Benefit adjustment: Benefits are adjusted on an ad hoc basis according to available resources.

Administrative Organization

Temporary disability benefits: State Fund of Social Insurance (http://www.sif.am) provides general supervision.

Enterprises and employers pay benefits to their employees.

Permanent disability and survivor pensions: Ministry of Labor and Social Affairs (http://www.mss.am) is responsible for policy.

Council of the State Fund of Social Insurance provides general coordination and oversight.

Regional and provincial branches of the State Fund of Social Insurance (http://www.sif.am) administer the program.

Medical benefits: Ministry of Health and health departments of local governments provide general supervision and coordination. The Ministry of Health and local health departments administer the provision of medical services through clinics, hospitals, maternity homes, and other facilities.

Unemployment

Regulatory Framework

First law: 1921.

Current laws: 1991 (employment), implemented in 1992; and 2005 (social protection), implemented in 2006.

Type of program: Social insurance system.

Coverage

All employed and self-employed persons.

Source of Funds

Insured person: See source of funds under Old Age, Disability, and Survivors, above.

Self-employed person: See source of funds under Old Age, Disability, and Survivors, above.

Employer: See source of funds under Old Age, Disability, and Survivors, above.

Government: Subsidies from central and local governments as needed.

Qualifying Conditions

Unemployment benefits: Must be unemployed as a result of enterprise reorganization, staff reduction, or the cancellation of a collective agreement; a partial benefit is paid if dismissed for a breach of discipline or for voluntary unemployment.

The insured must have a minimum of 12 months of covered employment before unemployment began; a minimum of 12 months of covered employment between two episodes of unemployment; be seeking to rejoin the labor force after a lengthy period of unemployment; or seeking a first job. The insured must be registered at an employment office and be able and willing to work.

Unemployment Benefits

If involuntarily unemployed, the monthly benefit is equal to 100% of the base benefit; if voluntarily unemployed, 80% of the base benefit; if dismissed for a breach of discipline, 60% of the base benefit.

The base benefit is equal to 60% of the national minimum wage (9,000 dr. a month).

The national monthly minimum wage is 15,000 dr.

The benefit is paid for up to 12 months.

Benefit adjustment: Benefits are adjusted on an ad hoc basis according to available resources.

Administrative Organization

State Fund of Social Insurance (http://www.sif.am) and the Ministry of Labor and Social Affairs (http://www.mss.am) provide general oversight.

Employment Service and regional Departments of Labor and Employment administer the program.

Family Allowances

Regulatory Framework

First law: 1944.

Current law: 2005 (social benefits).

Type of program: Universal and social assistance system.

Coverage

Families with children.

Source of Funds

Insured person: None.

Self-employed person: None.

Employer: None.

Government: The total cost.

Qualifying Conditions

Family allowances: The beneficiary must be employed at the time of the child's birth. Benefits are payable for children up to age 18.

Family Allowance Benefits

Family allowances: If the mother is not working, 2,300 dr. a month is paid for a child younger than age 2; if the mother is working, 1,150 dr. a month.

Cash benefits: Each child younger than age 18 receives 7,000 dr. (base sum), plus between 4,000 dr. and 6,500 dr. (supplementary sum), a month.

Benefit adjustment: Benefits are adjusted on an ad hoc basis according to available resources.

Administrative Organization

Ministry of Labor and Social Affairs (http://www.mss.am) is responsible for the program.

Australia

Exchange rate: US$1.00 equals
1.32 Australian dollars (A$).

Old Age, Disability, and Survivors

Regulatory Framework

First laws: 1908 (old-age and disability) and 1942 (widows).

Current laws: 1991 (social security), 1992 (superannuation guarantee), and 1999 (new tax system).

Type of program: Social assistance and mandatory occupational pension system.

Coverage

Social assistance (social security): All persons residing in Australia.

Mandatory occupational pension (superannuation): Employed persons older than age 17 but younger than age 70 earning more than A$450 a month.

Exclusions: Self-employed persons.

Source of Funds

Insured person

Social security: None.

Mandatory occupational pension (superannuation): None required, but voluntary contributions are encouraged.

Self-employed person

Social security: None.

Mandatory occupational pension (superannuation): Voluntary contributions are tax deductible up to a maximum of A$5,000 plus 75% of contributions in excess of this amount or the age-based contribution (younger than age 35, A$15,260; aged 35 to 49, A$42,385; aged 50 or older, A$105,113), whichever is lower. There is no upper limit for voluntary contributions.

Employer

Social security: None.

Mandatory occupational pension (superannuation): 9% of basic wages, up to a maximum of A$35,240 a quarter.

Employer contributions are tax deductible up to certain limits, depending on the age of the employee. For an employee younger than age 35, the maximum annual tax deductible wage is A$15,260; if aged 35 to 49, A$42,385; or if aged 50 or older, A$105,113.

Government

Social security: The total cost from general revenue.

Mandatory occupational pension (superannuation): Matches voluntary contributions made by the insured on the basis of A$1.50 for each A$1.00 contributed, up to A$1,500 a year for low-income earners.

Qualifying Conditions

Old-age pension

Social security (means-tested unless blind): Age 65 (men) or age 63 (women, as of July 1, 2005, and rising gradually to age 65 by July 1, 2013), must reside in Australia at the time of the claim and have 10 years of continuous residence (5 continuous years if the total residence period exceeds 10 years).

Deferred pension (pension bonus scheme): People who work may defer claiming the pension. The minimum deferral period is 12 months, and the covered person must complete at least 960 hours of work each year. The maximum deferral period is 5 years. The bonus is not paid to persons receiving income support or for deferred years after age 75.

The pension is payable abroad indefinitely if the pension begins before the insured leaves the country. The pension benefit may be reduced after 26 weeks.

Carer payment (means-tested): Paid to the provider of constant care at home for a person with an assessed disability, a severe medical condition, or who is frail and elderly.

Rent assistance (means-tested): Paid according to marital status and the level of rent. Special rules apply to people living in retirement villages.

Pharmaceutical allowance: Flat-rate allowances are paid automatically to pensioners.

Telephone allowance: Paid to pensioners to assist with the rental of a telephone line or mobile phone.

Remote area supplement: A tax-free allowance, subject to residence requirements.

Pensioner concession card: Social security recipients are entitled to the concession card that provides reduced costs on certain federal, state or territory, and local government services.

Mandatory occupational pension (superannuation): Aged 55 or older and permanently retired.

Disability pension

Social security (means-tested unless blind): Aged 16 to 65 (men) or aged 16 to 61 (women). A minimum degree of assessed disability of 20% and an inability to work for at least 30 hours a week at full wages, or the inability to be retrained for such work for at least the next 2 years due to a physical or mental impairment or permanent blindness. The person must reside in Australia.

If the assessed disability began before becoming an Australian resident, must reside in Australia at the time of the claim and have 10 years of continuous residence (5 continuous years if the total residence period exceeds 10 years); there is no minimum residence requirement for an Australian resident with an assessed disability.

The pension is payable abroad under specific circumstances but may be reduced.

Mobility allowance (not means-tested): Paid to a disabled person aged 16 or older who cannot use public transportation without substantial assistance.

Rent assistance (means-tested): Paid according to marital status and the level of rent. Special rules apply to people living in retirement villages.

Telephone allowance: Paid to pensioners to assist with the rental of a telephone line or mobile phone.

Remote area supplement: A tax-free allowance, subject to residency requirements.

Pensioner concession card: Social security recipients are entitled to the concession card that provides reduced costs on certain federal, state or territory, and local government services.

Carer payment (means-tested): Paid to the provider of constant care at home for a person who is assessed as disabled (including a child with a profound disability), has a severe medical condition, or is frail and elderly; or for two or more disabled children who are assessed as disabled or who have a severe medical condition.

Carer allowance: Paid to the provider of daily care and attention to a person who is assessed as disabled, has a severe medical condition, or is frail and elderly. The carer and the person receiving care must satisfy residency requirements.

Mandatory occupational pension (superannuation): Benefits may be payable when a superannuation fund member leaves the workforce as the result of a total and permanent disability.

Survivor pension

Social security (means-tested): A widow(er) with dependent children is entitled to benefits under the family tax benefit (Part B). See Family Allowances, below.

Rent assistance (means-tested): Paid according to the level of rent. Special rules apply to people living in retirement villages.

Pensioner concession card: Social security recipients are entitled to the concession card that provides reduced costs on certain federal, state or territory, and local government services.

Double orphan payment: Payable for a child younger than age 16 (aged 16 to 21 if a student not receiving the Youth Allowance) if both parents are dead (or one parent is dead and the other is in a hospital or an institution on a long-term basis, has been in prison for at least 10 years, or whose whereabouts is unknown) or for refugee children under certain circumstances.

Bereavement allowance: Paid to a surviving partner, subject to residence requirements. The surviving partner must have been living with the deceased immediately before his or her death.

Benefits are payable abroad indefinitely if the benefit is in payment before the person leaves the country. The benefit may be reduced after 26 weeks.

Mandatory occupational pension (superannuation): Benefits are payable to the survivors of superannuation fund members.

Old-Age Benefits

Old-age pension

Social security (means-tested unless blind): Up to A$499.70 is paid every 2 weeks for a single person; A$417.20 each for a couple.

Deferred pension (pension bonus scheme): The value of the pension bonus depends on how long the person deferred receiving the old-age pension. Eligible persons receive the bonus and the old-age pension at retirement. The bonus is paid as a lump sum. The maximum bonus is paid for 5 bonus years.

Carer payment (means-tested): Up to A$499.70 is paid every 2 weeks.

Rent assistance (means-tested): Up to A$95.40 is paid every 2 weeks, according to marital status and the level of rent. Special rules apply to people living in retirement villages.

Pharmaceutical allowance: A$5.80 is paid every 2 weeks for a single person; A$2.90 each for a couple.

Telephone allowance: A$81.60 is paid annually to telephone subscribers.

Remote area supplement: A$18.20 is paid every 2 weeks for a single person (A$15.60 each for a couple), plus A$7.30 every 2 weeks for each dependent.

Pensioner concession card: Social security recipients are entitled to the concession card that provides reduced costs on certain federal, state or territory, and local government services.

Benefit adjustment: Most benefits are adjusted in March and September according to changes in the price index (the single-person rate of the old-age pension is maintained as a percentage of average weekly earnings).

Mandatory occupational pension (superannuation): Usually a lump sum equal to the value of total contributions, plus interest minus administrative fees and taxes.

Permanent Disability Benefits

Disability pension

Social security (means-tested unless blind): Up to A$499.70 is paid every 2 weeks for a single person aged 21 or older; A$417.20 each is paid for a married couple. For single people younger than age 18 and living away from the family home, up to A$408.60 is paid every 2 weeks; A$264.40 if living in the family home. For single people aged 18 to 20 and living away from the family home, up to A$408.60 is paid every 2 weeks; A$299.80 if living in the family home. Single disability pensioners younger than age 21 are eligible for the youth disability supplement of A$90.10 every 2 weeks, which is included in the rates of the disability pension payable to pensioners younger than age 21.

Mobility allowance (not means-tested): A$68 is paid every 2 weeks.

Rent assistance (means-tested): Up to A$95.40 is paid every 2 weeks, according to marital status and the level of rent. Special rules apply to people living in retirement villages.

Pharmaceutical allowance: A$5.80 is paid every 2 weeks for a single person; A$2.90 each for a couple.

Telephone allowance: A$81.60 is paid annually to telephone subscribers.

Pensioner concession card: Social security recipients are entitled to the concession card that provides reduced costs on certain federal, state or territory, and local government services.

Carer payment (means-tested): Up to A$499.70 is paid every 2 weeks.

Carer allowance: A$94.70 is paid every 2 weeks.

Benefit adjustment: Benefits are adjusted in March and September according to changes in the price index.

Mandatory occupational pension (superannuation): Benefits may be payable for a total and permanent disability.

Survivor Benefits

Survivor pension

Social security (means-tested): Up to A$464.20 is paid every 2 weeks.

Rent assistance: Up to A$95.40 is paid every 2 weeks, according to marital status and the level of rent. Special rules apply to people living in retirement villages.

Pensioner concession card: Social security recipients are entitled to the concession card that provides reduced costs on certain federal, state or territory, and local government services.

Double orphan payment: See Family Allowances, below.

Bereavement allowance: The difference between the value of the social security pension paid to a single person and that paid to a member of a couple is paid to the surviving partner for 14 weeks after a pensioner's death; one pension payment is credited to the estate of a single pensioner.

Benefit adjustment: Benefits are adjusted in March and September according to changes in the price index.

Mandatory occupational pension (superannuation): Benefits are payable to the survivors of superannuation fund members. Survivor benefits receive favorable tax treatment.

Administrative Organization

Department of Families, Community Services, and Indigenous Affairs (http://www.facsia.gov.au) provides general supervision.

Centrelink (http://www.centrelink.gov.au) administers the programs through 401 customer service centers and 16 area support offices.

Australian Taxation Office (http://www.ato.gov.au) ensures employers make compulsory superannuation contributions.

Australian Prudential Regulation Authority (http://www. apra.gov.au) and the Australian Taxation Office (http://www. ato.gov.au) regulate private superannuation funds.

Sickness and Maternity

Regulatory Framework

First laws: 1944 (cash sickness benefits), 1947 (pharmaceutical benefits), and 1948 (national health).

Current laws: 1973 (national health), with 1983 (health) amendment; and 1991 (social security).

Type of program: Social assistance (cash sickness benefits) and universal (medical benefits) system.

Coverage

Cash sickness benefits: Gainfully employed persons, including self-employed persons, with limited income; and others meeting the qualifying conditions.

Cash maternity benefits: See Family Allowances, below.

Medical and pharmaceutical benefits: All persons residing in Australia.

Source of Funds

Insured person

Sickness benefits: None.

Medical benefits: 1.5% levy on income above A$26,523 for couples and single parents (increased by A$2,253 per child); A$15,718 for single persons with no dependents.

Higher income thresholds apply to low-income earners and to senior citizens.

Exemption from the levy: Veterans, war widows, and armed forces personnel with dependents (half levy if no dependents).

Pharmaceutical benefits scheme: Cost sharing for prescription drugs.

Self-employed person

Sickness benefits: None.

Medical benefits: 1.5% levy on income above A$26,523 for couples and single parents (increased by A$2,253 per child); A$15,718 for single persons with no dependents.

Higher income thresholds apply to low-income earners and to senior citizens.

Exemption from the levy: Veterans, war widows, and armed forces personnel with dependents (half levy if no dependents).

Pharmaceutical benefits scheme: Cost sharing for prescription drugs.

Employer

Sickness benefits: None.

Medical benefits: None.

Pharmaceutical benefits scheme: None.

Government

Sickness benefits: The total cost of cash benefits.

Medical benefits: Rebates for medical and hospital benefits.

Pharmaceutical benefits scheme: Assistance is provided toward the cost of a wide range of prescription drugs.

Government funding is provided for residential and community aged care.

Federal government general revenue grants and medicare grants provided to states and territories for public hospital operating costs meet approximately 40% to 50% of the total funding of the medical benefits program.

Qualifying Conditions

Cash sickness benefits (means-tested): Age 21 (age 25 if a full-time student) or older, not receiving the old-age pension, and residing in Australia. Sickness or injury prevents work and the claimant must have a job to return to or intends to resume full-time studies.

Dependent's supplement (means-tested): Payable for a cohabiting opposite-sex partner (regardless of marriage) and dependent children.

Cash maternity benefits: See Family Allowances, below.

Medical and pharmaceutical benefits: Must reside in Australia.

Sickness and Maternity Benefits

Sickness benefit (means-tested): Up to A$351.10 each is paid every 2 weeks for a couple; up to A$389.20 is paid every 2 weeks for a single person aged 21 or older with no dependents, up to A$421 every 2 weeks if single with

dependents, or up to A$426.80 if single and aged 60 or older.

For benefits for children, see Family Allowances, below.

Benefits are payable every 2 weeks after a 7-day waiting period for as long as the person is qualified.

Rent assistance (means-tested): Up to A$95.40 is paid every 2 weeks, according to marital status and the level of rent. Special rules apply to people living in retirement villages.

Pharmaceutical allowance: A$5.80 is paid every 2 weeks for a single person; A$2.90 each for a couple.

Telephone allowance: A$81.60 is paid annually to telephone subscribers.

Remote area supplement: A$18.20 is paid every 2 weeks for a single person (A$15.60 each for a couple), plus A$7.30 every 2 weeks for each dependent.

Concession card: Provided with a health care card that makes available additional health, household, and transportation assistance from state, territory, and local governments.

Benefit adjustment: Most benefits are adjusted in March and September according to changes in the price index.

Maternity benefits: See Family Allowances, below.

Workers' Medical Benefits

The patient pays 15% of the scheduled fee for outpatient ambulatory care or A$50.10, whichever is less (indexed annually for price changes).

Hospital benefits: Free standard ward inpatient treatment is provided by staff doctors in public hospitals.

Private benefit organizations pay for private hospital stays, or public hospitals charge for those who choose treatment by their own physician in public hospitals.

Pharmaceutical benefit: A fee of up to A$22.40 per prescription applies to most prescribed medicines. Pensioners, benefit recipients, and low-income persons pay a A$3.60 fee per prescription.

Dependents' Medical Benefits

The same medical and hospital benefits as for the head of the family. The patient pays 15% of the scheduled fee for outpatient ambulatory care or A$50.10, whichever is less (indexed annually for price changes).

Hospital benefits: Free standard ward inpatient treatment is provided by staff doctors in public hospitals.

Family membership in a private benefit organization will also cover dependents. Private benefit organizations pay for private hospital stays, or public hospitals charge for those who choose treatment by their own physician in public hospitals.

Pharmaceutical benefit: A fee of up to A$22.40 per prescription applies to most prescribed medicines. Pensioners, benefit recipients, and low-income persons pay a A$3.60 fee per prescription.

Administrative Organization

Sickness benefits: Department of Families, Community Services, and Indigenous Affairs (http://www.facsia.gov.au) provides general supervision.

Centrelink (http://www.centrelink.gov.au) administers the programs through 401 customer service centers and 16 area support offices.

Medical and pharmaceutical benefits: Medicare Australia (http://www.medicareaustralia.gov.au) administers the program.

Department of Health and Aging (http://www.health.gov.au) is responsible for policy development.

Work Injury

Regulatory Framework

First laws: For the six states, enacted between 1902 (Western Australia) and 1918 (Tasmania); 1911 (seamen's compensation); 1912 (commonwealth government employees); 1931 (Northern Territory); and 1946 (Australian Capital Territory).

Current laws: 1942, 1987, and 1998 (New South Wales); 1958, 1985, and 1993 (Victoria); 1986 (South Australia); 1986 (Northern Territory); 1988 (Tasmania); 1988 (federal government employees); 1989 (Australian Capital Territory); 1996 (Queensland); and 2001 (Western Australia).

Type of program: Employer-liability system, involving compulsory insurance with a public or private carrier under schemes established and run by state and territory governments.

Note: Some states still allow common-law actions for negligence against an employer.

Coverage

Employed persons.

Self-employed persons may self-insure.

Exclusions: Self-employed persons are not usually covered.

Source of Funds

Insured person: None.

Self-employed person: The total cost of self-insurance on a voluntary basis.

Employer: The total cost for employees is met through insurance premiums. The cost of premiums varies with the assessed degree of risk. Some employers are permitted to self-insure.

Government: None, except as a self-insurer for its own employees.

Qualifying Conditions

Work injury benefits: There is no minimum qualifying period.

Temporary Disability Benefits

The benefit varies depending on the state or territory in which the award is made. Generally, the benefit is equal to at least 95% of earnings and is paid for a minimum of 26 weeks. Benefits may be payable for an extended period at reduced levels.

The maximum benefit levels are determined by the states and territories. Usually, the maximum benefit is set by a ceiling on the weekly benefit payment or is based on a total lump-sum value.

Income from the temporary disability benefit is taken into account in the calculation of entitlement to means-tested disability benefits payable under Old Age, Disability and Survivors, above.

Benefit adjustment: Benefits are adjusted in March and September according to changes in the price index.

Permanent Disability Benefits

Permanent disability pension: Payable for a total disability.

Partial disability pension: The pension is determined by the amount of earnings lost subject to a limit; lump-sum payments are made for specific injuries.

Income from the permanent disability pension is taken into account in the calculation of entitlement to means-tested disability benefits payable under Old Age, Disability, and Survivors, above.

Lump-sum payments made for specified permanent injuries and for pain and suffering vary among states and territories.

Benefit adjustment: Benefits are adjusted in March and September according to changes in the price index.

Workers' Medical Benefits

Benefits include the reasonable cost of medical care, hospitalization, transportation, nursing care, and rehabilitation.

Survivor Benefits

Survivor benefit: A lump sum is paid for the survivor, plus a lump sum or a weekly payment for each child. In some cases, the benefit for a child may include a lump sum as well as a weekly payment.

Benefit adjustment: Benefits are adjusted in March and September according to changes in the price index.

Funeral grant: The reasonable cost of a funeral.

Administrative Organization

Worker's Compensation Board or Commission administers claims in most states (except Australian Capital Territory, Northern Territory, Tasmania, and Western Australia, which have multi-insurer systems with claims administered by insurers).

Worker's Compensation Board or Commission administers claims for Commonwealth employees.

Australian government agencies: Safety, Rehabilitation, and Compensation Commission (http://www.comcare.gov.au/src_commission); and Seafarers Safety, Rehabilitation, and Compensation Authority (Seacare Authority) (http://www.seacare.gov.au).

Unemployment

Regulatory Framework

First law: 1944.

Current law: 1991 (social security, job search, and newstart), with 1998 (youth allowance) amendment.

Type of program: Social assistance system.

Coverage

Gainfully employed persons (also payable to those not previously gainfully employed who meet the qualifying conditions), including self-employed persons.

Source of Funds

Insured person: None.

Self-employed person: None.

Employer: None.

Government: The total cost from general revenue.

Qualifying Conditions

Youth allowance (means-tested): Unemployed young people aged 16 to 20 (age 24 if a full-time student, aged 15 or older if old enough to leave school) who undertake approved education, training, job search, or other activity to prepare for employment or are incapacitated for work because of an illness or injury. The allowance is means-tested in terms of both parental and personal income and assets.

Newstart allowance (means-tested): Aged 21 or older but younger than the pensionable age and unemployed. Must reside permanently in Australia and be present in the country during the period of payment. Must be unemployed, capable of undertaking and actively seeking work, or temporarily incapacitated for work because of an illness. Unemployment is not due to voluntary leaving, a labor dispute, or the refusal of a suitable job offer. Otherwise, the benefit may be paid at a reduced rate for up to 26 weeks or postponed for up to 8 weeks.

Mature age allowance (means-tested): Payable to an unemployed person who is aged 60 or older but younger than the pensionable age. Must have received the newstart allowance for the preceding 9 months, or a nonactivity-tested payment in the 13 weeks before the claim, and have no recent workforce experience. Recipients are not required to look for work. (No new mature age allowances have been awarded since September 20, 2003.)

Partner allowance (means-tested): A member of a couple (born on or before July 1, 1955) whose partner receives a social security pension or allowance. Must have no recent workforce experience, no dependent children younger than age 16, and must not have received unemployment allowances or the sickness benefit in the 13 weeks before the claim. Recipients are not required to look for work. A couple refers to cohabiting opposite-sex partners, regardless of marriage. (No new partner allowances have been awarded since September 20, 2003.)

Parenting payment (income-tested): Payable for a child younger than age 16 who satisfies residency requirements.

Unemployment Benefits

Youth allowance (means-tested): Between A$174.30 and A$417.40 is paid every 2 weeks depending on age, living arrangements, marital status, and whether the recipient has dependent children. A child is assessed as dependent according to specified criteria, including the legal relationship with the claimant; the child's age, income, and residency status; and whether the child is a full-time student or is receiving social security benefits.

Newstart allowance (means-tested): Up to A$351.10 is paid every 2 weeks for each member of a couple older than age 21; A$389.20 every 2 weeks if single, older than age 21, and with no dependents; A$421 every 2 weeks if single with dependents, or A$426.80 every 2 weeks if single, older than age 60, and after receiving the allowance for 9 months. The allowance is payable after a 7-day waiting period for as long as the person remains qualified.

If exempt from having to actively seek work, a recipient of the newstart allowance may be paid for up to 26 weeks of temporary overseas absence in certain circumstances.

Mature age allowance (means-tested): Up to A$351.10 is paid every 2 weeks for each member of a couple; A$389.20 every 2 weeks if single. The allowance is payable after a 7-day waiting period for as long as the person remains qualified.

Partner allowance (means-tested): Up to A$351.10 is paid every 2 weeks. The allowance is payable after a 7-day waiting period for as long as the person remains qualified.

Parenting payment: Up to A$351.10 is paid every 2 weeks for parents living as a couple; A$464.20 every 2 weeks for a single parent.

Rent assistance (means-tested): Up to A$95.40 is paid every 2 weeks, according to marital status and the level of rent. Special rules apply to people living in retirement villages. Single recipients younger than age 25 and living with their parents are not eligible for rent assistance.

Remote area supplement: A$18.20 is paid every 2 weeks for a single person (A$15.60 each for a couple), plus A$7.30 every 2 weeks for each dependent.

Concession card: Provided with a health care card, or a pensioner concession card if older than age 60, after receiving social security benefits for 9 months.

Benefit adjustment: The youth allowance and newstart allowance are adjusted in March and September according to changes in the price index.

Administrative Organization

Department of Families, Community Services, and Indigenous Affairs (http://www.facsia.gov.au) provides general supervision.

Centrelink (http://www.centrelink.gov.au) administers the programs through 401 customer service centers and 16 area support offices.

Family Allowances

Regulatory Framework

First law: 1941 (family allowances).

Current laws: 1991 (orphan pension) and 1999 (family assistance).

Type of program: Universal and social assistance system.

Coverage

All persons residing in Australia with one or more children.

Source of Funds

Insured person: None.

Self-employed person: None.

Employer: None.

Government: The total cost from general revenue.

Qualifying Conditions

Family tax benefit, Parts A and B: Paid to families with dependent children up to and including age 20 (age 24 if a full-time student) for Part A; younger than age 16 (up to age 18 if a full-time student) for Part B.

The maximum family tax benefit (Part A) rate is paid if annual family income is not greater than A$40,000. Families receive some benefit under Part A for annual family income up to A$94,718 with one dependent child younger than age 18 (the income ceiling is raised for each additional dependent child younger than age 18 and for each dependent aged 18 to 24).

In addition, family tax benefit (Part B) provides extra assistance for single-income families (including single parents) with children. A higher rate is paid to families caring for children younger than age 5. The maximum Part B rate is paid if the annual income of the secondary earner is not greater than A$4,234. (Single parents are not subject to an income test.) Couples receive some benefit under Part B if the secondary earner's annual income is less than A$21,572 and the youngest child is younger than age 5; less than A$16,790 and the youngest child is between ages 5 and 18.

Large family supplement: Paid for families with three or more children. The supplement is paid as part of family tax benefit (Part A).

Multiple birth allowance: Paid for the birth of three or more children. The allowance is paid every 2 weeks until the children are age 6. The supplement is paid as part of family tax benefit (Part A).

Rent assistance: Payable to people receiving the family tax benefit (Part A) and paying rent to private landlords.

Double orphan pension: Payable to a child younger than age 16 (age 21 if a student and not receiving the youth allowance). If both parents are dead (or one parent is dead and the other is in a hospital or an institution on a long-term basis, has been in prison for at least 10 years, or whose whereabouts is unknown) or for refugee children under certain circumstances. The pension is not income-tested.

Maternity payment: A universal payment for persons with a newborn child. Includes persons with adopted babies, still-born babies, and babies who died shortly after birth.

Maternity immunization allowance: A universal payment for persons who are caring for a child aged 24 months or younger. The allowance is paid after the child receives all immunizations recommended for a child up to age 18 months or valid exemption from immunization.

Child care benefit: Paid to families with children residing in Australia who meet the immunization requirements or are exempt and who pay for child care with an approved or registered care provider.

Health care card: Provided to recipients of the maximum family tax benefit (Part A). A low-income health care card is also provided to those satisfying an income test on average gross weekly income in the 8 weeks immediately before the claim is made.

Income test: The income test is based on annual adjusted taxable income.

Family Allowance Benefits

Family tax benefit, Part A: The minimum and maximum rates of payment vary with the age of the dependent child.

The minimum rate per 2-week period for a child younger than age 18 is A$45.36 (for ages 18 to 24, A$61.04).

The maximum rate per 2-week period for a child younger than age 13 is A$140.84; for ages 13 to 15, A$179.76; for ages 16 to 17, A$45.36; and for ages 18 to 24, A$61.04. (An annual supplement of A$646.05 is also paid as a lump sum at the end of the financial year.)

Large family supplement: A$9.80 is paid every 2 weeks for each child after the second.

Multiple birth allowance: A$118.02 is paid every 2 weeks for triplets; A$157.36 for quadruplets or more. The allowance is usually added to the family tax benefit.

Rent assistance: A$0.75 is paid for each A$1.00 of rent paid above a determined rent threshold. The maximum rate of assistance for each 2-week period depends on whether the claimant is single or partnered, the number of children, and the level of the rent.

Family tax benefit, Part B: The maximum rate for a child younger than age 5 is A$120.96 every 2 weeks; for ages 5 to 18, A$84.28 every 2 weeks. (An annual supplement of A$313.90 is also paid as a lump sum at the end of the financial year.)

Double orphan pension: A$47.50 is paid every 2 weeks.

Maternity payment: A lump sum of A$4,000 is paid for each child.

Maternity immunization allowance: A single lump-sum payment of A$222.30.

Child care benefit: The rate of benefit depends on family income, the number of children, the number of hours of care paid for each week, the age of the children, and the status of the care provider. Low-income families using approved services receive higher benefits.

Health care card: The card makes available additional health, household, and transportation assistance from state, territory, and local governments.

Income test: The income test is based on annual adjusted taxable income.

Benefit adjustment: Most benefits are adjusted on July 1 each year according to changes in the price index.

Administrative Organization

Department of Families, Community Services, and Indigenous Affairs (http://www.facsia.gov.au) provides general supervision.

Family Assistance Offices administer the program.

Azerbaijan

Exchange rate: US$1.00 equals
0.92 new manat (AZN).

Old Age, Disability, and Survivors

Regulatory Framework

First law: 1956.

Current laws: 1992 (military pensions); 1992 (disability); 1997 (social insurance), with amendments; and 2006 (labor pensions).

Type of program: Social insurance and social assistance system.

Coverage

Social insurance: All workers residing in Azerbaijan, including self-employed persons, members of collective farms, landowners, and foreign citizens.

Social pension: Persons not eligible for social insurance pensions.

Source of Funds

Insured person

Social insurance: 3% of gross earnings.

There are no minimum and maximum earnings for contribution purposes.

The insured person's contributions also finance sickness and maternity benefits, temporary disability benefits, funeral grants, unemployment benefits, and child care benefits.

Social pension: None.

Self-employed person

Social insurance: 70% of the national minimum monthly wage if engaged in trade, transport, or construction; different rates apply for all other self-employed professions. Rates may vary in different regions of the country.

There are no minimum and maximum earnings for contribution purposes.

The self-employed person's contributions also finance sickness and maternity benefits, temporary disability benefits, funeral grants, unemployment benefits, and child care benefits.

Social pension: None.

Employer

Social insurance: 22% of payroll.

There are no minimum and maximum earnings for contribution purposes.

The employer's contributions also finance sickness and maternity benefits, temporary disability benefits, funeral grants, unemployment benefits, and child care benefits.

Social pension: None.

Government

Social insurance: Provides subsidies; contributes as an employer on behalf of employees.

There are no minimum and maximum earnings for contribution purposes.

Social benefit: The total cost.

Qualifying Conditions

Old-age labor pension: Age 62 (men) or age 57 (women) with at least 5 years of covered employment.

Covered employment includes noncontributory periods of active military and alternative national service; providing care for a Group I disabled person, a disabled child younger than age 16, and persons aged 70 or older; periods receiving unemployment allowance or employment training; and periods receiving a Group I or II disability pension as a result of an occupational disease or a work injury.

Early pension: A reduced pension is paid at age 57 with at least 25 years of covered employment (men), including at least 12.6 years of work in unhealthy or arduous conditions; age 52 with at least 20 years of covered employment (women), including at least 10 years of work in unhealthy or arduous conditions. An early pension is also provided for mothers who have reared at least three children or one disabled child from birth until age 8.

Gradual retirement pension: Paid to pensioners who continue working after the normal pension age.

Social pension (old-age): Paid to nonworking citizens from age 67 (men) or age 62 (women) who are not eligible for the old-age labor pension; from age 57 for some mothers who have reared at least three children.

Old-age pensions are payable abroad under bilateral agreement.

Disability labor pension: The pension is paid according to three assessed degrees of disability (Groups I to III): Group I (totally disabled, incapable of doing any work, and requiring constant attendance); Group II (disabled, incapable of doing any work, but not requiring constant attendance); and Group III (incapable of usual work).

The minimum degree of assessed disability for entitlement to a pension is 25%. The degree of disability is assessed and periodically reviewed by a medical commission.

The pension for different categories of insured person is determined according to minimum periods of covered employment. Persons younger than age 19 must have at least a year of covered employment; persons aged 19 or older must have 1 year plus 4 months for every subsequent year from age 19.

Covered employment includes noncontributory periods of active military and alternative national service; periods in education or professional training; periods providing care for a disabled person, a disabled child younger than age 16, and persons aged 70 or older; and periods of unemployment.

Social pension (disability): Paid to Group I (totally disabled, incapable of doing any work, and requiring constant attendance); Group II (disabled, incapable of doing any work, but not requiring constant attendance); and Group III (incapable of usual work) disabled persons who are not eligible for a disability labor pension, including persons who participated in the containment of the Chernobyl catastrophe and persons disabled from childhood.

Disability pensions are payable abroad under bilateral agreement.

Survivor labor pension: The deceased had at least 1 to 15 years of work, depending on age at the time of death.

Eligible survivors are a retired or disabled spouse, a non-working spouse, a spouse caring for a child younger than age 8, a war widow(er), and children younger than age 18 (age 23 if a full-time student, no limit if first disabled before age 18).

Other eligible survivors are the parents of an insured person killed in combat (regardless of whether they were dependent on the insured); retired or disabled parents (who were dependent on the insured); or parents (regardless of age or dependency) who do not work but care for one or more of the insured's children younger than age 8. Brothers and sisters who satisfy the age conditions and whose parents are incapable of work or are not working but are caring for one or more of the insured's children, brothers, sisters, or grandchildren younger than age 8. Grandparents who do not work but care for one or more of the insured's children, brothers, sisters, or grandchildren younger than age 8 and there is no one else capable of caring for them.

Funeral grant: Paid for the death of a labor pensioner.

Social pension (survivors): Paid to a dependent survivor if the deceased was not eligible for a labor pension.

Survivor pensions are payable abroad under bilateral agreement.

Old-Age Benefits

Old-age labor pension: The pension is equal to 60% of average gross monthly earnings (base pension) plus 2% for each year of employment over the minimum required period (25 years for men or 20 years for women), up to a maximum of 85% average gross monthly earnings.

Average gross monthly earnings are calculated on earnings during any continuous 60-month period of employment or the last 24 months before applying for a pension.

The minimum monthly base pension of the old-age labor pension is 35 AZN.

Early pension: The reduction applied to early pensions varies by profession.

Gradual retirement pension: Pensioners receive 100% of the base pension if they continue working after the normal pension age.

Special supplements: Rehabilitated victims of political repression receive 10% of the base pension of the old-age labor pension; war veterans receive 10%; disabled veterans (if eligible for the old-age labor pension) receive 100% (Group I), 70% (Group II), or 50% (Group III).

Social pension (old-age): 20 AZN a month. (The national monthly minimum wage is 30 AZN.)

Benefit adjustment: The social pension is indexed to the consumer price index and adjusted by presidential decree.

Permanent Disability Benefits

Disability labor pension: The base pension of the disability labor pension is paid as follows: Group I disabled persons (totally disabled, incapable of any work, and requiring constant attendance) receive 120% of the base pension of the old-age labor pension (Group I visually impaired persons receive 200%); Group II disabled persons (disabled, incapable of any work, but not requiring constant attendance) receive 100%; and Group III disabled persons (incapable of usual work) receive 55%.

The base pension of the old-age labor pension is equal to 60% of average gross monthly earnings. Average gross monthly earnings are calculated on earnings during any continuous 60-month period of employment or the last 24 months before the disability began.

The minimum monthly base pension of the old-age labor pension is 35 AZN.

The maximum monthly earnings for pension calculation purposes are 51 AZN.

Dependent's supplement: A cash supplement is paid for the spouse and children of Group I or II disabled persons.

Care supplement: A cash supplement is paid for Group I disabled persons and all war-disabled persons (including dependent pensioners).

Special supplements (disability): Group I disabled persons receive 120% of the base pension of the old-age labor pension (Group I visually impaired persons, 200%); Group II, 100%; and Group III, 55%.

Social pension (disability): Group I disabled persons receive 25 AZN; Group II, 20 AZN; and Group III, 15 AZN. All disabled children younger than age 16 receive 25 AZN.

Persons who became disabled while defending Azerbaijan receive 65 AZN (Group I), 55 AZN (Group II), or 50 AZN (Group III).

Military personnel who became disabled during military service or through participating in the containment of the Chernobyl catastrophe receive 60 AZN (Group I), 55 AZN (Group II), or 40 AZN (Group III).

In addition, persons who participated in the containment of the Chernobyl catastrophe, and who became disabled as a result, receive an annual benefit of 110 AZN for medical treatment.

Benefit adjustment: The social pension is indexed to the consumer price index and adjusted by presidential decree.

Survivor Benefits

Survivor labor pension

Spouse's pension: 100% of the base pension of the deceased's old-age labor pension.

The base pension of the old-age labor pension is equal to 60% of the deceased's average gross monthly earnings.

Survivor's supplement: The spouse and children of deceased National Heroes of Azerbaijan receive 100% of the base pension of the deceased's old-age labor pension; the spouse and children of citizens who died during the country's struggle for independence, 30%.

Orphan's pension: 100% of the base pension of the deceased's old-age labor pension is paid for each full orphan, the children of an unwed mother, or the deceased's only child.

Other eligible survivors: 50% of the base pension of the deceased's old-age labor pension.

Funeral grant: The minimum grant is 60 AZN.

Benefit adjustment: Benefits are indexed to the annual consumer price index and adjusted at least once a year.

Social pension (survivors): 20 AZN is paid a month. (The national monthly minimum wage is 30 AZN.)

Benefit adjustment: The social pension is indexed to the consumer price index and adjusted by presidential decree.

Administrative Organization

State Social Protection Fund is responsible for the program.

Regional and local branches of the State Social Protection Fund administer the program.

Sickness and Maternity

Regulatory Framework

First law: 1912.

Current laws: 1998 (social insurance), with 2005 amendment; and 1999 (health insurance).

Type of program: Social insurance (cash benefits) and universal (medical benefits) system.

Coverage

Cash benefits: All workers residing in Azerbaijan, including self-employed persons, members of collective farms, landowners, and foreign citizens.

Medical benefits: All persons residing permanently in Azerbaijan.

Source of Funds

Insured person

Cash sickness and maternity benefits: See source of funds under Old Age, Disability, and Survivors, above.

Medical benefits: None.

Self-employed person

Cash sickness and maternity benefits: See source of funds under Old Age, Disability, and Survivors, above.

Medical benefits: None.

Employer

Cash sickness and maternity benefits: See source of funds under Old Age, Disability, and Survivors, above.

Medical benefits: None.

Government

Cash sickness and maternity benefits: None; contributes as an employer on behalf of employees.

Medical benefits: The total cost.

Qualifying Conditions

Cash sickness and maternity benefits: Must be in covered employment.

Medical benefits: Residing in Azerbaijan.

Sickness and Maternity Benefits

Sickness benefit: A worker with at least 8 years of employment receives 100% of the last month's earnings; with between 5 and 8 years, 80%; with less than 5 years, 60%.

A working disabled person receives 150% of the last month's earnings, up to a maximum.

100% of the last month's earnings is paid for persons wounded during the military conflicts in Afghanistan or Karabakh; for those wounded in 1990 in Baku or in the Lankaran and Neftchala districts; for the parents, wives, and children of soldiers killed in combat; for those who participated in the containment of the Chernobyl catastrophe, and for some other groups of workers.

The benefit is paid from the first day of incapacity until recovery or assessed as permanently incapable of work.

The employer pays the benefits for the first 14 days.

Maternity benefit: The benefit is equal to 100% of gross average monthly earnings and is paid for 126 days (70 days before and 56 days after the expected date of childbirth).

A birth grant and child care benefits are provided under Family Allowances, below.

Maternity leave: For insured women in the nonagricultural sector, leave is provided for 70 days before and 56 days after (for multiple births or for a childbirth with complications, 70 days after) the expected date of childbirth. For insured women in the agricultural sector, leave is provided for 70 days before and 70 days after (for a childbirth with complications, 86 days after; for multiple births, 110 days after) the expected date of childbirth.

Workers' Medical Benefits

Compulsory medical insurance is organized by employers and covers medical services provided directly to patients by public and private facilities contracted by the health insurance agencies.

Free medical services include the provision of wheelchairs, immunization and vaccination services, and home nursing care for Group I (totally disabled, incapable of doing any work, and requiring constant attendance) disabled persons. There is compensation for transportation expenses for disabled persons and for authorized medical treatment abroad.

Group I (totally disabled, incapable of doing any work, and requiring constant attendance) and Group II (disabled but not requiring constant attendance) disabled persons and persons with long employment records are entitled to free dental prostheses and medicines prescribed by a doctor. Prosthesis, eyeglasses, and hearing aids are free for all disabled persons and for those with long employment records. General dental care is free for children up to age 16 and vulnerable groups of the population, including the disabled.

Dependents' Medical Benefits

Medical benefits are provided on an individual basis to all persons residing permanently in Azerbaijan.

Administrative Organization

Cash benefits: State Social Protection Fund is responsible for the program.

Medical benefits: Ministry of Health (http://www.mednet. az) administers the program.

Work Injury

Regulatory Framework

First law: 1956.

Current law: 1999 (labor code).

Type of program: Social insurance (cash benefits) and universal (medical benefits) system.

Coverage

Cash benefits: All employees.

Exclusions: Self-employed persons.

Medical benefits: All persons residing permanently in Azerbaijan.

Source of Funds

Insured person: None for permanent disability benefits. For temporary disability and survivor benefits, see source of funds under Old Age, Disability, and Survivors, above.

Self-employed person: Not applicable.

Employer: The total cost of permanent disability benefits. For temporary disability and survivor benefits, see source of funds under Old Age, Disability, and Survivors, above.

Government: None; contributes as an employer on behalf of employees.

Qualifying Conditions

Work injury benefits: There is no minimum qualifying period.

Temporary Disability Benefits

The benefit is equal to 55% of the base pension of the old-age labor pension.

The base pension of the old-age labor pension is equal to 60% of average gross monthly earnings. Average gross monthly earnings are calculated on earnings during any continuous 60-month period of employment or the last 24 months before the disability began.

The minimum monthly base pension of the old-age labor pension is 35 AZN.

The maximum monthly earnings for pension calculation purposes are 51 AZN.

The degree of disability is assessed and periodically reviewed by a medical commission.

Permanent Disability Benefits

Permanent disability pension: The pension is paid for a Group I (totally disabled, incapable of doing any work, and requiring constant attendance) or Group II (disabled, incapable of doing any work, but not requiring constant attendance) disability.

The minimum degree of assessed disability for entitlement to a pension is 25%. The degree of disability is assessed and periodically reviewed by a medical commission.

Group I disabled persons receive 120% of the base pension of the old-age labor pension (Group I visually impaired persons receive 200%); Group II disabled persons receive 100% of the base pension of the old-age labor pension.

The base pension of the old-age labor pension is equal to 60% of average gross monthly earnings.

The pension is paid by the employer.

Constant-attendance allowance: 3.50 AZN a month is paid for a Group I disabled person.

Benefit adjustment: Benefits are adjusted according to changes in earnings in the disabled person's place of work.

Workers' Medical Benefits

Medical services are provided directly to patients by state health providers. Benefits include general and specialist care, hospitalization, laboratory services, transportation, and the full cost of appliances and medicines. Rehabilitation and vocational training are available to disabled persons. All costs are paid by the employer.

Annual lump sum: A lump sum of 110 AZN is paid annually to victims of the Chernobyl catastrophe for a medical treatment.

Survivor Benefits

Eligible survivors are a retired or disabled spouse, a non-working spouse, a spouse caring for a child younger than age 8, a war widow(er), and children younger than age 18 (age 23 if a full-time student, no limit if first disabled before age 18).

Other eligible survivors are the parents of an insured person killed in combat (regardless of whether they were dependent on the insured); retired or disabled parents (who were dependent on the insured); or parents (regardless of age or dependency) who do not work but care for one or more of the insured's children younger than age 8. Brothers and sisters who satisfy the age conditions and whose parents are incapable of work or are not working but are caring for one or more of the insured's children, brothers, sisters, or grandchildren younger than age 8. Grandparents who do not work but care for one or more of the insured's children, brothers, sisters, or grandchildren younger than age 8 and there is no one else capable of caring for them.

Spouse's pension: 100% of the base pension of the deceased's old-age labor pension.

The base pension of the old-age labor pension is equal to 60% of the deceased's average gross monthly earnings.

Survivor's supplement: The spouse and children of deceased National Heroes of Azerbaijan receive 100% of the base pension of the deceased's old-age labor pension; the spouse and children of citizens who died during the country's struggle for independence, 30%.

Orphan's pension: 100% of the base pension of the deceased's old-age labor pension is paid for each full orphan, the children of an unwed mother, or the deceased's only child.

Other eligible survivors: 50% of the base pension of the deceased's old-age labor pension.

Benefit adjustment: Benefits are indexed to the annual consumer price index and adjusted at least once a year.

Funeral grant: The employer pays for the funeral.

Administrative Organization

Temporary disability benefits: Employers pay benefits directly to employees.

Pensions: State Social Protection Fund provides coordination and supervision of the program.

State Social Protection Fund, via its regional branches, collects and manages contributions and finances benefits.

Regional and local departments of the State Social Protection Fund administer the program.

Medical benefits: Ministry of Health (http://www.mednet.az) and health departments of local governments provide general supervision and coordination.

Medical services are delivered through clinics, hospitals, and other facilities administered by the Ministry of Health (http://www.mednet.az) and local health departments.

Unemployment

Regulatory Framework

First law: 1991.

Current laws: 1999 (labor code) and 2001 (employment).

Type of program: Social insurance system.

Coverage

All persons residing in Azerbaijan.

Source of Funds

Insured person: See source of funds under Old Age, Disability, and Survivors, above.

Self-employed person: See source of funds under Old Age, Disability, and Survivors, above.

Employer: See source of funds under Old Age, Disability, and Survivors, above.

Government: Subsidies as required from national and local governments.

Qualifying Conditions

Unemployment benefit: Must have at least 26 weeks of covered employment in the 12 months before unemployment. The insured must be between age 15 and the normal pension age, registered with the state employment services, and actively seeking and willing to work.

The benefit is suspended for 3 months for refusing two acceptable job offers or for failing to register each month at the employment service without a valid reason. The benefit ceases for filing false or fraudulent claims or for refusing to attend vocational training.

Unemployment Benefits

The benefit is equal to 70% of average gross monthly earnings in the 12 months before unemployment. The benefit must not exceed the national average monthly wage. The benefit is paid for a maximum of 26 weeks in any 12-month period.

The national average monthly wage is 156 AZN.

Administrative Organization

Ministry of Labour and Social Protection of the Population provides general oversight.

State Employment Service, with its local branch offices, is responsible for administering the program, paying benefits, providing services for unemployed persons (including training), and for creating new jobs.

Family Allowances

Regulatory Framework

First law: 1944.

Current laws: 1992 (pensions insurance), implemented in 1993, with 2005 amendment; and 2005 (social assistance).

Type of program: Social insurance and social assistance system.

Coverage

Social insurance benefits: Insured persons with at least one child.

Social assistance benefits: Low-income families.

Source of Funds

Insured person: See source of funds for social insurance under Old Age, Disability, and Survivors, above.

Self-employed person: See source of funds for social insurance under Old Age, Disability, and Survivors, above.

Employer: See source of funds for social insurance under Old Age, Disability, and Survivors, above.

Government: The total cost of social assistance and the child benefit.

Qualifying Conditions

Social assistance (income-tested): Paid to low-income families.

Income test: Average per capita monthly family income must be less than 30 AZN.

Child benefit (income-tested): Paid to persons residing in Azerbaijan younger than age 16 (age 18 if a student with no student allowance).

Income test: Average per capita monthly family income must be less than 30 AZN.

Child care benefit: Paid for employees who leave work to rear a child. There is no minimum qualifying period.

Birth and adoption grants: Paid to the mother (or other recognized carer).

Full orphan's special benefit: Paid to a full orphan until age 16.

Family Allowance Benefits

Social assistance (income-tested): The benefit raises average per capita family income to 30 AZN a month.

Child benefit (income-tested): Low-income families with a child younger than age 1 receive 10 AZN a month.

A child with a parent in active military service receives 20 AZN a month; children whose parents were disabled as the result of a war or armed conflict, children of persons who became totally disabled or died as a result of the Chernobyl catastrophe, and children of persons who participated in the containment of the Chernobyl catastrophe receive 5 AZN a month.

Child care benefit: 3.50 AZN a month is paid until the child is age 3.

Birth and adoption grants: A lump sum of 30 AZN is paid.

Full orphan's special benefit: 5 AZN a month is paid.

Benefit adjustment: Benefits are adjusted by presidential decree.

Administrative Organization

Ministry of Labour and Social Protection of the Population provides general oversight.

Local branches of the Ministry of Labour and Social Protection of the Population are responsible for administering social benefits and paying benefits to unemployed parents.

State Social Protection Fund, through its departments and regional branches, collects and manages contributions and finances benefits.

Bahrain

Exchange rate: US$1.00 equals 0.37 dinars.

Old Age, Disability, and Survivors

Regulatory Framework

First and current law: 1976 (social insurance), with amendments.

Type of program: Social insurance system.

Coverage

Bahraini employed persons in establishments with one or more employees.

Exclusions: Domestic servants, certain groups of agricultural employees, casual workers, temporary noncitizen workers, and other groups as specified in law.

Voluntary coverage for persons with 5 or more years of previous compulsory social security coverage but who are no longer covered on a compulsory basis, for self-employed persons, and for Bahrainis working abroad. Voluntary contributors are covered for old-age, disability, and survivor benefits.

Special system for public-sector employees.

Source of Funds

Insured person: 5% of total monthly salary; voluntary contributors, 12% of declared monthly income.

The maximum monthly earnings for contribution purposes are 4,000 dinars.

Self-employed person: 12% of monthly income on a voluntary basis.

The monthly income for contribution purposes is chosen by the self-employed person when joining the system but must be between 200 dinars and 1,000 dinars; thereafter, the monthly income for contribution purposes may be increased or decreased annually by up to 5% but must be between 200 dinars and 1,500 dinars.

Employer: 7% of the employee's monthly salary.

The maximum monthly earnings for contribution purposes are 4,000 dinars.

Government: None.

Qualifying Conditions

Old-age pension

Men: Age 60 with 15 years of coverage; older than age 60 with 10 years of coverage and 36 consecutive monthly contributions in the last 5 years.

Women: Age 55 with 10 years of coverage; older than age 55 with 10 years of coverage and 36 consecutive monthly contributions in the last 5 years.

Early pension: Regardless of age with 20 years of coverage (men) or 15 years of coverage (women).

Lump-sum compensation for prolonged service: Paid for a contribution period exceeding 40 years.

Retirement from usual employment is necessary. Pensioners may work in a new job, providing that the combined income from a pension and the job does not exceed the amount earned in the last job before retirement.

Old-age settlement: Paid if the insured is ineligible for an old-age pension.

Disability pension: The insured had at least 6 consecutive months of contributions immediately before the onset of disability; or 12 nonconsecutive months of contributions, 3 months of which were consecutive and immediately before the onset of disability. The pension is also payable if the disability begins within 1 year of the cessation of contributions. The insured must be younger than age 60 (men) or age 55 (women) at the onset of disability.

Disability settlement: Paid if the insured is ineligible for a disability pension.

Survivor pension: The insured was a pensioner at the time of death; had at least 6 consecutive months of contributions immediately before the date of death; or 12 nonconsecutive months of contributions, 3 months of which were consecutive and immediately before the date of death. The pension is also payable if death occurs within 1 year of the cessation of contributions, regardless of age.

Lump-sum compensation for prolonged service: Paid if the deceased had a contribution period exceeding 40 years.

Eligible survivors are a widow, a disabled widower, orphans, and the deceased's dependent parents, brothers, and sisters.

Entitlement to a survivor pension for widows, daughters, or sisters ceases on marriage but may be reinstated if she is subsequently divorced or widowed.

Marriage grant: A lump sum is paid to each female heir receiving a survivor pension who marries. The grant is paid to each survivor only once.

If a widow remarries or dies after the death of her insured or pensioner spouse, her pension is paid to eligible sons and daughters.

A son's pension ceases at age 22 (up to age 26 if a full-time student, no limit if disabled) or if personal earnings are at least equal to the pension.

A daughter's pension ceases on marriage (or if personal earnings are at least equal to the pension) but will be reinstated if she is subsequently divorced or widowed.

Survivor settlement: Paid to survivors if the deceased was ineligible for a pension.

Eligible survivors are a widow, a disabled widower, orphans, and the deceased's dependent parents, brothers, and sisters.

Death grant: Paid for the death of the insured or a pensioner. The grant is paid to a widow, the deceased's eldest son, or the person who paid for the funeral.

Old-Age Benefits

Old-age pension: The monthly pension is equal to 2% of the insured's monthly average earnings in the last 2 years times the number of years of contributions.

The maximum contribution period for pension calculation purposes is 40 years (up to 5 years of credited contributions may be used for pension calculation purposes, subject to the insured's total contribution period not exceeding 30 years).

The minimum pension is equal to the insured's average contributory wage during the last 2 years or 150 dinars a month, whichever is less. The contributory wage is equal to the total monthly wage received in January of each year. The minimum pension for every family member (including the pensioner) must be at least equal to 30 dinars a month, provided that the total does not exceed the average contributory wage over the last 2 years.

The maximum pension is equal to 88% of average earnings, calculated on the basis of 80% of the insured's average earnings plus an additional 10% of the pension (equal to 8% of average earnings).

Early pension: The pension is reduced by 20% if the insured retires before age 45, by 15% if aged 45 to 49, or by 10% if aged 50 to 54.

Lump-sum compensation for prolonged service: For a contribution period exceeding 40 years, the insured is entitled to a lump sum equal to 11% of average earnings in the last 2 years for each contribution year exceeding 40.

Old-age settlement: A lump sum is paid equal to 15% of the insured's average monthly earnings in the last 2 years, multiplied by 12 times the number of years of contributions, plus 5% interest from the date coverage stops until the date the settlement is paid.

Benefit adjustment: Benefits are adjusted on an ad hoc basis according to changes in the cost of living.

Permanent Disability Benefits

Disability pension: The pension is equal to 44% of the insured's average monthly earnings in the last year of contributions before the onset of disability or 2% of the insured's average earnings during the last year of contributions times the number of years of contributions, whichever is higher.

The minimum pension is equal to 44% of the insured's average monthly earnings in the last year of contributions or 150 dinars, whichever is higher; an insured person with income less than 150 dinars receives a pension equal to 100% of his or her average contributory wage in the last year.

The contributory wage is equal to the total monthly wage received in January of each year.

The maximum pension is equal to 88% of average earnings, calculated on the basis of 80% of the insured's average earnings plus an additional 10% of the pension (equal to 8% of average earnings).

Disability settlement: A lump sum is paid equal to 15% of the insured's monthly average earnings in the last 2 years, multiplied by 12 times the number of years of contributions, plus 5% interest from the date the insured ceased employment because of the onset of disability until the date the settlement is paid.

Benefits are payable abroad in limited circumstances.

Benefit adjustment: Benefits are adjusted on an ad hoc basis according to changes in the cost of living.

Survivor Benefits

Survivor pension

Widow(er)'s pension: 37.5% of the deceased's pension is paid; 50% in the absence of orphans.

Orphan's pension: 50% of the deceased's pension is split equally among the insured's children (a son must be younger than age 22, younger than age 26 if a full-time student); 62.5% if there are no other eligible survivors except the widow.

In the absence of any other survivors, a full orphan receives 100% of the deceased's pension; in the absence of a widow but with the presence of other eligible survivors (see below), a full orphan receives 87.5%.

Other eligible survivors: 12.5% of the deceased's pension is split equally among dependent parents, brothers, and sisters.

The minimum pension is 44% of the deceased's average earnings in the last year of contributions or 150 dinars a month, whichever is higher; if the deceased's monthly income was less than 150 dinars, the minimum pension is equal to 100% of the deceased's average contributory wage in the last year. The minimum pension for every surviving family member must be at least equal to 30 dinars a month even if the total exceeds 44% of the deceased's average earnings or 150 dinars, but the total must not exceed the average contributory wage during the last year.

The maximum pension is equal to 88% of the deceased's average earnings, calculated on the basis of 80% of the deceased's average earnings plus an additional 10% of the pension (equal to 8% of average earnings).

Lump-sum compensation for prolonged service: If the deceased had a contribution period exceeding 40 years, the survivor is entitled to a lump sum calculated on the basis of 11% of average earnings in the last 2 years for each contribution year exceeding 40.

Survivor pensions are paid monthly.

The survivor pension for a widow, daughter, or sister is suspended on marriage but may be reinstated if she is subsequently divorced or widowed.

Marriage grant: A lump sum equal to 15 times the monthly pension is paid.

Survivor settlement: A lump sum equal to 15% of the deceased's monthly average earnings in the last 2 years, multiplied by 12 times the number of years of contributions, plus 5% interest from the date of death until the date the settlement is paid.

Death grant: Six months' earnings (if the deceased was employed at the time of death) or pension (if retired) is paid, plus 300 dinars for funeral expenses; 400 dinars if the insured died abroad and regardless of the place of burial.

Benefits are payable abroad in limited circumstances.

Benefit adjustment: Benefits are adjusted on an ad hoc basis according to changes in the cost of living.

Administrative Organization

Ministry of Labor and Social Affairs (http://www.bah-molsa.com) provides general supervision.

Managed by a board of directors, the General Organization for Social Insurance (http://www.gosi.org.bh) administers the program.

Work Injury

Regulatory Framework

First and current law: 1976 (social insurance), with amendments.

Type of program: Social insurance system.

Coverage

Employed persons in establishments with one or more employees.

Exclusions: Domestic servants, casual employees, family labor, self-employed persons, and agricultural workers.

Special system for public-sector employees.

Source of Funds

Insured person: None.

Self-employed person: Not applicable.

Employer: 3% of the employee's basic salary; 1% if the employer pays cash benefits to an insured worker who is receiving medical treatment and pays the insured's transportation expenses to the place of treatment or provides medical care to insured workers in employer-owned hospital facilities.

The maximum monthly earnings for contribution purposes are 4,000 dinars.

Government: None.

Qualifying Conditions

Work injury benefits: There is no minimum qualifying period.

Temporary Disability Benefits

The daily allowance is equal to 100% of the insured's contributory daily wage. The employer pays the wage for the day of the injury; thereafter, the benefit is paid by the General Organization for Social Insurance until recovery or certification of permanent disability.

The degree of disability is assessed by the Medical Committee. The General Organization for Social Insurance may request periodic medical examinations during the first 4 years of disability. The insured may also request medical reexamination during this period.

Permanent Disability Benefits

Permanent disability pension: The base pension is equal to 80% of the insured's last monthly earnings. In addition, a supplement equal to 15% of the pension is paid if the pension is less than 50 dinars a month; 10% if the pension is 50 dinars or more. If the insured is totally disabled, the total pension amounts to 88% or 92% of the insured's average monthly earnings.

The minimum pension is 150 dinars a month or 88% or 92% of the insured's contributory wage, whichever is higher; for those earning less than 150 dinars, the pension equals 100% of his or her contributory wage. The contributory wage is equal to the insured's total monthly wage received in January of each year. The minimum pension for every family member (including the insured) must be at least 30 dinars a month, provided that the total does not exceed the insured's last contributory wage.

Partial disability: A percentage of the full pension is paid according to the assessed degree of disability. For a loss of working capacity of less than 30%, a lump sum is paid equal to 36 times the monthly permanent disability pension multiplied by the assessed percentage of disability.

The degree of disability is assessed by the Medical Committee. The General Organization for Social Insurance may request periodic medical examinations during the first 4 years of disability. The insured may also request medical reexamination during this period.

Survivor Benefits

Survivor pension: The base pension is equal to 80% of the deceased's last monthly earnings. In addition, a supplement equal to 15% of the pension is paid if the pension is less than 50 dinars a month; 10% if the pension is 50 dinars or more. The total pension amounts to 88% or 92% of the deceased's average monthly earnings.

Eligible survivors are a widow, a disabled widower, orphans, and the deceased's dependent parents, brothers, and sisters.

Widow(er)'s pension: 37.5% of the deceased's pension is paid; 50% in the absence of orphans.

If a widow remarries or dies after the death of her insured or pensioner spouse, her share is paid to eligible sons and daughters.

Orphan's pension: 50% of the deceased's pension is split equally among the insured's children (a son must be younger than age 22; younger than age 26 if a full-time student); 62.5% if there are no other eligible survivors except the widow.

A daughter's pension ceases on marriage (or if personal earnings are at least equal to the pension) but will be reinstated if she is subsequently divorced or widowed.

In the absence of any other survivors, a full orphan receives 100% of the deceased's pension; in the absence of a widow but with the presence of other eligible survivors (below), a full orphan receives 87.5%.

Other eligible survivors: 12.5% of the deceased's pension is split equally among dependent parents, brothers, and sisters.

The minimum pension is 150 dinars a month or 88% or 92% of the deceased's contributory wage, whichever is higher; if the deceased's monthly income was less than 150 dinars, the minimum pension is equal to 100% of the deceased's average contributory wage in the last year. The contributory wage is equal to the deceased's total monthly wage received in January of each year. The minimum pension for every family member must be at least 30 dinars a month, provided that the total does not exceed the deceased's last contributory wage.

The maximum pension is 88% of average earnings, calculated as 80% of the deceased's average earnings plus an additional 10% of the pension.

Marriage grant: A lump sum equal to 15 times the monthly pension is paid to each female heir receiving a survivor pension who marries. The grant is paid to each survivor only once. Entitlement to a survivor pension for widows, daughters, or sisters ceases on marriage but may be reinstated if she is subsequently divorced or widowed.

Death grant: Six months' earnings (if employed at the time of death) or monthly pension (if retired) is paid, plus 300 dinars for funeral expenses; 400 dinars if the insured died abroad and regardless of the place of burial. The grant is paid to a widow, the deceased's eldest son, or the person who paid for the funeral.

Benefit adjustment: Benefits are adjusted on an ad hoc basis according to changes in the cost of living.

Administrative Organization

Ministry of Labor and Social Affairs (http://www.bahmolsa.com) provides general supervision.

Managed by a board of directors, the General Organization for Social Insurance (http://www.gosi.org.bh) administers the program.

Bangladesh

Exchange rate: US$1.00 equals 69 takas.

Old Age, Disability, and Survivors

Regulatory Framework

First and current law: 1998.

Type of program: Social assistance system.

Coverage

Low-income citizens aged 62 or older.

Special system for public-sector employees.

Source of Funds

Insured person: None.

Self-employed person: None.

Employer: None.

Government: The total cost.

Qualifying Conditions

Old-age pension: Aged 62 or older, residing in Bangladesh, and selected for eligibility. Only one member from each family can receive the pension.

Disability pension: No benefits are provided.

Survivor pension: No benefits are provided.

Old-Age Benefits

Old-age pension: The monthly pension is 180 takas and is paid quarterly.

Permanent Disability Benefits

Disability pension: No benefits are provided.

Survivor Benefits

Survivor pension: No benefits are provided.

Administrative Organization

Ministry of Social Welfare administers the program.

Old-age pensions are disbursed by local branches of the government-run Sonali Bank.

Sickness and Maternity

Regulatory Framework

First law: 1939.

Current law: 2006 (labor law).

Type of program: Social insurance system.

Coverage

Cash sickness benefits: Employees of factories in manufacturing industries employing five or more workers and employees of shops and establishments with five or more workers.

Exclusions: Domestic workers, self-employed persons, and informal labor.

Cash maternity benefits: Employed women.

Medical benefits: Medical facilities are provided by some employers in the public and private sectors through dispensaries in their establishments; workers can also use general hospital facilities run by the government.

Source of Funds

Insured person: None.

Self-employed person: Not applicable.

Employer: The total cost.

Government: Provides hospital facilities.

Qualifying Conditions

Cash sickness benefits: Must be in insured employment.

Cash maternity benefits: Must have at least 6 months' service with the same employer on the expected date of childbirth.

Sickness and Maternity Benefits

Sickness benefit: The benefit is equal to 50% of wages for factory workers and 100% of wages for workers in shops, establishments, and large factories and is payable for up to 14 days a year.

Maternity benefit: A cash benefit, depending on the level of the insured's wages, is paid for 6 weeks before and 6 weeks after childbirth.

Workers' Medical Benefits

A medical allowance of 100 takas a month is paid to workers whose employer does not provide medical facilities.

Administrative Organization

Ministry of Labor and Manpower administers the program.

Public Health Service administers public health services.

Work Injury

Regulatory Framework

First law: 1923.

Current law: 2006 (labor law).

Type of program: Employer-liability system for accidental injuries and 33 listed occupational diseases.

Coverage

Employees of railways, factories with five or more workers, and estate and dock employees.

Exclusions: Domestic workers, self-employed persons, and informal labor.

Source of Funds

Insured person: None.

Self-employed person: Not applicable.

Employer: The total cost.

Government: None.

Qualifying Conditions

Work injury benefits: There is a 3-day waiting period.

Temporary Disability Benefits

The benefit is equal to the insured's full wages for the first 2 months, 2/3 of wages for the next 2 months, and half of wages for subsequent months of disability or for a maximum of a year, whichever is shorter.

Permanent Disability Benefits

The maximum benefit is 125,000 takas, regardless of the insured's earnings.

Survivor Benefits

The maximum benefit is 125,000 takas, regardless of the deceased's previous earnings.

Administrative Organization

Ministry of Labor and Manpower administers the program.

Commissioner of Workmen's Compensation provides supervision.

Unemployment

Regulatory Framework

No statutory unemployment benefits are provided.

The 2006 labor law requires employers to provide a termination benefit, a retrenchment and layoff benefit, and a benefit for discharge from service on the grounds of ill health to workers in shops and commercial and industrial establishments.

Monthly rated permanent employees receive half of the average basic wage for 120 days (plus 1 month's salary for each year of service); casual workers, for 60 days (plus a lump-sum payment of 14 days' wages for each year of service); and temporary workers, for 30 days.

Brunei

Exchange rate: US$1.00 equals
1.57 Brunei dollars (B$).

Old Age, Disability, and Survivors

Regulatory Framework

First and current laws: 1955 (old-age and disability pensions), with 1984 (universal pension) amendment; and 1992 (employees' trust fund).

Type of program: Provident fund and universal old-age and disability pension system.

Coverage

Provident fund: All employees up to age 55 who are citizens or residing permanently in Brunei, including government civil servants who began service on or after January 1, 1993. (Civil servants who began service before January 1, 1993, are covered by the government pension scheme.)

Voluntary coverage for self-employed persons and persons aged 55 or older.

Exclusions: Foreign workers.

Special systems for armed forces personnel, police force personnel, and prison wardens.

Universal old-age and disability pension: All persons residing in Brunei.

Source of Funds

Insured person

Provident fund: 5% of monthly earnings if monthly earnings exceed B$80. (Additional voluntary contributions are permitted with prior notification given to the employer.)

There are no minimum or maximum earnings for contribution purposes.

Universal old-age and disability pension: None.

Self-employed person

Provident fund: Voluntary contributions only.

There are no minimum or maximum declared earnings for contribution purposes.

Universal old-age and disability pension: None.

Employer

Provident fund: 5% of monthly payroll. (Additional voluntary contributions on behalf of employees are permitted.)

There are no minimum or maximum earnings for contribution purposes.

Universal old-age pension: None.

Government

Provident fund: None.

Universal old-age and disability pension: The total cost.

Qualifying Conditions

Old-age benefit

Provident fund: Age 55. Retirement is not necessary.

Early withdrawal: Age 50.

Drawdown payment: Fund members with at least B$40,000 in their individual account or who have been provident fund members for at least 10 years can draw down funds from their account for building or purchasing a house for their personal residence.

A lump sum is payable to members of any age if emigrating permanently from the country.

Universal old-age pension: Age 60 and residing in Brunei. Persons born in Brunei must have 10 years of residence immediately before claiming the pension; for persons born outside Brunei, 30 years of residence immediately before claiming the pension.

Disability benefit

Provident fund: The fund member must be unable to work as the result of a physical or mental disability. The degree of disability is assessed by the Medical Board.

Universal disability pension: Must be unable to work and have resided in Brunei in the 10 years immediately before the disability began. Must participate in suitable medical treatment and rehabilitation.

Survivor benefit (provident fund): Paid to the next of kin or named survivors.

Old-Age Benefits

Old-age benefit (provident fund): A lump sum is paid equal to total employee and employer contributions plus compound interest.

Early withdrawal: Fund members may draw down 25% of accumulated assets.

Drawdown payment: The fund member may draw down up to 45% of accumulated assets in the individual account only once before age 55 for building or purchasing a house.

Interest rate adjustment: Set by the government annually according to the financial health of the fund, bank saving rates, and inflation rates. The current rate is 4.25%.

Universal old-age pension: A flat-rate amount is paid.

Benefit adjustment: The pension is adjusted on an ad hoc basis.

Permanent Disability Benefits

Disability benefit (provident fund): A lump sum is paid equal to total employee and employer contributions plus compound interest.

Interest rate adjustment: Set by the government annually according to the financial health of the fund, bank saving rates, and inflation rates. The current rate is 4.25%.

Universal disability pension: A flat-rate amount is paid.

Benefit adjustment: The pension is adjusted on an ad hoc basis.

Survivor Benefits

Survivor benefit (provident fund): A lump sum is paid equal to total employee and employer contributions plus compound interest.

Interest rate adjustment: Set by the government annually according to the financial health of the fund, bank saving rates, and inflation rates. The current rate is 4.25%.

Administrative Organization

Under the supervision of the Employees' Trust Fund Board, the Employees' Trust Fund Department (http://www.tap.gov.bn) of the Ministry of Finance is responsible for the administration of contributions and benefits and the investment of funds.

Department of Community Development of the Ministry of Culture, Youth, and Sports (http://www.belia-sukan.gov.bn) administers the universal benefit program.

Sickness and Maternity

Regulatory Framework

The government provides all persons residing in Brunei with access to medical benefits, including outpatient and inpatient care provided by registered physicians and, upon referral by the physician, in approved hospitals. The Ministry of Health (http://www.moh.gov.bn) registers physicians and approves hospitals to provide services to residents.

Work Injury

Regulatory Framework

First and current law: 1957 (workmen's compensation), with 1984 amendment.

Type of program: Employer-liability system.

Coverage

All employees who are citizens or who reside permanently in Brunei, including government civil servants.

Exclusions: Domestic servants, home workers, and security personnel.

There is no voluntary coverage.

Source of Funds

Insured person: None.

Self-employed person: Not applicable.

Employer: The total cost, met through the direct provision of benefits.

Government: None.

Qualifying Conditions

Work injury benefits: There is no minimum qualifying period.

Temporary Disability Benefits

A monthly benefit is paid equal to 2/3 of the employee's average monthly earnings in the 6 months before the disability began.

The maximum monthly benefit is B$130.

The benefit is paid after a 4-day waiting period for up to 5 years. If the disability lasts more than 14 days, the benefit is paid retroactively for the first 4 days.

Permanent Disability Benefits

A lump sum is paid equal to 48 times the employee's average monthly earnings in the 6 months before disability began.

The maximum benefit is B$9,600.

Constant-attendance supplement (total permanent disability): If the insured requires the constant attendance of others to complete daily tasks, a lump sum is paid equal to 25% of the total permanent disability benefit.

Partial disability: A lump sum is paid equal to the total permanent disability benefit times the assessed percentage of disability, according to a schedule.

If temporary disability benefits were paid for a period exceeding 6 months before the determination of total or partial permanent disability, the temporary disability benefits paid after the duration of 6 months are deducted from the permanent disability benefit.

Workers' Medical Benefits

The employer must pay for the examination and treatment of the insured by a registered physician and, upon referral by the physician, in approved hospitals.

Survivor Benefits

A lump sum is paid equal to 36 times the insured's average monthly earnings in the last 6 months before death.

The maximum benefit is B$7,200.

Eligible survivors are dependent members of the deceased's family (including the spouse, children, parents, and brothers and sisters).

In the absence of eligible survivors, the employer must pay for the insured's funeral.

Administrative Organization

Workmen's Compensation, Health and Safety Section, of the Department of Labor (http://www.labour.gov.bn) enforces the law. The Department of Labor is part of the Ministry of Home Affairs.

Individual employers must pay compensation directly to employees or dependent survivors.

An arbitrator settles disputes regarding the determination and provision of benefits.

Burma (Myanmar)

Exchange rate: US$1.00 equals 450 kyats.

Old Age, Disability, and Survivors

Regulatory Framework

No statutory old-age, disability, and survivor benefits are provided. (A funeral grant is provided under Sickness and Maternity, below.)

Special systems for civil servants, permanent employees of state boards and corporations and municipal authorities, and armed forces personnel.

Sickness and Maternity

Regulatory Framework

First and current law: 1954 (social security), implemented in 1956.

Type of program: Social insurance system. Cash and medical benefits.

Coverage

Certain groups of employees of state enterprises, certain types of civil servant, and temporary and permanent employees of public or private firms with five or more workers in industry and commerce or in specified industries and services (railways, ports, mines, and oilfields).

Coverage is being extended gradually to different regions. Coverage is provided in Yangon, Mandalay, Mawlamyaing, Pathein, Bago, and 92 townships.

Exclusions: Self-employed persons, workers in private shops and establishments with less than five employees, construction workers, agricultural workers, and fishermen.

Source of Funds

Insured person: 1.5% of monthly earnings, according to 10 wage classes.

The minimum monthly earnings for contribution and benefit purposes are 100 kyats for monthly earnings in the lowest wage class of less than 150 kyats.

The maximum earnings for contribution and benefit purposes are 1,000 kyats for monthly earnings in the highest wage class of more than 950 kyats.

The insured's contributions also finance the work injury funeral grant.

Self-employed person: Not applicable.

Employer: 1.5% of monthly payroll, according to 10 wage classes.

The minimum monthly earnings for contribution and benefit purposes are 100 kyats for monthly earnings in the lowest wage class of less than 150 kyats.

The maximum earnings for contribution and benefit purposes are 1,000 kyats for monthly earnings in the highest wage class of more than 950 kyats.

The employer's contributions also finance the work injury funeral grant.

Government: Subsidies as required.

Qualifying Conditions

Cash sickness benefits: Must have 17 weeks of contributions in the last 26 weeks. A medical officer of the Social Security Board must certify the insured as incapable of work.

Coverage is provided for up to 26 weeks after the last day of covered employment for involuntarily unemployed persons registered as unemployed who had fulfilled the contribution conditions on the date of dismissal.

Cash maternity benefit: Must have 26 weeks of contributions in the 52 weeks before the expected date of childbirth.

Medical benefits: Must be in insured employment. There is no minimum qualifying period. Coverage is provided for up to 26 weeks after the last day of covered employment for involuntarily unemployed insured persons registered as unemployed.

Sickness and Maternity Benefits

Sickness benefit: The benefit is equal to 50% of the insured's average covered earnings in the 17 weeks before the onset of incapacity, according to 10 wage classes. The benefit is payable from the first day of incapacity for up to 26 weeks for one illness.

The minimum daily benefit is 2.55 kyats.

Maternity benefit: The benefit is equal to 66.6% of the insured's average covered earnings in the 17 weeks before maternity leave, according to 10 wage classes. The benefit is payable for a maximum of 12 weeks (6 weeks before and 6 weeks after) the expected date of childbirth.

The minimum daily benefit is 2.55 kyats.

Funeral grant: Paid to the person who paid for the funeral. The benefit is 1,000 kyats for the deceased's surviving spouse or child; otherwise, the benefit equals the actual cost of the funeral, up to a maximum of 1,000 kyats.

Workers' Medical Benefits

Medical services are provided directly to patients through the Social Security Board's dispensaries and hospitals, the dispensaries of large employers, and public hospitals.

Insured persons are registered with a dispensary and are covered only for services provided by this dispensary (except in the cases of emergency or upon referral from the dispensary). Medical benefits include medical care at the dispensary, emergency domiciliary care, specialist and laboratory services at a diagnostic center, necessary hospitalization, maternity care, and medicines.

The duration of benefits is 26 weeks for one illness (may be extended for medical reasons or if in the interest of public health).

Dependents' Medical Benefits

Pediatric care is provided for an insured woman's newborn child up to the age of 6 months.

Administrative Organization

Ministry of Labor provides general supervision.

Social Security Board administers contributions and benefits.

Work Injury

Regulatory Framework

First law: 1923 (workmen's compensation).

Current law: 1954 (social security), implemented in 1956.

Type of program: Social insurance system.

Note: The 1923 law is still in force for agricultural workers and nonagricultural employees not covered by the current law.

Coverage

Certain groups of employees of state enterprises, certain types of civil servant, and temporary and permanent employees of public or private firms with five or more workers in industry and commerce or in specified industries and services (railways, ports, mines, and oilfields).

Coverage is being extended gradually to different regions. Coverage is provided in Yangon, Mandalay, Mawlamyaing, Pathein, Bago, and 92 townships.

Exclusions: Self-employed persons, workers in private shops and establishments with less than five employees, construction workers, agricultural workers, and fishermen.

Employer liability under the Workmen's Compensation Act applies to all employees not covered by the Social Security Act.

Source of Funds

Insured person: None; see source of funds under Sickness and Maternity for the funeral grant.

Self-employed person: Not applicable.

Employer: 1% of monthly payroll, according to 10 wage classes; see source of funds under Sickness and Maternity for the funeral grant.

The minimum monthly earnings for contribution and benefit purposes are 100 kyats for monthly earnings in the lowest wage class of less than 150 kyats.

The maximum earnings for contribution and benefit purposes are 1,000 kyats for monthly earnings in the highest wage class of more than 950 kyats.

Government: None.

Qualifying Conditions

Work injury benefits: There is no minimum qualifying period.

Temporary Disability Benefits

The benefit is equal to 66.6% of the insured's average covered earnings in the 17 weeks before the disability began, according to 10 wage classes. The benefit is payable from the first day of incapacity for up to 52 weeks.

Permanent Disability Benefits

Permanent disability pension: If totally disabled (100%), the benefit is equal to 66.6% of the insured's average covered earnings in the 17 weeks before the disability began, according to 10 wage classes.

Constant-attendance supplement: If totally disabled, 25% of the insured's pension is paid for the constant attendance of another person, as certified by a medical officer of the Social Security Board.

Partial disability: A percentage of the full pension is paid according to the assessed loss of capacity; if the loss of capacity is less than 20%, a lump sum is paid equal to 5 years' pension.

The percentage loss of capacity is assessed by medical officers of the Social Security Board and may be reassessed at any time at the request of the board. The board can temporarily or permanently suspend benefits if the insured fails to attend requested medical examinations.

Workers' Medical Benefits

Medical services are provided directly to patients through the Social Security Board's dispensaries and hospitals, the dispensaries of large employers, and public hospitals. Insured persons are registered with a dispensary and are covered only for services provided by this dispensary (except in the cases of emergency or upon referral from the dispensary). Medical benefits include medical care at the dispensary, emergency domiciliary care, specialist and laboratory services at a diagnostic center, necessary hospitalization, physiotherapy, prostheses, appliances, and medicines.

There is no limit to duration.

Survivor Benefits

Survivor pension: Between 28 kyats and 267 kyats is paid a month, according to 10 wage classes. The pension is paid to the widow (the benefit ceases on remarriage). The average benefit is 27% of the deceased's covered earnings.

Orphan's pension: Between 14 kyats and 133.50 kyats is paid a month, according to 10 wage classes for each orphan younger than age 16; between 21 kyats and 200 kyats a month, according to 10 wage classes for each full orphan younger than age 16. The average pension is 13% (20% for a full orphan) of the deceased's covered earnings.

Other eligible survivors (in the absence of the above): A pension is payable to a disabled widower and aged or disabled relatives who were dependent on the deceased. The pension for other eligible survivors is determined by the Social Security Board, depending on the nature of the survivor's relationship with the deceased, personal income, working capacity, and other related conditions.

The maximum total survivor pension is equal to 66.6% of the deceased's average covered earnings in the 17 weeks before death, according to 10 wage classes. If the total of all survivor pensions exceeds the maximum, the pensions are reduced proportionally.

Funeral grant: Paid to the person who paid for the funeral. The benefit is 1,000 kyats for the deceased's surviving spouse or child; otherwise, the benefit equals the actual cost of the funeral, up to a maximum of 1,000 kyats.

Administrative Organization

Ministry of Labor provides general supervision.

Social Security Board administers contributions and benefits.

China

Exchange rate: US$1.00 equals 8.02 yuan.

Old Age, Disability, and Survivors

Regulatory Framework

First law: 1951.

Current laws: 1953 (regulations) and 1978, 1995, 1997, 1999, and 2005 (directives).

Type of program: Social insurance and mandatory individual account system.

Note: China does not yet have national social security legislation. Provincial and city/county social insurance agencies and employers adapt central government guidelines to local conditions.

Coverage

Employees in urban enterprises and urban institutions managed as enterprises and the urban self-employed. In some provinces, coverage for the urban self-employed is voluntary. (Urban enterprises comprise all state-owned enterprises, regardless of their location.) According to region, special arrangements are made for former farmers who migrate to work in urban areas.

Old-age provision in rural areas is based mainly on family support and through community and state financial support. Pilot schemes in the form of individual accounts, supported at the town and village level and subject to preferential support by the state, operate in some rural areas.

Employees of government and communist party organizations and employees of cultural, educational, and scientific institutions (except for institutions financed off-budget) are covered under special government-funded, employer-administered systems.

Source of Funds

Insured person

Basic pension insurance: None, or as determined by local government regulations.

Mandatory individual account: 8% of gross insured earnings.

The minimum earnings for contribution and benefit purposes are equal to 60% of the local average wage for the previous year.

The maximum earnings for contribution and benefit purposes vary but may be as much as 300% of the local average wage for the previous year.

Self-employed person

Basic pension insurance: Around 12% of the local average wage.

Mandatory individual pension account: Around 8% of the local average wage.

Employer

Basic pension insurance: The maximum contribution is 20% of payroll, depending on local government regulations. Contribution rates vary among provinces.

Mandatory individual account: None. (Employer contributions to individual accounts on behalf of employees ceased on December 31, 2005.)

Government

Basic pension insurance: Central and local government subsidies are provided to city/council retirement pension pools as needed.

Mandatory individual account: Central and local government subsidies are provided to city/council retirement pension pools as needed.

Qualifying Conditions

Old-age pension

Basic pension insurance (central government guidelines): Age 60 (men); age 60 (professional women), age 55 (non-professional salaried women), or age 50 (other categories of women). The insured must have a minimum of 15 years of coverage.

Age 55 (men) or age 45 (women) with at least 15 years of coverage, if employed in arduous or unhealthy work.

Early pension (basic pension insurance): Age 50 (men) or age 45 (women) with 10 years of coverage and if totally disabled.

Mandatory individual account (central government guidelines): Age 60 (men); age 60 (professional women), age 55 (nonprofessional salaried women), or age 50 (other categories of women). The insured must have a minimum of 15 years of coverage.

Age 55 (men) or age 45 (women) with at least 15 years of coverage, if employed in arduous or unhealthy work.

Lump-sum settlement (mandatory individual account): Paid if the insured has less than 15 years of contributions to the mandatory individual account.

Disability pension

Basic pension insurance (central government guidelines): Assessed with a total incapacity for work and not eligible for the early old-age pension. Medical experts of the Labor Ability Appraisal Committee assess the degree of disability.

Mandatory individual account (central government guidelines): No cash benefit is provided.

Survivor pension

Basic pension insurance (central government guidelines): The deceased was in covered employment or was a pensioner.

Eligible survivors include the spouse, children, and parents.

Funeral grant: Paid for the death of the insured or an immediate family member who was dependent on the insured.

Mandatory individual account (central government guidelines): The deceased was in covered employment.

The eligible survivor is the deceased's legal heir.

Old-Age Benefits

Old-age pension

Basic pension insurance (central government guidelines): The pension is calculated on the basis of the mean value of the average local wage of the preceding year before retirement and the average individual monthly wage for contribution purposes.

Early pension: A pension is provided.

The minimum pension is paid with 15 years of coverage and is equal to 1% of the calculated mean value for each year of coverage.

Mandatory individual account (central government guidelines): The monthly benefit is calculated on the basis of the balance in the insured's individual account divided by the actuarial month.

The actuarial month is determined by the insured's retirement age, the average life expectancy for the urban population, and the interest rate (transitional arrangements are provided by local governments for workers who began employment before the introduction of mandatory individual accounts in 1997 and who retired on or after January 1, 2006). After the monthly benefits from the mandatory individual account are exhausted, benefits are paid out of a reserve fund. The reserve fund constitutes balances of employer contributions made before January 1, 2006, to individual accounts that were subsequently closed as the result of the death of the individual account holder (see mandatory individual account under survivor benefits, below).

The minimum pension is set by provincial and city/county governments according to the local standard of living.

Lump-sum settlement (mandatory individual account): A lump sum is paid equal to the balance of the insured's total contributions plus interest.

Permanent Disability Benefits

Basic pension insurance (central government guidelines): The pension is equal to 40% of the insured's monthly wage. (Local governments' regulations may vary.)

The minimum pension is set by provincial and city/county governments according to the local standard of living.

Mandatory individual account (central government guidelines): No cash benefit is provided. (Local governments' regulations may vary.)

Survivor Benefits

Survivor pension

Basic pension insurance (central government guidelines): A lump sum of between 6 and 12 months of the deceased's last monthly wage, according to the number of surviving dependents.

Funeral grant: For the death of the insured, a lump sum equal to 2 months' average local wage in the previous year is payable to the spouse, children, parents, and grandparents. For the death of an immediate family member who was dependent on the insured, from 1/3 to 1/2 of the monthly average local or enterprise wage in the previous year is payable, depending on the age of the deceased.

Mandatory individual account (central government guidelines): A lump sum equal to the balance of the deceased's contributions, plus interest, is payable to the deceased's legal heir. (If the insured died before the normal retirement age, the balance of any employer contributions made before January 1, 2006, to the deceased's individual account is transferred to a reserve fund.)

Administrative Organization

Ministry of Labor and Social Security, Department of Pensions, provides general guidance and ensures that local regulations follow central government guidelines.

Provincial or city/county social insurance agencies administer their respective retirement pension pools and individual accounts.

Mandatory individual account funds are deposited in state-owned banks.

Provincial labor and social security authorities are responsible for regulatory funds to which locally pooled funds in the jurisdiction must pay a percentage of their revenue.

Sickness and Maternity

Regulatory Framework

First law: 1951.

Current laws: 1953; 1978 (permanent employees); 1986 (contract workers); 1988 and 1994 (women employees); 1998, 1999, 2000, and 2002 (medical insurance); and 2006 (rural cooperative medicare).

Type of program: Social insurance and mandatory individual account system.

Note: China does not yet have national social security legislation. The social insurance program applies to urban areas.

Coverage

The maternity insurance program covers all employees in urban enterprises. (Urban enterprises comprise all state-owned enterprises, regardless of their location.)

The urban medical insurance program covers all employees in urban areas (working in government organizations, enterprises, social groups, and nonprofit bodies).

A rural cooperative medicare program covers certain farmers (coverage is being gradually extended).

Source of Funds

Insured person: Around 2% of gross wages for medical benefits only (local government may adjust contribution rates according to local factors). The contribution is paid into the insured's individual account. (Employees do not contribute for maternity benefits.)

The minimum earnings for contribution and benefit purposes are equal to 60% of the local average wage for the previous year.

The maximum earnings for contribution and benefit purposes are equal to 300% of the local average wage for the previous year.

Self-employed person: Not applicable. (Farmers covered by the rural cooperative medicare program contribute a flat-rate 10 yuan to the program's pooling fund.)

Employer: Around 6% of total payroll for medical benefits (local government may adjust contribution rates according to local factors). The employer contribution is split 30/70 between the insured's individual account and the social insurance fund, respectively. (Nonparticipating enterprises pay directly for the cost of benefits.) A maximum of 1% of total payroll for maternity benefits (to be decided by local government).

Government: Central and local governments provide tax concessions and subsidies for administrative costs and finance complementary medical insurance systems for civil servants. Central and local governments finance most of the cost of the rural cooperative medicare program.

Local governments and employers adapt central government guidelines on contribution rates to local conditions.

Qualifying Conditions

Sickness, maternity, and medical benefits: There is no minimum qualifying period.

Sickness and Maternity Benefits

Sickness benefit (central government guidelines for permanent workers): According to length of service, 60% to 100% of the insured's last monthly wage is payable by the employer for up to 6 months each year; thereafter, 40% to 60% is payable by the employer until recovery or the determination of permanent disability.

Contract workers receive the same benefits as permanent workers.

Maternity benefit (central government guidelines for permanent workers): The average monthly wage of the enterprise for the previous year is paid by the maternity social insurance fund for up to 90 days for the birth of a child, 42 days for a pregnancy that lasted at least 4 months (15 to 30 days for less than 4 months), or 42 days for at least 4 months of gestation before an abortion.

Workers' Medical Benefits

Medical benefits (central government guidelines): Covered workers receive medical benefits at a chosen accredited hospital or clinic on a fee-for-service basis.

Cost sharing: The individual account is used to finance medical benefits only, up to a maximum equal to 10% of the local average annual wage. The social insurance fund reimburses the cost of medical benefits from 10% to 400% of the local average annual wage, according to the schedule. Medical treatment in high-grade hospitals results in lower percentage reimbursements, and vice versa. Reimbursement for payments beyond 400% of the local average annual wage must be covered by private insurance or public supplementary systems.

Under the rural cooperative medicare program, farmers are reimbursed annually for medical costs up to a maximum that varies according to the region.

Dependents' Medical Benefits

Medical benefits (central government guidelines): No benefits are provided. The individual account must not be used to pay for dependents' medical benefits.

Administrative Organization

Ministry of Labor and Social Security, Department of Medical Care Insurance, provides general guidance to local governments' medical insurance programs and ensures that local regulations follow central government guidelines.

Ministry of Labor and Social Security, Department of Medical Care Insurance, supervises the provision of benefits by nonparticipating enterprises.

Local government social insurance agencies and participating enterprises administer medical benefits insurance with the social insurance funds.

Local government social insurance agencies contract with accredited clinics and hospitals for the provision of medical benefits.

Ministry of Public Health provides general guidance to medical care providers.

Individual state-run enterprises administer cash benefit programs.

Local government social insurance agencies manage individual medical savings accounts.

County-level public health authorities administer the rural cooperative medicare pooling fund.

Work Injury

Regulatory Framework

First law: 1951.

Current laws: 1953, 1978 (permanent employees), 1986 (contract workers), 1996, 2003 (employment injury), and 2004 (rural migrants).

Type of program: Local government-administered social insurance system. (Employer-liability system for nonparticipating enterprises.)

Note: China does not yet have national social security legislation. Local governments and employers adapt central government guidelines to local conditions.

Coverage

Employees in all enterprises; self-employed persons and their employees.

Employees of government and communist party organizations; employees of cultural, educational, and scientific institutions (except for institutions financed off-budget); and university students are covered under special government-funded, employer-administered systems.

Source of Funds

Insured person: None.

Self-employed person: Contributes as an employer on behalf of employees.

Employer

Social insurance: Contributions vary according to three categories of industry and the assessed degree of risk. The average contribution rate in provinces is 1% of total payroll.

Employer-liability: The total cost for employers not participating in social insurance.

Government: Central and local government subsidies to guarantee reserve funds as needed.

Qualifying Conditions

Work injury benefits: There is no minimum qualifying period.

Temporary Disability Benefits

Temporary disability benefit (central government guidelines): 100% of the insured's wage is paid by the employer for a maximum of 12 months; may be extended for another 12 months.

Medical experts of the municipal Labor Ability Appraisal Committee assess the degree of disability. The benefit is suspended on the award of the permanent disability pension.

The employer provides necessary nursing care.

Permanent Disability Benefits

Permanent disability pension (central government guidelines): The pension is awarded according to 10 degrees of assessed disability.

Medical experts of the municipal Labor Ability Appraisal Committee assess the degree of disability.

For a total disability (degrees 1–4), a lump sum is paid equal to 24 months of the previous wage plus a monthly pension equal to 90% of the previous wage (1st degree); a lump sum equal to 22 months' wages plus a pension equal to 85% of the previous wage (2nd degree); a lump sum equal to 20 months' wages plus a pension equal to 80% of the previous wage (3rd degree); or a lump sum equal to 18 months' wages plus a pension equal to 75% of the previous wage (4th degree).

The pension ceases on the award of the old-age pension. If the old-age pension is less than the permanent disability pension, the work injury fund pays the difference.

To receive a pension for an assessed total disability, the insured and the former employer must contribute to the basic medical insurance system.

For a moderate permanent disability (degrees 5–6), a lump sum is paid equal to 16 months' wages (5th degree) or 14 months' wages (6th degree). If the employer cannot offer the insured an appropriate job, a monthly benefit is paid equal to 70% of the insured's wage before the onset of disability (5th degree) or 60% of the insured's wage (6th degree).

Employers pay social insurance contributions for pensioners assessed with a 5th or 6th degree disability. If the permanent disability pension is less than the local minimum wage, the employer pays the difference. If the insured voluntarily ceases the employment relationship with the employer, the insured receives a lump-sum work injury medical treatment subsidy and a disability employment subsidy. Provincial governments set the subsidy rates.

For a minor permanent disability (degrees 7–10), a lump sum is paid equal to 12 months' wages (7th degree), 10 months' wages (8th degree), 8 months' wages (9th degree), or 6 months' wages (10th degree). If the labor contract expires or the insured voluntarily ceases the employment relationship with the employer, the insured receives a lump-sum work injury medical treatment subsidy and a disability employment subsidy. Provincial governments set the subsidy rates.

For all degrees of disability, employers are required to pay higher lump-sum compensation if the injured worker was employed illegally.

The minimum pension is equal to the local minimum wage.

Workers' Medical Benefits

Benefits are provided by accredited hospitals and clinics. Medical benefits include treatment, surgery, nursing, medicine, appliances, transportation, and hospitalization.

Survivor Benefits

Survivor pension (central government guidelines): The spouse receives 40% of the deceased's last monthly wage; 30% is paid to each other dependent.

Widow(er)'s and orphan's supplements: Each receives 10% of the deceased's last monthly wage.

Other eligible survivors include parents, grandparents, grandchildren, brothers, and sisters.

The maximum total survivor pension is equal to 100% of the deceased's last monthly wage.

Death allowance: A lump sum is paid equal to between 48 months and 60 months of the local average wage.

Funeral grant: A lump sum is paid equal to 6 months of the local average wage.

Administrative Organization

Participating enterprises: Ministry of Labor and Social Security, Department of Medical Care Insurance, provides general guidance and ensures that local regulations follow central government guidelines.

Local government social insurance agencies and participating enterprises administer programs.

Unemployment

Regulatory Framework

First and current laws: 1986, 1993, and 1999.

Type of program: Local government-administered social insurance programs.

Note: China does not yet have national social security legislation. Local governments and employers adapt central government guidelines to local conditions.

Coverage

All employees of urban enterprises and institutions.

Source of Funds

Insured person: 1% of gross earnings.

Self-employed person: Not applicable.

Employer: 2% of payroll.

Government: Provincial regulatory fund and local governments provide subsidies to unemployment funds as required.

Qualifying Conditions

Unemployment benefit: Must have at least 1 year in covered employment; be involuntarily employed; not be receiving old-age benefits; be registered at, and regularly reporting to, a local employment-service agency; and be actively seeking employment. The claim to the unemployment benefit must be made within 60 days after the labor contract expires or is terminated. The benefit may cease or be suspended for refusing a suitable job offer.

Unemployment Benefits

The benefit amount is set by local governments at a level higher than the local public assistance benefit but lower than the local minimum wage. The benefit is payable for a maximum of 1 year with less than 5 years of coverage, for a maximum of 1.5 years with 5 or more but less than 10 years, or for a maximum of 2 years with 10 or more years of coverage.

Administrative Organization

Ministry of Labor and Social Security, Department of Unemployment, provides general guidance and ensures that local regulations follow central government guidelines.

Local government social insurance agencies pay benefits.

Local government social insurance agencies and the tax authorities collect contributions.

Family Allowances

Regulatory Framework

A tax-financed, means-tested minimum guarantee system provides benefits to urban families whose per capita income is below the stipulated minimum level.

A similar program has been implemented in some rural areas.

Note: China does not yet have national social security legislation.

Fiji

Exchange rate: US$1.00 equals
1.71 Fiji dollars (F$).

Old Age, Disability, and Survivors

Regulatory Framework

First and current law: 1966 (provident fund), with 1976, 1985, 2000, and 2005 amendments.

Type of program: Provident fund system.

Coverage

Employed workers aged 15 to 55, except members of equivalent private plans approved by the Fiji National Provident Fund Board.

Voluntary coverage for domestic workers, self-employed persons, students, and informal-sector workers.

Special system for civil servants and military and police personnel who began employment before November 1971 and elected to continue under the Civil Service Pension Scheme.

Source of Funds

Insured person: 8% of earnings; F$25 is deducted annually from each eligible member's provident fund account to finance the death benefit.

The maximum annual total contributions for pension calculation purposes are 16% of earnings (F$4,800 a year for voluntary contributors).

Self-employed person: A minimum annual contribution of F$84 up to a maximum of 30% of earnings; F$25 is deducted annually from each eligible member's provident fund account to finance the death benefit.

The maximum annual total contributions for pension calculation purposes are 16% of earnings (F$4,800 a year for voluntary contributors).

Employer: A minimum of 8% of payroll up to a maximum of 30% of payroll.

The maximum annual total contributions for pension calculation purposes are 16% of earnings.

Government: None.

Qualifying Conditions

Old-age benefit: Age 55; at any age if leaving the country permanently. Fund members with at least 10 years of contributions may elect to receive a monthly pension; a reduced pension may be paid for contributions of less than 10 years.

Disability benefit: Incapacity for work in covered employment. The disabled fund member may elect to receive a lump sum or a monthly pension.

Medical certification is required. A medical board appointed by the Fiji National Provident Fund Board may request the scheme member to have a medical examination.

Survivor benefit: On the death of the fund member before retirement age, and if the surviving spouse is the only survivor, the spouse may elect to receive a lump sum or a monthly pension.

Eligible survivors are named by the fund member.

Death benefit: A lump sum is paid to survivors named by the deceased.

Old-Age Benefits

A lump sum equal to total employee and employer contributions plus accumulated interest or, optionally, a monthly pension based on an annuity factor equal to 16% (for a single person) of employee and employer contributions (additional voluntary contributions are excluded) plus accumulated interest. A couple may elect to receive a monthly pension of 2/3 of the pension for a single person plus accumulated interest for as long as either spouse lives.

The annuity factor is being reduced by 1% each year until it reaches 15% (for a single person) for the financial year 2008/2009.

Drawdown payment: Workers who are members of the provident fund for at least 2 years and whose individual balance exceeds a prescribed minimum amount (F$1,000) can withdraw 2/3 of the balance for housing costs. Workers can also make withdrawals equal to 1/3 of the balance for education assistance and medical assistance.

Permanent Disability Benefits

A lump sum equal to total employee and employer contributions plus accumulated interest or, optionally, a monthly pension based on an annuity factor equal to 16% (for a single person) of employee and employer contributions (additional voluntary contributions are excluded) plus accumulated interest. A couple may elect to receive a monthly pension of 2/3 of the pension for a single person plus accumulated interest for as long as either spouse lives.

The annuity factor is being reduced by 1% each year until it reaches 15% (for a single person) for the financial year 2008/2009.

Survivor Benefits

Survivor benefit: A lump sum equal to total employee and employer contributions plus accumulated interest is paid to named survivors. A monthly pension based on an annuity factor equal to 16% of employee and employer contributions (additional voluntary contributions are excluded) may be paid in lieu of the lump sum to a spouse.

The annuity factor is being reduced by 1% each year until it reaches 15% for the financial year 2008/2009.

Death benefit: The maximum lump sum is F$7,000.

Benefit adjustment: The death benefit is reviewed annually.

Administrative Organization

Appointed by the Minister of Finance, the Fiji National Provident Fund Board (http://www.fnpf.com.fj) provides general supervision and enforces the law.

Work Injury

Regulatory Framework

First and current law: 1965 (workmen's compensation), with amendments.

Type of program: Employer-liability system.

Coverage

Employed persons and apprentices.

Exclusions: Casual labor, family labor, armed forces personnel, and some public-sector employees and other workers designated by the government.

Source of Funds

Insured person: None.

Self-employed person: Not applicable.

Employer: The total cost, met through the direct provision of benefits.

Government: None.

Qualifying Conditions

Work injury benefits: The insured must be totally incapacitated for work for at least 3 days.

Temporary Disability Benefits

The benefit is equal to 66% of the insured's weekly earnings and is paid after a 2-day waiting period for up to 260 weeks.

The maximum total benefit is F$16,000. The benefit may be converted to a lump-sum payment in certain cases.

The assessed degree of disability is established according to the schedule in law and following an examination by a doctor chosen by the employer. Periodic assessment of the degree of disability may be required.

Permanent Disability Benefits

For a total disability, a lump sum is paid equal to 260 weeks' earnings.

Constant-attendance supplement: Equal to 25% of the lump sum if totally disabled and in need of the constant help of another person.

Partial disability: A percentage of the lump sum payable for a total disability is paid according to the assessed degree of disability.

The assessed degree of disability is established according to the schedule in law and following an examination by a doctor chosen by the employer. Periodic assessment of the degree of disability may be required.

Workers' Medical Benefits

Medical and hospital care, surgery, medicines, appliances, and transportation.

Survivor Benefits

A lump sum is paid equal to 208 weeks of the deceased's earnings.

Eligible survivors are individuals who were fully or partially dependent on the insured. Survivor benefits are split among all eligible survivors.

The minimum benefit is F$9,000.

The maximum total benefit is F$24,000.

Administrative Organization

Permanent Secretary for Labor and Industrial Relations (http://www.fiji.gov.fj) enforces work injury law.

Individual employers pay compensation directly to their own employees, except for lump-sum payments and survivor benefits.

Local courts administer lump-sum payments and survivor benefits.

Disputes regarding the provision of medical benefits are settled by the courts.

Georgia

Exchange rate: US$1.00 equals 1.80 lari.

Old Age, Disability, and Survivors

Regulatory Framework

First law: 1956 (state pensions).

Current laws: 1990 (pension security), with 1995 amendments; 2003 (mandatory social security); 2003 (individual registration and accounts); and 2005 (state pensions).

Type of program: Social insurance and social assistance system.

Local authorities and employers may provide supplementary benefits out of their own budgets.

Coverage

Social insurance: All employed persons residing in Georgia.

Special system for employees of the Ministry of Security, the Ministry of Internal Affairs, and the Ministry of Defense.

Social assistance: Older persons, disabled persons, and survivors according to need as determined by local government authorities.

Source of Funds

Insured person

Social insurance: None.

Social assistance: None.

Self-employed person

Social insurance: None, if no employees; 20% of declared profits for those with employees.

Social assistance: None.

Employer

Social insurance: 20% of payroll.

The employer's contributions also finance sickness, maternity, and work injury benefits.

Social assistance: None.

Government

Social insurance: Subsidies as needed.

Social assistance: The total cost.

Qualifying Conditions

Old-age pension (social insurance): Age 65 (men) or age 60 (women), with at least 5 years of covered employment.

Earnings test: Pensioners in gainful employment must satisfy an earnings test.

Social pension (old-age): Aged 70 or older (men) or aged 65 or older (women). The pension is paid to an individual or to a family without other means of support.

Disability pension (social insurance): No benefits are provided.

Social pension (disability): Must be assessed as disabled. The pension is paid to an individual or family without other means of support.

Survivor pension (social insurance): No benefits are provided.

Social pension (survivors): The pension is paid to a surviving individual or family without other means of support.

Old-Age Benefits

Old-age pension (social insurance): 35 lari a month is paid.

Benefit adjustment: Benefits are adjusted on an ad hoc basis.

Social pension (old-age): 35 lari a month is paid.

Benefit adjustment: Benefits are adjusted on an ad hoc basis.

Permanent Disability Benefits

Disability pension (social insurance): No cash benefits are provided; there are certain reductions on hospital and medical charges if the disability is certified by local medical and health departments.

Social pension (disability): The monthly pension for an eligible single disabled person is 22 lari; 35 lari if the disabled person lives in a family of two or more.

Benefit adjustment: Benefits are adjusted on an ad hoc basis.

Survivor Benefits

Survivor pension (social insurance): No cash benefits are provided.

Social pension (survivors): The monthly pension for a single survivor is 22 lari; 35 lari for a family of two or more survivors.

Benefit adjustment: Benefits are adjusted on an ad hoc basis.

Administrative Organization

Ministry of Labor, Health, and Social Affairs (http://www.molhsa.ge) provides general supervision and coordination.

Department of Labor, Health, and Social Affairs (http://www.molhsa.ge) administers the program locally.

Sickness and Maternity

Regulatory Framework

First law: 1964 (health).

Current laws: 1994 (health care), 1955 (health care system), and 1997 (medical insurance).

Type of program: Social insurance (maternity benefits) and social assistance (medical benefits) system.

Coverage

Cash sickness benefits: No benefits are provided.

Cash maternity benefits: Employed and self-employed women.

Medical benefits: Persons residing in Georgia assessed as needy.

Source of Funds

Insured person: None.

Self-employed person: Not applicable.

Employer: See source of funds under Old Age, Disability, and Survivors, above.

Government: None for cash benefits; the total cost of medical benefits for needy persons residing in Georgia.

Qualifying Conditions

Cash sickness benefits: No cash benefits are provided.

(Private employers may voluntarily provide benefits if an employee's incapacity is certified by a doctor. The employee pays the cost of medical certification.)

Cash maternity benefits: There is no minimum qualifying period.

Medical benefits: Citizens residing in Georgia who satisfy a needs test.

Sickness and Maternity Benefits

Sickness benefit: No cash benefits are provided.

(Private employers may voluntarily pay 100% of earnings for up to 30 days a year.)

Maternity benefit: 200 lari is paid to a mother for medical services; 400 lari to a mother from a low-income family.

Maternity leave: Leave without pay is provided for up to 8 weeks after childbirth to care for an infant; may be extended up to 3 years.

Workers' Medical Benefits

Medical services are provided through government clinics, hospitals, maternity homes, and other facilities to the needy and disabled.

Dependents' Medical Benefits

Medical services are provided through government clinics, hospitals, maternity homes, and other facilities to the needy and disabled.

Administrative Organization

Cash maternity benefits: Ministry of Labor, Health, and Social Affairs (http://www.molhsa.ge) provides general supervision.

Maternity benefits are provided by the State United Social Insurance Fund (http://www.susif.ge).

Medical benefits: Ministry of Labor, Health, and Social Affairs (http://www.molhsa.ge) provides general supervision and coordination.

Work Injury

Regulatory Framework

First laws: 1955 (short-term benefits); and 1991 (pensions), with amendment.

Current law: 1999 (workmen's compensation).

Type of program: Social insurance and social assistance system.

Coverage

Work injury benefits: All employed persons.

Source of Funds

Insured person: None.

Self-employed person: Not applicable.

Employer: See source of funds under Old Age, Disability, and Survivors, above. If the employer is determined liable for the insured's disability or death, the employer pays the total cost of benefits.

Government: See source of funds under Old Age, Disability, and Survivors, above; the total cost of medical benefits.

Qualifying Conditions

Work injury benefits

Cash benefits: There is no minimum qualifying period.

Medical benefits: The Ministry of Labor, Health, and Social Affairs determines eligibility for medical benefits at the local level.

Temporary Disability Benefits

The benefit is equal to 100% of earnings and is paid for a maximum of 6 months; 10 months for tuberculosis. If the employer is determined liable for the insured's disability, the employer pays the total cost of benefits.

A special local commission, consisting of local health and medical officials, the employee, and the employer, determines liability and assesses the degree of disability.

Permanent Disability Benefits

Permanent disability pension: The benefit is calculated on the basis of the insured's average monthly earnings during the last 3 months and the percentage loss in working capacity. The duration of the payment depends on the assessed degree of disability and the extent to which the employer was at fault. If the employer is determined liable for the insured's disability, the employer pays the total cost of benefits.

A special local commission, consisting of local health and medical officials, the employee, and the employer, determines liability and assesses the degree of disability.

Workers' Medical Benefits

Medical services are provided directly by government health providers. If the employer is determined liable for the insured's disability, the employer pays the total cost of benefits.

Survivor Benefits

Survivor pension: If the employer is at fault for the insured's death, the pension is based on the deceased's average monthly earnings in the last 3 months. If the employer is not at fault, a social pension of 22 lari a month is paid for a single survivor; 35 lari for a family of two or more.

Administrative Organization

Temporary disability benefits: If the employer is at fault, enterprises and employers pay benefits to their employees.

Permanent disability and survivor pensions: Ministry of Labor, Health, and Social Affairs (http://www.molhsa. ge) provides general supervision and coordination. If the employer is at fault, enterprises and employers pay benefits to their employees.

Medical benefits: Ministry of Labor, Health, and Social Affairs (http://www.molhsa.ge) and health departments of local governments provide general supervision and coordination. Medical services are provided through clinics, hospitals, and other facilities administered by the Ministry of Labor, Health, and Social Affairs and local health departments. If the employer is at fault, enterprises and employers pay the cost of medical benefits for their employees.

Unemployment

Regulatory Framework

First law: 1991 (unemployment).

Current law: 2006 (employment).

Type of program: Social insurance system.

Coverage

Citizens between ages 16 and 65 (men) or ages 16 and 60 (women).

Source of Funds

Insured person: None.

Self-employed person: None.

Employer: None.

Government: The total cost.

Qualifying Conditions

Unemployment benefit: Must be registered at an employment office and be able and willing to work. The benefit may be reduced, suspended, or terminated if the insured is discharged for violating work discipline, leaving employment without good cause, violating the conditions for job placement or vocational training, or filing a fraudulent claim.

Unemployment Benefits

No cash benefits are currently provided.

Administrative Organization

Ministry of Labor, Health, and Social Affairs (http://www. molhsa.ge) provides general supervision.

Social Assistance and Employment State Agency and its regional and local branches administer the program.

Family Allowances

Regulatory Framework

First and current law: 2006.

Type of program: Social assistance system.

Coverage

All persons residing in Georgia.

Source of Funds

Insured person: None.

Self-employed person: None.

Employer: None.

Government: The total cost.

Qualifying Conditions

Family benefit: Families assessed as needy. (Families assessed as needy can receive social pensions at the same time as family benefits, subject to conditions.)

Family Allowance Benefits

Family benefit: 35 lari a month is paid for a family of two or more; 22 lari for a single person.

Administrative Organization

State United Social Insurance Fund (http://www.susif.ge) and the Social Assistance and Employment State Agency administer the programs.

Hong Kong

Exchange rate: US$1.00 equals
7.75 Hong Kong dollars (HK$).

Old Age, Disability, and Survivors

Regulatory Framework

First and current laws: 1971 (social assistance); 1973 (universal old-age and disability allowance); 1988 (universal higher-rate disability allowance); 1993 (comprehensive social security assistance); and 1995 (mandatory provident funds), implemented in 2000, with 2002 amendment.

Type of program: Universal old-age and disability pension, mandatory occupational benefit (mandatory provident fund schemes), and social assistance (comprehensive social security assistance) system.

Note: The mandatory occupational plans operating under the name of mandatory provident funds are privately run and should not be confused with publicly run national provident funds found in other countries.

Coverage

Universal allowances and comprehensive social security assistance: All persons residing in Hong Kong.

Mandatory occupational benefit: All employees holding a contract of 60 or more days (employees in the catering and construction industry who are employed for periods shorter than 60 days or are covered on a daily basis) and self-employed persons between ages 18 and 65.

Exclusions: Self-employed hawkers; domestic employees; persons covered by statutory pension plans or provident funds, such as civil servants or teachers; members of occupational retirement plans who are granted exemption certificates; and foreign citizens working in Hong Kong for less than 13 months or covered by another country's retirement system.

Source of Funds

Insured person

Universal allowances and comprehensive social security assistance: None.

Mandatory occupational benefit: A minimum of 5% of monthly earnings. Voluntary additional contributions are permitted.

The minimum monthly earnings for contribution purposes are HK$5,000.

The maximum monthly earnings for contribution purposes are HK$20,000.

Contributions are tax-deductible up to HK$12,000 a year.

Self-employed person

Universal allowances and comprehensive social security assistance: None.

Mandatory occupational benefit: A minimum of 5% of monthly or yearly income. Voluntary additional contributions are permitted.

The minimum earnings for contribution purposes are HK$5,000 a month or HK$60,000 a year.

The maximum earnings for contribution purposes are HK$20,000 a month or HK$240,000 a year.

Contributions are tax-deductible up to HK$12,000 a year.

Employer

Universal allowances and comprehensive social security assistance: None.

Mandatory occupational benefit: A minimum of 5% of monthly payroll. Voluntary additional contributions are permitted.

There are no minimum earnings for contribution purposes.

The maximum monthly earnings for contribution purposes are HK$20,000.

Government

Universal allowances and comprehensive social security assistance: The total cost.

Mandatory occupational benefit: None.

Qualifying Conditions

Old-age pension

Old-age allowance (universal)

Lower-rate allowance: Persons aged 65 to 69 who have resided in Hong Kong for at least 7 years (requirement waived for persons who became Hong Kong residents before January 1, 2004), including 1 year of residence immediately before claiming the benefit. The allowance is income-tested (monthly income must not exceed HK$5,910 if single or HK$9,740 if married) and asset-tested (assets must not exceed HK$169,000 if single or HK$254,000 if married).

Higher-rate allowance: Persons aged 70 or older who have resided in Hong Kong for at least 7 years (requirement waived for persons who became Hong Kong residents before January 1, 2004), including 1 year of residence immediately before claiming the benefit.

Mandatory occupational benefit (old-age): Age 65 (men and women).

Early retirement: Age 60 (men and women) if ceasing employment permanently. (Funds may be withdrawn before retirement if the member leaves Hong Kong permanently.)

Old-age benefit (comprehensive social security assistance): Persons aged 60 or older who have resided in Hong Kong for at least 7 years (requirement waived for persons who became Hong Kong residents before January 1, 2004), including 1 year of residence immediately before claiming the benefit. The benefit is income-tested and asset-tested on an individual basis if living alone; if living with other family members, the total income and assets of all family members are taken into account for determining the family's eligibility.

Disability pension

Disability allowance (universal)

Lower-rate allowance: Persons who have resided in Hong Kong for at least 7 years (requirement waived for persons who became Hong Kong residents before January 1, 2004), including 1 year of residence immediately before claiming the benefit. There are no requirements for length of residence for claimants younger than age 18 residing in Hong Kong. Must be certified by the Director of Health or the Chief Executive of the Hospital Authority (or, in exceptional cases, a registered doctor in a private hospital) to have a 100% loss of earning capacity or to be profoundly deaf.

Higher-rate allowance: Persons who have resided in Hong Kong for at least 7 years (requirement waived for persons who became Hong Kong residents before January 1, 2004), including 1 year of residence immediately before claiming the benefit. There are no requirements for length of residence for claimants younger than age 18 residing in Hong Kong. Must be certified by the Director of Health or the Chief Executive of the Hospital Authority (or, in exceptional cases, a registered doctor in a private hospital) as needing the constant attendance of others to carry out daily activities and must not be receiving care in a government-owned (or government-subsidized) residential institution or Hospital Authority residential medical institution.

Mandatory occupational benefit (disability): Assessed by a registered medical practitioner as having a total and permanent incapacity for work. Employment must have ceased.

Disability benefit (comprehensive social security assistance): Disabled persons who have resided in Hong Kong for at least 7 years (requirement waived for persons who became Hong Kong residents before January 1, 2004), including 1 year of residence immediately before claiming the benefit. There are no requirements for length of residence for disabled claimants younger than age 18 residing in Hong Kong. The benefit is income-tested and asset-tested on an individual basis if living alone; if living with other family members, the total income and assets of all family members are taken into account for determining the family's eligibility.

The disability must be certified by a public medical officer.

Partial disability: The benefit is paid for an assessed degree of disability of 50% or more, involving the loss of at least 50% of earning capacity but less than 100%, or to a person

assessed by the Director of Health or the Chief Executive of the Hospital Authority as having a degree of disability equivalent to a 50% loss in earning capacity.

The benefit is also paid for a work-related disability.

Survivor pension

Mandatory occupational benefit (survivors): Paid for the death of the insured before retirement. The benefit is paid to the named survivor.

Burial grant (comprehensive social security assistance): The deceased received comprehensive social security assistance. The lump sum is paid to the person who incurred the funeral expense.

Old-Age Benefits

Old-age pension

Old-age allowance (universal): The benefit is HK$625 a month (lower rate) or HK$705 a month (higher rate).

Mandatory occupational benefit (old-age): A lump sum is paid equal to total employee and employer contributions plus accrued interest.

Old-age benefit (comprehensive social security assistance): HK$2,280 to HK$3,885 a month is paid for a person living alone or HK$2,150 to HK$3,560 a month if living with other family members, subject to the recipient's health and whether constant attendance is needed; plus special grants to meet the specific individual needs of recipients.

Permanent Disability Benefits

Disability pension

Disability allowance (universal): The benefit is HK$1,125 a month (lower rate) or HK$2,250 a month (higher rate).

Mandatory occupational benefit (disability): A lump sum is paid equal to total employee and employer contributions plus accrued interest.

Disability benefit (comprehensive social security assistance): HK$1,930 to HK$4,165 a month is paid for a person living alone or HK$1,750 to HK$3,850 a month if living with other family members, subject to the recipient's age, the assessed degree of disability, and whether constant attendance is needed; plus special grants to meet the specific individual needs of recipients.

Survivor Benefits

Mandatory occupational benefit (survivors): A lump sum is paid equal to total employee and employer contributions plus accrued interest.

Burial grant (comprehensive social security assistance): The cost of the funeral, up to HK$10,430.

Administrative Organization

Universal pension and comprehensive social security assistance: Social Welfare Department (http://www.info.gov.hk/swd) administers the program.

Mandatory occupational benefits: Under the direction of an executive director and an advisory committee, the Mandatory Provident Fund Schemes Authority (MPFA) (http://www.mpfahk.org) supervises mandatory provident funds. The MPFA is responsible for registering provident funds and ensuring that approved trustees administer the provident funds in a prudent manner.

Sickness and Maternity

Regulatory Framework

First and current laws: 1968 (employment ordinance), with 1997 amendment; and 1971 (social assistance).

Type of program: Employer-liability (cash benefits only) and social assistance (comprehensive social security assistance) system.

Note: Hong Kong does not yet have social security legislation for the comprehensive social security assistance program.

Coverage

Employer-liability system: All employed persons.

Comprehensive social security assistance: All persons residing in Hong Kong.

Source of Funds

Insured person

Employer liability: None.

Comprehensive social security assistance: None.

Self-employed person

Employer liability: Not applicable.

Comprehensive social security assistance: None.

Employer

Employer liability: The total cost through the direct provision of benefits.

Comprehensive social security assistance: None.

Government

Employer liability: None.

Comprehensive social security assistance: The total cost.

Qualifying Conditions

Cash sickness benefits (employer liability): Must have at least 1 month of continuous employment.

The employee must accumulate a sufficient number of paid sickness days. Paid sickness days accumulate at the rate of 2 days for each complete month of employment during the first 12 months of employment and 4 days for each month of employment thereafter, up to a maximum of 120 days. The sick leave period must last at least 4 consecutive days, and the employee must provide an appropriate medical certificate issued by a registered medical practitioner or dentist.

Cash maternity benefits (employer liability): Must have at least 40 weeks of continuous employment. The employee must provide notice to the employer of her intention to take maternity leave after the pregnancy has been confirmed by a registered medical practitioner.

Comprehensive social security assistance: Persons aged 15 to 59 who have resided in Hong Kong for at least 7 years (requirement waived for persons who became Hong Kong residents before January 1, 2004), including 1 year immediately before claiming the benefit. There are no requirements for length of residence for claimants younger than age 18 residing in Hong Kong. Benefits are income-tested and asset-tested on an individual basis if living alone; if living with other family members, the total income and assets of all family members are taken into account for determining the family's eligibility.

Must be certified by a public medical officer as having limited working capacity or being incapable of work.

The benefit is also paid for a work-related temporary incapacity.

Sickness and Maternity Benefits

Sickness benefit (employer liability): The benefit is equal to 80% of the employee's normal earnings and is payable for the number of paid sickness days accumulated by the employee.

Maternity benefit (employer liability): The benefit is equal to 80% of the employee's normal earnings and is payable for 10 weeks. The benefit is payable from 2 to 4 weeks before the expected date of childbirth or from the date of childbirth if it occurs earlier.

Comprehensive social security assistance: HK$1,930 to HK$3,530 a month is paid for a person living alone or HK$1,750 to HK$3,205 a month if living with other family members, subject to the assessed degree of reduced working capacity and whether constant attendance is needed; plus special grants to meet the specific individual needs of recipients.

Workers' Medical Benefits

Comprehensive social security assistance: Free medical treatment is provided in public hospitals and clinics for recipients of comprehensive social security assistance.

Dependents' Medical Benefits

Comprehensive social security assistance: Free medical treatment is provided in public hospitals and clinics for recipients of comprehensive social security assistance.

Administrative Organization

Employer liability: Labor Department (http://www.labour.gov.hk) administers the program.

Comprehensive social security assistance: Social Welfare Department (http://www.info.gov.hk/swd) administers the program.

Work Injury

Regulatory Framework

First and current law: 1953 (employee's compensation ordinance), with 2005 amendment.

Type of program: Employer-liability system, involving compulsory insurance with private carriers.

Coverage

Employees including domestic workers, agricultural employees, and crew members of Hong Kong ships.

Exclusions: Outworkers, family helpers, and certain casual employees.

Source of Funds

Insured person: None.

Self-employed person: Not applicable.

Employer: The total cost of the employer-liability program. (The minimum insurance coverage must be at least HK$100 million for employers with up to 200 employees or at least HK$200 million for employers with more than 200 employees.)

Government: None.

Qualifying Conditions

Work injury benefits: There is no minimum qualifying period.

Temporary Disability Benefits

The benefit is equal to 80% of the difference between the employee's monthly earnings before and after the accident. The benefit is paid for up to 36 months, after which a disability is considered to be permanent.

The employee's monthly earnings for benefit calculation purposes are the earnings in the month immediately before the accident or average monthly earnings in the last 12 months before the accident, whichever is higher.

The minimum monthly earnings for benefit calculation purposes are HK$3,490. There are no maximum monthly earnings for benefit calculation purposes.

Incapacity for work must be certified by a registered medical practitioner or an Employees' Compensation Assessment Board appointed by the Commissioner for Labor.

Benefit adjustment: Employees' monthly earnings are adjusted according to the average rate of increase of earnings of employees in similar employment with the same employer or, in the absence of such employees, according to the rate of increase in the consumer price index at the end of each 12-month period of receipt of a temporary disability benefit.

Permanent Disability Benefits

Permanent disability grant: If totally disabled (100%), a lump sum is paid equal to 48 months' times the insured's earnings if aged 56 or older; 72 months' earnings if aged 40 but younger than age 56; or 96 months' earnings if younger than age 40.

The insured's earnings for benefit calculation purposes are the earnings in the month immediately before the accident or average monthly earnings in the last 12 months before the accident, whichever is higher.

The maximum monthly earnings for benefit calculation purposes are HK$21,000.

The minimum lump sum for a permanent total disability is HK$344,000, regardless of age.

The maximum lump sum for a permanent total disability is HK$1,008,000 if aged 56 or older; HK$1,512,000 if aged 40 but younger than age 56; or HK$2,016,000 if younger than age 40.

Partial disability: A percentage of the full benefit is paid according to the assessed degree of disability and the schedule in law.

Constant-attendance supplement: The actual cost of constant attendance, up to HK$412,000. The supplement is paid as a lump sum or as periodic payments for up to 2 years.

The degree of disability is assessed by an Employees' Compensation Assessment Board appointed by the Commissioner for Labor.

Workers' Medical Benefits

Examination and treatment by a registered medical practitioner including dental care, physiotherapy and chiropractic services, and appliances.

The maximum limits on employers' liability for treatment costs are HK$200 a day for in-patient care, HK$200 a day for outpatient care, or HK$280 if both types of care are needed during the same day. The maximum limits on costs for appliances are initially HK$33,000 and HK$100,000 for subsequent repair and renewal of the appliance.

Survivor Benefits

Survivor grant: A lump sum is paid equal to 36 months of the deceased's earnings if the deceased was aged 56 or older; 60 months' earnings if aged 40 but younger than age 56; or 84 months' earnings if younger than age 40.

The deceased's earnings for benefit calculation purposes are earnings in the month immediately before the accident or average monthly earnings in the last 12 months before the accident, whichever is higher.

The maximum monthly earnings for benefit calculation purposes are HK$21,000.

The minimum lump sum is HK$303,000, regardless of age.

The maximum lump sum is HK$756,000 if the deceased was aged 56 or older; HK$1,260,000 if aged 40 but younger than age 56; or HK$1,764,000 if younger than age 40.

Eligible survivors are the deceased's spouse, children, parents, grandparents, and other family members who had been living with the deceased as a member of the same household for at least 24 months immediately before the accident. The grant is split depending on the number and type of eligible survivors (with spouse and children receiving the major share of the benefit in all cases). If the only survivors are the spouse and children, the spouse receives 50% of the grant and the children share the remaining 50% in equal amounts.

Funeral grant: A lump sum is paid to the person who incurred the funeral expense, up to a maximum of HK$35,000.

Administrative Organization

Labor Department (http://www.labour.gov.hk) administers the employer-liability program.

Employers take out insurance policies with private insurance carriers.

Unemployment

Regulatory Framework

First and current law: 1977.

Type of program: Social assistance (comprehensive social security assistance) system.

Note: Hong Kong does not yet have social security legislation for the comprehensive social security assistance program.

Coverage

All persons residing in Hong Kong.

Source of Funds

Insured person: None.

Self-employed person: None.

Employer: None.

Government: The total cost.

Qualifying Conditions

Comprehensive social security assistance (unemployment): Persons between ages 15 and 59 with at least 7 years of residence (requirement waived for persons who became Hong Kong residents before January 1, 2004), including 1 year of residence immediately before claiming the benefit. There are no requirements for length of residence for claimants younger than age 18 residing in Hong Kong. Benefits are income-tested and asset-tested on an individual basis if living alone; if living with other family members, the total income and assets of all family members are taken into account for determining the family's eligibility.

Recipients must be capable of work, actively seeking full-time jobs, and participating in the Support for Self-reliance Scheme of the Social Welfare Department.

Unemployment Benefits

Comprehensive social security assistance (unemployment): HK$1,610 a month for a person living alone or HK$1,150 to HK$1,435 a month if living with other family members, subject to the number of family members; plus special grants to meet the specific individual needs of recipients.

Administrative Organization

Social Welfare Department (http://www.info.gov.hk/swd) administers the program.

Family Allowances

Regulatory Framework

First and current law: 1971 (social assistance).

Type of program: Social assistance (comprehensive social security assistance) system.

Note: Hong Kong does not yet have social security legislation for the comprehensive social security assistance program.

Coverage

All persons residing in Hong Kong.

Source of Funds

Insured person: None.

Self-employed person: None.

Employer: None.

Government: The total cost.

Qualifying Conditions

Comprehensive social security assistance (family):
Persons who have resided in Hong Kong for at least 7 years
(requirement waived for persons who became Hong Kong
residents before January 1, 2004), including 1 year of residence immediately before claiming the benefit. There are no
requirements for length of residence for claimants younger
than age 18 residing in Hong Kong. Benefits are income-
tested and asset-tested on an individual basis if living alone;
if living with other family members, the total income and
assets of all family members are taken into account for
determining the family's eligibility.

Family Allowance Benefits

Comprehensive social security assistance (family): From
HK$1,150 to HK$1,750 a month, subject to the number of
family members; plus special grants to meet the specific
individual needs of recipients.

Administrative Organization

Social Welfare Department (http://www.info.gov.hk/swd)
administers the program.

India

Exchange rate: US$1.00 equals 46.10 rupees.

Old Age, Disability, and Survivors

Regulatory Framework

First and current laws: 1952 (employees' provident funds), with amendments; 1972 (payment of gratuity); 1976 (employees' deposit-linked insurance); 1995 (employees' pension scheme); and 1995 (national social assistance program).

Type of program: Provident fund with survivor (deposit-linked) insurance and pension fund; gratuity schemes for industrial workers; and social assistance system.

Note: In 2004, a voluntary old-age, disability, and survivors benefits scheme, part of the Unorganized Sector Social Security Scheme for employees and self-employed persons aged 36 to 50 with monthly earnings of 6,500 rupees or less but without mandatory coverage, was introduced as a pilot program in 50 districts. Contributions are income related and flat rate.

Coverage

Provident fund and survivor (deposit-linked) insurance: Employees, including casual, part-time, and daily wage workers and those employed through contractors, with monthly earnings of 6,500 rupees or less working in establishments with a minimum of 20 employees in one of the 182 categories of covered industry (the establishment remains covered even if the number of employees falls below 20); employees of other establishments specified by law, including cooperatives with more than 50 employees and establishments with less than 20 employees; newspaper employees; and cinemas and theaters employing 5 or more persons.

Employees covered by equivalent occupational private plans may contract out.

Voluntary coverage for employees of covered establishments with monthly earnings of more than 6,500 rupees, with the agreement of the employer. Voluntary coverage for establishments with less than 20 employees if the employer and a majority of the employees agree to contribute.

Exclusions: Self-employed persons, agricultural workers, and cooperatives employing less than 50 workers.

Pension scheme: Employees with monthly earnings of 6,500 rupees or less.

Voluntary coverage is possible.

Exclusions: Self-employed persons, agricultural workers, and cooperatives employing less than 50 workers.

Gratuity scheme: Employees of factories, mines, oil-fields, plantations, ports, railways, and shops with at least 10 workers.

Exclusions: Self-employed persons, agricultural workers, and cooperatives employing less than 50 workers. There is no coverage in the states of Jammu and Kashmir.

Special systems for coal miners, railway employees, and public-sector employees.

Social assistance: Needy older persons and poor households on the death of the primary breadwinner.

Source of Funds

Insured person

Provident fund: 12% of basic wages (10% of basic wages in five specified categories of industry) in covered establishments with less than 20 employees and some other specific cases.

The maximum monthly earnings for contribution purposes are 6,500 rupees.

Survivor (deposit-linked) insurance scheme: None.

Pension scheme: None.

Gratuity scheme: None.

Social assistance: None.

Self-employed person

Provident fund: Not applicable.

Survivor (deposit-linked) insurance scheme: Not applicable.

Pension scheme: Not applicable.

Gratuity scheme: Not applicable.

Social assistance: None.

Employer

Provident fund: 3.67% of monthly payroll, plus 1.1% of monthly payroll for administrative costs.

Survivor (deposit-linked) insurance scheme: 0.5% of monthly payroll, plus 0.01% of monthly payroll for administrative costs.

The maximum monthly earnings for contribution purposes are 6,500 rupees.

Pension scheme: 8.33% of monthly payroll.

The maximum monthly earnings for contribution purposes are 6,500 rupees.

Gratuity scheme: An average of 4% of monthly payroll.

Social assistance: None.

Government

Provident fund: None.

Survivor (deposit-linked) insurance scheme: None.

Pension scheme: 1.16% of the insured's basic wages.

The maximum monthly earnings for contribution purposes are 6,500 rupees.

Gratuity scheme: None.

Social assistance: The total cost.

Qualifying Conditions

Old-age benefits

Provident fund: Age 55 and retired from covered employment; at any age if leaving the country permanently, if covered employment ends involuntarily, on the termination of service under a voluntary retirement scheme, on changing employment from an establishment covered by the scheme to one that is not, or after 2 months of unemployment.

Early retirement: Age 54 or within 1 year before actual retirement, whichever is later.

Drawdown payment: Partial drawdown is permitted before retirement for special purposes, including the purchase of life insurance; the purchase or construction of a home; loan repayment; to pay for children's education fees, a child's marriage, or care costs for a serious illness; to compensate for damage resulting from a natural disaster; or to meet costs relating to the onset of disability.

Pension scheme: Age 58 or retired with a minimum of 10 years' coverage.

Early pension: Age 50 with a minimum of 10 years' coverage. Employment must cease.

Gratuity scheme: Must have at least 5 years of continuous employment.

Old-age pension (social assistance): Needy persons aged 65 or older.

Disability benefits

Provident fund: Must be assessed with a permanent and total incapacity for normal work.

Pension scheme: Must be assessed as permanently and totally disabled as the result of an occupational injury. The insured must have at least 1 month of contributions.

Gratuity scheme: Paid for an assessed disability caused by a disease or an accident.

Survivor benefits

Provident fund: Paid for the death of the provident fund member before retirement.

Survivor (deposit-linked) insurance scheme: Paid for the death of the provident fund member before retirement.

Pension scheme: The deceased scheme member had at least 1 month of contributions (paid regardless of whether the insured was employed or retired at the time of death).

Gratuity scheme: Paid for the death of the insured as the result of an illness or an accident.

Survivor grant (social assistance): Paid to needy households (under the National Family Benefit Scheme) on the death of the primary breadwinner between ages 18 and 65.

Old-Age Benefits

Provident fund: A lump sum is paid equal to total employee and employer contributions plus interest.

Drawdown payment: According to circumstances, the value of the minimum payment varies from 1 month's wages to total employee and employer contributions plus accrued interest.

Pension scheme: With 10 or more years of coverage, a monthly pension is paid based on a member's pensionable service and earnings, subject to a minimum pension; with less than 10 years, a lump sum is paid equal to total employee and employer contributions plus interest.

Optionally, one-third of the pension can be taken as a lump sum.

There are no fixed amounts for the minimum and maximum pension.

Early pension: The basic pension is reduced by 3% for each year that retirement is taken before age 58.

Pension adjustment: The pension is adjusted annually by the central government according to an actuarial evaluation.

Gratuity scheme: Based on the insured's final salary, a lump sum is paid equal to 15 days' wages for each year of continuous service (a reduced amount is paid for part years in excess of 6 months).

The maximum benefit is 350,000 rupees.

For seasonal employees, employers pay the gratuity at the rate of 7 days' wages for each season worked.

Old-age pension (social assistance): 75 rupees a month is paid.

Permanent Disability Benefits

Provident fund: A lump sum is paid equal to total employee and employer contributions plus interest.

Pension scheme: A monthly pension is paid based on the member's pensionable earnings subject to a minimum of 250 rupees or, optionally, a lump sum equal to total employee and employer contributions plus interest.

Pension adjustment: The pension is adjusted annually by the central government according to an actuarial evaluation.

Gratuity scheme: Based on the insured's last wage, a lump sum is paid equal to 15 days' wages for each year of continuous service before the onset of disability (a reduced amount is paid for part years in excess of 6 months).

The maximum benefit is 350,000 rupees.

For seasonal employees, employers pay the gratuity at the rate of 7 days' wages for each season worked.

Social assistance (disability): No benefits are provided.

Survivor Benefits

Provident fund: A lump sum is paid equal to total employee and employer contributions plus interest. The lump sum is paid to a named survivor or split equally among all members of the deceased's family.

Death grant: Up to 2,000 rupees is paid.

Survivor (deposit-linked) insurance scheme: A lump sum is paid equal to the average balance of the deceased's provident fund account during the 12 months before death or during the period of membership, whichever is less.

The maximum benefit is 60,000 rupees (and is paid in addition to the provident fund survivor benefit).

Widow(er)'s pension (pension scheme): 50% of the deceased's pension is paid. The pension ceases on the remarriage of the widow(er).

The minimum monthly pension is 450 rupees.

Orphan's pension (pension scheme): Paid for one or two orphans up to age 25 (no limit if totally and permanently disabled). The pension is equal to 25% of the widow(er)'s pension, subject to a minimum of 150 rupees a month; full orphans receive 75% of the widow(er)'s pension, subject to a minimum of 250 rupees a month.

Other eligible survivors (pension scheme): In the absence of the above, up to 75% of the deceased's pension is paid to a named survivor or to a dependent father or mother.

Benefit adjustment: The pension is adjusted annually by the central government according to an actuarial evaluation.

Gratuity scheme: Based on the deceased's last wage, a lump sum is paid equal to 15 days' wages for each year of continuous service (a reduced amount is paid for part years in excess of 6 months). The benefit is paid to a named survivor or to the deceased's heirs.

The maximum benefit is 350,000 rupees.

For the death of seasonal employees, employers pay the gratuity at the rate of 7 days' wages for each season worked.

Funeral grant: See Sickness and Maternity, below.

Survivor grant (social assistance): A lump sum of 10,000 rupees is paid.

Administrative Organization

Ministry of Labor and Employment (http://www.labour.nic.in) provides general supervision for all schemes.

Employees' Provident Fund Organization (http://www.epfindia.com) is organized and administered through regional, subregional, inspectorate, and subaccounts offices.

Central Board of Trustees of the Employees' Provident Fund administers the funds through a tripartite body comprising representatives of government, employers, and employees.

Gratuity scheme is administered by central and state authorities.

National Social Assistance Scheme administers social assistance old-age pensions.

National Family Benefit Scheme administers survivor grants.

Sickness and Maternity

Regulatory Framework

First and current laws: 1948 (employees' state insurance) and 1995 (social assistance).

Type of program: Social insurance and social assistance system.

Notes: Under a 1961 law (Maternity Benefit Act No. 53), implemented in 1963, maternity benefits are provided by employers to employees in factories and establishments not covered by the Employees' State Insurance Act of 1948.

In 2004, a voluntary sickness and maternity benefits scheme, part of the Unorganized Sector Social Security Scheme for employees and self-employed persons aged 36 to 50 with monthly earnings of 6,500 rupees or less but without mandatory coverage, was introduced as a pilot program in 50 districts. Contributions are income related and flat rate.

Coverage

Social insurance: Employees with monthly earnings of 10,000 rupees or less (October 2006), working in power-using manufacturing establishments with 10 or more workers or in nonpower-using establishments with 20 or more workers, including shops, hotels, restaurants, cinemas, road transport agencies, and newspaper establishments.

Employees of establishments run by the government that are covered by equivalent private plans may contract out.

Coverage is being extended gradually to different districts, with 728 industrial centers currently covered. (The scheme still does not apply to the states of Nagaland, Manipur, Tripura, Sikkim, Arunachal Pradesh, and Mizoram.)

Exclusions: Self-employed persons, employees in seasonal work (less than 7 months a year), agricultural workers, and workers in certain other sectors.

Voluntary coverage for medical benefits is available to previously insured retired persons through the payment of a flat-rate monthly contribution of 10 rupees.

Social assistance: Needy pregnant women may receive assistance for the first two births.

Source of Funds

Insured person

Social insurance: 1.75% of earnings for employees whose average daily wage is at least 50 rupees.

The insured person's contributions also finance work injury benefits and the unemployment allowance.

Social assistance: None.

Self-employed person

Social insurance: Not applicable.

Social assistance: None.

Employer

Social insurance: 4.75% of payroll for covered employees.

The employer's contributions also finance work injury benefits and the unemployment allowance.

Social assistance: None.

Government

Social insurance: State governments pay 12.5% of the cost of medical benefits.

State government contributions also finance work injury medical benefits and the cost of necessary medical care to unemployment allowance beneficiaries and their dependents.

Social assistance: The total cost.

Qualifying Conditions

Cash sickness benefits (social insurance): Must have been in insured employment for 78 days during a 6-month period.

Cash maternity benefits (social insurance): Must have been in insured employment for 70 days during two designated and consecutive 6-month periods.

Cash maternity grant (social assistance): Paid to needy pregnant women for the first two live births.

Funeral grant (social insurance): Paid for the death of the insured.

Medical benefits: Must be currently in insured employment or qualified for cash sickness benefit.

Sickness and Maternity Benefits

Sickness benefit: The benefit varies but is around 50% of the average daily wage. The benefit is payable after a 2-day waiting period for up to 91 days in any two consecutive designated 6-month periods.

Family planning (sterilization): Cash sickness benefit is paid at double rate for 7 days (men) or 14 days (women); may be extended in case of complications.

Maternity benefit: The benefit is equal to 100% of average earnings, according to wage class, and is payable for up to 12 weeks (including a maximum of 6 weeks before the expected date of childbirth); 6 weeks in the case of a miscarriage. The benefit may be extended by 4 weeks for medical reasons.

The minimum daily benefit is 10 rupees.

Cash maternity grant (social assistance): A lump sum of 1,000 rupees is paid.

Funeral grant (social insurance): A lump sum is paid equal to the funeral cost, up to a maximum of 2,500 rupees. The grant is paid to the oldest member of the family or to the person who pays for the funeral.

Workers' Medical Benefits

State governments arrange for the provision of medical care on behalf of the Employees' State Insurance Corporation, except in New Delhi and the Noida area of Uttar Pradesh where the Corporation administers medical care directly. Services are provided in different states through social insurance dispensaries and hospitals, state government services, or private doctors under contract. Benefits include outpatient treatment; specialist consultations; hospitalization; surgery and obstetric care; imaging and laboratory services; transportation; and the free supply of drugs, dressings, artificial limbs, aids, and appliances.

The duration of benefits is from 3 months to 1 year, according to the insured's contribution record.

Dependents' Medical Benefits

Benefits are currently provided in most states and districts. Services are provided in different states through social insurance dispensaries and hospitals, state government services, or private doctors under contract. Benefits include outpatient treatment; specialist consultations; hospitalization; surgery and obstetric care; imaging and laboratory services; transportation; and the free supply of drugs, dressings, artificial limbs, aids, and appliances.

Eligible dependents are the spouse, children until age 18 (age 21 if a student, no limit if disabled), a widowed mother, an unmarried daughter, and dependent parents.

Administrative Organization

Ministry of Labor and Employment (http://www.labour.nic.in) provides general supervision.

Employees' State Insurance Corporation (http://www.esic.nic.in), which is managed by a tripartite board and a Director General, administers the social insurance program through regional and local offices.

State governments administer the provision of medical benefits through agreement with, and reimbursement by, the Employees' State Insurance Corporation.

Employees' State Insurance Corporation administers the provision of medical benefits in some cases.

Work Injury

Regulatory Framework

First law: 1923 (workmen's compensation).

Current law: 1948 (employees' state insurance).

Type of program: Social insurance system.

Coverage

Employees with monthly earnings of 10,000 rupees or less (October 2006) working in power-using manufacturing establishments with 10 or more workers or in nonpower-using establishments with 20 or more workers, including shops, hotels, restaurants, cinemas, road transport agencies, and newspaper establishments.

Employees of establishments run by the government that are covered by equivalent private plans may contract out.

Coverage is being extended gradually to different districts, with 728 industrial centers currently covered. The scheme has not been implemented in the states of Nagaland, Manipur, Tripura, Sikkim, Arunachal Pradesh, and Mizoram.

Exclusions: Employees in seasonal work (working less than 7 months a year), agricultural workers, and workers in certain other sectors.

Source of Funds

Insured person: See source of funds under Sickness and Maternity, above.

Self-employed person: Not applicable.

Employer: See source of funds under Sickness and Maternity, above.

Government: See source of funds under Sickness and Maternity, above.

Qualifying Conditions

Work injury benefits: There is no minimum qualifying period.

Temporary Disability Benefits

The benefit varies but is around 70% of the average daily wage. The benefit is payable for the entire duration of the disability, subject to a minimum period of incapacity of 3 days.

Permanent Disability Benefits

Permanent disability pension: The pension is paid according to the assessed loss of earning capacity.

Separate medical boards assess the loss of earning capacity resulting from a work injury or an occupational disease.

The maximum daily rate is equal to the temporary disability benefit rate per day (around 70% of the average daily wage).

If the daily value of the pension is equal to 5 rupees or less, the benefit may be paid as a lump sum provided the total value of the benefit payable does not exceed 30,000 rupees.

Partial disability: A percentage of the full pension is paid according to the assessed loss of earning capacity.

Benefit adjustment: Benefits are reviewed periodically by the Employees' State Insurance Corporation and adjusted for inflation.

Workers' Medical Benefits

Services are provided in different states through social insurance dispensaries and hospitals, state government services, or private doctors under contract. Benefits include outpatient treatment; specialist consultations; hospitalization; surgery and obstetric care; imaging and laboratory services; transportation; and the free supply of drugs, dressings, artificial limbs, aids, and appliances. The scale of services provided varies among states.

Survivor Benefits

Survivor pension (widow's pension): The pension is equal to 60% of the deceased's total disability pension (the average pension is equal to 70% of the deceased's earnings).

Orphan's pension: 40% of the deceased's pension (the average pension is equal to 70% of the deceased's earnings) is paid for an orphan younger than age 18 (no limit if disabled or an unmarried daughter).

Eligible dependents are the spouse and children until age 18 (age 21 if a student, no limit if disabled or an unmarried daughter).

The maximum total survivor pension is 100% of the deceased's pension.

Other eligible survivors (in the absence of the above): Parents, grandparents, and other dependents younger than age 18.

The minimum daily benefit is 14 rupees.

The maximum total pension for other eligible survivors is 50% of the deceased's pension.

Funeral grant: A lump sum is paid equal to the funeral cost, up to a maximum of 2,500 rupees. The grant is paid to the oldest member of the family or to the person who pays for the funeral.

Administrative Organization

Ministry of Labor and Employment (http://www.labour.nic.in) provides general supervision.

Employees' State Insurance Corporation (http://www.esic.nic.in), which is managed by a tripartite board and a Director General, administers the program through regional and local offices.

State governments administer the provision of medical benefits through agreement with, and reimbursement by, the Employees' State Insurance Corporation.

Employees' State Insurance Corporation administers the provision of medical benefits in some cases.

Unemployment

Regulatory Framework

First and current law: 1948 (state insurance).

Type of program: Social insurance system.

Coverage

Employees with monthly earnings of 10,000 rupees or less (October 2006) working in power-using manufacturing establishments with 10 or more workers or in nonpower-using establishments with 20 or more workers, including shops, hotels, restaurants, cinemas, road transport agencies, and newspaper establishments.

Source of Funds

Insured person: See source of funds under Sickness and Maternity.

Self-employed person: Not applicable.

Employer: See source of funds under Sickness and Maternity.

Government: See source of funds under Sickness and Maternity.

Qualifying Conditions

Unemployment allowance: Must be involuntarily unemployed as the result of retrenchment or a nonwork-related permanent disability. The insured must have contributed for a minimum of 5 years.

Unemployment Benefits

Unemployment allowance: The benefit is equal to 50% of the insured's average wages and is payable for up to 6 months.

Access to medical care is also provided to beneficiaries and their dependents.

Administrative Organization

Employees' State Insurance Corporation (http://www.esic.nic.in), which is managed by a tripartite board and a Director General, administers the program through regional and local offices.

Indonesia

Exchange rate: US$1.00 equals
9,200 rupiah (Rp).

Old Age, Disability, and Survivors

Regulatory Framework

First law: 1977.

Current law: 1992 (employees' social security).

Type of program: Provident fund and social insurance system.

Coverage

Establishments with 10 or more employees or a monthly payroll of Rp1 million or more. Employees with contracts of less than 3 months are covered for social insurance death benefits only.

Exclusions: Self-employed persons.

Coverage is being extended to employees of smaller establishments and to organized informal-sector workers, including family labor, fishermen, and employees of rural cooperatives.

Special systems for public-sector employees and military personnel.

Source of Funds

Insured person

Provident fund: 2% of gross monthly earnings.

Social insurance: None.

Self-employed person: Not applicable.

Employer

Provident fund: 3.7% of monthly payroll.

Social insurance: 0.3% of monthly payroll.

Government: None.

Qualifying Conditions

Old-age benefit (provident fund): Age 55 (men and women). Retirement from employment is not required.

Deferred old-age benefit: There is no maximum age for deferral.

Drawdown payments: At any age if emigrating permanently, if starting work as a public employee or beginning military service, or if unemployed for at least 6 months after at least 5 years of fund membership.

Disability benefit (provident fund): Younger than age 55 with a total permanent incapacity for work as a result of a work injury. A medical doctor must certify the incapacity.

Survivor benefit (provident fund): The provident fund member was younger than age 55 at the time of death. The benefit is paid to the spouse or, in the absence of a spouse, to dependent children.

Death grant and funeral grant (social insurance): Paid for the death of the insured.

Old-Age Benefits

Old-age benefit (provident fund): A lump sum is paid equal to total employee and employer provident fund contributions plus accrued interest; optionally, a periodic pension is payable to members with more than Rp50 million in their provident fund account.

Drawdown payments: The maximum lump sum is equal to total employee and employer provident fund contributions plus accrued interest.

Permanent Disability Benefits

Disability benefit (provident fund): A lump sum is paid equal to total employee and employer provident fund contributions plus accrued interest; optionally, a periodic pension is payable to members with more than Rp50 million in their provident fund account.

Survivor Benefits

Survivor benefit (provident fund): A lump sum is paid equal to total employee and employer provident fund contributions plus accrued interest; optionally, eligible survivor(s) may receive a periodic pension if the deceased had more than Rp50 million in his or her provident fund account.

If the deceased was receiving a periodic pension, the survivor benefit is equal to the total employee and employer provident fund contributions plus accrued interest minus the amounts already paid to the deceased member.

Death grant and funeral grant (social insurance): A lump-sum death grant of Rp5 million and a lump-sum funeral grant of Rp1 million are paid.

Eligible survivors (in order of priority) are the spouse, children, parents, grandchildren, grandparents, siblings, or parents-in-law. In the absence of eligible survivors, the benefit is paid to a person named by the deceased; in the absence of a named survivor, only the funeral benefit is paid to the person who pays for the funeral.

Benefit adjustment: Social insurance benefits are adjusted every 2 years.

Administrative Organization

Ministry of Manpower and Transmigration (http://www.nakertrans.go.id) provides general supervision.

Employees Social Security System (Jamsostek) (http://www. jamsostek.co.id) collects contributions, administers benefits, and manages the investment of funds.

Sickness and Maternity

Regulatory Framework

First law: 1957.

Current law: 1992 (employees' social security).

Type of program: Social insurance system. Medical benefits only.

Coverage

Establishments with 10 or more employees or a monthly payroll of Rp1 million or more.

Exclusions: Employees whose employer provides benefits that are more comprehensive than those provided by the Jamsostek program, employees with labor contracts of less than 3 months, and self-employed persons.

Coverage is being extended to employees of smaller establishments and to organized informal-sector workers, including family labor, fishermen, and employees of rural cooperatives.

Special system for civil servants, civil service pensioners, military and police pensioners, veterans, national independence pioneers, and for their respective dependents up to age 25.

Source of Funds

Insured person: None.

Self-employed person: Not applicable.

Employer: 3% of monthly payroll for single employees; 6% for married employees.

The maximum monthly earnings for contribution purposes are Rp1 million.

Government: None.

Qualifying Conditions

Cash sickness and maternity benefits: No benefits are provided.

Medical benefits: Must be currently covered.

Sickness and Maternity Benefits

Sickness benefit: No benefits are provided.

Maternity benefit: No benefits are provided.

Workers' Medical Benefits

Public- and private-sector contractors provide services. Insured persons must register with a primary care provider who is under contract. A doctor's referral is required for access to specialist and inpatient care (except for emergencies). Medical benefits include primary and specialist outpatient care, hospitalization, medicines, emergency care, dental care, and eye care.

The cost of maternity care for up to three children, up to a maximum of Rp150,000 each.

The maximum limit on duration for inpatient care is 60 days a year.

Dependents' Medical Benefits

Public- and private-sector contractors provide services. A doctor's referral is required for access to specialist and inpatient care (except for emergencies). Medical benefits include primary and specialist outpatient care, hospitalization, medicines, emergency care, dental care, and eye care.

The cost of maternity care for up to three children, up to a maximum of Rp150,000 each.

The maximum limit on duration for inpatient care is 60 days a year.

Eligible dependents are the dependent spouse and up to three dependent children (unmarried and unemployed) younger than age 21.

Administrative Organization

Ministry of Manpower and Transmigration (http://www. nakertrans.go.id) provides general supervision and grants exemption to employers providing benefits that are more comprehensive than those provided by the Jamsostek program.

Employees Social Security System (Jamsostek) (http://www. jamsostek.co.id) collects contributions and contracts with health care providers for medical benefits.

Work Injury

Regulatory Framework

First law: 1951 (workmen's compensation).

Current law: 1992 (employees' social security).

Type of program: Social insurance system.

Coverage

Establishments with 10 or more employees or a monthly payroll of Rp1 million or more.

Exclusions: Self-employed persons, family labor, fishermen, and employees of rural cooperatives.

Coverage is being extended to employees of smaller establishments and to organized informal-sector workers, including family labor, fishermen, and employees of rural cooperatives.

Special system for public-sector employees.

Employers not covered by the law must provide similar benefits to their employees.

Source of Funds

Insured person: None.

Self-employed person: Not applicable.

Employer: The total cost; contributions vary according to five classes of business activity risk: class I, 0.24% of monthly payroll; class II, 0.54%; class III, 0.89%; class IV, 1.27%; or class V, 1.74%.

Government: None.

Qualifying Conditions

Work injury benefits: Must be assessed with a partial or total disability before age 55. There is no minimum qualifying period.

Temporary Disability Benefits

The monthly benefit is equal to 100% of the insured's wage in the month before the disability began and is paid for the first 4 months; 75% for the next 4 months; thereafter, 50% until rehabilitation or the determination of permanent disability.

Based on a health examination by a medical doctor, the degree of disability is assessed by Jamsostek.

Permanent Disability Benefits

A lump sum is paid equal to 49 months of the insured's wage in the month before the disability began, plus a monthly benefit of Rp50,000 paid for 24 months.

Partial disability: A lump sum is paid equal to 70 months of the insured's wage in the month before the disability began times the assessed degree of disability according to the schedule in law.

The degree of disability is assessed by Jamsostek, based on an examination by a medical doctor.

Workers' Medical Benefits

Medical benefits include medical treatment, hospital care, dental and eye care, and prostheses.

The maximum limit on the cost of medical treatment and hospital expenses is Rp6,400,000 per accident.

Transportation costs from the place of the accident to the hospital are provided up to a maximum of Rp400,000, depending on the method of transport used.

Survivor Benefits

Survivor benefit: A lump sum is paid equal to 42 months of the deceased's wage in the month before death, plus a monthly benefit of Rp50,000 paid for 24 months.

Eligible survivors (in order of priority) are the spouse, children, parents, grandchildren, grandparents, siblings, or parents-in-law. In the absence of eligible survivors, the benefits are paid to a person named by the deceased; in the absence of a named survivor, only the funeral grant is paid to the person who pays for the funeral.

Funeral grant: Rp1 million is paid to the survivor eligible for the survivor benefit; in the absence of an eligible survivor, the grant is paid to the person who pays for the funeral.

Administrative Organization

Ministry of Manpower and Transmigration (http://www. nakertrans.go.id) provides general supervision.

Employees Social Security System (Jamsostek) (http://www. jamsostek.co.id) collects contributions, administers benefits, and contracts with health care providers for medical services.

Iran

Exchange rate: US$1.00 equals 8,229 rials.

Old Age, Disability, and Survivors

Regulatory Framework

First law: 1953.

Current laws: 1975 (social security); and 1986 (self-employed insurance), implemented in 1987.

Type of program: Social insurance system.

Coverage

All employed and self-employed persons.

Voluntary coverage for previously insured persons and for drivers of commercial vehicles.

Special systems for government employees and armed forces personnel.

Source of Funds

Insured person: 7% of earnings. Voluntary insured persons contribute 26% of earnings; commercial drivers contribute 27% of earnings.

The minimum monthly earnings for contribution and benefit purposes for salaried employees are 1,500,000 rials.

The insured's contributions also finance medical, sickness, maternity, and work injury benefits.

Self-employed person: 12% of earnings for old-age; 14% for old-age and survivors; or 18% for old-age, disability, and survivors.

Employer: 20% of payroll.

The minimum monthly earnings for contribution and benefit purposes on behalf of salaried employees are 1,500,000 rials.

The employer's contributions also finance medical, sickness, maternity, and work injury benefits.

Government: 3% of payroll.

Qualifying Conditions

Old-age pension: Age 60 (men) or age 55 (women) with at least 14 years of contributions; age 50 (men) or age 45 (women) with at least 30 years of contributions; at any age with at least 35 years of contributions; women aged 42 with at least 20 years of contributions.

At any age with at least 20 continuous years or 25 noncontinuous years of work in an unhealthy working environment or in a physically demanding natural environment.

Retirement from insured employment is necessary.

The old-age pension is not payable abroad.

Disability pension: Must be assessed as totally disabled (2/3 loss of earning capacity).

The disability pension is not payable abroad.

Survivor pension: The deceased was an old-age or a total disability pensioner at the time of death; had paid at least a year of contributions in the last 10 years, including 90 days in the year before death; had paid at least 20 years of contributions; with more than 10 years but less than 20 years of contributions, a lump sum is paid equal to one month's minimum wage for each year of service.

Eligible survivors are a widow or dependent widower, children younger than age 18 (age 20 if a student or disabled), an unmarried daughter until she marries, and aged dependent parents (a father older than age 60; a mother older than age 55).

The survivor pension is not payable abroad.

Old-Age Benefits

Old-age pension: The pension is equal to 1/30th of the insured's average earnings during the last 24 months times the number of years of contributions. The maximum number of years of contributions for pension calculation purposes is 35.

For insured persons working in difficult or hazardous occupations, each year of paid contributions counts as 1.5 years.

The minimum pension is equal to the minimum wage of an unskilled laborer (1,500,000 rials a month).

Benefit adjustment: Benefits are adjusted annually according to wage changes.

Permanent Disability Benefits

Disability pension: The pension is equal to 1/30th of the insured's average earnings times the number of years of contributions.

The minimum pension is equal to 50% of the insured's average earnings or 100% of the minimum wage of an unskilled laborer (1,500,000 rials a month).

The maximum pension is equal to 100% of the insured's average earnings.

Pension supplement: If the pension is less than 60% of the insured's average earnings and the insured has dependents, an additional 10% of the pension is paid up to a maximum of 60% of the insured's average earnings.

Benefit adjustment: Benefits are adjusted annually according to changes in wages.

Survivor Benefits

Survivor pension: The widow(er) receives 50% of the deceased's pension. If there is more than one legitimate widow, the pension is split equally between them.

The minimum widow(er) pension is equal to 20% of the deceased's pension.

Orphan's pension: 25% of the deceased's pension (50% for a full orphan) is paid for each orphan younger than age 18; no limit if a student, disabled, or an unmarried daughter.

Parent's pension: 20% of the deceased's pension is paid for each dependent aged parent (a father older than age 60 or disabled; a mother older than age 55 or disabled).

The minimum total survivor pension is equal to the minimum wage of an unskilled laborer (1,500,000 rials a month).

The maximum total survivor pension is equal to 100% of the deceased's pension. If the total survivor pension exceeds 100% of the deceased's pension, the survivor pensions are reduced proportionately.

Benefit adjustment: Benefits are adjusted annually according to changes in wages.

Funeral grant: 750,000 rials is paid to survivors living in a city with a population of less than 500,000; 1,000,000 rials in cities with populations greater than 500,000.

Administrative Organization

Ministry of Welfare and Social Security provides general supervision.

Social Security Organization (http://www.tamin.org.ir) administers the program through provincial branch offices and local agencies.

Sickness and Maternity

Regulatory Framework

First law: 1949.

Current laws: 1975 (social security); and 1986 (self-employed insurance), implemented in 1987.

Type of program: Social insurance system.

Coverage

All employed persons.

Self-employed persons are covered for medical benefits only.

Voluntary coverage for previously insured persons and for drivers of commercial vehicles.

Special systems for government employees and armed forces personnel.

Source of Funds

Insured person: See source of funds under Old Age, Disability, and Survivors, above.

Self-employed person: Medical benefits are financed according to set tariffs.

Employer: See source of funds under Old Age, Disability, and Survivors, above.

Government: See source of funds under Old Age, Disability, and Survivors, above.

Qualifying Conditions

Cash sickness and medical benefits: There is no minimum qualifying period.

Cash maternity benefits: Must have at least 60 days of contributions in the year before the expected date of childbirth for the first three children.

Sickness and Maternity Benefits

Sickness benefit: The benefit is equal to 75% of the insured's average earnings in the previous 3 months for a worker with dependents; 66.6% of the insured's average earnings for a single worker.

The benefit is reduced to 50% of the insured's average earnings if unmarried and hospitalized in a Social Security Organization hospital; there is no reduction if the insured person has dependents.

The benefit is payable after a 3-day waiting period (unless hospitalized) until recovery.

Maternity benefit: The benefit is equal to 66.6% of the insured woman's average earnings in the previous 3 months and is payable for up to a maximum of 4 months, including at least 1 month after the expected date of childbirth.

Workers' Medical Benefits

Direct system: Medical care and medicines are provided directly to patients through medical facilities belonging to the Social Security Organization.

Dental grant: 250,000 rials for a half set of dentures or 450,000 rials for a full set.

Other medical expenses are payable according to set tariffs.

If the insured must be transferred to another city for outpatient medical treatment, 100% of the daily sickness benefit is paid for each day. If the insured requires a travel companion, 50% of the insured's daily wage is paid to the travel companion in addition to travel expenses, subject to a decision by the insured's doctor.

Indirect system: Medical services are provided through public and private hospitals and clinics, as well as through university hospitals and contracted-out physicians. The cost of inpatient care and outpatient care varies among medical care providers, as does the degree of cost sharing and the rate of reimbursement.

Dependents' Medical Benefits

Direct system: Medical care and medicines are provided directly to patients through medical facilities belonging to the Social Security Organization.

Dental grant: 250,000 rials for a half set of dentures or 450,000 rials for a full set.

Other medical expenses are payable according to set tariffs.

Indirect system: Medical services are provided through public and private hospitals and clinics, as well as through university hospitals and contracted-out physicians. The cost of inpatient care and outpatient care varies among medical care providers, as does the degree of cost sharing and the rate of reimbursement.

Eligible dependents are a wife and the first three children younger than age 18 (age 20 if a student, disabled, or an unmarried daughter), a disabled dependent husband older than age 60, and aged dependent parents. Voluntary insurance can be taken from the Social Security Organization for the fourth and subsequent children.

Administrative Organization

Social Security Organization (http://www.tamin.org.ir) administers the program.

Work Injury

Regulatory Framework

First law: 1936.

Current law: 1975 (social security).

Type of program: Social insurance system.

Coverage

All employed and self-employed persons.

Voluntary coverage for previously insured persons and for drivers of commercial vehicles.

Special systems for government employees and armed forces personnel.

Source of Funds

Insured person: See source of funds under Old Age, Disability, and Survivors, above.

Self-employed person: Not applicable.

Employer: See source of funds under Old Age, Disability, and Survivors, above.

Government: See source of funds under Old Age, Disability, and Survivors, above.

Qualifying Conditions

Work injury benefits: There is no minimum qualifying period.

Temporary Disability Benefits

The daily benefit is equal to 75% of the insured's last daily wage for a worker with dependents; 66.6% for a worker without dependents.

The benefit is reduced to 50% of the insured's last daily wage if the insured is hospitalized.

The benefit is paid from the first day of incapacity until recovery or certification of permanent disability.

Permanent Disability Benefits

Permanent disability pension: With an assessed degree of disability of at least 66% (total disability), the pension is equal to 1/30th of the insured's average earnings times the number of years of contributions.

The minimum pension is equal to 50% of the insured's average earnings or 100% of the minimum wage of an unskilled laborer (1,500,000 rials a month).

The maximum pension is equal to 100% of the insured's average earnings.

Pension supplement: If the pension is less than 60% of the insured's average earnings and the insured has dependents, an additional 10% of the pension is paid up to a maximum of 60% of the insured's average earnings.

Partial disability: With an assessed degree of disability of between 33% and 65%, a percentage of the full pension is paid according to the assessed degree of disability.

Benefit adjustment: Benefits are adjusted annually according to changes in wages.

Disability grant: With an assessed degree of disability of between 10% and 32% and a disability that is the result of losing a limb, a lump sum is paid equal to 36 times the insured's disability pension times the assessed degree of disability.

Workers' Medical Benefits

Medical care and medicines are provided directly to patients through medical facilities belonging to the Social Security Organization. There is no qualifying period for prostheses.

Survivor Benefits

Survivor pension: 50% of the deceased's pension is paid to a widow of any age or to a dependent widower. If there is more than one legitimate widow, the pension is split equally between them.

Orphan's pension: 25% of the deceased's pension (50% for a full orphan) is paid for each orphan younger than age 18 (age 20 if a student or disabled) and to an unmarried daughter until she marries.

Parent's pension: 20% of the deceased's pension is paid for each dependent aged parent (a father older than age 60 or disabled; a mother older than age 55 or disabled).

The minimum survivor pension is equal to the minimum wage of an unskilled laborer (1,500,000 rials a month).

The maximum total survivor pension is equal to 100% of the deceased's pension. If the total survivor pension exceeds 100% of the deceased's pension, the survivor pensions are reduced proportionately.

Benefit adjustment: Benefits are adjusted annually according to changes in wages.

Funeral grant: 750,000 rials is paid to survivors living in a city with a population of less than 500,000; 1,000,000 rials in cities with populations greater than 500,000.

Administrative Organization

Ministry of Welfare and Social Security provides general supervision.

Social Security Organization (http://www.tamin.org.ir) administers the program through provincial branch offices and local agencies.

Unemployment

Regulatory Framework

First law: 1987.

Current law: 1990 (unemployment insurance).

Type of program: Social insurance system.

Coverage

All employed persons covered by the labor law.

Voluntary coverage for previously insured persons and foreign citizens.

Exclusions: Self-employed persons, retired persons, and totally disabled persons.

Source of Funds

Insured person: None.

Self-employed person: Not applicable.

Employer: 3% of payroll.

Government: Any deficit.

Qualifying Conditions

Unemployment benefit: Must have at least 6 months of insurance before the date of unemployment. Must be registered at an employment office and capable of, and available

for, work. Unemployment is not due to leaving voluntarily, misconduct, or the refusal of a suitable job offer.

Unemployment Benefits

The maximum duration of benefits depends on the length of coverage and marital status. If a married individual has between 6 and 24 months of coverage, the benefit is payable for up to 12 months (6 months if single); for between 25 and 120 months of coverage, up to 18 months (12 months if single); for between 121 and 180 months, up to 26 months (18 months if single); for between 181 and 240 months, up to 36 months (24 months if single); for 241 months and longer, up to 50 months (36 months if single).

The benefit is equal to 55% of the insured's average earnings, increased by 10% for each of the first four dependents.

The minimum benefit is equal to the minimum wage of an unskilled laborer (1,500,000 rials a month).

The maximum benefit is equal to 80% of the insured's average earnings.

Insured persons aged 55 or older may receive unemployment benefits up to the retirement age.

Benefit adjustment: Benefits are adjusted annually according to changes in wages.

Administrative Organization

Ministry of Labor provides general supervision.

Family Allowances

Regulatory Framework

First law: 1953.

Current law: 1975 (social security).

Type of program: Employment-related system.

Coverage

Employed persons.

Source of Funds

Insured person: None.

Self-employed person: Not applicable.

Employer: The total cost.

Government: None.

Qualifying Conditions

Family allowances: The child must be younger than age 18 (no limit if a student or disabled). The parent must have at least 720 working days of contributions.

Marriage grant: Must have at least 720 days of contributions before the date of marriage. The grant is paid once only.

Family Allowance Benefits

Family allowances: The monthly allowance is equal to three times the lowest daily wage of an unskilled laborer. The lowest daily wage is based on the minimum wage of an unskilled laborer (1,500,000 rials a month). The allowance is paid for a maximum of two children.

Benefit adjustment: Benefits are adjusted annually according to changes in wages.

Marriage grant: The grant is equal to 1 month of the insured's average earnings. If both spouses are insured, both the husband and wife will receive the grant.

Administrative Organization

Ministry of Labor provides general supervision.

Israel

Exchange rate: US$1.00 equals
4.50 new shekels (NS).

Old Age, Disability, and Survivors

Regulatory Framework

First and current laws: 1953 (national insurance), implemented in 1954; 1955 (survivor pensions); 1957 (old-age pensions), with 1996 amendment; 1970 (disability insurance); 1974 (pensions), with 1977, 1979, and 1981 amendments; 1980 (long-term care insurance); 1980 (income support); 1982 (benefits); and 1988 (benefits).

Type of program: Social insurance and social assistance system.

Coverage

Social insurance: All persons residing in Israel aged 18 or older.

Exclusions: Persons who immigrated to Israel when aged 60 to 62, depending on the month of birth.

Social assistance (income support programs, means-tested): All persons residing in Israel aged 20 or older (aged 18 or older for certain groups).

Exclusions: Persons living in institutions whose maintenance is paid entirely by the state, the Jewish Agency, a local authority, or religious institution; persons serving in the regular army and their spouses; members of a kibbutz or cooperative village; vehicle owners (unless disabled in the legs or dependent on the vehicle for medical reasons); and students in higher education.

Source of Funds

Insured person: 0.22% of earnings below, plus 3.85% of earnings above, 60% of the national average wage (old-age and survivor pensions); 0.11% of earnings below, plus 1.86% of earnings above, 60% of the national average wage (disability benefits); and 0.01% of earnings below, plus 0.14% of earnings above, 60% of the national average wage (long-term care).

The minimum earnings for contribution purposes are NS3,585 (equal to the minimum wage). (A person earning less than this amount pays contributions as if earning the minimum.)

The maximum earnings for contribution purposes are five times the national average wage as of January 1 each year.

The national average wage is NS7,383 (July 2006).

Self-employed person: 3.09% of earnings below, plus 5.21% of earnings above, 60% of the national average wage

(old-age and survivor pensions); 1.11% of earnings below, plus 1.86% of earnings above, 60% of the national average wage (disability benefits); and 0.12% of earnings below, plus 0.18% of earnings above, 60% of the national average wage (long-term care).

The minimum earnings for contribution purposes are NS1,846 (25% of the national average wage). (A person earning less than this amount pays contributions as if earning the minimum.)

The national average wage is NS7,383 (July 2006).

Employer: 1.87% of earnings below, plus 2.14% of earnings above, 60% of the national average wage (old-age and survivor pensions); 0.38% of earnings below, plus 0.44% of earnings above, 60% of the national average wage (disability benefits); and 0.06% of earnings below, plus 0.07% of earnings above, 60% of the national average wage (long-term care).

The minimum earnings for contribution purposes are NS3,585 (equal to the minimum wage). (A person earning less than this amount pays contributions as if earning the minimum.)

The maximum earnings for contribution purposes are five times the national average wage as of January 1 each year.

The national average wage is NS7,383 (July 2006).

Government: 0.25% of earnings (old-age and survivor pensions), 0.10% of earnings (disability benefits), and 0.02% of earnings (long-term care) on behalf of government employees; subsidizes old-age and survivor pensions at a rate of 15.78% of total employee and employer contributions; the total cost of special old-age and survivor benefits and long-term care benefits for new immigrants; the total cost of social assistance income support programs and the mobility allowance.

Qualifying Conditions

Old-age pension

Social insurance: The retirement age for the earnings-tested pension is age 66 (men) or age 61 (women); the pensionable age (absolute age for receiving the pension, without an earnings test) is age 70 (men) or age 66 (women).

The retirement age for the earnings-tested pension is rising gradually to age 67 (men) or age 62 (women), and the pensionable age (absolute age for receiving the pension, without an earnings test) is rising gradually to age 70 (men and women).

Reduced pension: The pension is reduced until age 70 (men) or age 65 (women) if income from work exceeds between 57% and 76% of the national average wage (according to the number of dependents). The national average wage is NS7,383 (July 2006).

Must have 5 years of coverage in the last 10 years or a total of 12 years of coverage; insured women who are widowed, divorced, deserted, married to an uninsured husband, or unmarried and aged 56 or older at the time of immigration are exempt from the qualifying period, as are women who received a disability pension for the 12 months preceding age 60.

Earnings test: The pension is reduced or suspended until the insured is of pensionable age if income from work exceeds 57% (for a single person) or 76% (for a person with dependents, according to the number of dependents) of the national average wage. There is no earnings test if the insured is of pensionable age. The national average wage is NS7,383 (July 2006).

Deferred pension: Paid between the earnings-tested age and the pensionable age to persons who were previously ineligible to receive the pension because of the earnings test.

Dependent's supplement (earnings-tested): Paid for a dependent spouse or child.

Seniority increment: The increment is paid for years of coverage exceeding 10 years. A housewife is not eligible.

Special old-age benefit (social assistance): A government-financed pension for new immigrants not insured because of their age at the time of immigration and insured persons who emigrated from Israel then returned and do not satisfy the qualifying period condition at the pensionable age.

Income support benefit (social assistance): Must have 24 months of continuous residence (12 accumulative months for new immigrants), subject to an earnings and employment test; incapable of providing self with earned income sufficient for subsistence.

A partial benefit is payable to individuals whose combined income from employment and benefits is less than the minimum income level for subsistence.

Benefits are payable abroad under bilateral agreement.

Disability pension: Must reside in Israel and be between ages 18 and the earnings-tested age for the old-age pension. There is no qualifying period. Must have a total assessed degree of medical disability (from one or more impairments) of at least 60% (a total assessed degree of medical disability of at least 40% if one impairment is assessed as at least 25%; a total assessed degree of medical disability of at least 50% for a disabled housewife) and a functional loss of earning capacity of at least 50%.

Additional monthly pension: Paid to those with an assessed functional loss of earning capacity of at least 75% who do not reside in an institution at the main expense (over 50%) of a public body and who have an assessed degree of medical disability of at least 50%.

Dependent's supplement: A supplement is paid for a spouse or a child with earnings below 57% of the average wage.

Attendance allowance: Paid to persons dependent on the help or supervision of others for performing everyday functions. Must be assessed as at least 60% disabled and

receiving the disability pension; if not receiving the disability pension, at least 75% disabled and subject to an earnings test.

Disabled child benefit: Must reside in Israel, must not be institutionalized or living with a foster family, and must not receive the mobility allowance (the mobility allowance may be received if the parent has two disabled children and under other permitted exceptional circumstances).

Long-term care benefit (earnings-tested): Must be of earnings-tested age for the old-age pension, must not be institutionalized, but must be dependent on the help or supervision of others for performing everyday functions. The benefit is not paid to a single person with income greater than 1.5 times the average wage, to a couple with income greater than 2.25 times the average wage, or to a person with a child with an additional income greater than 0.75 times the average wage for each child.

Mobility allowance: Must reside in Israel, be aged 3 or older but younger than the retirement age as defined in law for men (age 66 in July 2006), and have an assessed loss of mobility. A medical committee assesses the degree of loss of mobility.

Benefits are payable abroad under bilateral agreement.

Survivor pension (social insurance): Paid to a widow(er) or child up to age 18 (age 20 if in higher education or the premilitary framework, age 21 if in the military or volunteer service, up to age 22 in certain other cases) of an insured person who died from any cause, except war or hostile action. The deceased had 12 months of coverage in the year before death, 24 months of coverage in the last 5 years, 60 months in the last 10 years, or met the qualifying period for the old-age pension. The pension for a widow(er) ceases on remarriage.

A widow must have been married to the deceased for at least 1 year (6 months if aged 55 or older) or had a child with the deceased.

A widower must have been married to the deceased for at least 1 year (6 months if aged 55 or older) and must either have a child living with him or satisfy an earnings test.

Survivor pension with income supplement (social assistance): Paid to individuals whose combined income from employment and the survivor pension is less than the minimum income level for subsistence.

Survivor pension seniority increment: Paid if the insured (except a housewife) had more than 10 years of insurance coverage.

Survivor grant: Paid to a widow(er) younger than age 40 without dependent children or to a widower whose eligibility for a survivor pension has ceased.

Special survivor benefit: Paid to the widow and orphans of a person who resided in Israel but was not insured at the time of his immigration.

Marriage grant: Paid to a widow(er) who remarries. The widow(er)'s right to the survivor pension ceases on remarriage.

Death grant: The grant is paid to the widow(er) or children of a deceased pensioner.

Funeral grant: On the death of the insured, the grant is paid to the organization responsible for the funeral service.

Benefits are payable abroad under bilateral agreement.

Old-Age Benefits

Old-age pension

Social insurance: A single pensioner receives 16.2% of the old-age basic amount a month; a couple receive 24.3%.

The value of the old-age basic amount is NS7,152 (January 2006).

Dependent's supplement: 5.1% of the old-age basic amount is paid for each of the first two children up to age 18 (age 20 if in higher education or the premilitary framework, age 21 if in military or volunteer service, up to age 22 in certain other cases).

Income supplement: Paid if income, including the pension, is less than the minimum level for subsistence. Rates vary between 28.5% and 62.4% of the old-age basic amount a month, depending on marital status and the number of children. The resulting amount is increased by an additional 7%.

Deferred pension: The pension is increased by 5% for each year of deferred retirement.

Seniority increment: The pension is increased by 2% for each year of insurance coverage exceeding 10 years, up to a maximum equal to 50% of the pension.

Special old-age benefit (social assistance): The benefits are the same as the social insurance old-age pension.

Income support benefit (social assistance): A single pensioner receives from 20% to 25% of the old-age basic amount a month; a couple without children receive 27.5% to 37.5%. The benefit amount varies with age.

The value of the old-age basic amount is NS7,152 (January 2006).

Benefit adjustment: Benefits are adjusted annually in January according to the rise in the consumer price index in the previous year.

Permanent Disability Benefits

Disability pension: If the insured is assessed as at least 75% disabled, the full single disability pension is equal to 25% of the disability basic amount plus 7% of this amount. There is no earnings test.

The value of the disability basic amount is NS7,240 (January 2006).

Partial disability: A percentage of the full pension is paid according to the assessed degree of disability.

Additional monthly pension: 17% of the disability pension is paid if the assessed degree of disability is at least 80%; 14% for an assessed degree of disability between 70% and 79%; 11.5% for an assessed degree of disability between 50% and 69%.

Dependent's supplement (income-tested): Up to 12.5% of the disability basic amount is paid for a spouse; 10% for each of the first two children. The supplement is increased by 7%.

Income supplement: Payable if income, including the disability pension, is less than the minimum level for subsistence.

Attendance allowance: 50%, 100%, or 150% of the full single disability pension is paid, according to the assessed degree of dependence.

Attendance allowance increment: 14%, 28.5%, or 42.5% of the full disability pension is paid, according to the assessed degree of dependence.

Disabled child benefit: Between 30% and 120% of the full single disability pension is paid, according to the assessed degree of disability.

Disabled child benefit supplements: The cost of schooling for disabled students and an additional pension for severely disabled children.

The maximum total benefit is 137% of the full individual disability pension.

Long-term care benefit (earnings-tested): 93% of the full individual disability pension is paid if the beneficiary is largely dependent on the help of others; 150% if completely dependent. Benefits are normally paid directly to the organization providing the long-term care services, not to the beneficiaries. (If long-term care services are not available and the beneficiary lives with and is cared for by a family member, benefits are paid directly at 80%).

The benefit payment is reduced by 4%.

The benefit is reduced by 50% if income is higher than the average wage for a single person; by 1.5 times the average wage for a couple, plus 0.5 times the average wage for each child, up to a maximum.

Benefit adjustment: Benefits are adjusted annually in January according to the rise in the consumer price index in the previous year.

Mobility allowance: A monthly pension is paid to help cover mobility expenses. The pension varies depending on whether the insured has earned income, has a driver's license, and owns an automobile. Additional cash benefits may be provided to help cover automobile taxes and costs resulting from a loss in mobility.

Benefit adjustment: The pension is adjusted periodically according to increases in the cost of automobile maintenance.

Survivor Benefits

Survivor pension: 16.2% of the old-age basic amount is paid for a surviving spouse aged 50 or older or caring for a child.

The value of the old-age basic amount is NS7,152 (January 2006).

Child increment: 7.6% of the old-age basic amount is paid for each child.

A single child not covered by the survivor pension child increment receives 10.1% of the basic old-age amount; 7.6% of the old-age basic amount each if there is more than one child; 10.1% for each full orphan.

For a widow(er) between ages 40 and 49 with no children, the pension is 12.2% of the old-age basic amount.

If the survivor also receives the old-age pension, the survivor pension is reduced by 50%.

Survivor pension with income supplement (social assistance): A widow(er) with no children receives 28.5% of the old-age basic amount; a widow(er) with one child, 47.2% (minus NS148); a widow(er) with two or more children, 57.3% (minus NS148). The resulting pensions are increased by an additional 7%. For a single child (orphans and abandoned children), the pension is 25% of the old-age basic amount (minus NS148); for two children, 37.5% (minus NS296).

Survivor pension seniority increment: The pension is increased by 2% for each year the deceased had coverage exceeding 10 years, up to a maximum equal to 50% of the pension.

Survivor grant: For a widow(er) younger than age 40 with no children, a lump sum of 3 years' full pension is paid.

Special survivor benefit: The benefits are the same as for the social insurance survivor pension.

Marriage grant: The grant is equal to 36 months' pension and is paid in two installments (the first on marriage, the second 2 years after).

Death grant: A lump sum equal to the disability basic amount is paid to the widow(er) or children of a deceased pensioner. The value of the disability basic amount is NS7,240 (January 2006).

Funeral grant: The cost of the burial is paid, up to a fixed amount.

Benefit adjustment: Benefits are adjusted annually in January according to the rise in the consumer price index in the previous year.

Administrative Organization

Ministry of Social Affairs (http://www.molsa.gov.il) provides general supervision.

National Insurance Institute (http://www.btl.gov.il) administers the program, collects contributions, and pays benefits through its branch offices.

Sickness and Maternity

Regulatory Framework

First and current laws: 1953 (national insurance), implemented in 1954, with 1976 (vacation pay for adopting parents), 1986 (birth allowance), 1990 (risk pregnancy benefit), and 1997 (maternity allowance for father) amendments; 1976 (sick pay in collective agreements, not under social security law); and 1995 (national health insurance).

Type of program: Social insurance system.

Coverage

Sickness benefits: All employees are covered under collective agreement. (Cash sickness benefits are not provided under the 1953 law).

Maternity benefits: Employed persons, self-employed persons, and persons aged 18 or older undertaking vocational training.

Maternity grant: Insured women or the wife of the insured; persons not residing in Israel but who work there, including employed and self-employed women and the wives of employed and self-employed men. If not residing in Israel, the woman or her husband must have worked in Israel for at least 6 months immediately before the childbirth. The birth must occur in Israel.

Medical benefits: All persons residing in Israel.

Source of Funds

Insured person: 3.1% of earnings below, plus 5% of earnings above, 60% of the national average wage (medical benefits); 0.04% of earnings below, plus 0.87% of earnings above, 60% of the national average wage (maternity benefits). (Cash sickness benefits are not provided under the 1953 law.)

The minimum earnings for contribution purposes are NS3,585 (equal to the minimum wage).

The maximum earnings for contribution and benefit purposes are five times the national average wage.

The national average wage is NS7,383 (July 2006).

Self-employed person: 3.1% of earnings below, plus 5% of earnings above, 60% of the national average wage (medical benefits); 0.56% of earnings below, plus 0.82% of earnings above, 60% of the national average wage (maternity benefits). (Cash sickness benefits are not provided under the 1953 law.)

The minimum earnings for contribution purposes are NS1,846 (25% of the national average wage).

The national average wage is NS7,383 (July 2006).

Employer: None for medical benefits; 0.16% of earnings below, plus 0.17% of earnings above, 60% of the national average wage for maternity benefits. (Cash sickness benefits are not provided under the 1953 law.)

The minimum earnings for contribution purposes are NS3,585 (equal to the minimum wage).

The maximum earnings for contribution and benefit purposes are five times the national average wage.

The national average wage is NS7,383 (July 2006).

Government: None for medical benefits; 0.09% of earnings for maternity benefits. (Cash sickness benefits are not provided under the 1953 law.)

Qualifying Conditions

Cash sickness benefits: Sickness benefits are not provided under the 1953 law.

Cash maternity benefits: The full benefit is paid with 10 months of coverage in the last 14 months or 15 months in the last 22 months. A partial benefit is paid with at least 6 months of coverage in the last 14 months.

A father with 10 months of coverage in the last 14 months or 15 months in the last 22 months may share the maternity leave period with his wife (and take a period of leave of at least 21 consecutive days) if his employer authorizes the leave period and his wife agrees to waive part of her leave and return to work.

Vacation pay for adopting parents: Paid for the cessation of work as a result of adopting a child younger than age 10. At least one of the adopting parents must have 10 months of coverage in the last 14 months or 15 months in the last 22 months. An adopting father may take a period of at least 21 days of leave when the mother returns to work.

Risk pregnancy benefit: Paid for the cessation of work as a result of a risk to the pregnancy, in accordance with the medical authorization of a gynecologist. The insured must have 10 months of coverage in the last 14 months or 15 months in the last 22 months and must not receive a similar payment from any other source.

Maternity and hospitalization grant: Paid for a birth for which hospitalization was necessary.

Multiple birth allowance: Paid for the birth of three or more children, of which at least three survive past 30 days. The mother must be entitled to the maternity grant.

Hospital transportation costs: Provided for women who have to travel by ambulance to a hospital to give birth. If the ambulance journey is more than 40 kilometers, the National Insurance Institute pays the cost of transportation beyond the first 20 kilometers. The hospital must be the one nearest to the woman's place of residence.

Special allowance and special benefit: Paid for a mother who was insured for the maternity grant and who died while giving birth or within a year of giving birth.

Benefits are payable abroad under bilateral agreement.

Sickness and Maternity Benefits

Sickness benefit: Benefits are provided to employees under collective agreement; 75% of earnings are paid for 90 days (up to 100% of earnings without limit if stipulated in a collective agreement).

Maternity allowance: The benefit is equal to 100% of the insured's average daily net income in the 3 months preceding the day on which the insured woman ceased work because of the pregnancy. The allowance is payable for 12 weeks; 6 weeks if only the lower contribution condition is satisfied.

Risk pregnancy grant: For each day of rest from work, a sum is paid equal to the average wage divided by 30 or the insured woman's income in the 3 months preceding the day she stopped work divided by 90, whichever is lower.

Maternity grant (layette): NS1,448 is paid for the first child, NS652 for the second child, and NS434 for the third or subsequent child (higher for multiple births) for the purchase of clothing and other necessities for a newborn child.

Hospitalization grant: A grant for the payment of hospitalization expenses is provided.

Multiple birth allowance: An allowance is paid for 20 months and calculated as a percentage of the disability basic amount in January of the year of childbirth.

The value of the disability basic amount is NS7,240 (January 2006).

Hospital transportation costs: In certain cases, a fixed payment is made for the cost of transportation to the hospital.

Special allowance: 30% of the national average wage is paid for a period of 24 months for each child of the last childbirth. The entitlement period is reduced to 12 months if the spouse is also receiving survivor or dependent benefits.

Special benefit: If the spouse stops working to care for the child(ren), a benefit is paid equal to the injury allowance (75% of earnings, up to a maximum) for up to 12 weeks.

All maternity benefit payments, except for the hospitalization grant, are reduced by 4%.

Workers' Medical Benefits

Services are provided by doctors in hospitals owned and operated by, or under contract to, the sick fund. Benefits include general and specialist care, medicines, laboratory services, hospitalization, and rehabilitation.

Cost sharing: Patients pay a set amount toward the cost of drugs and appliances, which varies according to the sick fund.

Dependents' Medical Benefits

Services are provided by doctors in hospitals owned and operated by, or under contract to, the sick fund. Benefits include general and specialist care, medicines, laboratory services, hospitalization, and rehabilitation.

Cost sharing: Patients pay a set amount toward the cost of drugs and appliances, which varies according to the sick fund.

Administrative Organization

Ministry of Social Affairs (http://www.molsa.gov.il) provides general supervision.

National Insurance Institute (http://www.btl.gov.il) administers the program, collects contributions, and pays benefits through its branch offices.

Sickness insurance and medical care are administered by four funds under the supervision of the Ministry of Health (http://www.health.gov.il): Leumit (National) Sick Fund (http://www.leumit.co.il); Clalit (General) Sick Fund (http://www.clalit.org.il); Maccabi Healthcare Services (http://www.maccabi-health.co.il); and Meuhedet (United) Sick Fund (http://www.meuhedet.co.il).

Work Injury

Regulatory Framework

First and current laws: 1953 (national insurance), implemented in 1954; and 1956 (self-employed persons), implemented in 1957.

Type of program: Social insurance system.

Coverage

Employed persons, self-employed persons, members of cooperatives, vocational trainees and those undergoing vocational rehabilitation, working prisoners, foreign residents working in Israel, migrant workers working in Israel, and, under certain conditions, Israelis working abroad.

Exclusions: Police, prison service, and defense force employees.

Source of Funds

Insured person: None.

Self-employed person: 0.39% of earnings below, plus 0.68% of earnings above, 60% of the national average wage.

The minimum earnings for contribution purposes are NS1,846 (25% of the national average wage).

The national average wage is NS7,383 (July 2006).

Employer: 0.54% of earnings below, plus 0.61% of earnings above, 60% of the national average wage.

The minimum earnings for contribution purposes are NS3,585 (equal to the minimum wage).

The maximum earnings for contribution purposes are five times the national average wage as of January 1 each year.

The national average wage is NS7,383 (July 2006).

Government: 0.03% of payroll and earnings.

The minimum earnings for contribution purposes are NS3,585 (equal to the minimum wage).

The maximum earnings for contribution purposes are five times the national average wage as of January 1 each year.

The national average wage is NS7,383 (July 2006).

Qualifying Conditions

Work injury benefits

Temporary disability benefit (injury allowance): Paid for a work incapacity and absence from work as the result of a work injury or prescribed occupational disease. There is no minimum qualifying period.

Temporary disability pension: Paid to a worker assessed as disabled as the result of a work injury, with a temporary assessed degree of disability of at least 5%. There is no minimum qualifying period.

Permanent disability pension: Paid to a worker recognized as disabled as the result of a work injury, with a permanent assessed degree of disability of at least 20%. There is no minimum qualifying period.

Disability grant: Paid to a worker with a permanent degree of assessed disability of at least 5% but less than 20%. There is no minimum qualifying period.

Special pension and special grant: Paid for an assessed degree of disability of at least 75%; 65% to 74% for those who have difficulty walking.

Survivor pension: Paid to a widow who is aged 40 or older; regardless of age with a dependent child or if unable to support herself. Also payable to a widower who has a dependent child; regardless of dependent children if unable to support himself or has income below a determined level.

Survivor grant: Paid to a widow who is not entitled to a survivor pension.

Marriage grant: Paid to a widow(er) who remarries. The widow(er)'s right to the survivor pension ceases on remarriage.

Death grant (work injury-related death): Paid to the deceased's spouse and children if the deceased received a disability pension for an assessed degree of disability of at least 50%, had reached the earnings-tested age for the old-age pension, or received a dependent's allowance.

Death grant (nonwork injury-related death): Paid to the deceased's spouse and children if the deceased had an assessed degree of disability of at least 50% for at least 36 months before death and was receiving a work injury disability pension throughout this period.

Funeral grant: Paid for the insured's funeral.

Temporary Disability Benefits

Temporary disability benefit (injury allowance): The daily benefit is calculated on the basis of 75% of covered earnings in the 3 months before the injury, up to a maximum.

The benefit is paid after a 2-day waiting period (waived if the incapacity for work lasts at least 12 days) for a maximum of 13 weeks. The benefit is paid by the National Insurance Institute, which is reimbursed by the employer for the first 12 days. Self-employed persons are not eligible for the benefit for the first 12 days of incapacity.

The benefit is reduced by 4%.

Temporary disability pension: A percentage of the insured's monthly wage is paid according to the assessed degree of medical disability. The pension is paid monthly.

Permanent Disability Benefits

Permanent disability pension: If the insured is totally (100%) disabled, the monthly pension is equal to 75% of the insured's earnings.

Partial disability: A percentage of the full pension is paid according to the insured's wages and assessed degree of disability.

Income support: Low-income recipients of disability pensions may receive an income supplement.

Disability grant: A lump sum is paid equal to 43 months' pension.

Special pension and special grant: Financial aid is provided to help meet personal expenses and transportation costs, up to a maximum.

Benefit adjustment: Benefits are normally adjusted annually in January according to changes in the consumer price index.

Survivor Benefits

Survivor pension: The pension is equal to between 40% and 100% of the disability pension that the deceased would have been entitled to if assessed as totally disabled, including supplements for children.

Survivor grant: A lump sum equal to 36 months' survivor pension.

Orphan's pension: 20% of the disability pension that the deceased would have been entitled to if assessed as totally disabled is paid for the first orphan and 10% each for the second and third. The pension is paid to the surviving spouse in addition to the survivor pension.

Full orphan's pension: 60% of the disability pension that the deceased would have been entitled to if assessed as totally disabled is paid for the first orphan, 20% for the second, and 10% each for the third and fourth.

Other dependent relatives (in the absence of the above): 50% of the disability pension that the deceased would have been entitled to if assessed as totally disabled is paid for one dependent, up to a maximum of 100% for four or more dependents.

Income support: Low-income recipients of disability pensions may receive an income supplement.

Marriage grant: A widow(er) who remarries receives a grant equal to 36 months' pension. The grant is paid in two installments (the first, on marriage; the second, 2 years later).

Death grant (work injury-related): A lump sum is paid equal to the disability basic amount. The value of the disability basic amount is NS7,240 (January 2006).

Death grant (nonwork injury-related): The grant is equal to 60% of the disability pension that the deceased would have been entitled to if assessed as totally disabled multiplied by 36. The grant is paid in two installments.

Funeral grant: On the death of the insured, the grant is paid to the organization responsible for the funeral service. The cost of the funeral is paid, up to a fixed amount.

Administrative Organization

Ministry of Social Affairs (http://www.molsa.gov.il) provides general supervision.

National Insurance Institute (http://www.btl.gov.il) administers the program, collects contributions, and pays benefits through its branch offices.

Unemployment

Regulatory Framework

First and current laws: 1970 (unemployment insurance) and 1973 (payment of benefits).

Type of program: Social insurance system.

Coverage

Employed persons residing permanently or temporarily in Israel and aged 20 (under certain circumstances, aged 18) to the earnings-tested pension age as defined in law for men (age 66, rising gradually to age 67).

Israel

Source of Funds

Insured person: 0.21% of earnings above, plus 0.01% of earnings below, 60% of the national average wage.

The minimum earnings for contribution purposes are NS3,585 (equal to the minimum wage).

The maximum earnings for contribution purposes are five times the national average wage as of January 1 each year.

The national average wage is NS7,383 (July 2006).

Self-employed person: Not applicable.

Employer: 0.04% of earnings above, plus 0.03% of earnings below, 60% of the national average wage.

The minimum earnings for contribution purposes are NS3,585 (equal to the minimum wage).

The maximum earnings for contribution purposes are five times the national average wage as of January 1 each year.

The national average wage is NS7,383 (July 2006).

Government: 0.06% of earnings on behalf of government employees.

The minimum earnings for contribution purposes are NS3,585 (equal to the minimum wage).

The maximum earnings for contribution purposes are five times the national average wage as of January 1 each year.

The national average wage is NS7,383 (July 2006).

Qualifying Conditions

Unemployment benefits: Must be involuntarily unemployed, aged 20 (under certain circumstances, aged 18) to the earnings-tested pension age as defined in law for men (age 66, rising gradually to age 67), registered at the labor exchange, and ready and able to perform any suitable work.

Regular employee: Must have 360 days of contributions in the last 540 days before unemployment.

Daily employee: Must have 300 days of contributions in the last 540 days before unemployment.

There is no qualifying period for demobilized soldiers or for young women who completed a period of national service (for up to 1 year after completion).

Unemployment Benefits

A daily benefit is paid equal to between 20% and 80% of the insured's average daily wage in the last 75 days of work before unemployment.

The maximum daily benefit is NS295 for the first 5-month period and NS197 for the second period (from the sixth month onward). The benefit is payable after a 5-day waiting period (the waiting period is also applied each time the insured has received unemployment benefits for 4 consecutive months).

The maximum duration of payment varies according to the category of beneficiary, from 50 to 175 days.

Administrative Organization

Ministry of Social Affairs (http://www.molsa.gov.il) provides general supervision.

National Insurance Institute (http://www.btl.gov.il) administers the program, collects contributions, and pays benefits through its branch offices.

Family Allowances

Regulatory Framework

First law: 1959.

Current laws: 1975 (children's insurance), 1984 (income test), and 1993 (universal).

Type of program: Universal system.

Coverage

All persons residing in Israel with one or more children.

Source of Funds

Insured person: None.

Self-employed person: 2.4% of earnings above, plus 1.39% of earnings below, 60% of the national average wage.

The minimum earnings for contribution purposes are NS1,846 (25% of the national average wage).

The national average wage is NS7,383 (July 2006).

Employer: 2.17% of earnings above, plus 1.91% of earnings below, 60% of the national average wage.

The minimum earnings for contribution purposes are NS3,585 (equal to the minimum wage).

The maximum earnings for contribution purposes are five times the national average wage as of January 1 each year.

The national average wage is NS7,383 (July 2006).

Government: 0.1% of earnings plus an amount equal to 191.8% of all receipts from insurance contributions, the funding of the study grant, and payments to new immigrant children.

The minimum earnings for contribution purposes are NS3,585 (equal to the minimum wage).

The maximum earnings for contribution purposes are five times the national average wage as of January 1 each year.

The national average wage is NS7,383 (July 2006).

Qualifying Conditions

Family allowances: The child must be younger than age 18 and residing in Israel.

Family Allowance Benefits

Family allowances: NS148 a month is paid for each of the first two children, NS178 for the third, and NS329 for the fourth and each subsequent child.

For children born on or after June 1, 2003, a uniform rate of NS148 per child is paid regardless of the child's place in the family. For those born before that date, a gradual reduction will take place in the rates so that by January 2009 the same rate will be payable for each child, regardless of the child's place in the family.

Benefit adjustment: Benefits are normally adjusted annually in January according to changes in the consumer price index.

Administrative Organization

Ministry of Social Affairs (http://www.molsa.gov.il) provides general supervision.

National Insurance Institute (http://www.btl.gov.il) administers the program, collects contributions, and pays benefits through its branch offices.

Japan

Exchange rate: US$1.00 equals 112.26 yen.

Old Age, Disability, and Survivors

Regulatory Framework

First law: 1941 (employees' pension insurance).

Current laws: 1954 (employees' pension insurance); and 1959 (national pension), with 1985 amendment.

Type of program: A social insurance system involving a flat-rate benefit for all residents under the national pension program and earnings-related benefits under the employees' pension insurance program or other employment-related program.

Coverage

National pension program: Persons residing in Japan aged 20 to 59; voluntary coverage for persons residing in Japan aged 60 to 64 and for citizens residing abroad (aged 20 to 64; age 69 in special cases).

Employees' pension insurance: Employees of covered firms in industry and commerce, including seamen. (Partial contracting-out from employees' pension insurance is allowed if corporate plans provide equivalent or higher benefits.)

Source of Funds

Insured person

National pension program: The contribution is included in the insured person's contribution to the employees' pension insurance or other employment-related program. A proportionate amount is transferred to the national pension program.

All other insured persons contribute 13,860 yen a month. Contributions for the low-income spouses of workers insured under the employment-related program are optional.

Employees' pension insurance: 7.32% (September 2006) of basic monthly earnings and salary bonuses before tax, according to 30 wage classes; miners and seamen contribute 7.852% (September 2006) of basic monthly earnings including salary bonuses before tax.

If the employer has contracted-out, the contribution is between 4.47% and 5.77% of monthly earnings including salary bonuses before tax.

The minimum monthly earnings for contribution and benefit purposes are 98,000 yen.

The maximum monthly earnings for contribution and benefit purposes are 620,000 yen.

The minimum and maximum earnings levels are adjusted on an ad hoc basis in line with the increase in the national average wage.

Self-employed person

National pension program: 13,860 yen a month.

Employees' pension insurance: Not applicable.

Employer

National pension program: The contribution is included in the employer's contribution to the employees' pension insurance or other employment-related program. A proportionate amount is transferred to the national pension program.

Employees' pension insurance: 7.32% (September 2006) of monthly payroll including salary bonuses before tax, according to 30 wage classes; contributions for miners and seamen, 7.852% (September 2006) of payroll including salary bonuses before tax.

If the employer is contracted-out, the contribution is between 5.47% and 5.77% of monthly payroll including salary bonuses before tax.

The minimum monthly earnings for contribution and benefit purposes are 98,000 yen.

The maximum monthly earnings for contribution and benefit purposes are 620,000 yen.

The minimum and maximum earnings levels are adjusted on an ad hoc basis in line with the increase in the national average wage.

Government

National pension program: One-third plus 25/1000 (increasing to 1/2 by the end of fiscal year 2009) of the cost of benefits and 100% of administrative costs are financed by the national tax.

Employees' pension insurance: The total cost of administration is financed by the national tax.

Qualifying Conditions

Old-age pension

National pension program: Age 65 with a minimum of 25 years of contributions (the coverage period can include years of coverage under any employment-related program belonging to the insured's dependent or common-law spouse). There is no requirement to cease employment, and the pension is not earnings tested.

Early pension: An early pension is payable between ages 60 and 64.

Deferred pension: The insured must satisfy the qualifying conditions for the old-age national pension until age 65 and must not claim the pension before age 66.

Dependent's supplement: No supplements are paid for a spouse or children. (If the insured receives a supplement for a spouse under the employees' pension insurance scheme, when the spouse reaches age 65 and starts to receive the old-age national pension, he or she will receive an additional pension.)

Employees' pension insurance: Age 60 (age 57 for seamen and miners) with 25 years of coverage. There is no requirement to cease employment. The pension is reduced if the pension and salary combined exceed a certain limit. The reduction is greater for those aged 60 to 64 than for those aged 65 to 69.

Dependent's supplement: Paid for a dependent spouse younger than age 65. When the spouse reaches age 65, and receives a pension in his or her own right under the national pension program, the supplement ceases. Paid for children up to the end of the fiscal year in which they reach age 18 (age 20 if disabled).

Disability pension

National pension program: Must be assessed with a total disability requiring constant attendance (Group I) or a degree of disability that severely restricts the person's ability to live independently (Group II). The insured must satisfy the qualifying conditions for the old-age national pension at the onset of disability or have paid or credited contributions during 2/3 of the period between age 20 and the onset of disability. Credited contributions may be awarded to low-income or disabled persons or to those receiving public aid. The pension amount is reduced for credited contribution periods.

Dependent's supplement: Paid for children up to the end of the fiscal year in which they reach age 18 (age 20 if disabled).

Employees' pension insurance: Must be assessed with a total disability requiring constant attendance (Group I), a degree of disability that severely restricts the person's ability to live independently (Group II), or a degree of disability that severely restricts the person's ability to work (Group III). The insured must satisfy the qualifying conditions for the old-age national pension at the onset of disability or have paid or credited contributions during 2/3 of the period between age 20 and the onset of disability. Credited contributions may be awarded to low-income or disabled persons or to those receiving public aid. The pension amount is reduced for credited contribution periods.

Dependent's supplement: Paid to persons with a Group I or II disability for a dependent spouse younger than age 65. When the spouse reaches age 65 and receives a pension in his or her own right under the national pension program, the supplement ceases.

Disability grant (employees' pension insurance): Paid for a degree of disability assessed as less severe than Group III. Contributions must have been paid or credited during 2/3 of the period between age 20 and the onset of disability.

Credited contributions may be awarded to low-income or disabled persons or for those receiving public aid. The pension amount is reduced for credited contribution periods.

Survivor pension

National pension program: The deceased was an old-age or disability pensioner or was insured at the time of death with contributions paid or credited during 2/3 of the period between age 20 and the date of death.

Dependent's supplement: Paid for children up to the end of the fiscal year in which they reach age 18 (age 20 if disabled).

Eligible survivors include the widow living with, and caring for, the deceased's children up to the end of the fiscal year in which the child reaches age 18 (age 20 if disabled), and the deceased's children up to the end of the fiscal year in which the child reaches age 18 (age 20 if disabled).

Death grant (national pension program): The deceased was not an old-age or disability pensioner at the time of death and had paid at least 3 years of contributions.

Employees' pension insurance: The deceased satisfied the qualifying conditions for the old-age or disability (Group I or II) pension or was insured at the time of death with contributions paid or credited during 2/3 of the period between age 20 and the date of death.

Eligible survivors include a widow, a widower aged 55 or older, children or grandchildren up to the end of the fiscal year in which the child reaches age 18 (age 20 if disabled), and parents or grandparents older than age 55, if they were financially dependent on the deceased at the time of death. The pension is paid to the first eligible survivor in the following order of priority: spouse, children, parents, grandparents, and grandchildren.

Dependent's supplement: Paid for a surviving parent or children up to the end of the fiscal year in which the child reaches age 18 (age 20 if disabled).

Old-Age Benefits

National pension program (old-age): If fully insured (480 months of paid contributions), the pension is 792,100 yen a year. If not fully insured, a reduced pension is paid according to the number of contributions paid and credited. The pension is paid every 2 months.

Early pension: For those born on or after April 2, 1941, the reduction is 0.5% times the number of months between the date of application and age 65. For older cohorts, the benefit is actuarially reduced by between 42% and 11%, depending on the age at which the pension is taken between ages 60 and 64.

Deferred pension: For those born on or after April 2, 1941, the increase is 0.7% times the number of months between age 65 and the month of application. For older cohorts, the pension that was payable at age 65 is increased by between 12% and 88%, depending on the age at which the pension is taken between ages 66 and 70. Different rates apply if the pension is deferred until age 71 or older.

Dependent's supplement: The supplement is paid directly to a qualifying spouse aged 65 or older. The supplement ranges from 15,300 yen to 227,900 yen a year, depending on the spouse's age.

Benefit adjustment: Automatic annual adjustment for changes in the cost of living.

Employees' pension insurance (old-age): The pension is calculated on the basis of the insured's average monthly wage over the full career times a coefficient determined by the insured's date of birth times the number of months of coverage. The pension is paid every 2 months.

Pensioners between ages 60 and 64 receive an additional 1,676 yen a month for each month of coverage.

Working pensioner (aged 60 to 64): The full pension is paid for continued employment between ages 60 and 64 if the combined total of monthly earnings and the pension is no greater than 280,000 yen; if the combined total is greater than 280,000 yen a month, the pension is reduced by 50% of the value of the monthly earnings; if the wage exceeds 480,000 yen a month, the pension is reduced by the value of the monthly earnings.

Working pensioner (aged 65 to 69): If the combined total monthly earnings and pension exceeds 480,000 yen, the pension is reduced by 50% of the value of monthly earnings.

Dependent's supplement: 227,900 yen a year is paid for a spouse; 227,900 yen a year for each of the first two children and 75,900 yen a year for each subsequent child up to the end of the fiscal year in which the child reaches age 18 (age 20 if disabled).

Benefit adjustment: Automatic annual adjustment for changes in the cost of living.

Permanent Disability Benefits

National pension program (disability): The pension is 990,100 yen a year for a Group I disability (total disability requiring constant attendance) or 792,100 yen a year for a Group II disability (a degree of disability that severely restricts the person's ability to live independently).

Dependent's supplement: 227,900 yen a year is paid for each of the first two children and 75,900 yen a year for each subsequent child up to the end of the fiscal year in which the child reaches age 18 (age 20 if disabled).

Benefits are paid every 2 months.

Benefit adjustment: Automatic annual adjustment for changes in the cost of living.

Employees' pension insurance (disability): For a Group I disability, the pension is equal to 125% of the old-age pension plus additional benefits for dependents; for Group II, 100% of the old-age pension plus additional benefits for dependents; and for Group III, 100% of the old-age pen-

sion. For persons with less than 300 months of coverage, the pension is calculated on the basis of a contribution period of 300 months.

The minimum benefit is 594,200 yen a year.

Dependent's supplement: 227,900 yen a year for a spouse.

Benefits are paid every 2 months.

Disability grant: A lump sum is paid equal to 150% of the old-age pension. The minimum lump sum is 1,168,000 yen.

Benefit adjustment: Automatic annual adjustment for changes in the cost of living.

Survivor Benefits

National pension program (survivors)

Widow's pension: 792,100 yen a year is paid for a widow. (No benefit is payable for a widower.)

Dependent's supplement: 227,900 yen a year is paid for each of the first two children and 75,900 yen a year for each additional child up to the end of the fiscal year in which the child reaches age 18 (age 20 if disabled).

Full orphan's pension: The benefit is the same as for a widow plus dependent supplements and is split equally among all eligible full orphans.

Benefits are paid every 2 months.

Death grant: A lump sum of between 120,000 yen and 320,000 yen is paid, according to the length of the period of paid contributions between 3 and 35 years.

Benefit adjustment: Automatic annual adjustment for changes in the cost of living.

Employees' pension insurance (survivors): 75% of the old-age pension is paid to the first eligible survivor for the death of an insured worker.

Dependent's supplement: 227,900 yen a year is paid for each of the first two children and 75,900 yen for each additional child up to the end of the fiscal year in which the child reaches age 18 (age 20 if disabled). If there are no children, a supplement of 594,200 yen a year is paid for a widow between ages 40 and 65 if she was aged 35 or older when the insured died.

Benefits are paid every 2 months.

Benefit adjustment: Automatic annual adjustment for changes in the cost of living.

Administrative Organization

Pension Bureau of the Ministry of Health, Labor, and Welfare (http://www.mhlw.go.jp) designs both programs.

Social Insurance Agency (http://www.sia.go.jp) administers both programs nationally.

Regional Social Insurance Bureaus and Social Insurance Offices (part of the Social Insurance Agency) administer contributions and benefits for both programs locally.

Sickness and Maternity

Regulatory Framework

First and current laws: 1922 (employees' health insurance), implemented in 1927, with 2000 and 2006 amendments; 1938 (national health insurance), with 1958 and 2006 amendments; and 1982 (medical system for the elderly), implemented in 1983, with 2006 amendment.

Type of program: Social insurance system.

Coverage

National health insurance: All persons residing in Japan not covered under the employees' health insurance program.

Special national health insurance societies provide coverage for certain occupations.

Employees' health insurance

Society-managed health insurance: Members of an occupational health insurance society.

Government-managed health insurance: Employees of firms in industry and commerce with five or more employees are covered by the government-managed program, unless the insured is a member of an occupational health insurance society.

Voluntary coverage for employees in private-sector workplaces with less than five workers and for agricultural, forestry, or fishery workers.

Special systems for seamen, private-school employees, and local and national government employees.

A health and medical services program operates for persons aged 75 or older (the insured person may also be covered by the national health insurance or the employees' health insurance program).

Source of Funds

Insured person

National health insurance: The contribution is fixed by the insurer but must not exceed 530,000 yen a year per household. (The average annual contribution in 2003 was 81,523 yen per insured person, or 160,282 yen per household.)

Contributions may be reduced for low-income persons residing in Japan.

Employees' health insurance: 4.1% of the basic monthly earnings including salary and bonuses before tax, according to 39 wage classes (government-managed program). The annual average contribution in 2004 was 3.74% of basic monthly earnings including salary and bonuses before tax, according to 39 wage classes (society-managed program).

The minimum monthly basic earnings for contribution and benefit purposes are 98,000 yen.

The maximum monthly basic earnings for contribution and benefit purposes are 980,000 yen.

The minimum and maximum earnings levels are adjusted on an ad hoc basis in line with any increase in the national average wage.

Self-employed person

National health insurance: The contribution is fixed by the insurer but must not exceed 530,000 yen a year per household. (The average annual contribution in 2003 was 81,523 yen per insured person, or 160,282 yen per household.)

Contributions may be reduced for low-income persons residing in Japan.

Employees' health insurance: 4.1% of the basic monthly earnings including salary and bonuses before tax, according to 39 wage classes (government-managed program). The annual average contribution in 2004 was 3.74% of basic monthly earnings including salary and bonuses before tax, according to 39 wage classes (society-managed program).

The minimum monthly basic earnings for contribution and benefit purposes are 98,000 yen.

The maximum monthly basic earnings for contribution and benefit purposes are 980,000 yen.

The minimum and maximum earnings levels are adjusted on an ad hoc basis in line with any increase in the national average wage.

Employer

National health insurance: None.

Employees' health insurance: 4.1% of the basic monthly payroll including bonuses before tax, according to 39 wage classes (government-managed program). The annual average contribution in 2004 was 3.74% of basic monthly payroll including bonuses before tax, according to 39 wage classes (society-managed program).

The minimum monthly basic earnings for contribution and benefit purposes are 98,000 yen.

The maximum monthly basic earnings for contribution and benefit purposes are 980,000 yen.

The minimum and maximum earnings levels are adjusted on an ad hoc basis in line with any increase in the national average wage.

Government

National health insurance: A subsidy equal to 50% (43% from national government and 7% from the prefecture) of the cost of medical care.

Employees' health insurance: 13% of benefit costs, 16.4% of the cost of health care for older people, the total cost of administration for the government-managed program, and part of the cost of administration for the society-managed program.

Also, 50% of the cost (excluding the cost covered by the insured) of medical care provided under the health and medical services program for older people.

Qualifying Conditions

National health insurance: Must reside in Japan.

Employees' health insurance: Must be in covered employment. If an insured person leaves employment but was in covered employment during the previous 2 months, the insured may be covered on a voluntary basis for up to 2 years.

Eligible dependents are spouses, parents, grandparents, younger sisters and brothers, children, and grandchildren whether or not residing with the insured person; and fathers- and mothers-in-law, uncles, aunts, nephews, nieces, and older brothers and sisters, provided they reside with the insured.

Sickness and Maternity Benefits

National health insurance: Each insurer provides maternity and child care allowances and funeral grants, according to the municipality.

Employees' health insurance

Sickness and injury allowance: 60% of the average daily basic wage is paid, according to wage class. The benefit is payable after a 3-day waiting period for up to 18 months. Health insurance societies may provide more generous benefits. If the insured receives wages, benefits are suspended or partially reduced.

Maternity allowance: 60% of the average daily basic wage is paid, according to wage class, for 42 days before (98 days for expected multiple births) and 56 days after the expected date of childbirth. If the insured receives wages, benefits are suspended or partially reduced.

Child care allowance: A lump sum of 350,000 yen is paid to an insured person or the dependent of an insured person whose pregnancy lasts 4 or more months.

Funeral grant: A lump sum of 50,000 yen is paid to a dependent who organizes the funeral. If there is no dependent, the actual cost is paid to the person who organizes the funeral, up to a maximum of 50,000 yen.

Workers' Medical Benefits

National health insurance: Medical care and treatment is usually provided by clinics, hospitals, and pharmacists under contract with, and paid by, the insurer (some insurers provide services directly through their own clinics and hospitals). Benefits include medical treatment, surgery, hospitalization, nursing care, dental care, maternity care (only for a difficult childbirth), and medicines.

There is no limit to duration.

Cost sharing: The amount depends on the person's age: younger than age 3, 20% of the cost; ages 3 to 69, 30% of the cost; aged 70 or older, 10% of the cost or 30% for those with a certain level of income.

Inpatients also pay a daily fee toward the cost of meals and other living expenses. The daily fee for meals and other living expenses depends on family income and the duration of the hospital stay.

Employees' health insurance: Benefits include medical treatment, surgery, hospitalization, nursing care, dental care, maternity care (only for a difficult childbirth), and medicines.

There is no limit to duration.

Cost sharing: The amount depends on the person's age: younger than age 3, 20% of the cost; ages 3 to 69, 30% of the cost; aged 70 or older, 10% of the cost or 20% for those with an income of 1,240,000 yen or more.

Inpatients also pay a daily fee toward the cost of meals and other living expenses. The daily fee for meals and other living expenses depends on family income and the duration of the hospital stay.

Dependents' Medical Benefits

National health insurance: Not applicable.

Employees' health insurance: Benefits include medical treatment, surgery, hospitalization, nursing care, dental care, maternity care (only for a difficult childbirth), and medicines.

There is no limit to duration.

Cost sharing: The amount depends on the person's age: younger than age 3, 20% of the cost; ages 3 to 69, 30% of the cost; aged 70 or older, 10% of the cost or 20% for those with an income of 1,240,000 yen or more.

Inpatients also pay a daily fee toward the cost of meals and other living expenses. The daily fee for meals and other living expenses depends on family income and the duration of the hospital stay.

Administrative Organization

Health Insurance Bureau of the Ministry of Health, Labor, and Welfare (http://www.mhlw.go.jp) governs public health insurance programs.

Regional Social Insurance Bureaus, Social Insurance Offices, Regional Bureaus of Health and Welfare, and prefectures supervise the programs locally.

National health insurance: Municipalities administer the program.

Employees' health insurance: Social Insurance Agency (http://www.sia.go.jp) provides the national administration for the government-managed program, and 1,756 health insurance societies administer the society-managed program nationwide.

Municipalities administer the health and medical services program for older people.

Work Injury

Regulatory Framework

First law: 1911.

Current law: 1947 (workmen's accident compensation insurance), with 1980, 1986, 1995, and 2000 amendments.

Type of program: Social insurance system.

Coverage

Employees of all firms in industry and commerce not included under voluntary coverage or special systems.

Voluntary coverage for employees in agricultural, forestry, and fishery establishments with less than five workers.

Special systems for seamen and civil servants.

Source of Funds

Insured person: None.

Self-employed person: Not applicable.

Employer: 0.45% to 11.8% of payroll, according to a 3-year accident rate.

Government: Provides subsidies, set within the limits of the national budget.

Qualifying Conditions

Work injury benefits: There is no minimum qualifying period.

Temporary Disability Benefits

The benefit is equal to 60% of the insured's average daily wage in the preceding 3 months plus a temporary disability supplement equal to 20% of the insured's average daily wage. The benefit is payable after a 3-day waiting period until the end of the 18th month (the employer pays 60% of the average daily wage for the first 3 days).

The minimum daily benefit is 4,100 yen.

The maximum daily benefit ranges from 13,300 yen to 24,026 yen, depending on the insured's age.

Benefit adjustment: Automatic quarterly adjustment for wage changes greater than 10% from the previous quarter.

From the 19th month, less severely disabled persons receive the same level of benefit as before until recovery; more severely disabled persons receive the disease compensation pension (annual benefit is equal to 100% of the average daily wage in the preceding 3 months multiplied by between 245 and 313 days until recovery, according to the degree of

disability), plus a special supplement based on the worker's annual salary bonus.

Benefits are paid every 2 months.

Benefit adjustment: Automatic annual adjustment for changes in wages.

Permanent Disability Benefits

Permanent disability pension: Seriously disabled persons (Groups 1 to 7) receive an annual pension of between 131 and 313 times their average daily wage in the preceding 3 months. The pension varies with the assessed degree of disability.

Less seriously disabled persons (Groups 8 to 14) receive a lump-sum benefit of between 56 and 503 times their average daily wage in the preceding 3 months. The pension varies with the assessed degree of disability.

Constant-attendance allowance (Groups 1 and 2): 104,590 yen a month if requiring full-time care (56,7180 yen if the care is provided by family members); 52,300 yen a month if requiring part-time care (28,360 yen if the care is provided by family members).

Benefits are paid every 2 months.

Benefit adjustment: Automatic annual adjustment for changes in wages.

Workers' Medical Benefits

Benefits include medical treatment, surgery, hospitalization, nursing, dental care, medicines, appliances, and transportation.

There is no limit on the duration of benefits.

Survivor Benefits

Survivor pension: An annual pension is paid equal to the insured's average daily wage in the preceding 3 months multiplied by between 153 and 245 days, according to number of survivors.

Eligible survivors include a widow or widower (aged 60 or older), children and grandchildren (up to the end of the fiscal year in which the child reaches age 18), parents and grandparents (aged 60 or older), and dependent brothers and sisters up to the end of the fiscal year in which the child reaches age 18; or aged 60 or older.

Benefits are paid every 2 months.

Benefit adjustment: Automatic annual adjustment for changes in wages.

Death grant (if no eligible survivors): A lump sum equal to the insured's average daily wage in the preceding 3 months multiplied by 1,000 days is paid to a nondependent survivor.

Funeral grant: The grant is equal to 60 days of the insured's average daily wage in the 3 months preceding death or 315,000 yen plus 30 days' wages, whichever is greater.

Administrative Organization

Ministry of Health, Labor, and Welfare (http://www.mhlw. go.jp) provides general supervision and administration.

Work Injury Compensation Division within the Ministry of Health, Labor, and Welfare's Bureau of Labor Standards administers the program through prefecture labor standards offices and local labor standards inspection offices.

Unemployment

Regulatory Framework

First law: 1947.

Current law: 1974 (employment insurance), with 2003 amendment.

Type of program: Social insurance system.

Coverage

Employees younger than age 65.

Voluntary coverage for employees in agricultural, forestry, and fishery establishments with less than five regular employees.

Exclusions: Seasonal workers whose term of employment is 4 months or less.

Special systems for daily workers, seamen, and civil servants.

Source of Funds

Insured person: 0.8% of earnings; 0.9% for agricultural, forestry, fishery, or sake brewing industry workers.

Self-employed person: Not applicable.

Employer: 1.15% of payroll; 1.25% of payroll for agricultural, forestry, fishery, or sake brewing industry workers; and 1.35% of payroll for construction workers.

Government: 25% of the cost of unemployment benefits and special allowances, 33.3% of the cost of benefits for daily workers, and 12.5% of the cost of benefits for insured persons on child care leave and for older workers.

Qualifying Conditions

Unemployment benefit: Must have 6 months of insurance during the last 12 months (or 1 year of contributions during the last 2 years for part-time workers). Must be registered with the Public Employment Security Office and be capable of, and willing to, work. The unemployed person must report to the Public Employment Security Office once every 4 weeks. Unemployment must not be due to voluntary leaving, serious misconduct, refusal of a suitable job offer, or nonattendance at vocational training (otherwise, the benefit may be limited to 1 to 3 months).

Special daily or monthly allowances: Includes vocational training, transportation for job search activities, moving, and lodging expenses. The allowances are payable to cover the cost of vocational training and while seeking employment in the wider area. The insured must have at least 3 years of coverage to receive education and training benefits and must take designated educational and training courses.

Older worker benefit: Paid to workers between ages 60 and 64 with more than 5 years of coverage whose wage has been reduced by 75% from the wage paid at age 60.

Child care leave benefit: Paid to insured persons who take child care leave to care for a newborn child up to age 1; up to age 18 months subject to conditions.

Nursing care leave benefit: Paid to insured persons who take leave to provide nursing care for family members.

Unemployment Benefits

The benefit is between 50% and 80% of the insured's average daily wage (higher percentages are awarded to lower-wage earners) in the 6 months before unemployment; 45% to 80% if between ages 60 and 64. The benefit is payable after a 7-day waiting period for between 90 and 150 days, according to the length of coverage, age, reasons for unemployment, and employment prospects. Additional days of benefit are payable for between 90 days and 330 days if the insured becomes unemployed from an industry in recession, has a physical or mental illness, or is undergoing training.

The minimum daily benefit is 1,688 yen.

The maximum daily benefit is 7,935 yen.

Special daily or monthly allowances: Allowances are paid to cover the cost of vocational training and while seeking employment in the wider area.

Older worker benefit: The maximum benefit is equal to 15% of the wage after age 60, depending on the percentage of wage reduction.

Child care leave benefit: A monthly benefit is paid equal to 40% of the insured's average daily wage in the 6 months before the leave period times 30.

Nursing care leave benefit: The benefit is equal to 40% of the insured's wage before the leave period.

Administrative Organization

Ministry of Health, Labor, and Welfare (http://www.mhlw. go.jp) provides general supervision and management.

Employment Security Bureau in the Ministry of Health, Labor, and Welfare, the Employment Security Sections of prefectural Labor Bureaus, and Public Employment Security Offices are responsible for the national administration of the program and the collection of contributions.

Family Allowances

Regulatory Framework

First and current law: 1971 (children's allowance), implemented in 1972, with 1981, 1985, 1991, 1994, 2000, 2004, and 2006 amendments.

Type of program: Employer-liability and social assistance system.

Coverage

Residents with one or more children younger than age 12.

Source of Funds

Insured person: None.

Self-employed person: None.

Employer

Children's allowance: 70% of the cost (about 0.09% of wages) for children younger than age 3.

Special allowance: 100% of the cost for children younger than age 3.

Government

Children's allowance: National Treasury, 10% of the cost for employees' children younger than age 3; prefecture, 10%; and municipalities, 10%. National Treasury, 33.3% of the cost for employees' children between ages 3 and 12; prefecture, 33.3%; and municipalities, 33.3%. National Treasury, 33.3% of the cost for self-employed and unemployed persons' children between ages 0 and 12; prefecture, 33.3%; and municipalities, 33.3%.

Special allowance: National Treasury, 33.3% of the cost for employees' children between ages 3 and 12; prefecture, 33.3%; and municipalities, 33.3%.

Qualifying Conditions

Family allowances

Children's allowance: For a family of four, the parent's income must be less than 7,800,000 yen in the previous year. The allowance is paid for children younger than age 12.

Special allowance: For a family of four, allowances are provided for private- and public-sector employees with income greater than 7,800,000 yen but less than 8,600,000 yen in the previous year.

Family Allowance Benefits

Family allowances

Children's allowance: 5,000 yen a month is paid for each of the first two children and 10,000 yen a month for each subsequent child.

Special allowance: 5,000 yen a month is paid for each of the first two children and 10,000 yen a month for each subsequent child.

Allowances are paid every 4 months (in February, June, and October) based on eligibility in January, May, and September, respectively.

Benefit adjustment: Benefits are adjusted on an ad hoc basis.

Administrative Organization

Ministry of Health, Labor, and Welfare (http://www.mhlw.go.jp) supervises the program through its Equal Employment, Children, and Families Bureau.

Insurance division of prefecture Welfare Department and Social Insurance Office collects contributions.

Municipalities deliver allowances.

Jordan

Exchange rate: US$1.00 equals 0.70 dinars.

Old Age, Disability, and Survivors

Regulatory Framework

First law: 1978.

Current law: 2001 (social security).

Type of program: Social insurance system.

Coverage

Employees older than age 16 working in private establishments with at least five workers; government and public-sector employees not covered under civil or military pension laws; employees of universities, municipalities, and village councils; and Jordanian citizens working at diplomatic missions or for international organizations.

Voluntary coverage for all Jordanian citizens residing in the Kingdom or abroad who cease to be compulsorily covered, subject to a minimum income requirement and a maximum earnings ceiling.

Exclusions: Public-sector employees covered under civil or military pension laws, foreign employees serving in international organizations or foreign political or military missions, and casual labor. The law is yet to be implemented with regard to coverage for the following categories of employees: agricultural workers, seamen, fishermen, and domestic servants.

Special systems for public-sector employees covered under civil or military pension laws.

Source of Funds

Insured person: 5.5% of gross earnings; insured workers can also contribute lump-sum amounts for previous work periods not covered.

Voluntary contributors pay 14.5% of income between 100 dinars and 1,000 dinars.

Self-employed person: May contribute voluntarily in certain circumstances. Voluntary contributors pay 14.5% of income between 100 dinars and 1,000 dinars.

Employer: 9% of payroll.

Government: Any deficit.

Qualifying Conditions

Old-age pension: Age 60 (men) or age 55 (women) with 180 months of coverage, including 60 months of paid contributions.

An insured person with at least 10 years of contributions before reaching the statutory retirement age may continue to contribute up to age 65 (men) or age 60 (women) in order to meet the minimum qualifying conditions.

Dependent's supplement: Eligible dependents are a dependent wife; a dependent disabled husband; a disabled son; an unmarried dependent daughter; and dependent parents, brothers, and sisters.

Early pension: A reduced old-age pension is payable from age 45 with at least 18 years (men) or 15 years (women) of contributions.

Benefits are payable abroad.

Disability pension: The insured must be assessed with a total or partial incapacity for work and have 60 months of contributions of which 36 months are consecutive.

The Central Medical Committee and Appeals Medical Committee are responsible for assessing the degree of disability.

Benefits are payable abroad.

Survivor pension: The deceased had 24 months of contributions of which 12 months were consecutive. If more than one survivor is eligible, the pension is split between survivors according to the schedule in law.

Eligible survivors include a widow; a disabled widower; the insured's male children up to age 26 if a student or until the completion of the first university degree, whichever comes first; all dependent daughters if unmarried, widowed, or divorced; brothers (younger than age 18) who were supported by the deceased; sisters supported by the deceased; parents; and an unborn child.

The pension for a widow, daughter, or sister is suspended on marriage but is resumed if she is subsequently widowed or divorced.

Benefits are payable abroad.

Old-Age Benefits

Old-age pension: The pension is calculated on the basis of 2.5% of the insured's average monthly wage in the last 2 years times the number of years of contributions.

The maximum pension is equal to 75% of the insured's average monthly wage in the last 2 years.

Dependent's supplement: The pension is increased by 10% for the first dependent and 5% each for the second and third. The maximum supplement is equal to 20% of the pension.

Early pension: The pension is calculated on the basis of 2.5% of the insured's average monthly wage in the last 2 years times the number of years of contributions but is subject to scaled reductions based on gender and age at the time the pension is first received.

For men, the scaled reductions range from 1% if retiring between ages 58 and 59 to 18% if retiring between ages 45 and 46; for women, the reduction is 10% if retiring between ages 45 and 50 or 5% if retiring between ages 50 and 54; no reduction for women retiring at age 54 or 55.

If an insured person reaches the retirement age, becomes disabled, or dies without entitlement to a pension, a lump sum is paid equal to 15% of the insured's average annual wage in the last 2 years for each year of contributions; if the contribution period is less than 2 years, the lump sum is equal to 15% of the average monthly wage multiplied by the number of months of contributions.

If an insured person ceases work before the retirement age without entitlement to a pension but has between 12 and 59 months of contributions, a lump sum is paid equal to 10% of the insured's average annual wage; with 60 to 179 months, 12% of the average annual wage; with at least 180 months, 15% of the average annual wage.

Lump-sum benefits can also be paid for certain cases as determined by the Board of Directors of the Social Security Corporation.

Since January 1, 1996, all newly awarded pension benefits are increased by 10% of the pension value (by a minimum of 30 dinars up to a maximum of 50 dinars).

Benefit adjustment: Benefits are adjusted periodically by the Council of Ministers according to changes in the cost of living.

Permanent Disability Benefits

Disability pension: The pension is equal to 50% of the insured's average monthly wage.

The average monthly wage is calculated on the basis of average earnings on which contributions were paid in the last 36 months.

The pension is increased by 0.5% for each full year of contributions if the insured has at least 60 months of contributions; by 1% for each full year of contributions if the insured has at least 120 months of contributions.

Constant-attendance allowance: Equal to 25% of the pension.

Since January 1, 1996, all newly awarded pension benefits are increased by 10% of the pension value (by a minimum of 30 dinars up to a maximum of 50 dinars).

There is no maximum pension.

Benefit adjustment: Benefits are adjusted periodically by the Council of Ministers according to changes in the cost of living.

Survivor Benefits

Survivor pension: The pension is equal to 50% of the average monthly wage in the last year of contributions or, if the deceased was a pensioner, 100% of the insured's pension.

The pension is increased by 0.5% for each full year of contributions if the deceased had at least 60 months of con-

tributions; by 1% for each full year of contributions if the deceased had at least 120 months of contributions.

Funeral grant: 500 dinars.

Since January 1, 1996, all newly awarded pension benefits are increased by 10% of the pension value (by a minimum of 30 dinars up to a maximum of 50 dinars).

Benefit adjustment: Benefits are adjusted periodically by the Council of Ministers according to changes in the cost of living.

Administrative Organization

Social Security Corporation (http://www.ssc.gov.jo) administers the program.

Work Injury

Regulatory Framework

First law: 1978.

Current law: 2001 (social security).

Type of program: Social insurance system.

Coverage

Employees older than age 16 working in private establishments with at least five workers; government and public-sector employees not covered under civil or military pension laws; employees of universities, municipalities, and village councils; Jordanian citizens working at diplomatic missions and for international organizations; and apprentices younger than age 16.

Exclusions: Public-sector employees covered under civil or military pension laws, foreign employees serving in international organizations or foreign political or military missions, and casual labor. The law is yet to be implemented with regard to providing coverage for the following categories of employees: agricultural workers, seamen, fishermen, and domestic servants.

Special system for public-sector employees covered under civil or military pension law.

Source of Funds

Insured person: None.

Self-employed person: Not applicable.

Employer: 2% of payroll (may be reduced to 1% if the employer assumes the full cost of medical treatment and the payment of daily allowances for temporary disability). No contribution is required on wages paid to apprentices.

Government: Any deficit.

Qualifying Conditions

Work injury benefits: There is no minimum qualifying period.

Temporary Disability Benefits

The benefit is equal to 75% of the insured's daily wage. The employer pays the wage for the day the accident occurred; thereafter, the Social Security Corporation pays the daily benefit. Payment continues until the insured resumes work, is assessed as permanently disabled, or dies.

Permanent Disability Benefits

Permanent disability pension: If the insured is assessed as totally disabled, the pension is equal to 75% of the monthly wage used for contribution purposes on the day of the injury.

Constant-attendance allowance: Equal to 25% of the pension.

Partial disability: If assessed as at least 30% disabled, a percentage of the total disability pension is paid according to the assessed degree of disability multiplied by the insured's monthly wage. If assessed as less than 30% disabled, a lump sum is paid equal to a percentage of the total disability pension according to the assessed degree of disability multiplied by 36 monthly wages.

The Central Medical Committee and Appeals Medical Committee are responsible for assessing the degree of disability.

Workers' Medical Benefits

Medical treatment, hospitalization, transportation, and rehabilitation services (including artificial limbs).

Survivor Benefits

Survivor pension: The pension is equal to 60% of the covered monthly wage used for contribution purposes on the day of the injury. If there is more than one eligible survivor, the pension is split according to the schedule in law.

Eligible survivors include a widow; a disabled widower; the insured's male children up to age 26 if a student or until the completion of the first university degree, whichever comes first; all dependent daughters if unmarried, widowed, or divorced; brothers (younger than age 18) who were supported by the deceased; sisters supported by the deceased; parents; and an unborn child.

The pension for a widow, daughter, or sister is suspended on marriage but is resumed if she is subsequently widowed or divorced.

Since January 1, 1996, all newly awarded pension benefits are increased by 10% of the pension value (by a minimum of 30 dinars up to a maximum of 50 dinars).

Funeral grant: 500 dinars.

Administrative Organization

Social Security Corporation (http://www.ssc.gov.jo) administers the program.

Kazakhstan

Exchange rate: US$1.00 equals 123 tenge.

Old Age, Disability, and Survivors

Regulatory Framework

First law: 1991.

Current laws: 1997 (pensions), implemented in 1997 and 1998, with 2006 amendment; 1997 (social allowances), implemented in 1997; and 2003 (compulsory social insurance), implemented in 2005.

Type of program: Mandatory individual accounts, social insurance, and social assistance system.

Note: In 1998, the old social insurance system was replaced by mandatory individual accounts. Benefits continue to be paid for rights earned under the old system (solidarity system). In 2005, a new complementary social insurance program (disability and survivor benefits) was implemented.

Coverage

Mandatory individual account: All employed persons residing in Kazakhstan.

Solidarity pension: All employed Kazakh citizens with at least 6 months of contributions before January 1, 1998.

Social insurance: Employed (excluding working pensioners) and self-employed persons, including foreign citizens and persons without citizenship who work and reside permanently in Kazakhstan.

Special systems for government employees, teachers, professional athletes, specific categories of performing artists, truck drivers, machine operators, railway employees, and test pilots.

State social benefits: Pensioners with pension income less than a government-set minimum level and persons without entitlement to contributory benefits.

Source of Funds

Insured person

Mandatory individual account: 10% of monthly earnings.

In addition, pension fund administrators charge, on average, 15% of annual investment returns for annual administrative fees.

Old-age solidarity pension: None.

Social insurance: None.

State social benefits: None.

Self-employed person

Mandatory individual account: 10% of monthly income, but not less than 10% of the minimum wage and not more than 10% of 70 times the minimum wage.

In addition, pension fund administrators charge, on average, 15% of annual investment returns for annual administrative fees.

Old-age solidarity pension: 18% of monthly income is paid to the state budget.

Social insurance: 2% (3% in 2007) of the monthly minimum wage.

The mandatory social insurance contributions finance disability, survivor, and unemployment benefits.

State social benefits: None.

Employer

Mandatory individual account: None.

Old-age solidarity pension: 18% of monthly payroll is paid to the state budget.

Social insurance: 2% (3% in 2007) of monthly payroll.

The mandatory social insurance contributions finance disability, survivor, and unemployment benefits.

State social benefits: None.

Government

Mandatory individual account: The cost of the guaranteed minimum pension.

Old-age solidarity pension: Subsidies as needed.

Social insurance: None; contributes as an employer.

State social benefits: The total cost.

Qualifying Conditions

Old-age pension

Mandatory individual account: Age 63 (men) or age 58 (women) with at least 35 years of contributions. Age 50 (men) or age 45 (women) and lived in ecologically damaged zones or in zones with a maximum radiation risk for at least 10 years between August 29, 1949, and July 5, 1963; age 53 for mothers living in rural areas with five or more children older than age 8.

Early pension: Age 55 (men and women) if the accumulated capital is sufficient to finance a benefit at least equal to the minimum pension. Also paid if unemployed, aged 55 or older, and with at least 35 years of contributions.

Old-age solidarity pension: Age 63 with 25 years of contributions (men) or age 58 with 20 years of contributions (women). Age 50 with 25 years of contributions (men) or age 45 with 20 years of contributions (women) and lived in ecologically damaged zones or in zones with a maximum radiation risk for at least 10 years between August 29, 1949, and July 5, 1963; age 53 for mothers living in rural areas with five or more children older than age 8.

Partial pension: Paid if the insured has insufficient years of covered employment for the full pension at the normal retirement age.

State basic pension supplement (old-age): Paid to recipients of the mandatory individual account or the old-age solidarity pension.

State social benefits (old-age): Paid to persons not eligible for an old-age solidarity pension.

Social insurance (disability): Paid to persons covered by mandatory social insurance and assessed as disabled.

State social benefits (disability): Paid to persons assessed as disabled.

Social insurance (survivors): Paid to survivors on the death of the insured family breadwinner.

Eligible survivors are dependents who are not able to work, including children younger than age 18 (age 23 if a full-time student; no limit if disabled before age 18); a widow(er) of retirement age or disabled or taking care of children, brothers, and grandchildren younger than age 18; grandparents or any other relative taking care of children, brothers, and grandchildren younger than age 18.

State social benefits (survivors): Paid to survivors on the death of the family breadwinner.

Eligible survivors are dependents who are not able to work, including children younger than age 18 (age 23 if a full-time student; no limit if disabled before age 18); a widow(er) of retirement age or disabled or taking care of children, brothers, and grandchildren younger than age 18; grandparents or any other relative taking care of children, brothers, and grandchildren younger than age 18.

Old-Age Benefits

Old-age pension

Mandatory individual account: The benefit is based on the insured's contributions plus accrued interest.

The benefits may be paid monthly, quarterly, or annually; if the value of the insured's contributions plus accrued interest is less than 100,000 tenge or less than 12 times the minimum pension, a lump sum is paid.

Minimum pension guarantee: 6,700 tenge. Only the difference between the insured's benefit (contributions plus accrued interest) and the amount of the minimum pension is paid.

Benefit adjustment: The minimum pension is set annually in the national budget.

Old-age solidarity pension: The monthly pension is equal to 60% of earnings in the best 3 consecutive years after 1995,

plus 1% of earnings for each year in excess of 25 years (men) or 20 years (women) of work.

Partial pension: A percentage of the full pension is paid according to the number of years below the required number of years of coverage.

Benefit adjustment: Benefits are adjusted periodically according to changes in the consumer price index.

State basic pension supplement: 3,000 tenge a month.

Benefit adjustment: The benefit is set annually in the national budget.

State social benefit (old-age): A monthly amount is paid calculated on the basis of the value of the living wage.

Benefit adjustment: The benefit is set annually in the national budget.

Permanent Disability Benefits

State social benefit (disability): A flat-rate monthly benefit is paid according to the assessed degree of disability and the prescribed category of disability.

Social insurance (disability): The amount of the monthly benefit is based on the difference between average monthly insured earnings in the last 24 months and 80% of the legal minimum wage, multiplied by the income replacement rate, the loss of working capacity rate, and the covered period rate.

The income replacement rate is 0.6.

The loss of working capacity rate is 0.7 for a loss of working capacity of between 80% and 100%; 0.5 for a loss of between 60% and 79%; 0.3 for a loss of between 30% and 59%.

The covered period rate is 0.1 with less than 6 months of coverage; 0.7 with between 6 and 11 months; 0.75 with between 12 and 23 months; 0.85 with between 24 and 35 months; 0.9 with between 36 and 47 months; 0.95 with between 48 and 59 months; and 1.0 with 60 or more months.

The disability pension ceases at the old-age pension age and is replaced by the old-age pension.

Benefit adjustment: Benefits are adjusted periodically according to changes in the consumer price index.

Survivor Benefits

State social benefit (survivors): A flat-rate monthly benefit is paid according to family size and whether any family members are disabled.

Social insurance (survivors): The amount of the monthly benefit is based on the difference between average monthly insured earnings in the last 24 months and 80% of the legal minimum wage, multiplied by the income replacement rate, the number of survivors rate, and the covered period rate.

The income replacement rate is 0.6.

The number of survivors rate is 0.4 for one dependent survivor; 0.5 for two; 0.6 for three; and 0.8 for four or more.

The covered period rate is 0.1 with less than 6 months of coverage; 0.7 with between 6 and 11 months; 0.75 with between 12 and 23 months; 0.85 with between 24 and 35 months; 0.9 with between 36 and 47 months; 0.95 with between 48 and 59 months; and 1.0 with 60 or more months.

Benefit adjustment: Benefits are adjusted periodically according to changes in the consumer price index.

Administrative Organization

Individual account: Kazakhstan Agency for Financial Market and Financial Organizations supervises pension funds and insurance companies.

Old-age solidarity pension: Ministry of Labor and Social Protection (http://www.enbek.kz) provides general coordination and supervision. Regional departments of the Ministry of Labor and Social Protection administer the program.

Social insurance: Ministry of Labor and Social Protection (http://www.enbek.kz) provides general coordination and supervision.

State Fund of Social Insurance (http://www.gfss.kz) manages the program finances.

State social benefits: Regional departments of the Ministry of Labor and Social Protection (http://www.enbek.kz) administer the program.

Sickness and Maternity

Regulatory Framework

First and current law: 1999 (employer-financed benefits).

Type of program: Employer-liability (cash benefits) and universal (medical care) system.

Coverage

Cash benefits: Employed citizens.

Medical benefits: All persons residing permanently in Kazakhstan.

Source of Funds

Insured person

Cash benefits: None.

Medical benefits: None.

Self-employed person

Cash benefits: Not applicable.

Medical benefits: None.

Employer

Cash benefits: The total cost.

Medical benefits: None.

Government

Cash benefits: None.

Medical benefits: The total cost.

Qualifying Conditions

Cash sickness and maternity benefits: There is no minimum qualifying period.

Medical benefits: There is no minimum qualifying period.

Sickness and Maternity Benefits

Sickness benefit: The daily benefit is calculated on the basis of average earnings, according to the schedule in law.

Benefit adjustment: Periodic benefit adjustment according to changes in the consumer price index.

Maternity benefit: The benefit is equal to 100% of earnings and is payable for a total of 126 calendar days before and after the expected date of childbirth (may be extended to 140 days if there are complications during childbirth); 170 days for women affected by radiation (may be extended to 184 days if there are complications during childbirth or for multiple births).

Benefit adjustment: Benefits are adjusted periodically according to changes in the consumer price index.

Workers' Medical Benefits

Medical services are provided directly to patients through government or enterprise-administered health providers. Benefits include general and specialist care, hospitalization, laboratory services, dental care, maternity care, and transportation.

Administrative Organization

Cash benefits: Benefits are paid by the employer.

Ministry of Labor and Social Protection (http://www.enbek.kz) provides general coordination and supervision.

Medical benefits: Ministry of Health (http://www.dari.kz) and health departments of local governments provide general supervision and coordination.

Medical services are provided through clinics, hospitals, and other facilities administered by the Ministry of Health and local health departments.

Work Injury

Regulatory Framework

First law: 1955 (short-term benefits).

Current laws: 1993 (work injury), with 1995 and 1999 amendments; and 2005 (employer-liability).

Type of program: Employer-liability and social assistance system.

Coverage

Employed persons.

Exclusions: Self-employed persons.

Source of Funds

Insured person: None.

Self-employed person: Not applicable.

Employer: The cost of certain benefit payments.

Government: The cost of disability and survivor benefits.

Qualifying Conditions

Work injury benefits: There is no minimum qualifying period.

Temporary Disability Benefits

The monthly benefit is equal to 100% of earnings and is paid from the first day of incapacity until recovery or the award of a permanent disability pension.

Permanent Disability Benefits

State social benefit (permanent disability): A flat-rate monthly benefit is paid according to the assessed degree of disability and the prescribed category of disability.

Benefit adjustment: Benefits are adjusted periodically according to changes in the consumer price index.

Lump-sum grant: Depending on the nature of the disability, employers provide compensation to meet any additional costs caused by a work injury or an occupational disease, in accordance with collective agreement but not less than five times annual earnings for a Group I disability (incapable of any work) or Group II disability (incapable of usual work); twice annual earnings for a Group III disability (disabled but capable of work); or 100% of annual earnings for the permanent loss of working capacity but no disability group determined.

Benefit adjustment: Benefits are adjusted periodically according to changes in the consumer price index.

Workers' Medical Benefits

The employer pays for all medical benefits, including appliances and rehabilitation.

Survivor Benefits

State social benefit (survivors): A flat-rate monthly allowance according to family size and whether any family members are disabled.

Payable on the death of the family breadwinner to dependents who are not able to work, including children younger than age 18 (age 23 if a full-time student; no limit if disabled before age 18); a widow(er) of retirement age or disabled or taking care of children, brothers, and grandchildren younger than age 18; grandparents or any other relative taking care of children, brothers, and grandchildren younger than age 18.

Benefit adjustment: Periodic benefit adjustment according to changes in the consumer price index.

Funeral benefit: The employer pays the cost of the funeral if the death was the result of a work injury or an occupational disease.

Administrative Organization

Temporary disability benefits: Enterprises and employers pay benefits to employees.

Pensions: Regional departments of Ministry of Labor and Social Protection (http://www.enbek.kz) administer the program.

Medical benefits: Ministry of Health (http://www.dari.kz) and health departments of local governments provide general supervision and coordination.

Medical services are provided through clinics, hospitals, and other facilities administered by the Ministry of Health and local health departments.

Medical Insurance Fund finances approved medical treatments.

Unemployment

Regulatory Framework

First and current law: 2003 (compulsory social insurance), implemented in 2005.

Type of program: Social insurance system.

Coverage

Employed (excluding working pensioners) and self-employed persons, including foreign citizens and persons without citizenship who work and reside permanently in Kazakhstan.

Source of Funds

Insured person: None.

Self-employed person: See source of funds under Old Age, Disability, and Survivors, above.

Employer: See source of funds under Old Age, Disability, and Survivors, above.

Government: See source of funds under Old Age, Disability, and Survivors, above.

Qualifying Conditions

Unemployment benefit: Must have at least 6 months of coverage.

Unemployment Benefits

The monthly benefit is based on average monthly insured earnings in the last 24 months multiplied by the income replacement rate and the covered period rate.

The income replacement rate is 0.3.

The covered period rate is 0.7 with between 6 and 11 months of coverage; 0.75 with between 12 and 23 months; 0.85 with between 24 and 35 months; 0.9 with between 36 and 47 months; 0.95 with between 48 and 59 months; and 1.0 with 60 or more months.

The unemployment benefit period varies according to the length of the covered period.

Administrative Organization

Ministry of Labor and Social Protection (http://www.enbek. kz) provides general coordination and supervision.

State Fund of Social Insurance (http://www.gfss.kz) manages the program finances.

Family Allowances

Regulatory Framework

First and current law: 2001 (social assistance), implemented in 2002.

Type of program: Social assistance system.

Coverage

Citizens, refugees, noncitizens, and stateless persons residing in Kazakhstan who satisfy a needs test and an income test; disabled persons; persons in full-time education or training; persons aged 80 or older; and children younger than age 7.

Source of Funds

Insured person: None.

Self-employed person: None.

Employer: None.

Government: The total cost.

Qualifying Conditions

Family allowances: Must reside in Kazakhstan and satisfy needs and income tests.

Family Allowance Benefits

Family allowance: Cash benefits are determined in relation to an individual or family satisfying a needs test and an income test. (Income from state social benefits is not included.)

Benefit adjustment: Benefits are adjusted periodically according to changes in the consumer price index.

Administrative Organization

Ministry of Labor and Social Protection (http://www.enbek. kz) provides general coordination and supervision. Regional departments of labor and social protection administer the program.

Kiribati

Exchange rate: US$1.00 equals
1.32 Australian dollars (A$).

Old Age, Disability, and Survivors

Regulatory Framework

First and current law: 1976 (provident fund), with amendments.

Type of program: Provident fund system.

Coverage

Employed persons aged 14 or older earning at least A$10 a month, including employees in government service, public enterprises, cooperatives, and the private sector.

Voluntary coverage for former employees with at least 2 consecutive years of contributions who have not made any withdrawals.

Exclusions: Domestic servants.

Source of Funds

Insured person: 7.5% of gross wages.

The special death benefit is financed by deducting A$5 a year from all employee accounts from which no withdrawals have ever been made.

Self-employed person: Not applicable.

Employer: 7.5% of payroll.

Government: None; contributes as an employer.

Qualifying Conditions

Old-age benefit: Age 50; at any age for a woman who marries and has never withdrawn payments from her account; at any age (men and women) if emigrating permanently.

Early withdrawal: Age 45 if retired permanently from employment or on providing evidence of the intention to retire permanently.

Disability benefit: Must be assessed with a physical or mental incapacity for work.

Survivor benefit: The deceased fund member had not withdrawn any part of the amount credited to his or her account.

Special death benefit: Paid for the death of a fund member.

Old-Age Benefits

A lump sum is paid equal to the total employee and employer contributions plus accumulated interest. (If the fund member makes a partial withdrawal at age 45, the remaining amount cannot be withdrawn until age 50.)

The interest rate is 11% a year.

Interest rate adjustment: The interest rate is reviewed every 3 years by the National Provident Fund Board.

Loan scheme: Up to 70% of the member's account balance may be taken as a loan. In the event of default on the loan, the outstanding sum is payable from the account.

Permanent Disability Benefits

A lump sum is paid equal to total employee and employer contributions plus accumulated interest.

The interest rate is 9% a year.

Interest rate adjustment: The interest rate is reviewed every 3 years by the National Provident Fund Board.

Survivor Benefits

Survivor benefit: A lump sum is paid equal to total employee and employer contributions plus accumulated interest. The lump sum is paid to a named survivor.

The interest rate is 11% a year.

Interest rate adjustment: The interest rate is reviewed every 3 years by the National Provident Fund Board.

Special death benefit: The benefit is equal to 50% of the amount credited to the deceased member's fund at the time of death.

The maximum death benefit is A$1,500.

Administrative Organization

Organized on a tripartite basis and consisting of two representatives each from government, employers, and employees, the National Provident Fund Board administers the program.

Work Injury

Regulatory Framework

First and current law: 1949 (workmen's compensation), with amendments.

Type of program: Employer-liability system, involving compulsory insurance with a private carrier.

Coverage

Employed persons earning A$10,000 or less a year, including seamen employed on Kiribati ships.

Exclusions: Casual employees.

Source of Funds

Insured person: None.

Self-employed person: Not applicable.

Employer: The total cost.

Government: None.

Qualifying Conditions

Work injury benefits: There is no minimum qualifying period. For occupational diseases, the incapacity or death must have occurred during employment or within 12 months after employment ended.

Temporary Disability Benefits

The benefit is equal to 100% of earnings for monthly earnings up to a maximum of A$40; 75% of earnings for monthly earnings greater than A$40 up to a maximum of A$60; or 66.6% of earnings for monthly earnings greater than A$60.

The benefit is payable after a 3-day waiting period.

The maximum benefit is A$160 a month.

The total maximum benefit is equal to the lump sum payable for total or partial permanent disability.

Permanent Disability Benefits

Permanent disability grant: A lump sum is paid equal to 48 months' earnings.

The minimum grant is A$500.

The maximum grant is A$25,000.

Constant-attendance supplement: Equal to 25% of the permanent disability grant.

Partial disability: A percentage of the permanent disability grant is paid according to the assessed degree of disability and the schedule in law. The total payment must not exceed the full benefit payable under permanent total disability.

Workers' Medical Benefits

Medical and surgical care are provided.

Survivor Benefits

Survivor grant: A lump sum is paid equal to 48 months' earnings.

The minimum grant is A$400.

The maximum grant is A$25,000.

Funeral grant: Burial expenses of up to A$30 are paid if there are no eligible survivors.

Administrative Organization

Ministry of Labor, Employment, and Cooperatives administers claims and calculates the benefits due.

Employers insure work injury liability with the Kiribati Insurance Corporation.

Korea, South

Exchange rate: US$1.00 equals 945.30 won.

Old Age, Disability, and Survivors

Regulatory Framework

First law: 1973 (national welfare pension).

Current law: 1986 (national pension), with 1989, 1993, 1995, 1997, 1998, 1999, and 2000 amendments.

Type of program: Social insurance system.

Coverage

Employed and self-employed persons between ages 18 and 59. (Employed and self-employed persons between ages 60 and 64 may contribute on a voluntary basis.)

Special systems for civil servants, private-school employees, military personnel, and employees of the special post office.

Source of Funds

Insured person: 4.5% of standard monthly earnings before tax, according to 45 levels of standard monthly earnings. Voluntarily insured persons contribute 9% of monthly earnings based on the previous year's median monthly income of all insured persons.

The minimum monthly earnings for contribution purposes are 220,000 won.

The maximum monthly earnings for contribution purposes are 3,600,000 won.

Self-employed person: Self-employed persons, including farmers and fishermen, and nonemployed persons contribute 9% of monthly earnings, according to 45 levels of standard monthly earnings.

The minimum monthly earnings for contribution purposes are 220,000 won.

The maximum monthly earnings for contribution purposes are 3,600,000 won.

Employer: 4.5% of the standard monthly payroll before tax, according to 45 levels of standard monthly earnings.

The minimum monthly earnings for contribution purposes are 220,000 won.

The maximum monthly earnings for contribution purposes are 3,600,000 won.

Government: Part of the cost of administration; an amount equal to 1/2 of the monthly contribution per person for farmers and fishermen with average monthly earnings ranging from 220,000 won to 440,000 won; a flat-rate contribution of 21,600 won per person for farmers and fishermen with average monthly earnings greater than 440,000 won.

Qualifying Conditions

Old-age pension: Age 60 (to be raised gradually to age 65 by 2033) with at least 20 years of coverage. If younger than age 65, taxable monthly income or earnings from gainful activity must not exceed 1,566,567 won.

Reduced old-age pension: Aged 60 or older with between 10 and 19 years of coverage and monthly income or earnings from gainful activity not exceeding 1,566,567 won. There is no retirement test if aged 65 or older.

Active old-age pension: Age 60 with at least 10 years of coverage and in gainful activity with monthly taxable income exceeding 1,566,567 won.

Early pension: Age 55 with at least 10 years of coverage and taxable monthly income or earnings from gainful activity not exceeding 1,566,567 won.

Dependent's supplement: Paid for eligible dependents, including the spouse, children younger than age 18 or disabled (assessed with a first- or second-degree disability), and parents (including the spouse's parents) aged 60 or older or disabled (assessed with a first- or second-degree disability).

Lump-sum refund (old-age): Paid if the insured is aged 60, ceases gainful activity, and has less than 10 years of coverage; at any age if the insured emigrates from Korea permanently or loses Korean nationality; under bilateral agreement to insured foreigners who leave Korea.

Disability pension: Must be assessed with a first-degree (total loss of work capacity and requiring constant attendance), second-degree (severe loss of work capacity), or third-degree disability (less severe loss of work capacity) as the result of a disease or injury that began while insured. The insured must have paid 2/3 of scheduled contributions on time.

The National Pension Corporation assesses the degree of disability.

At the request of the beneficiary, the National Pension Corporation may reassess the degree of disability and adjust the benefit amount.

Dependent's supplement: Paid for eligible dependents, including the spouse, children younger than age 18 or disabled (assessed with a first- or second-degree disability), and parents (including the spouse's parents) aged 60 or older or disabled (assessed with a first- or second-degree disability).

Lump-sum disability benefit: Paid for a fourth-degree disability (partial loss of work capacity). The insured must have paid 2/3 of scheduled contributions on time.

Survivor pension: Payable for the death of an insured person (the deceased must have paid 2/3 of scheduled contributions on time), an old-age pensioner, or a disability pensioner with a first- or second-degree disability.

Eligible survivors include a widow, a widower aged 60 or older (at any age with a first- or second-degree disability), parents and grandparents (including the spouse's parents or grandparents) aged 60 or older or disabled and assessed with a first- or second-degree disability, and children and grandchildren younger than age 18 (any age if assessed with a first- or second-degree disability). The pension is paid to eligible survivors in the following order of priority: spouse, children, parents, grandchildren, and grandparents.

Dependent's supplement: Paid for eligible dependents, including children younger than age 18 or disabled (assessed with a first- or second-degree disability) and parents (including the spouse's parents) aged 60 or older or disabled (assessed with a first- or second-degree disability).

Lump-sum refund (survivors): Paid on the death of an insured or formerly insured person if the qualifying conditions for the survivor pension are not satisfied.

Lump-sum death benefit: Paid to dependent survivors (direct blood-relatives including cousins) in the absence of eligible survivors for the survivor pension or lump-sum refund.

Old-Age Benefits

Old-age pension: With 20 years of coverage, the basic monthly pension amount (BPA) is equal to 1.8 times the sum of the average indexed national monthly wage in the 3 years immediately before the year in which the pension is first payable and the insured's average monthly wage over the insured's total contribution period.

Pension increment: An increment is paid for each year of coverage exceeding 20 years.

Reduced old-age pension: The pension ranges from 47.5% to 92.5% of the monthly BPA if the insured has at least 10 years but less than 20 years of coverage.

Active old-age pension: The pension is based on the insured's BPA, adjusted according to the total number of years of coverage and the insured's age.

Early pension: The pension is based on the insured's BPA, adjusted according to the total number of years of coverage and the insured's age when the pension is first paid.

Dependent's supplement: 195,910 won a year for a spouse and 130,600 won a year per child or parent is paid to all pensioners, except those receiving the active old-age pension.

Benefit adjustment: Benefits are adjusted annually according to changes in the consumer price index for the previous year.

Lump-sum refund (old-age): Equal to the insured's total contributions (including any employer contributions) plus interest calculated at the basic bank rate on the date of the refund.

Permanent Disability Benefits

Disability pension: The pension is calculated according to the insured's basic monthly pension amount (BPA) and assessed degree of disability.

The BPA is equal to 1.8 times the sum of the average indexed national monthly wage in the 3 years immediately before the year in which the pension is first payable and the insured's average monthly wage over the insured's total contribution period. An increment is paid for years of coverage exceeding 20 years.

Total disability: 100% of the insured's BPA is paid for a first-degree disability (total loss of work capacity and requiring constant attendance).

Moderate disability: 80% of the insured's BPA is paid for an assessed second-degree disability (severe loss of work capacity); 60% for an assessed third-degree disability (less severe loss of work capacity).

Dependent's supplement: 195,910 won a year for a spouse and 130,600 won a year per child or parent is paid to disabled insured persons with an assessed first-, second-, or third-degree disability.

Benefit adjustment: Benefits are adjusted annually according to changes in the consumer price index for the previous year.

Lump-sum disability benefit: 225% of the BPA is paid to insured persons with a fourth-degree disability (partial loss in work capacity).

Survivor Benefits

Survivor pension: If the deceased had at least 20 years of contributions, the pension is equal to 60% of the deceased's BPA; between 10 and 19 years of contributions, 50%; less than 10 years of contributions, 40%.

The BPA is equal to 1.8 times the sum of the average indexed national monthly wage in the 3 years immediately before the year in which the pension is first payable and the insured's average monthly wage over the insured's total contribution period. An increment is paid for years of insurance coverage exceeding 20 years.

Dependent's supplement: 130,600 won a year is paid per child or parent.

Benefit adjustment: Benefits are adjusted annually according to changes in the consumer price index for the previous year.

Lump-sum refund (survivors): Equal to the deceased's total contributions (including employer contributions) plus interest calculated at the basic bank rate on the date of the refund.

Lump-sum death benefit: Equal to the deceased's total contributions (including employer contributions) plus interest based on the average annual bank interest rate.

The maximum lump-sum death benefit is four times the deceased's last covered monthly wage, or the average covered monthly wage for the entire insured period, whichever is higher.

Administrative Organization

Ministry of Health and Welfare (http://www.mohw.go.kr) supervises the program.

National Pension Corporation (http://www.npc.or.kr) administers the program, collects contributions, and pays benefits.

Sickness and Maternity

Regulatory Framework

First laws: 1963 (voluntary medical insurance for employees); and 1976 (compulsory national medical insurance), implemented in 1977.

Current laws: 1999 (national health insurance), implemented in 2000, with 2005 amendment; and 2002 (financial stability of national health insurance), with 2004 amendment.

Type of program: Social insurance system. Medical benefits only.

Coverage

All Korean citizens and employees (foreigners residing in Korea may contribute on a voluntary basis), except for those with low income and covered by the medical aid program.

Source of Funds

Insured person: 2.24% of standard monthly earnings before tax, according to 50 levels of standard monthly earnings.

The minimum monthly earnings for contribution purposes are 280,000 won.

The maximum monthly earnings for contribution purposes are 5,080,000 won.

Self-employed person: An amount calculated on the basis of personal factors including property ownership, income, age, and gender.

There are no minimum or maximum earnings for contribution purposes.

Employer: 2.24% of standard monthly payroll (private-school boards contribute 1.344%), according to 50 levels of standard monthly payroll.

The minimum monthly earnings for contribution purposes are 280,000 won.

The maximum monthly earnings for contribution purposes are 5,080,000 won.

Government: 2.24% of standard monthly earnings for government employees and 0.895% for private-school employees, according to 50 levels of standard monthly payroll. Of the total benefit expenditure for insured self-employed persons, 40% is financed from general revenue, and 10% of total benefit expenditure for older cohorts (older than age 65) of insured self-employed persons is financed from an earmarked tax on tobacco.

The minimum monthly earnings for contribution purposes are 280,000 won.

The maximum monthly earnings for contribution purposes are 5,080,000 won.

Qualifying Conditions

Cask sickness and maternity benefits: No cash benefits are provided.

Medical benefits: Must not have missed more than 2 months' contributions since first becoming insured.

Sickness and Maternity Benefits

Sickness benefit: No cash benefits are provided.

Maternity benefit: No cash benefits are provided.

Workers' Medical Benefits

Benefits include medical treatment, surgery, hospitalization, and medicines. Medical services are provided by doctors, clinics, hospitals, and pharmacists under contract to the National Health Insurance Corporation (NHIC). Benefits are payable for up to 365 treatment days a year, with each individual medical service used being counted as a day of treatment. If the treatment days exceed 365, the patient pays all subsequent costs. If the total amount paid by the NHIC for 365 days does not exceed 1,500,000 won per patient per year, the NHIC may continue to pay benefits up to that limit.

Maternity care is provided, with no limit on the number of children. There are no cash maternity benefits.

Cost sharing: The insured pays 20% of hospitalization costs and between 30% and 50% of outpatient care (50% if provided by a specialized general hospital, 50% if provided by a general hospital, 35% to 40% if provided by a hospital, or 30% if provided by a clinic). The NHIC refunds 50% of the patient's costs exceeding 1,200,000 won in 30 days. The overall limit paid by each patient is 3,000,000 won every 6 months.

Dependents' Medical Benefits

Benefits include medical treatment, surgery, hospitalization, and medicines. Medical services are provided by doctors, clinics, hospitals, and pharmacists under contract to the National Health Insurance Corporation (NHIC). Benefits are payable for up to 365 treatment days a year, with each individual medical service used being counted as a day of treatment. If the treatment days exceed 365, the patient pays all subsequent costs. If the total amount paid by the NHIC for 365 days does not exceed 1,500,000 won per patient per year, the NHIC may continue to pay benefits up to that limit.

Maternity care is provided to the insured's dependents, with no limit on the number of children. There are no cash maternity benefits.

Cost sharing: The insured or his or her dependents pay 20% of hospitalization costs and between 30% and 50% of outpatient care (50% if provided by a specialized general hospital, 50% if provided by a general hospital, 35% to 40% if provided by a hospital, or 30% if provided by a clinic). The NHIC refunds 50% of the patient's costs exceeding 1,200,000 won in 30 days. The overall limit paid by each patient is 3,000,000 won every 6 months.

Dependents include the spouse, children up to age 18 (or until the completion of university studies), parents and grandparents of the insured and of his or her spouse, and brothers and sisters who have no income or salary and who are mainly supported by the insured.

Administrative Organization

Ministry of Health and Welfare (http://www.mohw.go.kr) provides general supervision.

National Health Insurance Corporation (http://www.nhic.or.kr) administers the national health insurance program, levies and collects contributions, and pays medical service providers.

Health Insurance Review Agency (http://www.hira.or.kr) examines and reviews medical claims and evaluates the quality of medical services.

Work Injury

Regulatory Framework

First law: 1953 (law still applies to employees if the duration of incapacity due to a work-related injury or an occupational disease is less than 3 days).

Current law: 1963 (industrial accident compensation insurance), implemented in 1964, with 1970, 1994, 1997, 1999, 2003, 2004, and 2005 amendments.

Type of program: Social insurance system.

Coverage

Employees of establishments with at least one employee.

Voluntary coverage for agriculture, forestry, hunting, and fishery businesses with fewer than five employees; certain small business employers with less than 50 employees; persons working on small-scale construction projects (when net construction costs are below 20,000,000 won); electricians; telecommunications workers; fire service personnel; certain self-employed persons; and domestic employees.

Special systems for civil servants, military personnel, private-school employees, and seamen.

Source of Funds

Insured person: None.

Self-employed person: Between 0.5% and 61.1% of declared earnings or payroll is contributed on a voluntary basis.

There are no minimum or maximum earnings for contribution purposes. The contribution rate is reviewed annually.

Employer: Between 0.5% and 61.1% of annual payroll (for compulsorily and voluntarily insured employers), according to the assessed degree of risk. The average contribution is 1.78% of annual payroll.

There are no minimum or maximum earnings for contribution purposes. The contribution rate is reviewed annually.

Government: None.

Qualifying Conditions

Work injury benefits: There is no minimum qualifying period.

Temporary Disability Benefits

70% of the insured's average daily wage in the 3 months before the onset of disability is paid if the insured is unable to work and receiving medical treatment.

After 24 months and if still receiving medical treatment, persons assessed with a first-degree (total loss of work capacity and requiring constant attendance), second-degree (severe loss of work capacity), or third-degree disability (less severe loss of work capacity) receive the injury and disease compensation pension (ranging from 70.4% to 90.1% of the insured's average daily wage) for 257, 291, or 329 treatment days according to the assessed degree of disability. The benefit is payable until recovery or the award of the permanent disability pension.

The minimum daily benefit is 24,800 won.

The maximum daily benefit is 155,360 won.

Benefit adjustment: The minimum and maximum benefits are adjusted annually according to wage changes.

Permanent Disability Benefits

Permanent disability benefit: The benefit varies according to the assessed degree of disability, in order of decreasing severity from grades one to seven. The annual pension is equal to the insured's average daily wage in the 3 months before the onset of disability multiplied by 138, 164, 193, 224, 257, 291, or 329, according to the assessed degree of disability. Insured persons with an assessed disability of four to seven (medium severity) may choose between the pension or a lump sum equal to the insured's average daily wage multiplied by 616, 737, 869, or 1,012, according to the assessed degree of disability.

The minimum daily benefit is 45,700 won.

The maximum daily benefit is 155,360 won.

Partial disability: A lump sum is paid for an assessed degree of disability from grades eight to fourteen (lower severity). The benefit is equal to the insured's average daily wage in the 3 months before the date of injury multiplied by between 55 and 495, according to the assessed degree of disability.

Nursing benefit: Paid for nursing services for insured persons with a residual chronic disability after receiving medical treatment. The benefit varies between 24,940 won and 37,420 won a day, according to assessed needs.

Benefit adjustment: The minimum and maximum benefits are adjusted annually according to changes in wages.

Workers' Medical Benefits

Medical benefits include medical treatment, surgery, hospitalization, medicines, nursing, dental care, rehabilitation appliances, and transportation.

Survivor Benefits

Survivor pension: 52% of annual earnings (calculated as the insured's average daily wage in the 3 months before the date of death multiplied by 365) is paid for a single person; the pension is increased by 5% for each additional survivor up to 67% for a family of four or more. The pension is paid monthly.

Eligible survivors include the dependent spouse, parents and grandparents older than age 60, children and grandchildren younger than age 18, and siblings older than age 60 or younger than age 18. The pension is paid to eligible survivors in the following order of priority: spouse, children, parents, grandchildren, grandparents, and brothers or sisters.

Benefit adjustment: The minimum and maximum benefits are adjusted annually according to changes in wages.

Lump-sum grant: If there are no eligible survivors for the survivor pension, a lump sum equal to the insured's average daily wage in the 3 months before the date of death multiplied by 1,300 is payable to nondependent survivors.

Funeral grant: A lump sum equal to the insured's average daily wage in the 3 months before the date of death multiplied by 120 is paid to the person who paid for the funeral.

The minimum funeral grant is 7,525,147 won.

The maximum funeral grant is 10,814,947 won.

Benefit adjustment: The minimum and maximum benefits are adjusted annually according to changes in wages.

Administrative Organization

Ministry of Labor (http://www.molab.go.kr) provides general supervision.

Korea Labor Welfare Corporation (http://www.welco.or.kr) collects contributions, pays benefits, and administers the program through its own medical care institutions.

Unemployment

Regulatory Framework

First and current law: 1993 (employment insurance), implemented in 1995, with 1997, 1999, 2002, 2003, and 2005 amendments.

Type of program: Social insurance system.

Coverage

All employees younger than age 65.

Voluntary coverage for agriculture, forestry, hunting, and fishery businesses with fewer than five employees; small-scale construction projects (when net construction costs are below 20,000,000 won); electricians; telecommunications workers; fire service personnel; self-employed persons; and domestic employees.

Exclusions: Persons working less than 60 hours a month or less than 15 hours a week, family labor, and self-employed persons.

Special systems for civil servants, private-school employees, military personnel, and employees of the special post office.

Source of Funds

Insured person: 0.45% of annual wages before tax.

There are no maximum earnings for contribution purposes.

Self-employed person: 0.25% of declared wages are contributed on a voluntary basis.

There are no maximum earnings for contribution purposes.

Employer: Between 0.7% and 1.3% (depending on the type of business) of annual payroll.

There are no maximum earnings for contribution purposes.

Government: None.

Qualifying Conditions

Unemployment benefits: Must have at least 6 months of coverage during the last 18 months, be registered at an employment security office, and be capable of and available for work. Unemployment must not be due to voluntary leaving, misconduct, a labor dispute, or the refusal of a suitable job offer.

Additional allowances are payable to unemployed persons to encourage retraining or job search. Allowances include the early reemployment allowance, vocational ability development allowance, and transportation and home moving allowance.

Unemployment Benefits

The benefit is equal to half of the insured's average daily earnings during the 3 months immediately before unemployment. The benefit is paid after a 7-day waiting period for up to 90 days to those with between 6 and 12 months of coverage; for up to 240 days with more than 10 years of coverage or aged 50 or older or disabled.

The minimum daily benefit is 90% of the minimum daily wage. (The minimum daily wage is 24,800 won.)

The maximum daily benefit is 40,000 won.

Administrative Organization

Ministry of Labor (http://www.molab.go.kr) provides general supervision of the program.

Employment Security Offices (part of the Ministry of Labor) pay unemployment benefits.

Korea Labor Welfare Corporation (http://www.welco.or.kr) collects contributions.

Kuwait

Exchange rate: US$1.00 equals 0.28 dinars.

Old Age, Disability, and Survivors

Regulatory Framework

First and current laws: 1976 (civilians), implemented in 1977; 1980 (military), implemented in 1981; and 1992 (supplementary), implemented in 1995.

Type of program: Social insurance system.

Coverage

Basic system: Civil servants, oil and private-sector workers, self-employed persons, and military personnel.

Supplementary system: Employees with covered monthly earnings greater than 1,250 dinars and those with sources of earnings not covered by the basic system.

Voluntary coverage for self-employed persons.

Source of Funds

Basic system

Insured person: 5% of gross earnings.

The minimum monthly earnings for contribution and benefit purposes are 230 dinars.

The maximum monthly earnings for contribution and benefit purposes are 1,250 dinars.

Self-employed person: 5% to 15% of monthly income, chosen by the self-employed person from 22 income bands.

The minimum monthly earnings for contribution and benefit purposes are 200 dinars.

The maximum monthly earnings for contribution and benefit purposes are 1,250 dinars.

Employer: 10% of payroll.

The minimum monthly earnings for contribution purposes are 230 dinars.

The maximum monthly earnings for contribution purposes are 1,250 dinars.

Government: A subsidy equal to 10% of the total payroll for employees, 32.5% of the total payroll for military personnel, and 25% of total declared income for self-employed persons.

Benefit adjustments under the basic and supplementary systems are financed by a combined additional monthly contribution by the insured person (1%), self-employed person (1%), employer (1%), and government (2%) on total earnings, up to 2,500 dinars.

Supplementary system

Insured person: 5% of earnings exceeding 1,250 dinars.

The maximum monthly earnings for contribution and benefit purposes are the first 1,000 dinars of earnings exceeding 1,250 dinars.

Self-employed person: 5% of declared income exceeding 1,250 dinars, on a voluntary basis.

The maximum monthly earnings for contribution and benefit purposes are the first 1,000 dinars of earnings exceeding 1,250 dinars.

Employer: 10% of the payroll exceeding the maximum payroll covered by the basic system.

The maximum monthly earnings for contribution and benefit purposes are the first 1,000 dinars of earnings exceeding 1,250 dinars.

Government: None.

Qualifying Conditions

Old-age pension

Basic system: Age 50 with 15 years of contributions for men and women. (The pensionable age will increase gradually to age 55 by 2020.)

Age 47 with 20 years of contributions for men and unmarried women with no children. (The pensionable age will increase gradually to age 55 by 2020.)

Age 40 with 15 years of contributions for married women and women with children. (The pensionable age will increase gradually to age 50 by 2020.)

At any age with 20 years of contributions for those in arduous work.

Retirement is necessary, except if moving from the public sector to the private sector, with certain requirements as to the length of service in the public sector.

Age 65 with 15 years of contributions or age 55 with 20 years of contributions for self-employed persons.

Age 50 with 15 years of contributions or age 45 with 20 years of contributions for military personnel, subject to other conditions.

Benefits are not payable abroad.

Supplementary system: Paid at the same time as the old-age pension under the basic system.

Deferred supplementary pension: The supplementary pension may be deferred.

Benefits are not payable abroad.

Disability pension

Basic system: An assessed degree of incapacity for work of more than 50%.

The degree of disability is assessed by the general medical council.

Benefits are not payable abroad.

Supplementary system: An assessed degree of incapacity for work of more than 50%.

The degree of disability is assessed by the general medical council.

Benefits are not payable abroad.

Survivor pension: The insured met the coverage requirements for a pension or was a pensioner at the time of death.

Death grant: Paid on the death of an insured person or a pensioner.

Benefits are not payable abroad.

Old-Age Benefits

Old-age pension

Basic system: The benefit is equal to 65% (75% for military personnel) of the insured's last monthly earnings (average monthly insured income in the last 3 years for self-employed persons), plus 2% for each year of contributions exceeding 15 years, up to a maximum of 95% of earnings (100% for military personnel).

At the pensioner's request, part of the pension may be paid as a lump sum before age 65.

An additional lump sum is paid to persons with more than the required number of years of insurance coverage.

Benefit adjustment: Flat-rate adjustments are made to benefits every 3 years.

Supplementary system: The benefit is equal to the accrued sum in the insured's account divided by a fixed amount varying from 202 dinars to 120 dinars, according to the insured's age.

The accrued sum is calculated on the basis of 15% to 25% (according to the insured's age) of the insured's average monthly earnings during the total contribution period increased by 2.5% for each year of contributions.

Deferred pension (supplementary system): The benefit is increased by 5% for each year of deferral.

At the pensioner's request, part of the pension may be paid as a lump sum before age 65.

Benefit adjustment: Flat-rate adjustments are made to benefits every 3 years.

Permanent Disability Benefits

Disability pension

Basic system: The benefit is equal to 65% (75% for military personnel) of the insured's last monthly earnings, plus 2%

for each year of contributions exceeding 15 years, up to a maximum of 95% of earnings (100% for military personnel). The insured is credited with contribution years from the date of the onset of disability up to age 60.

Benefit adjustment: Flat-rate adjustments are made to benefits every 3 years.

Supplementary system: The benefit is equal to the accrued sum in the insured's account divided by a fixed amount varying from 202 dinars to 120 dinars, according to the insured's age.

The accrued sum is calculated on the basis of 15% to 25% (according to the insured's age) of the insured's average monthly earnings during the total contribution period increased by 2.5% for each year of contributions.

The insured is credited with contribution years from the date of the onset of disability up to age 60.

Benefit adjustment: Flat-rate adjustments are made to benefits every 3 years.

Survivor Benefits

Survivor pension: The maximum pension is equal to 100% of the deceased's pension, according to the number and category of eligible survivors. The survivor pension for different eligible categories of survivor is set according to the schedule in law.

Eligible survivors include widows, dependent widowers (if disabled and incapable of work), children, parents, brothers, sisters, and a son's children. Sons must be younger than age 26 (age 28 if a full-time student). There is no limit for unmarried female survivors or disabled male survivors.

The pension is suspended on marriage but is reinstated if subsequently divorced or widowed.

The pension is suspended or ceases if the survivor (except the widow) starts working.

If a survivor's eligibility for the pension ceases, the pension is split among all remaining eligible survivors.

The minimum monthly pension is 180 dinars for a widow or a dependent widower, 145 dinars for each parent, or 94 dinars for each of the other survivors.

Marriage grant: The deceased's daughter or sister or the daughter of the deceased's son receives a grant equal to 6 months of her share in the pension. The grant is paid to each survivor only once.

Death grant: The grant is equal to twice the deceased's last monthly earnings or pension. The minimum grant is twice the minimum wage in the oil and private sectors.

Benefit adjustment: Benefits are adjusted on an ad hoc basis, often at the same time as wage increases for civil servants.

Administrative Organization

Public Institution for Social Security (http://www.pifss.gov.kw), managed by a board of directors and chaired by the Minister of Finance, administers the program.

Work Injury

Regulatory Framework

First and current law: 1976 (social insurance), not yet implemented.

Type of program: Social insurance system.

There is no specific program for work injury. Cash benefits for a work-related injury are provided through the basic system of the Old Age, Disability, and Survivors program, above.

The government pays for any medical care required as the result of a work-related injury.

Kyrgyzstan

Exchange rate: US$1.00 equals 40.80 soms.

Old Age, Disability, and Survivors

Regulatory Framework

First law: 1922.

Current law: 1997 (state pension).

Type of program: Notional defined contribution (NDC) social insurance and social assistance system.

Coverage

Social insurance: All employed persons and members of cooperatives and state and collective farms.

Special system for armed forces personnel.

Special provisions for workers in aviation, the performing arts, and citizens with special merits.

Social assistance: Disadvantaged older persons, disabled persons, and survivors who are not eligible for social insurance benefits. Eligibility does not take into account the total household income of the recipient.

Source of Funds

Insured person: 8% of earnings.

The insured person's contributions also finance sickness and maternity, work injury, and unemployment benefits.

Self-employed person: A fixed amount is paid, depending on the type of work.

The self-employed person's contributions also finance work injury benefits.

Employer: 21% of payroll.

The employer's contributions also finance sickness and maternity and work injury benefits.

Government: The total cost of social assistance allowances and constant-attendance supplements for the disabled; part of the cost of work injury pensions; other subsidies as needed.

Qualifying Conditions

Old-age pension: In January 2006, age 62 with 25 years of covered employment (men) or age 57 and 8 months with 20 years of covered employment (women). The retirement age will increase gradually to age 63 (men) or age 58 (women) by 2007.

Covered employment includes periods of study, maternity leave, caring for disabled persons, unemployment, and other leave periods approved by special decree.

The qualifying conditions are reduced for periods of full-time underground work, full-time work in hazardous conditions, work associated with the Chernobyl catastrophe, and for mothers with five or more children or at least one disabled child.

Pension supplement (old-age): Aged 80 or older; veterans of the Second World War; carers of Group II (totally disabled with an 80% loss of mobility) disabled persons; and single Group II disabled persons.

Pensions are not payable abroad if the pensioner is leaving the country permanently.

Social assistance allowance (old-age): Paid to persons not eligible for an old-age pension. There is no income test.

Disability pension: There are three groups of assessed disability: totally disabled and requiring constant attendance (Group I); totally disabled with an 80% loss of mobility (Group II); and partially disabled with some loss in working capacity (Group III). The insured must have between 1 year and 5 years of covered employment, depending on the insured's age when the disability began.

Covered employment includes periods of study, maternity leave, caring for disabled persons, unemployment, and other leave periods approved by special decree.

The degree of disability is assessed by a Ministry of Labor and Social Protection expert commission.

Pension supplement (disability): Paid to Group I disabled persons, single Group II disabled persons, and persons who worked at the Chernobyl catastrophe.

Pensions are not payable abroad if the pensioner is leaving the country permanently.

Social assistance allowance (disability): Paid to persons not eligible for a disability pension. There is no income test.

Survivor pension: The deceased had between 1 year and 5 years of covered employment, depending on age at the time of death.

Covered employment includes periods of study, maternity leave, caring for disabled persons, unemployment, and other leave periods approved by special decree.

Eligible survivors are the spouse; surviving children younger than age 16 (age 21 if a student); nonworking dependents, including sisters, brothers, and grandchildren younger than age 16; and parents of pensionable age or disabled.

Pensions are not payable abroad if the pensioner is leaving the country permanently.

Social assistance allowance (survivors): Paid to survivors not eligible for a survivor pension. There is no income test.

Old-Age Benefits

Old-age pension: The monthly pension is the sum of a base element (293 soms, but not less than 12% of the average wage in the last year), an insurance element based on years of covered employment and earnings for the period before January 1, 1996, and an insurance element based on the value of accumulated contributions beginning January 1, 1996, onward.

The insurance element for the period before January 1, 1996, is calculated as average earnings for 60 consecutive working months times 1% for every complete year of insured employment. The insurance element for the period beginning January 1, 1996, onward is calculated as accumulated contributions (of at least 1 year) divided by 12 months and multiplied by a coefficient.

There is no maximum pension.

The maximum average earnings for benefit calculation purposes are equal to 20 times the minimum wage.

Partial pension: With at least 5 years of covered employment, a percentage of the full pension is paid according to the number of years of covered employment.

Pension supplement: The supplement is between 50% and 475% of the calculated pension amount.

Benefit adjustment: Benefits are adjusted periodically according to changes in the cost of living.

Social assistance allowance (old-age): The allowance is calculated on the basis of the guaranteed minimum standard of living (GM). There is no income test.

The GM is 175 soms and is adjusted periodically according to changes in wages.

Permanent Disability Benefits

Disability pension: If totally disabled and requiring constant attendance (Group I), the monthly pension is the sum of a base element (293 soms, but not less than 12% of the average wage in the last year), an insurance element based on years of covered employment and earnings for the period before January 1, 1996, and an insurance element based on the value of accumulated contributions beginning January 1, 1996, onward.

The insurance element for the period before January 1, 1996, is calculated as average earnings for 60 consecutive working months times 1% for every complete year of insured employment. The insurance element for the period from January 1, 1996, onward is calculated as accumulated contributions (of at least 1 year) divided by 12 months and multiplied by a coefficient.

Constant-attendance supplement: 100% of the calculated pension amount is paid a month.

The pension for a Group II disability is calculated in the same way as a Group I disability, plus a pension supplement for single disabled persons requiring constant attendance.

Pension supplement: The supplement is between 50% and 475% of the calculated pension.

Partial pension for total disability: With less than the required number of years of covered employment, a percentage of the full pension is paid according to the number of years of covered employment.

Partial disability (Group III): Equal to 50% of the calculated pension.

There is no minimum disability pension.

Benefit adjustment: Benefits are adjusted periodically according to changes in the cost of living.

Social assistance allowance (disability): 245% of the guaranteed minimum standard of living (GM) is paid to a Group I disabled person (320% if disabled since childhood); 150% of the GM for a Group II disabled person (170% if disabled since childhood); 95% of the GM for a Group III disabled person (150% if disabled since childhood).

Also, 320% of the GM is paid to disabled children up to age 18 diagnosed with cerebral palsy; 225% for disabled children younger than age 18 (age 21 if a full-time student) and children diagnosed with HIV or AIDS.

There is no income test.

The GM is 175 soms and is adjusted periodically according to changes in wages.

Survivor Benefits

Survivor pension: The monthly pension for one survivor is equal to 50% of the Group II disability pension that would have been payable to the deceased; 90% for two; 120% for three; or 150% for four or more survivors.

Full orphan's pension: Paid at the same rates as the survivor pension (above) but based on the Group II disability pensions that would have been payable for both parents.

Benefit adjustment: Benefits are adjusted periodically according to changes in the cost of living.

Social assistance allowance (survivors): 150% of the guaranteed minimum standard of living (GM) is paid a month for each orphan younger than age 16 (age 21 if a full-time student); 225% for a full orphan. There is no income test.

The GM is 175 soms and is adjusted periodically according to changes in wages.

Funeral grant: The lump sum paid for the death of an insured pensioner is equal to 10 times the deceased's base pension amount; if the deceased did not qualify for a pension, the lump sum paid is equal to 10 times the minimum wage.

Administrative Organization

Ministry of Labor and Social Protection (http://www.mlsp. kg) provides general coordination and oversight.

Provincial and county offices of the Ministry of Labor and Social Protection administer the program.

Social Fund administers benefits.

Sickness and Maternity

Regulatory Framework

First law: 1922.

Current laws: 1955, with amendments; 1996 (social insurance); and 1997 (medical insurance), with 2005 amendment.

Type of program: Social insurance (cash benefits) and universal (medical benefits) system.

Coverage

Cash sickness and maternity benefits: Employed persons, students, and members of cooperatives.

Medical benefits: All persons residing in the country.

Source of Funds

Insured person

Cash benefits: See source of funds under Old Age, Disability, and Survivors, above.

Medical benefits: See source of funds under Old Age, Disability, and Survivors, above.

Self-employed person

Cash benefits: Not applicable.

Medical benefits: None.

Employer

Cash benefits: See source of funds under Old Age, Disability, and Survivors, above.

Medical benefits: See source of funds under Old Age, Disability, and Survivors, above.

Government

Cash benefits: None.

Medical benefits: The total cost.

Qualifying Conditions

Cash sickness and maternity benefits: There is no minimum qualifying period.

Medical benefits: There is no minimum qualifying period.

Sickness and Maternity Benefits

Sickness benefit: The monthly benefit is equal to 75% of seven times the minimum wage; seven times the minimum wage with three or more dependent children, if a disabled veteran, or if disabled as a result of the Chernobyl catastrophe.

Benefit adjustment: Benefits are adjusted periodically according to changes in the cost of living.

Maternity benefit: The benefit is equal to seven times the minimum wage and is payable for a total of 126 calendar days before and after the expected date of childbirth (may be extended to 140 days if there are complications during childbirth).

Benefit adjustment: Benefits are adjusted periodically according to changes in the cost of living.

Workers' Medical Benefits

Medical services are provided directly to patients through government or enterprise-administered health providers. Benefits include general and specialist care, hospitalization, laboratory services, dental care, maternity care, and transportation.

Providers may charge fees for services.

Dependents' Medical Benefits

Medical services are provided directly to patients through government or enterprise-administered health providers. Benefits include general and specialist care, hospitalization, laboratory services, dental care, maternity care, and transportation.

Providers may charge fees for services.

Administrative Organization

Cash benefits: Social Fund provides general oversight and administers the program.

Employers pay cash benefits.

Medical benefits: Ministry of Health (http://www.med.kg) is responsible for policy.

Ministry of Health (http://www.med.kg) and health departments of local governments provide general supervision and coordination. The Ministry of Health and local health departments administer medical services delivered through clinics, hospitals, maternity homes, and other facilities.

Mandatory Health Insurance Fund provides health care benefits.

Work Injury

Regulatory Framework

First law: 1922.

Current laws: 1955 (short-term benefits); 1990 (pensions), with 1992 and 1994 amendments; and 2005 (labor safety).

Type of program: Social insurance (cash benefits) and universal (medical benefits) system.

Coverage

Employed persons, students, and members of cooperatives.

Source of Funds

Insured person

Cash benefits: See source of funds under Old Age, Disability, and Survivors, above.

Medical benefits: None.

Self-employed person

Cash benefits: Not applicable.

Medical benefits: None.

Employer

Cash benefits: See source of funds under Old Age, Disability, and Survivors, above.

Medical benefits: None.

Government

Temporary disability benefits: None.

Permanent disability and survivor benefits: See source of funds under Old Age, Disability, and Survivors, above.

Medical benefits: The total cost.

Qualifying Conditions

Work injury benefits: There is no minimum qualifying period.

Temporary Disability Benefits

100% of earnings is paid from the first day of incapacity until recovery or the award of a permanent disability pension.

The degree of disability is assessed by a Ministry of Labor and Social Protection expert commission.

Benefit adjustment: Benefits are adjusted periodically according to changes in the cost of living.

Permanent Disability Benefits

Permanent disability pension: The pension depends on the severity of the assessed disability: totally disabled and requiring constant attendance (Group I); totally disabled with an 80% loss in mobility (Group II); and partially disabled with some loss in working capacity (Group III).

If totally disabled and requiring constant attendance (Group I), the monthly pension is the sum of a base element (293 soms, but not less than 12% of the average wage in the last year), an insurance element based on years of covered employment and earnings for the period before January 1, 1996, and an insurance element based on the value of accumulated contributions beginning January 1, 1996, onward.

The insurance element for the period before January 1, 1996, is calculated as average earnings for 60 consecutive working months times 1% for every complete year of insured employment. The insurance element for the period beginning January 1, 1996, onward is calculated as accumulated contributions (of at least 1 year) divided by 12 months and multiplied by a coefficient.

Constant-attendance supplement: 50% of the minimum pension (100% if blind) a month.

The pension for a Group II disability pension is the same as the Group I pension, plus a pension supplement for single disabled persons requiring constant attendance.

Pension supplement: The supplement is between 50% and 475% of the calculated pension.

The degree of disability is assessed by a Ministry of Labor and Social Protection expert commission.

Partial disability (Group III): Equal to 50% of the calculated pension.

The minimum disability pension is equal to 100% of the minimum wage.

Pensions for a work injury or an occupational disease are payable abroad.

Benefit adjustment: Benefits are adjusted periodically according to changes in the cost of living.

Workers' Medical Benefits

All necessary medical care is provided.

Survivor Benefits

Survivor pension: The monthly pension for one survivor is equal to 50% of the Group II disability pension that would have been payable to the deceased; 90% for two; 120% for three, or 150% for four or more survivors.

Full orphan's pension: Paid at the same rates as the survivor pension (above) but based on the Group II disability pensions that would have been payable for both parents.

The minimum full orphan's pension is equal to 100% of the minimum wage (100 soms).

Benefit adjustment: Benefits are adjusted periodically according to changes in the cost of living.

Administrative Organization

Temporary disability benefits: Social Fund provides general supervision.

Enterprises and employers pay cash benefits to their employees.

Permanent disability and survivor pensions: Ministry of Labor and Social Protection (http://www.mlsp.kg) provides general coordination and oversight.

Provincial and county offices of the Ministry of Labor and Social Protection (http://www.mlsp.kg) administer the program.

Medical benefits: Ministry of Health (http://www.med. kg) and health departments of local governments provide general supervision and coordination. The Ministry of Health and local health departments administer the provision of medical services delivered through clinics, hospitals, maternity homes, and other facilities.

Unemployment

Regulatory Framework

First law: 1921.

Current law: 1998 (supporting employment), with 2000, 2001, and 2003 amendments.

Type of program: Social insurance system.

Coverage

Employed persons between age 16 and the pensionable age.

Source of Funds

Insured person: See source of funds under Old Age, Disability, and Survivors, above.

Self-employed person: Not applicable.

Employer: None.

Government: Subsidies as needed from central and local governments.

Qualifying Conditions

Unemployment benefit: Must be registered at an employment office and able and willing to work. The benefit may be reduced, suspended, or terminated if the worker is discharged for violating work discipline, leaving employment without good cause, violating conditions for a job placement or vocational training, or filing fraudulent claims.

Also payable to students who register as unemployed in the 12 months after graduation.

Unemployment Benefits

The minimum benefit is 100% of the minimum wage. The benefit is paid monthly for up to 6 calendar months.

Dependent's supplement: 10% of the unemployment benefit is paid for each dependent.

Administrative Organization

Employment Service and local employment centers administer the program.

Family Allowances

Regulatory Framework

First law: 1944.

Current law: 1998 (state allowances), with 2001 and 2002 amendments.

Type of program: Social assistance system.

Coverage

Children of single-parent families or of unwed mothers; students (younger than age 18) with disabled or unemployed parents.

For orphans, see social assistance allowances (survivor benefits) under Old Age, Disability, and Survivors, above.

Source of Funds

Insured person: None.

Self-employed person: None.

Employer: None.

Government: The total cost.

Qualifying Conditions

Family allowances (income tested): Household per capita income, based on average income during the 3 months before making the claim, must be lower than 100% of the guaranteed minimum standard of living (GM).

The GM is 175 soms and is adjusted periodically according to changes in wages.

Social assistance allowance: Paid for each child younger than age 16 (age 18 if a full-time student).

Birth grant: Paid for each newborn child.

Family Allowance Benefits

Family allowances (income tested): 100% of the guaranteed minimum standard of living (GM) is paid monthly for a mother on leave caring for a child younger than age 18 months or caring for two children younger than age 3; 150% of the GM if caring for three children younger than age 16.

The GM is 175 soms and is adjusted periodically according to changes in wages.

Social assistance allowance: The allowance is equal to the difference between family average per capita income and the GM.

The GM is 175 soms and is adjusted periodically according to changes in wages.

Kyrgyzstan

Birth grant: A lump sum equal to 300% of the GM for each newborn child.

The GM is 175 soms and is adjusted periodically according to changes in wages.

Administrative Organization

Ministry of Labor and Social Protection (http://www.mlsp.kg) and local offices administer the program.

Laos

Exchange rate: US$1.00 equals 10,065 kip.

Old Age, Disability, and Survivors

Regulatory Framework

First and current law: 1999 (employees in enterprises), implemented in 2001.

Type of program: Social insurance system.

Coverage

Employees in private-sector and state-owned enterprises with 10 or more employees; pensioners. (Coverage is currently available only in certain regions of the country.)

Exclusions: Self-employed persons and employees of embassies and international organizations operating in Laos.

Voluntary coverage for workers in smaller enterprises.

Special system for civil servants, the police, and armed forces personnel.

Source of Funds

Insured person: 4.5% of gross monthly earnings.

The insured's contributions also finance sickness, maternity, and funeral benefits.

The minimum earnings for contribution and benefit purposes are 290,000 kip.

The maximum earnings for contribution and benefit purposes are 1,500,000 kip.

Self-employed person: Not applicable.

Employer: 5% of monthly payroll.

The employer contributions also finance sickness, maternity, funeral, and work injury benefits.

The minimum earnings for contribution and benefit purposes are 290,000 kip.

The maximum earnings for contribution and benefit purposes are 1,500,000 kip.

Government: Administrative costs for the salaries of civil servants who work for the Social Security Organization.

Qualifying Conditions

Old-age pension: Age 60 with at least 5 years of covered employment. Retirement from gainful employment is not necessary.

Early pension: Age 55.

Deferred pension: Age 65.

Old-age lump-sum benefit: Paid if the insured reaches the pensionable age with less than 5 years of covered employment.

Disability pension: Paid for a permanent or long-term inability to earn normal income (for blue-collar workers, normal income must be more than the minimum wage; for white-collar workers, income must be equal to the typical earnings of such workers) as the result of an assessed disability. The insured must have at least 5 years of covered employment and have been in covered employment when the disability began.

The pension is awarded by the board of directors of the Social Security Organization on the basis of an investigation carried out by the organization's disability assessment unit.

The pension may be reduced or suspended if the pensioner refuses to undergo proposed medical treatment or rehabilitation.

Carer's benefit: Must have a need for the frequent or constant attendance of another person in order to complete routine daily activities.

Disability lump-sum benefit: Paid if the insured has less than 5 years of covered employment and has a permanent or long-term inability to earn normal income (for blue-collar workers, normal income must be more than the minimum wage; for white-collar workers, income must be equal to the typical earnings of such workers) as the result of an assessed disability.

Adaptation benefit: The deceased was in covered employment at the time of death. The benefit is paid to the surviving spouse and children up to age 18 (age 25 if a full-time student, no limit if disabled) for a 12-month period directly after the insured's death.

Other survivor benefits are only payable after the adaptation benefit ceases.

Survivor pension: The deceased had at least 5 years of covered employment. The spouse was married to the deceased at the time of death and must not have remarried. A widow must be at least age 44; a widow younger than age 44 must have dependents younger than age 15 (no limit if disabled) or be disabled or incapable of finding suitable employment; a widower must be disabled or incapable of finding suitable employment.

Orphan's pension: The pension is paid to orphans up to age 18 (age 25 if a full-time student, no limit if disabled).

Survivor lump-sum benefit: Paid if the deceased had less than 5 years of covered employment.

Death grant: The deceased was in covered employment for at least 12 of the last 18 months.

Old-Age Benefits

Old-age pension: The pension is calculated according to the insured's total pension points multiplied by the insured's average covered earnings in the last 12 months before retirement. The resulting amount is then multiplied by 1.5%.

Awarded pension points may be earned, purchased, or credited. For a pension point to be earned, the insured's covered annual earnings must be equal to the average earnings of all insured persons in that year.

For a working career that began before the program was introduced, workers are credited with 0.8 pension points per year for a minimum of 1 year (if they were age 31 when the program was introduced) increasing up to a maximum of 15 years (if they were aged 45 or older at that time).

Pension points may be purchased under certain conditions to be established in the regulations (not yet implemented).

Early pension: Pensions are reduced by 0.5% for each month the pension is taken before age 60.

Deferred pension: Pensions are increased by 0.5% for each month the pension is deferred after age 60.

Benefit adjustment: Benefits are adjusted at least once a year according to changes in the average insured earnings of all insured persons.

Old-age lump-sum benefit: A lump sum is paid equal to 70% of the insured's average covered earnings in the last 12 months multiplied by the number of months of coverage and divided by 12.

Permanent Disability Benefits

Disability pension: With a minimum of 5 years of covered employment, the pension is calculated on the basis of the average covered earnings of all insured persons in the last 12 months times the number of pension points times 1.5.

Awarded pension points may be earned, purchased, or credited. For a pension point to be earned, the insured's covered annual earnings must be equal to the average earnings of all insured persons in that year. Pension points are credited on the basis of the insured's average annual pension points over the insured period before the onset of disability until the insured reaches the normal pension age.

The disability pension is not reduced if the insured takes up employment.

Benefit adjustment: Benefits are adjusted at least once a year according to changes in the average insured earnings of all insured persons.

Carer's benefit: The benefit is calculated according to the number of hours of care needed per month times the minimum wage (not yet implemented).

Disability lump-sum benefit: A lump sum is paid equal to the actuarial value of the disability pension that the insured would have received.

Survivor Benefits

Adaptation benefit: A monthly benefit equal to 80% of the deceased's average covered earnings in the 12 months before death is paid for a 12-month period directly after the date of death. Other survivor benefits are payable only after the adaptation benefit ceases.

Survivor pension: The spouse receives 60% of the deceased's old-age pension. If the worker died before reaching the pensionable age, the pension is equal to 60% of the disability pension, calculated as if the worker was entitled to a disability pension at the time of death.

Orphan's pension: Each orphan receives 20% of the deceased's old-age pension or projected disability pension.

The maximum orphan pension is equal to 60% of the deceased's old-age pension or projected disability pension for three or more children.

The maximum total survivor benefit is equal to 80% of the deceased's old-age pension or 100% of the insured's projected disability pension.

Benefit adjustment: Benefits are adjusted at least once a year according to changes in the average insured earnings of all insured persons.

Survivor lump-sum benefit: A lump sum is paid equal to the actuarial value of the survivor pension that eligible survivors would have received.

Death grant: A lump sum is paid equal to the insured's average covered earnings in the 6 months before death.

Administrative Organization

Ministry of Labor and Social Welfare supervises the program.

Social Security Organization collects contributions and administers the payment of benefits.

Sickness and Maternity

Regulatory Framework

First and current law: 1999 (employees in enterprises), implemented in 2001.

Type of program: Social insurance system.

Coverage

Employees in private-sector and state-owned enterprises with 10 or more employees; pensioners. (Coverage is currently available only in certain regions of the country.)

Exclusions: Self-employed persons and employees of embassies and international organizations operating in Laos.

Voluntary coverage for workers in smaller enterprises.

Special system for civil servants, the police, and armed forces personnel.

Source of Funds

Insured person: See source of funds under Old Age, Disability, and Survivors, above.

Self-employed person: Not applicable.

Employer: See source of funds under Old Age, Disability, and Survivors, above.

Government: See source of funds under Old Age, Disability, and Survivors, above.

Qualifying Conditions

Sickness benefit: Must have been in covered employment for at least 3 of the last 12 months and be no longer eligible for statutory sick pay (payable by the employer for 30 days under the labor law).

The insured must provide a medical certificate issued by the hospital with which he or she is registered stating the probable duration of sickness.

The benefit may be reduced or suspended if the insured refuses proposed rehabilitation or partial reemployment.

Maternity benefit: Must have been in covered employment for at least 9 of the last 12 months. The benefit is paid to a female insured person who stops work because of pregnancy, childbirth, or a miscarriage. The benefit is also paid to a male or female insured person who stops work to adopt a child younger than age 1.

Birth grant: Must have been in covered employment for at least 12 of the last 18 months. The grant is paid to a female insured person or the wife of a male insured person. The grant is also paid to a male or female insured person who adopts a child younger than age 1.

Medical benefits: Must have been in covered employment for at least 3 of the last 12 months. Benefits are provided until 3 months after the date of the last payment of contributions or after last receiving the sickness benefit. The benefits may be extended for treatment for a life-threatening condition.

Sickness and Maternity Benefits

Sickness benefit: The benefit is equal to 60% of the insured's average covered earnings in the 6 months before the incapacity began; for the partial resumption of work, the benefit is 60% of the difference between the insured's earnings from partial activity and the insured's previous earnings.

The benefit is payable for up to 12 months; may be extended for up to 6 months if the insured is likely to return to work at the end of this period.

Maternity benefit: The benefit is equal to 100% of the insured's average covered earnings in the 6 months before stopping work and is paid for 3 months.

Birth grant: A lump sum is paid equal to 60% of the monthly minimum wage.

Workers' Medical Benefits

Benefits include preventive, curative, and rehabilitative services, including maternity care but excluding necessary treatment resulting from motor vehicle accidents. Accredited providers deliver medical services and are paid on a per capita basis.

The maximum duration for hospitalization is 3 months a year.

Each insured person must register with a hospital, and only services provided by that hospital are covered (except in the case of emergencies). The choice of hospital may be changed every 12 months.

There is no cost sharing.

Dependents' Medical Benefits

Benefits include preventive, curative, and rehabilitative services, including maternity care but excluding necessary treatment resulting from motor vehicle accidents. Accredited providers deliver medical services and are paid on a per capita basis.

The maximum duration for hospitalization is 3 months a year.

There is no cost sharing.

Eligible dependents include the spouse and children up to age 18 (age 25 if a full-time student, no limit if disabled).

Administrative Organization

Ministry of Labor and Social Welfare supervises the program.

Social Security Organization collects contributions, administers cash benefit payments, and contracts with hospitals to provide medical benefits. Contracts must be approved by the Ministry of Public Health.

Work Injury

Regulatory Framework

First and current law: 1999 (employees in enterprises), implemented in 2001.

Type of program: Social insurance system (with an employer-liability system for noncovered employees).

Coverage

Employees in all private-sector and state-owned enterprises with 10 or more employees, paid trainees, and volunteers for rescue operations.

Exclusions: Self-employed persons and employees of embassies and international organizations operating in Laos.

Special system for civil servants, the police, and armed forces personnel.

Employers must provide similar benefits for noncovered employees.

Source of Funds

Insured person: None.

Self-employed person: Not applicable.

Employer: See source of funds under Old Age, Disability, and Survivors, above.

Government: See source of funds under Old Age, Disability, and Survivors, above.

Qualifying Conditions

Work injury benefits: There is no minimum qualifying period.

Temporary Disability Benefits

The benefit is equal to 100% of the insured's average covered earnings in the 6 months before the disability began and is payable for up to 6 months; thereafter, 60% for up to 12 months. If the insured is reemployed part time, the benefit is calculated as the difference between the insured's part-time earnings and previous earnings.

The benefit may be reduced if the insured refuses proposed rehabilitation or part-time reemployment.

Permanent Disability Benefits

The monthly benefit is calculated as the percentage of permanent loss of earning capacity multiplied by 67.5% of the insured's average covered earnings during the last 12 months before the disability began.

The pension is awarded by the board of directors of the Social Security Organization following a determination of disability by the organization's disability assessment unit. The disability is reassessed every 3 years.

The pension may be reduced or suspended if the pensioner refuses proposed rehabilitation.

Benefit adjustment: Benefits are adjusted at least once a year according to changes in the average insured earnings of all insured persons.

Carer's benefit: Paid if there is a need for the frequent or constant attendance of another person in order to complete routine daily activities. The benefit is calculated according to the number of hours of care needed per month times the minimum wage.

An insured person with an assessed degree of permanent disability of less than 25% may opt for a lump sum equal to 12 times the insured's monthly disability pension.

Workers' Medical Benefits

Benefits include preventive, curative, and rehabilitative services, including the treatment of employment injuries and occupational diseases. Accredited providers deliver medical services and are paid on a per capita basis.

The maximum duration for hospitalization is 3 months a year.

Each insured person must register with a hospital, and only services provided by that hospital are covered (except in the case of emergencies). The choice of hospital may be changed every 12 months.

There is no cost sharing.

Survivor Benefits

Adaptation benefit: A monthly benefit equal to 80% of the deceased's average covered earnings in the 12 months before death is paid to the surviving spouse and children up to age 18 (age 25 if a full-time student, no limit if disabled) for a 12-month period directly after the date of death. Other survivor benefits are payable only after the adaptation benefit ceases.

Survivor pension: The spouse receives 50% of the insured's average covered earnings in the last 12 months before death.

The eligible survivor was married to the deceased at the time of death and has not remarried. A widow must be at least age 44; a widow younger than age 44 must have dependents younger than age 15 (no limit if disabled) or be disabled or incapable of finding suitable employment; a widower must be disabled or incapable of finding suitable employment.

Parent's pension: In the absence of an eligible spouse, dependent parents receive 50% of the deceased's average covered earnings in the last 12 months before death.

Orphan's pension: Each orphan up to age 18 (age 25 if a full-time student, no limit if disabled) receives 15% of the deceased's average covered earnings in the last 12 months before death. In the absence of an eligible surviving spouse or dependent parents, the orphan's pension is increased to 20% per child. The maximum total orphan pension is 60% of the deceased's average covered earnings.

The total benefit for all survivors must not exceed the maximum amount of permanent disability benefit to which the deceased could have been entitled.

Benefit adjustment: Benefits are adjusted at least once a year according to changes in the average insured earnings of all insured persons.

Death grant: A lump sum is paid equal to the deceased's average covered earnings in the 6 months before death. The benefit is paid to the relatives who pay for the funeral.

Administrative Organization

Ministry of Labor and Social Welfare supervises the program.

Social Security Organization collects contributions and administers the payment of benefits.

Lebanon

Exchange rate: US$1.00 equals 1,501 pounds.

Old Age, Disability, and Survivors

Regulatory Framework

First and current law: 1963.

Type of program: Social insurance system. Lump-sum benefits only.

Coverage

Employees in industry, commerce, and agriculture.

Exclusions: Temporary agricultural employees, all employees who opted in 1965 to continue with coverage under the labor code, and citizens of other countries not providing reciprocal coverage.

Special system for public-sector employees and teachers.

Source of Funds

Insured person: None.

Self-employed person: Not applicable.

Employer: 8.5% of payroll.

Government: None.

Qualifying Conditions

Old-age benefit: Payable from age 60 but is compulsory at age 64; at any age after 20 years of employment; at any age if a woman marries and leaves employment during the first year of marriage; if disabled (with at least 20 years of employment); or on death (with at least 6 years of employment).

Reduced benefit: A reduced benefit is paid at any age with between 5 and 19 years of employment if the insured is leaving employment permanently.

Employment must cease.

Disability benefit: Must have an assessed loss of at least 50% of normal working capacity.

Survivor benefit: The deceased was covered, or was previously covered, under the program.

Old-Age Benefits

A lump sum is paid equal to the final month's earnings (or average monthly earnings during the previous 12 months, if greater) times the number of years of service up to 20 years, plus 1.5 months' earnings per year of service beyond

20 years of service or age 64. (For benefit calculation purposes, the insured is credited with up to 20 years of coverage for service before 1963.)

Reduced benefit: A lump sum is paid equal to 50% of the benefit for 1 to 5 years of contributions; 65%, for 6 to 10 years; 75%, for 10 to 15 years; or 85%, for 15 to 20 years.

Permanent Disability Benefits

A lump sum is paid equal to the insured's last month's earnings times the number of years of service.

The minimum benefit is equal to 20 times the insured's last month's earnings.

Survivor Benefits

A lump sum is paid equal to the deceased's final month's earnings times the number of years of service.

The minimum benefit is equal to six times the deceased's final month's earnings.

Eligible survivors: The widow (or a widower aged 60 or older or disabled) receives 25% of the benefit; the remaining 75% is split equally among the deceased's children (no minimum or maximum age limit). If there are surviving parents (no minimum or maximum age limit), they receive 10%, with the remaining 90% going to the widow and children (split on the basis of 25% and 75% of the 90%, respectively). If there is no widow(er) and no children, 50% is paid to the parents and 50% to surviving brothers and sisters. If there are no surviving parents, their portion of the benefit is paid to surviving brothers.

Administrative Organization

Ministry of Labor provides general supervision and trusteeship.

National Social Security Fund, managed by a tripartite board and a director general, administers the program through its district offices.

Sickness and Maternity

Regulatory Framework

First and current law: 1963.

Type of program: Social insurance system. Cash and medical benefits.

Note: The program for sickness benefit has not been implemented.

Coverage

Employees in industry and commerce, certain categories of agricultural employees, and teachers.

Public-sector employees, university students, dock workers, and weekly and daily newspaper sellers are covered for medical benefits only.

Exclusions: Temporary agricultural employees and citizens of other countries without reciprocal agreements.

Voluntary coverage for workers previously covered by the mandatory system but without coverage in their present employment and self-employed persons.

Source of Funds

Insured person: 2% of earnings.

The maximum earnings for contribution purposes are 1,500,000 pounds.

Self-employed person: Voluntary contributions of 9% of earnings.

The maximum earnings for contribution purposes are 1,000,000 pounds (1,500,000 pounds for self-employed persons with employees).

Employer: 7% of payroll.

The maximum earnings for contribution purposes are 1,500,000 pounds.

Government: About 25% of the cost of benefits.

Qualifying Conditions

Cash sickness benefits: No benefits are provided.

Cash maternity benefits: Must have 3 months of coverage in the last 6 months.

Medical benefits: Must be currently covered.

Sickness and Maternity Benefits

Sickness benefit: No benefits are provided.

Maternity benefit: Information is not available.

Funeral grant: 150% of the minimum wage is paid. (The minimum wage is 300,000 pounds.)

Workers' Medical Benefits

The insured receives a partial cash refund for the cost of treatment from doctors (full refund for maternity care); service benefits are provided by hospitals under contract with, and paid directly by, the National Social Security Fund. Benefits include general and specialist care, hospitalization, maternity care, medicines, and laboratory services.

The insured is normally reimbursed by the fund for 80% of the cost of doctor's treatment (90% of the cost of hospital care and 100% of the cost of maternity care and kidney and cholesterol dialysis), according to the schedule in law.

The duration of benefits is 26 weeks; up to 52 weeks in special cases. For chronic illnesses, including heart disease and cancer, there is no limit to duration.

Dependents' Medical Benefits

The insured receives a partial cash refund for the cost of treatment for a dependent from doctors (full refund for maternity care); service benefits are provided by hospitals under contract with, and paid directly by, the National Social Security Fund. Benefits include general and specialist care, hospitalization, maternity care, medicines, and laboratory services.

The insured is normally reimbursed by the fund for 80% of the cost of doctor's treatment (90% of the cost of hospital care and 100% of the cost of maternity care and kidney and cholesterol dialysis) for a dependent, according to the schedule in law.

The duration of benefits is 26 weeks; up to 52 weeks in special cases. For chronic illnesses, including heart disease and cancer, there is no limit to duration.

Administrative Organization

Ministry of Labor provides general supervision and trusteeship.

National Social Security Fund administers the program.

Work Injury

Regulatory Framework

First and current law: 1943, with 1983 amendment.

Type of program: Employer-liability system, involving compulsory insurance with a private carrier.

Coverage

All wage earners covered by an employment contract.

Source of Funds

Insured person: None.

Self-employed person: Not applicable.

Employer: The total cost.

Earnings for contribution and benefit purposes are subject to a ceiling.

Government: None.

Qualifying Conditions

Work injury benefits: There is no minimum qualifying period.

Temporary Disability Benefits

75% of the covered worker's daily wage is paid from the day after the accident until full recovery, certification of permanent disability, or death.

Permanent Disability Benefits

If assessed as more than 50% disabled, the benefit is equal to 2/3 of earnings; if assessed as less than 50% disabled, the benefit is equal to half of the full permanent disability benefit.

If assessed as less than 30% disabled, a lump sum is paid equal to 3 years' earnings.

Partial disability: A percentage of the full benefit is paid according to the assessed loss of earning capacity.

Constant-attendance supplement: A set amount is paid according to the schedule in law.

Workers' Medical Benefits

Medical services are provided by hospitals under contract with, and paid directly by, the National Social Security Fund. Medical benefits include general and specialist care, hospitalization, medicines, laboratory services, and appliances.

There is no cost sharing for doctors' services.

Survivor Benefits

Survivor pension: A lump sum is paid equal to up to 500 days of the deceased's pay. For benefit calculation purposes, the deceased's pay includes only 1/4 of the amount exceeding the minimum wage and 1/8 of the amount exceeding twice the minimum wage.

Eligible survivors are the widow, an aged or disabled widower, children younger than age 16 (age 25 if a student or disabled), aged or disabled parents, and dependent brothers and sisters.

Funeral grant: 150% of the minimum wage is paid. (The minimum wage is 300,000 pounds.)

Administrative Organization

Ministry of Labor provides general supervision and trusteeship.

National Social Security Fund administers benefits.

Family Allowances

Regulatory Framework

First law: 1943.

Current law: 1963.

Type of program: Employment-related system.

Coverage

Employees and social insurance beneficiaries with a non-working wife or with children.

Coverage extends to five children only.

Source of Funds

Insured person: None.

Self-employed person: Not applicable.

Employer: 6% of payroll.

The maximum earnings for contribution purposes are 1,500,000 pounds.

Government: None.

Qualifying Conditions

Family allowances: The child must be younger than age 18 (age 25 if a full-time student or an unmarried unemployed daughter; no limit if disabled). The wife must not be gainfully employed.

Family Allowance Benefits

Family allowances: The maximum monthly allowance is 75% of the minimum wage, including a lump sum of 60,000 pounds payable to the wife (20% of the minimum wage) and 33,000 pounds for each child (11% of the minimum wage for each of up to five children).

Administrative Organization

Ministry of Labor provides general supervision and trusteeship.

National Social Security Fund administers allowances.

Malaysia

Exchange rate: US$1.00 equals
3.62 ringgits (M$).

Old Age, Disability, and Survivors

Regulatory Framework

First law: 1951 (provident fund).

Current laws: 1969 (social security); and 1991 (provident fund), with 2001 amendment.

Type of program: Provident fund and social insurance system.

Note: Employees' Provident Fund operates three types of mandatory individual accounts: Account 1, to finance old-age, disability, and survivor benefits and the purchase of approved investments; Account 2, to finance old-age, disability, and survivor benefits and the purchase of a house and education costs; and Account 3, to finance old-age, disability, and survivor benefits and to pay for designated critical illnesses and prosthetic appliances. A voluntary fourth account may be opened to finance periodic payments between ages 55 and 75.

Coverage

Provident fund: Private-sector employees and nonpensionable public-sector employees.

Voluntary coverage for domestic servants, foreign workers, self-employed persons, and pensionable public-sector employees.

Exclusions: Nomadic aborigines and prisoners or other persons detained in rehabilitation centers or psychiatric hospitals.

Special system for government employees.

Social insurance: Employees up to age 55 earning M$2,000 or less a month (or earning M$2,000 or less a month when first employed) and casual workers.

Voluntary coverage for employees earning more than M$2,000 a month, on agreement between the employer and the employee.

Exclusions: Domestic servants, foreign workers, and self-employed persons.

Special system for public-sector employees.

Source of Funds

Insured person

Provident fund: 11% of monthly earnings according to wage classes; pensionable public-sector employees may voluntarily contribute between M$50 and M$5,000 a month.

(60%, 30%, and 10% of monthly contributions are placed in Accounts 1, 2, and 3, respectively. If voluntary Account 4 is opened, it is credited with up to 50% of the balance of Account 1 and subsequently 50% of the contributions to Account 1 until the member is age 55.)

Insured persons can make voluntary additional contributions.

The minimum monthly earnings for provident fund contribution purposes are M$10.

There are no maximum earnings for provident fund contribution purposes.

The (mandatory and voluntary) provident fund contributions (up to M$5,000 a month) are tax deductible.

10% of the total insured person and employer provident fund contributions finance certain medical expenses (see Sickness and Maternity, below).

Social insurance: 0.5% of monthly earnings according to 24 wage classes.

There are no minimum monthly earnings for contribution purposes for social insurance (for the lowest wage class of under M$30, the contribution is based on M$20).

The maximum monthly earnings for contribution purposes for social insurance are M$2,000.

Social insurance contributions are tax deductible.

Self-employed person

Provident fund: Voluntary contributions of between M$50 and M$5,000 a month.

The voluntary provident fund contributions (up to M$5,000 a month) are tax deductible.

Social insurance: Not applicable.

Employer

Provident fund: 12% of monthly earnings according to wage classes. (60%, 30%, and 10% of monthly contributions are placed in Accounts 1, 2, and 3, respectively. If voluntary Account 4 is opened, it is credited with up to 50% of the balance of Account 1 and subsequently 50% of the contributions to Account 1 until the member is age 55.)

Employers can make voluntary additional contributions.

10% of the total insured person and employer provident fund contributions finance certain medical expenses (see Sickness and Maternity, below).

Social insurance: 0.5% of monthly payroll according to 24 wage classes.

There are no minimum monthly earnings for contribution purposes for social insurance (for the lowest wage class of under M$30, the contribution is based on M$20).

The maximum monthly earnings for contribution purposes for social insurance are M$2,000.

Government

Provident fund: None.

Social insurance: None.

Qualifying Conditions

Provident fund

Old-age benefit: Contributions are allocated to three separate accounts (an optional fourth account is opened for members participating in a monthly retirement payment scheme), and individual savings can be accessed under different specified conditions:

Account 1: All funds can be withdrawn at age 55 (at any age if a member permanently emigrates from Malaysia).

Drawdown payment: Funds can be drawn down before age 55. Members with at least M$55,000 in Account 1 may draw down up to 20% of the account balance over M$50,000 for investment in unit trusts through external fund management institutions approved by the Ministry of Finance. The minimum permitted withdrawal is M$1,000.

Account 2: All funds can be withdrawn at age 55 (at any age if a member permanently emigrates from Malaysia).

Drawdown payment: Funds can be drawn down before age 55 to purchase a home, to pay for a house loan, and to pay for education for the member or his or her children.

Account 3: All funds can be withdrawn at age 55 (at any age if a member permanently emigrates from Malaysia).

Drawdown payment: Funds can be drawn down before age 55 to pay for the treatment of designated critical illnesses and certain prosthetic appliances. A list of critical illnesses is provided by the Employees' Provident Fund Board.

The fund member is not required to retire at age 55. If the fund member withdraws all of his or her funds (Accounts 1, 2, and 3) at age 55, he or she can choose to rejoin and contribute to the Employees' Provident Fund if still in employment or if new employment is found. Fund members who do not withdraw funds at age 55 and who are still employed must continue to make contributions.

Account 4 (voluntary): The member must be aged 55 or older and have at least M$24,000 in Account 4 to receive a monthly payment. All funds may be withdrawn if a member permanently emigrates from Malaysia.

Incapacitation benefit: Must be certified by a medical doctor to be mentally or physically unable to work. Fund members may be referred to an Employees' Provident Fund panel clinic to confirm the disability certified by the medical doctor.

Additional benefit: A lump sum is paid, up to age 55.

Survivor benefit: The benefit is paid to the named beneficiary (non-Muslims) or administrator (Muslims). In the absence of a named beneficiary, the benefit is paid (in order of priority) to the administrator (Muslims), spouse, children, parents, and siblings.

Additional benefit: A lump sum is paid on the death of a fund member (up to age 55) to the dependent spouse (if married) or parents (if single).

The benefits are paid in addition to social insurance benefits.

All provident fund benefits are payable abroad.

Social insurance

Old-age pension: No benefits are provided.

Disability pension: Must have at least 24 months of contributions in the last 40 months; contributions for at least 2/3 of the months since first becoming insured, with a minimum of 24 months of contributions.

Reduced disability pension: A reduced pension is paid if contributions were paid for at least 1/3 of the months since first becoming insured, with a minimum of 24 months.

The degree of disability is assessed by the medical board appointed by the Social Security Organization in consultation with the Ministry of Health.

Invalidity grant: Paid if the insured is not eligible for a disability pension but has at least 12 months of contributions.

Survivor pension: The deceased had at least 24 months of contributions in the last 40 months; contributions for at least 2/3 of the months since first becoming insured, with a minimum of 24 months of contributions.

Reduced survivor pension: A reduced pension is paid if the deceased paid contributions for 1/3 of the months since first becoming insured, with a minimum of 24 months of contributions.

The survivor pension is split as follows: 60% of the benefit is paid to the widow (the widower if previously the insured's dependent) and 40% to unmarried children (60% to full orphans) younger than age 21 (until the completion of a first university degree, no limit if disabled).

The spouse pension ceases on remarriage.

Other eligible survivors (in the absence of the above): 40% of the benefit is paid to parents (grandparents if the parents are deceased) and 30% to unmarried dependent brothers and sisters younger than age 21.

Funeral grant: The deceased was a disability pensioner or fulfilled the contribution conditions for a full or reduced disability pension. The grant is paid to the person who paid for the funeral.

Old-Age Benefits

Provident fund

Accounts 1, 2, and 3: The withdrawal of total savings (employee and employer contributions plus compound interest, minus drawdown payments) in a lump sum, monthly installments, or a combination of both.

The minimum total amount to be paid in monthly installments is M$12,000 (the minimum duration for periodic payments is 60 months, and the minimum monthly benefit is M$200).

The interest rate is set annually by the government on the recommendation of the Employees' Provident Fund Board. The interest rate paid by the board in 2005 was 5%.

Account 4 (voluntary): The amount accumulated in Account 4 is divided by 240 and paid monthly over a 20-year period between ages 55 and 75, plus compound interest. The minimum monthly payment is M$100, corresponding to the minimum required savings of M$24,000.

The yearly compound interest can be withdrawn annually beginning at age 55, if some or all of the principal capital is left with the fund.

The interest rate is set annually by the government on the recommendation of the Employees' Provident Fund Board. The interest rate paid by the board in 2005 was 5%.

Old-age pension (social insurance): No benefits are provided.

Permanent Disability Benefits

Incapacitation benefit (provident fund): A lump sum equal to total employee and employer contributions (Accounts 1, 2, and 3) plus compound interest, minus drawdown payments.

The interest rate is set annually by the government on the recommendation of the Employees' Provident Fund Board.

Additional benefit (provident fund): A lump sum of M$5,000.

Disability pension (social insurance): The pension is equal to 50% of the insured's average monthly earnings in the 24 months before the disability began plus 1% of the insured's average monthly earnings in the 24 months before the disability began for each 12-month period of contributions exceeding 24 months.

The maximum pension is equal to 65% of the insured's average monthly earnings in the 24 months before the disability began.

Reduced disability pension: The pension is equal to 50% of the insured's average monthly earnings in the 24 months before the disability began.

The minimum monthly pension is M$171.43.

The maximum monthly earnings for calculating the disability pension are M$2,000.

Constant-attendance supplement: Equal to 40% of the insured's pension (up to a maximum of M$500 a month), if requiring the constant attendance of another person. The need for constant attendance is assessed by the Social Security Organization's medical board.

Invalidity grant (social insurance): A lump sum equal to total employer and employee contributions plus interest.

The minimum annual interest rate is 4%.

Benefit adjustment: Social insurance benefits are adjusted according to changes in the cost of living and the financial health of the fund.

Survivor Benefits

Survivor benefit (provident fund): A lump sum equal to the total employee and employer contributions (Accounts 1, 2, and 3) plus compound interest, minus drawdown payments.

The interest rate is set annually by the government on the recommendation of the Employees' Provident Fund Board. The interest rate paid by the board in 2005 was 5.05%.

Additional benefit (provident fund): A lump sum of M$2,500 is paid.

Survivor pension (social insurance): If the deceased was a disability pensioner, 100% of the disability pension is paid; if the deceased was employed, 50% of the insured's average monthly earnings in the 24 months before death plus 1% of the insured's average monthly earnings in the 24 months before death for each 12-month period of contributions exceeding 24 months.

The maximum survivor pension is equal to 65% of the deceased's average monthly earnings in the 24 months before death.

Reduced survivor pension: The pension is equal to 50% of the deceased's average monthly earnings in the 24 months before death.

The minimum monthly survivor pension is M$171.43.

The maximum monthly earnings for calculating the survivor pension are M$2,000.

Funeral grant (social insurance): Up to M$1,500 is paid to the person who paid for the funeral.

Benefit adjustment: Social insurance benefits are adjusted according to changes in the cost of living and the financial health of the fund.

Administrative Organization

Provident fund: Ministry of Finance (http://www.treasury.gov.my) provides general supervision for the program.

Managed by a tripartite governing board, the Employees' Provident Fund (http://www.kwsp.gov.my) administers contributions and benefits and is responsible for investing members' funds.

Social insurance: Ministry of Human Resources (http://www.mohr.gov.my) provides general supervision.

Managed by a tripartite governing board, the Social Security Organization (Perkeso) (http://www.perkeso.gov.my) administers contributions and benefits.

Sickness and Maternity

Regulatory Framework

First law: 1951 (provident fund).

Current law: 1991 (provident fund).

Type of program: Provident fund system. Medical benefits only.

Coverage

Cash sickness and maternity benefits: No coverage is provided.

Medical benefits: Private-sector employees and nonpensionable public-sector employees.

Voluntary coverage for domestic servants, foreign workers, self-employed persons, and pensionable public-sector employees.

Exclusions: Nomadic aborigines and prisoners or other persons detained in rehabilitation centers or psychiatric hospitals.

Special system for government employees.

Source of Funds

Insured person: See source of funds (provident fund) under Old Age, Disability, and Survivors, above.

Self-employed person: See source of funds (provident fund) under Old Age, Disability, and Survivors, above.

Employer: See source of funds (provident fund) under Old Age, Disability, and Survivors, above.

Government: See source of funds (provident fund) under Old Age, Disability, and Survivors, above.

Qualifying Conditions

Cash sickness and maternity benefits: No cash benefits are provided.

Medical benefits: Covered by the provident fund.

Sickness and Maternity Benefits

Sickness benefit: No benefits are provided.

Maternity benefit: No benefits are provided.

Workers' Medical Benefits

Fund members can withdraw savings from Account 3 to pay for medical treatment for a critical illness and for certain prosthetic appliances, if the employer does not provide full coverage for such treatment. A list of designated critical illnesses is provided by the Employees' Provident Fund Board.

Dependents' Medical Benefits

Fund members can withdraw savings from Account 3 to pay for medical treatment for the following dependents: spouse, children, parents, parents-in-law, and siblings. The covered critical illnesses and prosthetic appliances are the same as for the fund member.

Administrative Organization

Ministry of Finance (http://www.treasury.gov.my) provides general supervision for the program.

Managed by a tripartite governing board, the Employees' Provident Fund (http://www.kwsp.gov.my) administers contributions and benefits and is responsible for investing members' funds.

Work Injury

Regulatory Framework

First law: 1929.

Current law: 1969 (social security).

Type of program: Social insurance system.

Coverage

Employees earning M$2,000 or less a month (or earning M$2,000 or less a month when first employed) and casual workers.

Voluntary coverage for employees earning more than M$2,000 a month, on agreement between the employer and the employee.

Exclusions: Domestic servants, domestic drivers and gardeners, members of the armed forces, government servants, persons in detention institutions, prisoners, spouses of business owners, and self-employed persons.

Special systems for public-sector employees and foreign workers.

Source of Funds

Insured person: None.

Self-employed person: Not applicable.

Employer: 1.25% of monthly payroll according to 24 wage classes.

There are no minimum monthly earnings for contribution purposes (for the lowest wage class of under M$30, the contribution is based on M$20).

The maximum monthly earnings for contribution purposes are M$2,000.

Government: None.

Qualifying Conditions

Work injury benefits: There is no minimum qualifying period.

Temporary Disability Benefits

The benefit is equal to 80% of the insured's average daily wage in the 6 months before the disability began. The insured must be certified by a medical doctor to be unfit for work for a minimum of 4 days. The benefit is payable without limit with continuing medical certification.

The minimum daily benefit is M$10.

The maximum daily benefit is M$52.

Permanent Disability Benefits

Permanent disability pension: For a total (100%) disability, the pension is equal to 90% of the insured's average daily wage in the 6 months before the disability began.

The minimum daily benefit is M$10.

The maximum daily benefit is M$58.50.

Constant-attendance supplement (total permanent disability): Equal to 40% of the insured's pension (up to a maximum of M$500 a month), if requiring the constant attendance of another person. The need for constant attendance is assessed by the Social Security Organization's medical board.

Partial disability: A percentage of the full pension is paid according to the assessed degree of disability.

The minimum daily benefit for a permanent partial disability is M$10.

Partial lump sum: Up to one-fifth of the benefit may be paid as a lump sum when the assessed disability is greater than 20%.

If the disability is assessed as less than 20%, the insured can request to receive the benefit as a lump sum.

The degree of disability is assessed by the medical board appointed by the Social Security Organization in consultation with the Ministry of Health.

Benefit adjustment: Benefits are adjusted according to changes in the cost of living and the financial health of the fund.

Workers' Medical Benefits

Benefits include necessary medical treatment, hospitalization, medicines, artificial limbs and other prosthetic appliances, and physical and vocational rehabilitation.

Care is provided in government hospitals and by a panel of physicians under contract with the Social Security Organization.

Survivor Benefits

Survivor pension: The full daily benefit is equal to 90% of the insured's average daily wage in the 6 months before death and is split as follows: 60% of the full daily benefit is paid to the widow (the widower if previously the insured's dependent) and 40% to unmarried children (60% to full orphans) younger than age 21 (until the completion of a first university degree, no limit if disabled).

The spouse pension ceases on remarriage.

Other eligible survivors (in the absence of the above): 40% of the full daily benefit is paid to parents (grandparents if the parents are deceased) and 30% to unmarried dependent brothers and sisters younger than age 21.

The minimum daily survivor benefit is M$10.

The maximum daily survivor benefit is M$58.50.

Benefit adjustment: Benefits are adjusted according to changes in the cost of living and the financial health of the fund.

Funeral grant: Up to M$1,500 is paid to the person who paid for the funeral.

Benefit adjustment: Benefits are adjusted according to changes in the cost of living and the financial health of the fund.

Administrative Organization

Ministry of Human Resources (http://www.mohr.gov.my) provides general supervision.

Managed by a tripartite governing board, the Social Security Organization (Perkeso) (http://www.perkeso.gov.my) administers contributions and benefits and contracts with health service providers for the provision of medical services.

Marshall Islands

Exchange rate: Currency is the US dollar (US$).

Old Age, Disability, and Survivors

Regulatory Framework

First law: 1967.

Current law: 1990 (social security), with amendment.

Type of program: Social insurance system.

Coverage

Gainfully employed persons, including the self-employed.

Exclusions: Casual labor under certain circumstances.

Source of Funds

Insured person: 7% of earnings.

The maximum earnings for contribution and benefit purposes are US$5,000 a quarter.

Self-employed person: 14% of 3/4 of gross income.

The maximum earnings for contribution and benefit purposes are US$5,000 a quarter.

Employer: 7% of payroll; small business employers contribute 14% of twice the salary of the highest-paid employee.

The maximum earnings for contribution and benefit purposes are US$5,000 a quarter.

Government: None; contributes as an employer.

Qualifying Conditions

Old-age pension: Age 60 with 1 quarter of coverage for each year after June 30, 1968 (or since age 21, if later), with at least 12 quarters of coverage.

Early pension: Age 55 with at least 80 quarters of coverage.

Deferred pension: A deferred pension is possible.

Disability pension: Incapacity for usual work. Must have 1 quarter of coverage for each year after June 30, 1968 (or since age 21, if later), with at least 12 quarters of coverage including 6 quarters of coverage during the last 40 quarters.

Survivor pension: The deceased had 1 quarter of coverage for each year after June 30, 1968 (or since age 21, if later), or at least 6 quarters of coverage in the 40 quarters before death.

Eligible survivors are a widow(er) of any age and orphans younger than age 18 (age 22 if a full-time student, no limit if disabled before age 22).

Income test: The pension is reduced by US$1 for each US$3 of earnings above US$1,500 a quarter for pensioners who are younger than age 62.

Pensions are normally payable abroad to noncitizens for 6 months only; may be paid for longer under a reciprocal agreement.

Lump-sum survivor benefit: Paid when all eligible survivors no longer qualify for survivor benefits as a result of death, remarriage, or age conditions.

Old-Age Benefits

Old-age pension: The pension is calculated on the basis of 2% of indexed covered earnings, plus 14.5% of the first US$11,000 of cumulative covered earnings, plus 0.7% of cumulative covered earnings in excess of US$11,000 up to a maximum of US$44,000.

Early pension: The pension is reduced by 0.5% for each month the pension is taken before age 60.

Deferred pension: The pension is increased by 0.5% for each month the pension is deferred after age 60.

The minimum old-age pension is US$128.99 a month.

Permanent Disability Benefits

Disability pension: The pension is calculated on the basis of 2% of indexed covered earnings, plus 14.5% of the first US$11,000 of cumulative covered earnings, plus 0.7% of cumulative covered earnings greater than US$11,000 up to a maximum of US$44,000.

The minimum disability pension is US$128.99 a month.

Survivor Benefits

Survivor pension: The widow(er) receives 100% of the deceased's pension.

Orphan's pension: Each eligible orphan receives 25% of the deceased's pension.

The minimum survivor pension is US$128.99 a month.

The maximum survivor pension is 100% of the deceased's pension.

Lump-sum survivor benefit: A lump sum is paid equal to 4% of cumulative covered earnings minus the total value of the survivor benefits already paid.

Administrative Organization

Marshall Islands Social Security Administration administers the program.

Sickness and Maternity

Regulatory Framework

First law: 1991 (health fund).

Current law: 2002 (health fund administration).

Type of program: Social insurance program. Medical benefits only.

Coverage

Gainfully employed persons, including the self-employed.

Exclusions: Casual labor under certain circumstances.

Source of Funds

Insured person: 3.5% of earnings.

The maximum earnings for contribution and benefit purposes are US$5,000 a quarter.

Self-employed person: 10% of 3/4 of gross income.

The maximum earnings for contribution and benefit purposes are US$5,000 a quarter.

Employer: 3.5% of payroll; small business employers contribute 10% of twice the salary of the highest-paid employee.

The maximum earnings for contribution and benefit purposes are US$5,000 a quarter.

Government: None; contributes as an employer.

Qualifying Conditions

Cash sickness and maternity benefits: No cash benefits are provided.

Medical benefits: An insured employee or insured citizen.

Sickness and Maternity Benefits

Sickness benefits: No cash benefits are provided.

Maternity benefits: No cash benefits are provided.

Workers' Medical Benefits

General medical services are delivered through a public hospital and a private clinic in Majuro and through a public hospital in Ebeye.

Dependents' Medical Benefits

No information is available.

Administrative Organization

Ministry of Health Services administers the Social Security Health Fund.

Social Security Administration is responsible for the collection of contributions for the Social Security Health Fund.

Micronesia

Exchange rate: Currency is the US dollar (US$).

Old Age, Disability, and Survivors

Regulatory Framework

First law: 1967.

Current law: 1982 (social security), implemented in 1983, with 2005 amendment.

Type of program: Social insurance system.

Coverage

Gainfully employed and self-employed persons.

Exclusions: Persons engaged in casual labor working less than 1 week in any calendar month, certain self-employed persons, and family labor.

Special systems (individual retirement plans) for some government agency employees.

Source of Funds

Insured person: 6% of earnings.

The minimum earnings for contribution purposes are US$50 a quarter.

The maximum earnings for contribution purposes are US$5,000 a quarter.

Self-employed person: 2.5% of business annual gross revenue for the previous calendar year.

The maximum earnings for contribution purposes are US$5,000 a quarter.

Employer: 6% of twice the salary of the highest-paid employee per quarter.

Government: None; contributes as an employer.

Qualifying Conditions

Old-age pension (earnings-tested): Age 60 with 1 quarter of coverage for each year after June 1968 (or since age 21, if later) up to age 60, with at least 12 quarters of coverage.

Earnings test: The old-age pension is reduced by US$1 for each US$2 of earnings exceeding US$300 a quarter, if the pensioner is reemployed.

The pension is payable abroad to citizens of Palau, Marshall Islands, and the United States under reciprocal agreement. If eligible for an old-age pension at retirement age but not residing in Micronesia, a lump sum is paid equal to the total value of contributions made to Micronesia's Social Security Administration. The lump sum is reduced by the value of

any payments made by Micronesia's Social Security Administration to the insured before the lump sum is paid.

Old-age lump-sum benefit: Paid to insured persons who do not qualify for the old-age pension at retirement age.

The lump-sum benefit is also payable abroad to citizens of Palau, Marshall Islands, and the United States under reciprocal agreement.

Disability pension: Assessed as incapable of substantial gainful activity because of a disability that will last for at least a year or result in death. Must have 1 quarter of coverage for each year after June 1968 (or since age 21, if later), with at least 12 quarters of coverage or at least 8 quarters of coverage during the last 13 quarters.

Eligibility for the disability pension may cease if the insured's condition improves.

Periodic examinations to determine the degree of disability are carried out by Micronesia's Social Security Administration's certified disability examiner.

Dependent disabled child benefit: If an active insured person who was eligible to receive a pension dies, the benefit is payable to a dependent child who was disabled before reaching age 22. The benefit may continue for as long as the disability exists.

Disability benefits are payable abroad to citizens of Palau, Marshall Islands, and the United States under reciprocal agreement. If eligible for a pension when the disability began and not residing in Micronesia, a lump sum is paid equal to the total value of contributions made to Micronesia's Social Security Administration. The lump sum is reduced by the value of any payments made by Micronesia's Social Security Administration to the insured before the lump sum is paid.

Survivor pension (earnings-tested): The deceased had 1 quarter of coverage for each year after June 1968 (or since age 21, if later) or had at least 8 quarters of coverage in the 13 quarters before death. If the deceased was insured at the time of death but did not meet the qualifying conditions for a pension, surviving children may still receive the orphan's pension.

Eligible survivors are the insured's spouse and dependent unmarried children younger than age 18 (age 22 if a full-time student, no limit if disabled before age 22). The pension for a spouse ceases on remarriage.

Earnings test: The survivor's pension is reduced by US$1 for each US$2 of earnings exceeding US$300 a quarter.

The pension is payable abroad to citizens of Palau, Marshall Islands, and the United States under reciprocal agreement. If eligible for a pension at the time of death and not residing in Micronesia, a lump sum is paid to survivors equal to the total value of the deceased's contributions to Micronesia's Social Security Administration. The lump sum is reduced by the value of any payments made by Micronesia's Social

Security Administration to the deceased, the surviving spouse, or orphans before the lump sum is paid.

Survivor lump-sum benefit: Paid for the death of an insured person of retirement age who did not meet the qualifying conditions for a pension or for an insured worker who did not meet the qualifying conditions for a pension, subject to the condition that the value of any benefits previously received does not exceed 4% of the deceased's cumulative covered earnings. Also paid when all survivors are no longer eligible to receive a survivor pension on the grounds of age, remarriage, or death, subject to the condition that the value of any benefits previously received does not exceed 4% of the deceased's cumulative covered earnings.

Eligible survivors are (in order of priority) the deceased's spouse, children, parents, and legal heir.

The lump-sum survivor benefits are payable abroad to citizens of Palau and Marshall Islands under reciprocal agreement.

Old-Age Benefits

Old-age pension (earnings-tested): The monthly pension is based on 16.5% of the first US$10,000 of cumulative covered earnings, plus 3% of the next US$30,000 of cumulative earnings, plus 2% of cumulative earnings exceeding US$40,000.

The minimum monthly old age pension is US$50.

Benefit adjustment: Benefits are adjusted according to changes in the earnings test.

Old-age lump-sum benefit: 4% of the insured's cumulative covered earnings is paid.

Permanent Disability Benefits

Disability pension: The monthly pension is based on 16.5% of the first US$10,000 of cumulative covered earnings, plus 3% of the next US$30,000 of cumulative earnings, plus 2% of cumulative earnings exceeding US$40,000.

The minimum monthly disability pension is US$50.

Dependent disabled child benefit: The benefit is equal to 15% of the monthly disability pension that would have been payable to the deceased.

Survivor Benefits

Survivor pension (earnings-tested): 60% of the deceased's pension is paid to a widow(er), regardless of age.

If the surviving spouse is also eligible for an old-age or disability pension in his or her own right, the highest monthly benefit amount is paid. In addition, the surviving spouse receives a lump sum equal to 4% of the cumulative covered earnings used to calculate the lower benefit amount, minus the sum of all benefits already received on the basis of those cumulative covered earnings.

Orphan's pension (earnings-tested): 15% of the deceased's pension is paid for each eligible child.

The maximum half orphan's pension is 40% of the deceased's pension (if there are three or more children and if a survivor pension is paid to the spouse).

The monthly benefit paid to a full orphan is based on the higher of the two benefit amounts earned by the deceased parents. In addition, a full orphan receives a lump sum equal to 2% of the other deceased parent's cumulative covered earnings, minus the sum of any benefits received by the deceased parent.

The maximum full orphan's pension is 100% of the deceased's pension (if there are seven or more children).

The minimum monthly survivor pension is US$50.

The maximum survivor pension is 100% of the deceased's pension (may be higher if the survivor pension is calculated on the basis of the surviving spouse's own contribution record).

Benefit adjustment: Benefits are adjusted according to changes in the earnings test.

Survivor lump-sum benefit: 4% of the deceased's total cumulative covered earnings is paid (reduced by the amount of any benefits paid to the insured and his or her eligible dependents).

Administrative Organization

United States Social Security Administration (http://www.socialsecurity.gov) administers the program.

Federated States of Micronesia Social Security Administration (http://www.fm/fsmss) administers the program at the local level.

Nepal

Exchange rate: US$1.00 equals 73.85 rupees.

Old Age, Disability, and Survivors

Regulatory Framework

First and current laws: 1962 (provident fund); and 1994 (old-age allowance), with 1995, 1996 (widow's allowance and disability pension), and 2002 (eliminating drawdown payment) amendments.

Type of program: Provident fund and social assistance system.

Coverage

Provident fund: Compulsory coverage for government employees.

Voluntary coverage for any organization with 10 or more employees.

Exclusions: Self-employed persons, temporary workers, part-time workers, and domestic servants.

Special system for civil servants.

Social assistance: Nepalese citizens aged 75 or older, aged 60 or older and a widow, or aged 16 or older and assessed as disabled.

Source of Funds

Provident fund

Insured person: 10% of monthly earnings.

Self-employed person: Not applicable.

Employer: 10% of monthly payroll. (Additional voluntary contributions may be made by employers on behalf of employees.)

There are no maximum earnings for additional voluntary contributions.

Government: None.

Social assistance

Insured person: None.

Self-employed person: None.

Employer: None.

Government: The total cost.

Qualifying Conditions

Old-age benefit (provident fund): Paid on retirement or the termination of employment. The legal retirement age is age 55; retirement may be deferred in certain instances until age 60.

Additional benefit scheme: Paid at retirement age.

Loan scheme (provident fund): Loans are provided from the fund member's own account to help finance the cost of housing, education, and other needs. The qualifying conditions vary according to the nature of the loan.

Old-age allowance (social assistance): Paid to Nepalese citizens aged 75 or older.

Personal accident insurance (provident fund): Paid in the event of the partial or permanent disability or the accidental death of the fund member.

Disability pension (social assistance): Paid to disabled Nepalese citizens aged 16 or older. The person must be assessed as blind or having lost the use of feet or hands.

Survivor benefit (provident fund): Paid for the death of the fund member.

Funeral grant (provident fund): Paid for the death of the fund member.

Survivor allowance (social assistance): Paid to Nepalese widows aged 60 or older who satisfy a means test (no personal income, not receiving family support, and not receiving a pension on behalf of a deceased husband).

Old-Age Benefits

Old-age benefit (provident fund): A lump sum is paid equal to employer and employee contributions plus 5.25% interest a year.

Additional benefit scheme: A lump sum calculated on the basis of the value of the old-age lump-sum benefit times 0.75% times the number of years of contributions, up to a maximum.

Loan scheme (provident fund): The maximum amount that may be borrowed and the maximum borrowing period vary according to the nature of the loan.

Government employees also receive a monthly pension, up to a maximum of 100% of basic earnings.

Interest rate adjustment: The Board of Directors of the Provident Fund decides the rate of interest on the basis of the fund's annual income.

Old-age allowance (social assistance): 250 rupees a month is paid.

Permanent Disability Benefits

Personal accident insurance (provident fund): A lump sum of 55,000 rupees is paid for a permanent disability.

Partial disability: A lump sum ranging from 10,000 rupees to 25,000 rupees is paid, according to the assessed degree of disability.

Disability pension (social assistance): 250 rupees a month is paid.

Survivor Benefits

Survivor benefit (provident fund): 100% of the lump sum payable to the deceased is paid to a named survivor or to the deceased's heirs. In the case of more than one named survivor, the amount is split equally.

The surviving spouse of a deceased government employee also receives a pension for up to 7 years, up to a maximum of 100% of basic earnings.

Interest rate adjustment: The Board of Directors of the Provident Fund decides the rate of interest on the basis of the fund's annual income.

Funeral grant (provident fund): A lump sum of 5,000 rupees is paid.

Personal accident insurance (provident fund): A lump sum of 55,000 rupees is paid.

Survivor allowance (social assistance): 150 rupees a month is paid.

Administrative Organization

Provident fund: Employees' Provident Fund is an autonomous body operating under the general supervision of the Ministry of Finance.

Managed by a board of directors, the Employees Provident Fund (http://www.epfnepal.com) administers the program.

Social assistance: Ministry of Local Development administers the program.

Benefits are administered at the local level by Village Development Committees.

Sickness and Maternity

Regulatory Framework

No statutory cash benefits are provided.

The 1993 Labor Code requires private-sector employers to pay 50% of wages for sick leave for up to 15 days each year, provided the employee has been continuously employed by the same employer for at least a year.

The 1992 Civil Servant Act provides for maternity leave to employed women for up to 60 days before or after childbirth, for up to two births.

The 1983 Employment Act requires employers to pay 100% of wages for maternity leave of up to 52 days before or after childbirth. Maternity leave may be paid for up to two births. If both children subsequently die, the woman may take maternity leave for the birth of two more children.

Free medical treatment is provided to older persons through government hospitals.

The 1974 Bonus Act requires private-sector enterprises to provide employees and their dependents with basic medical benefits.

Work Injury

Regulatory Framework

First law: 1959.

Current law: 1992 (work injury), with 1993 amendment.

Type of program: Employer-liability system, involving compulsory insurance with a private carrier.

Coverage

Employees of establishments with 10 or more workers.

Exclusions: Self-employed persons and domestic servants.

Special system for miners.

Source of Funds

Insured person: None.

Self-employed person: Not applicable.

Employer: The total cost is met through the direct provision of benefits or the payment of insurance premiums.

Government: None.

Qualifying Conditions

Work injury benefits: There is no minimum qualifying period.

Temporary Disability Benefits

The benefit is equal to 50% of earnings; 100% of earnings if hospitalized. The benefit is paid from the first day of incapacity for up to a year.

The degree of disability is assessed by a recognized doctor, according to the schedule in law.

Permanent Disability Benefits

For a total disability (100%), a lump sum is paid equal to 5 years' earnings.

Partial disability: A percentage of the total disability lump sum is paid according to the assessed degree of disability.

The degree of disability is assessed by an authorized doctor, according to the schedule in law.

Workers' Medical Benefits

The total cost of necessary treatment.

The nature of necessary treatment is assessed by an authorized doctor, according to the schedule in law.

Survivor Benefits

A dependent survivor receives a lump sum equal to 3 years of the deceased's earnings.

Administrative Organization

Labor and Employment Promotion Department enforces the law.

Unemployment

Regulatory Framework

No statutory unemployment benefits are provided.

The 1992 Labor Act requires employers to pay lump-sum severance benefits to laid-off employees equal to 1 month's wages for each year of service in all establishments employing 10 or more workers.

The 1993 Labor Rules require employers in establishments with 10 or more workers to pay a cash benefit to workers with at least 3 years' employment when they retire or resign, as follows: 50% of monthly wages for each of the first 7 years of service, 66% of monthly wages for each year between 7 and 15 years, and 100% of monthly wages for each year of service exceeding 15 years.

The employee may choose to receive the cash benefit or the severance lump sum.

New Zealand

Exchange rate: US$1.00 equals
1.57 New Zealand dollars (NZ$).

Old Age, Disability, and Survivors

Regulatory Framework

First laws: 1898 (old-age pension), 1911 (widows' pension), 1924 (blind person's pension), and 1936 (disability pension).

Current law: 2001 (New Zealand superannuation).

Type of program: Universal and social assistance system.

Note: All net benefits reflect the primary tax rate applied.

Coverage

All persons residing in New Zealand.

Source of Funds

Insured person: None.

Self-employed person: None.

Employer: None.

Government: The total cost is financed from general revenues.

Qualifying Conditions

Old-age pension (New Zealand superannuation): Age 65 with 10 years' residence after age 20, including 5 years after age 50; no income or retirement test (except for a married pensioner with an unqualified spouse).

The pension is paid for up to 26 weeks if the beneficiary is not going abroad for more than 30 weeks. A reciprocal agreement is required for the full payment of the pension if the beneficiary is going abroad for longer; in other instances, partial payment up to 50% (100% for certain Pacific countries).

Assistance benefits (old-age): Other benefits may be provided.

Disability pension (invalids' benefit): Permanent and severe restriction in working capacity or total blindness and has resided in New Zealand for at least 10 years. The benefit is income-tested (the personal earnings of totally blind persons are exempt). The beneficiary must be a New Zealand citizen or reside permanently in New Zealand and be age 16 or older.

The disability pension may be paid for a limited period when the beneficiary is going abroad temporarily, depending on individual circumstances.

Assistance benefits (disability): Other benefits may be provided.

Survivor pension (widows' benefit, orphan's benefit, unsupported child's benefit): Paid to a widow or carer of orphans or unsupported children. The widow, carer, orphan, or unsupported child must reside in New Zealand. The widow's (carer's) benefit is income-tested. For benefits for orphans and unsupported children, there is an income test on the child's nonpersonal income (such as money from trusts).

The survivor pension may be paid for a limited period when the beneficiary is going abroad temporarily, depending on individual circumstances.

Domestic purposes benefit: Paid to single women living alone or single parents with dependent children.

Assistance benefits (survivors): Other benefits may be provided.

Old-Age Benefits

Old-age pension (New Zealand superannuation): NZ$263.90 (net) a week is paid for a single person living alone, NZ$243.60 (net) if sharing accommodation, or NZ$406 (net) for a married or civil-union couple living together and both spouses qualify for the pension.

The pension is not income-tested but may be reduced if the beneficiary is receiving a benefit or pension from an overseas government.

A married pensioner with a spouse younger than age 65 may receive half the married rate (NZ$203 [net] a week) with no income test (the spouse receives no payment), or a special married couple rate (NZ$387.14 [net] a week) with an income test.

Benefit adjustment: Benefits are adjusted annually according to changes in the consumer price index for the previous calendar year.

Assistance benefits: Other assistance benefits available to old-age pensioners (some needs-tested) include an accommodation supplement, a disability allowance, and special needs grants.

Permanent Disability Benefits

Disability pension (invalids' benefit): Up to NZ$175.91 (net) a week is paid for a single person aged 16 or 17; NZ$217.38 (net) for a single person aged 18 or older; NZ$181.16 (net) for each member of a married or civil-union couple, with or without children; NZ$285.57 (net) for a single person with children.

Income test: The benefit is reduced by NZ$0.30 for each dollar of gross earned income exceeding NZ$4,160 a year and by NZ$0.70 for each dollar of gross earned income exceeding NZ$9,360. The personal earnings of totally blind persons are exempt.

Dependent's supplement: Additional payments are provided for dependent children.

Benefit adjustment: Benefits are adjusted annually according to changes in the consumer price index for the previous calendar year.

Assistance benefits: Other assistance benefits available to pensioners (some needs-tested) include an accommodation supplement, a family support payment, an advance payment of benefit, a training incentive allowance, transition-to-work assistance, a disability allowance, a special benefit, and special needs grants.

Survivor Benefits

Survivor pension

Widows' benefit: Up to NZ$181.16 (net) is paid a week for a single woman without children whose partner has died; NZ$249.10 (net) if with children.

Domestic purposes benefit: NZ$181.16 (net) a week for a single woman with no dependent children; NZ$249.10 (net) for a single parent with dependent children.

Income test: The benefit is reduced by NZ$0.30 for each dollar of gross earned income exceeding NZ$4,160 a year and by NZ$0.70 for each dollar of gross earned income exceeding NZ$9,360.

Orphan's benefit: Up to NZ$133.05 (net) is paid a week, subject to age, for each full orphan younger than age 18 (not taxable). The benefit is not income-tested, except for the child's nonpersonal income (such as money from trusts).

Unsupported child's benefit: Up to NZ$133.05 (net) is paid a week, subject to age, for each full orphan younger than age 18 (not taxable). The benefit is not income-tested, except for the child's nonpersonal income (such as money from trusts).

Funeral grant: Up to NZ$1,662.58 is paid for funeral costs (not taxable but income- and asset-tested).

Benefit adjustment: Benefits are adjusted annually according to changes in the consumer price index for the previous calendar year.

Assistance benefits: Other assistance benefits available to pensioners (some needs-tested) include an accommodation supplement, an advance payment of benefit, a training incentive allowance, transition-to-work assistance, a disability allowance, and special needs grants.

Administrative Organization

Ministry of Social Development (Work and Income) (http://www.msd.govt.nz) administers pensions through its local offices.

Sickness and Maternity

Regulatory Framework

First law: 1938.

Current laws: 1964 (social security), implemented in 1965, with 2001 amendment; and 1987 (parental leave and employment protection), with 2002 amendment.

Type of program: Universal and social assistance system.

Coverage

Cash sickness benefits (sickness benefit): Persons temporarily incapacitated for full-time work.

Maternity benefits (sickness benefit): Single women.

Paid parental leave: All persons residing in New Zealand, subject to employment history.

Medical benefits: All persons residing in New Zealand.

Source of Funds

Insured person: None.

Self-employed person: None.

Employer: None.

Government: The total cost is financed from general revenues.

Qualifying Conditions

Cash sickness and maternity benefits (sickness benefit): Aged 18 or older (aged 16 or 17 if married or in a civil union with a dependent child) with at least 24 months of continuous residence in New Zealand. Must reside in New Zealand. Benefits are income-tested.

For persons with less than 24 months of residence in New Zealand, an income- and asset-tested benefit is possible in cases of hardship.

Paid parental leave: The recipient must have been employed by the same employer for more than 12 months before the expected date of childbirth or the adoption of a child younger than age 5 and have worked a minimum of 10 hours a week, including at least 1 hour a week or 40 hours a month.

Medical benefits: Must reside or have a stated intent to remain in New Zealand for at least 2 years. There is no income test.

Sickness and Maternity Benefits

Sickness benefit: Up to NZ$173.92 (net) a week is paid if aged 25 or older, single, and with no children; NZ$144.92 (net) if between ages 20 and 24, or if aged 18 or 19 and living away from home; NZ$115.94 (net) if aged 18 or 19 and living with a parent.

Up to NZ$249.10 (net) a week is paid for a single beneficiary with children; up to NZ$144.92 (net) for each member of a married or civil-union couple with or without children.

The benefit is paid after a waiting period of between 1 and 10 weeks, depending on previous income and family circumstances.

There is no limit on the period of eligibility for sickness benefit (unless paid because of pregnancy or a pregnancy-related medical complication, see below).

Income test: The benefit is reduced by NZ$0.70 for each dollar of gross earned income exceeding NZ$80 a week.

Benefit adjustment: Benefits are adjusted annually according to changes in the consumer price index for the previous calendar year.

Maternity benefit (sickness benefit): The benefit is normally paid to a single pregnant woman at the sickness benefit rate (see above) after the 26th week of pregnancy. Payment can continue for up to 13 weeks after childbirth.

Income test: The benefit is reduced by NZ$0.70 for each dollar of gross earned income exceeding NZ$80 a week.

Benefit adjustment: Benefits are adjusted annually according to changes in the consumer price index for the previous calendar year.

Paid parental leave: Paid leave is provided for up to 12 weeks to one parent or shared between both parents. The paid leave replaces 100% of previous earnings, up to NZ$346.63 of gross earnings a week.

Benefit adjustment: Benefits are adjusted annually according to any percentage movement upward in average ordinary-time weekly earnings. Average ordinary-time weekly earnings (employees) are determined by the quarterly employment survey published by Statistics New Zealand.

Workers' Medical Benefits

Subsidies are provided for those using health care. Free services include inpatient care in public hospitals, general practitioner care for children up to age 6, maternity services, and most laboratory services. Costs for care in a private hospital are not subsidized.

Cost sharing: Approved prescribed medicines are subsidized at various levels, depending on income.

Families with low income have access to a Community Services Card (CSC) that reduces prescription charges from a maximum of NZ$15 per item to a minimum of NZ$3 per item. If a family has paid for 20 items in a year, the charge falls to zero for CSC holders and NZ$2 per item for other persons. There is no reimbursement for CSC holders for dental treatment, physiotherapy, treatment for a work-related injury, or for expenses for eyeglasses for children younger than age 6.

A government prescription charge applies for prescription items that are subsidized by the government. In certain cases, a premium must be paid if the cost of manufacture is more than the government subsidy. There is no government prescription charge on items for children younger than age 6. Some items have an unsubsidized manufacturer's charge.

Dependents' Medical Benefits

Same as for the family head, with special subsidies for low-income families (defined according to predetermined annual gross family income levels and the number of family members) or those who need intensive medical care.

Administrative Organization

Ministry of Social Development (Work and Income) (http://www.msd.govt.nz) administers cash benefits through its branch and district offices.

Ministry of Social Development (Community Services Card Service Centre) administers Community Services Cards.

Ministry of Health (HealthPac) (http://www.moh.govt.nz/moh.nsf) administers medical benefits.

Inland Revenue Department (http://www.ird.govt.nz) administers statutory paid parental leave benefits.

Work Injury

Regulatory Framework

First law: 1908.

Current law: 2001 (injury prevention, rehabilitation, and compensation), implemented in 2002, with 2002 (employer levies; ancillary services) and 2005 (treatment of injuries; employer levies) amendments.

Type of program: Universal and employer-liability (with a public carrier) system. Employers may self-manage claims.

Coverage

The accident compensation scheme provides coverage for work injury and occupational disease for all New Zealand citizens and residents.

Note: The scheme also provides coverage for medical malpractice and certain criminal injuries for all New Zealand citizens and residents and temporary visitors to New Zealand including children and nonworking adults. In return, people do not have the right to sue for a personal injury covered by the scheme, other than for damages exceeding the amount needed for simple compensation.

Source of Funds

Insured person

Work injury: None.

Nonwork injury: Contributes for nonwork-related injuries.

Contribution rates are set each year based on the actual cost of injuries that have occurred, according to the schedule in law.

Self-employed person

Work injury: Contributes for work injuries.

Nonwork injury: Contributes for nonwork-related injuries.

Contribution rates are set each year based on the actual cost of injuries that have occurred, according to the schedule in law.

Employer: Contributes for employee work injuries.

Contribution rates are set each year on the basis of the actual cost of injuries that have occurred, according to the schedule in law.

Government

Work injury: Special earmarked taxes, including gas and motor vehicle licensing fees; contributes as an employer.

Nonwork injury: General revenues fund the program for nonearners.

Note: All of the above contributions are assigned to one of seven accounts. The type of injury claim determines from which account the compensation will be funded.

Qualifying Conditions

Work injury benefits: There is no minimum qualifying period.

Nonwork-related injury benefits: There is a 1-week waiting period.

Survivor benefits

Spouse: Payments continue until the latest of the following: the end of 5 consecutive years from the date on which the entitlement first became payable, the date the deceased's youngest child reaches age 18, the date the spouse no longer provides care for the deceased's children younger than age 18, or the date the spouse no longer provides care for any other qualifying dependent. (The spouse can choose between survivor benefits under superannuation or work injury.)

Orphan: Payments continue until the end of the calendar year in which he or she reaches age 18; the end of full-time study or age 21, whichever is earliest. A disabled orphan who was dependent on the deceased is eligible for weekly compensation after the end of the calendar year in which he or she reaches age 18 if his or her average earnings are less than or equal to the minimum full-time earner rate.

Other dependents: Average weekly earnings over a 12-month period must not be greater than the minimum full-time earner rate, regardless of age.

Temporary Disability Benefits

Temporary disability benefit (weekly compensation): 80% of the worker's average weekly earnings is paid until he or she is able to return to work. Weekly earnings are calculated under prescribed rules according to the worker's earnings in the period before the incapacity began. For work-related personal injuries, the employer pays for the first week of incapacity. (For nonwork-related personal injuries, there is a 1-week waiting period.) The benefit is paid for as long as a certified incapacity lasts or until age 65 (at which point New Zealand superannuation is paid). Claimants aged 65 or older can receive the benefit for up to 2 years.

Must be substantially unable to perform the usual job as a result of the injury. A medical practitioner must provide a medical certificate. Medical certificates are normally valid for 13 weeks. If incapacitated after 13 weeks, the worker must be reassessed by a registered medical practitioner and be given another medical certificate.

The minimum weekly benefit for incapacitated full-time earners is NZ$328 (gross) a week if aged 18 or older; NZ$262.40 (gross) if younger than age 18.

The maximum weekly benefit is NZ$1,535.65 (gross).

Earnings test: If a worker receives income from work during a period of incapacity, weekly compensation is reduced proportionately. No deduction is made for the first NZ$65.21 of earnings; NZ$0.24 is deducted for every dollar of earnings exceeding NZ$65.21 a week but less than NZ$104.28 a week; NZ$0.56 is deducted for every dollar of earnings exceeding NZ$104.28 a week. Thresholds are adjusted annually through indexation. A further reduction is applied if total weekly earnings plus the adjusted weekly benefit are greater than the pre-incapacity weekly earnings. The total earnings that a worker can receive from work and benefits are equal to the level of pre-incapacity earnings.

Employers may make an additional weekly payment to increase the employee's income during incapacity to the level of his or her normal wage. The additional payment is exempt from the benefit reduction.

Benefit adjustment: Benefits are increased annually according to changes in the labor cost index.

Permanent Disability Benefits

Permanent disability pension

Lump-sum payment: A single nontaxable payment is provided to compensate for a permanent impairment resulting from an injury. Assessment for entitlement begins 2 years after the onset of injury, or once the injury stabilizes, whichever is earlier.

The worker must be assessed as having a permanent impairment of 10% or more. The lump sum ranges from NZ$2,763.90 for an assessed impairment of 10% to NZ$110,555.80 for an assessed impairment of 80% or more.

Independence allowance: Paid for any long-term impairment resulting from an injury suffered before April 1, 2002. The allowance is paid on a quarterly basis for as long as the worker remains eligible. The allowance is paid in addition to other cash assistance.

The worker must be assessed as having a permanent impairment of 10% or more. The allowance per quarter ranges from NZ$139.49 for an assessed impairment of 10% to NZ$837.07 for an assessed impairment of 80% or more. The allowance is nontaxable.

Medical practitioners assess the degree of impairment.

Benefit adjustment: Benefits may increase if the initial assessed level of impairment increases.

Workers' Medical Benefits

Medical care: A minimum contribution must be made for entitlement to medical care and physical rehabilitation, as specified in legislation. In some cases, the minimum contribution may be the full cost. The cost of benefits that are not specified are paid in full. The full cost of elective surgery is generally fully funded.

Social rehabilitation: Provided without limit and includes attendant care, household help, child care, assistive devices and appliances, modification of motor vehicles or residential premises, and travel-related costs.

Vocational rehabilitation: Provided for up to 3 years to those entitled to compensation for loss of earnings and potential earnings, or to those who could be entitled if they did not receive vocational rehabilitation.

Attendant care: Provided to assist the worker achieve a maximum level of independence and rehabilitation. An assessor recommends the level of individual care required and the duration of the level of care. Up to NZ$3,000 a week is paid, subject to individual needs.

Survivor Benefits

Survivor pension: If the deceased was an earner at the time of death, the weekly benefit is based on a percentage of the deceased's earnings. The benefit is paid to a surviving spouse, child, or other dependent.

Spouse's benefit: The benefit is equal to 60% of the weekly compensation rate that would have been paid to the deceased.

Orphan's benefit (younger than age 18): The benefit is equal to 20% of the weekly compensation rate that would have been paid to the deceased; 40% for a full orphan.

Other dependents: The benefit is equal to 20% of the weekly compensation rate for a total incapacity that would have been paid to the deceased.

The maximum total weekly compensation payable to survivors is equal to 80% of the deceased's weekly earnings, subject to a maximum.

Survivor's grant: NZ$5,333.86 is paid to a spouse; NZ$2,666.94 to each child younger than age 18 or other dependent.

Child care (weekly compensation): NZ$113.42 a week is paid for one child; a total of NZ$158.79 a week for three or more children. The benefit is nontaxable.

Funeral grant: A grant of up to NZ$4,975.01 is paid to the deceased's personal representative.

Administrative Organization

Department of Labor (http://www.dol.govt.nz) provides a purchasing and monitoring function and administers the legislation.

Accident Compensation Corporation (http://www.acc.co.nz) administers benefits.

Unemployment

Regulatory Framework

First law: 1930.

Current law: 1964 (social security), implemented in 1965.

Type of program: Social assistance system.

Coverage

Unemployment benefit: All persons older than age 18 who are unemployed and actively seeking employment.

Independent youth benefit: Single persons aged 16 or 17 who are not living with their parents and who cannot be supported by their parents. Must be unemployed and actively seeking employment.

Exclusions: Superannuation pensioners, full-time students, and striking workers.

Source of Funds

Insured person: None.

Self-employed person: None.

Employer: None.

Government: The total cost is financed from general revenues.

Qualifying Conditions

Unemployment benefit: Aged 18 or older (aged 16 or 17 and married with a dependent child) and has resided in New Zealand for at least 24 months. The benefit is income-tested. If the person has resided in New Zealand for less than 24 months, an income- and asset-tested hardship or emergency benefit is possible at an equivalent rate to the unemployment benefit. The person must be registered at a labor office and actively seeking work.

The benefit is not paid if unemployment was voluntary or due to dismissal for serious misconduct or involvement in an industrial dispute. The beneficiary must comply with the work test, which includes acceptance of any offer of suitable employment. The benefit may be withheld for up to 13 weeks in cases of voluntary unemployment or the failure to meet employment-related obligations.

Independent youth benefit: Single persons aged 16 or 17 who are not living with, and cannot be supported by, parents. Must have lived continuously in New Zealand for at least 24 months; be available for and actively seeking full-time work; be in training; be sick, injured, or disabled; or be in school.

Unemployment Benefits

Up to NZ$173.92 (net) a week is paid if aged 25 or older, single, and with no children; NZ$144.92 (net) if between ages 20 and 24 or if aged 18 or 19 and living away from home; NZ$115.94 (net) if aged 18 or 19 and living with a parent.

Up to NZ$249.10 (net) a week is paid for a single beneficiary with children; up to NZ$144.92 (net) for each member of a married or civil-union couple, with or without children.

Income test: The benefit is reduced by NZ$0.70 for each dollar of gross earned income exceeding NZ$80 a week.

The benefit is paid after a waiting period of between 1 and 10 weeks, depending on previous income and family circumstances.

There is no maximum period for which the unemployment benefit can be paid.

Benefit adjustment: Benefits are adjusted annually according to changes in the consumer price index for the previous calendar year.

Independent youth benefit: Up to NZ$144.92 (net) a week is paid.

Income test: The benefit is reduced by NZ$0.70 for each dollar of gross earned income exceeding NZ$80 a week.

Benefit adjustment: Benefits are adjusted annually according to changes in the consumer price index for the previous calendar year.

Administrative Organization

Ministry of Social Development (Work and Income) (http://www.msd.govt.nz) administers benefits through its branch and district offices.

Family Allowances

Regulatory Framework

Current laws: 1973 (social security), 1978 (social security), and 1999 (taxation).

Type of program: Universal and social assistance system.

Coverage

Domestic purposes benefit: Single parents caring for a dependent child younger than age 18 or a person caring for someone (other than a spouse) who would otherwise be hospitalized.

Emergency maintenance allowance: Single parents who do not qualify for domestic purposes benefit on the grounds of residency or age or who are experiencing hardship. The allowance is paid at the same rate as the domestic purposes benefit.

Child disability allowance: Persons caring for children with physical or mental disabilities at home.

Family support: Working and beneficiary families with dependent children.

In-work payment: Working families with dependent children.

Family tax credit: Working families with dependent children.

Parental tax credit: Working families with dependent children.

Note: It is possible to be eligible for more than one tax credit and allowance.

Source of Funds

Insured person: None.

Self-employed person: None.

Employer: None.

Government: The total cost is financed from general revenues.

Qualifying Conditions

Family allowances

Domestic purposes benefit: Paid to single parents aged 18 or older or to parents who have been married or were in a civil union. The parent must reside in New Zealand and the dependent child was born in New Zealand; if the child was born overseas, one of the parents must satisfy the residence criteria.

Emergency maintenance allowance: As a substitute for the domestic purposes benefit, paid to single parents experiencing hardship and who do not meet the residence criteria for domestic purposes benefit; or the single parent is aged 16 or 17, has never been married or in a civil union, and cannot be supported by his or her parents.

Child disability allowance: The allowance is paid to a parent or guardian of a dependent child with serious disabilities and living at home.

Family support: Paid to families with dependent children aged 17 or younger (age 18 if a student) and not receiving other benefits. Qualifying income depends on the number of children in the family.

In-work payment: Paid to families with dependent children aged 17 or younger (age 18 if a student). A two-parent family must be working jointly more than 30 hours a week; single parents must be working more than 20 hours a week. Eligibility also requires that no parent is receiving superannuation or income-tested benefits.

Family tax credit: Paid to families with children aged 17 or younger (age 18 if a student) with annual income less than NZ$17,680 (net). A two-parent family must be working jointly more than 30 hours a week; single parents must be working more than 20 hours a week. Eligibility also requires that no parent is receiving superannuation or income-tested benefits.

Parental tax credit: Families with income under a certain level (depends on the number of children) on the birth of a child and not receiving superannuation or income-tested benefits.

Family Allowance Benefits

Family allowances

Domestic purposes benefit: NZ$249.10 (net) a week is paid for single parents. The benefit is paid after a waiting period of between 1 and 10 weeks, depending on previous income and family circumstances.

Income test: The benefit is reduced by NZ$0.30 for each dollar of gross earned income exceeding NZ$4,160 a year and by NZ$0.70 for each dollar of gross earned income exceeding NZ$9,360.

Emergency maintenance allowance: NZ$249.10 (net) a week is paid for single parents. The benefit is paid after a waiting period of between 1 and 10 weeks, depending on previous income and family circumstances.

Income test: The benefit is reduced by NZ$0.30 for each dollar of gross earned income exceeding NZ$4,160 a year and by NZ$0.70 for each dollar of gross earned income exceeding NZ$9,360.

Child disability allowance: NZ$38.46 a week is paid. There is no income test and the benefit is not taxable.

Family support: Up to NZ$85 a week is paid for the first child and NZ$75 a week for each additional child, depending on the age of the children.

Income test: The benefit is reduced by NZ$0.20 for each dollar of gross earned income exceeding NZ$35,000.

In-work payment: Up to NZ$60 is paid a week for up to three children and NZ$15 a week for each additional child.

Income test: The benefit is reduced by NZ$0.20 for each dollar of gross earned income exceeding an income threshold determined by the number of dependent children in the family.

Family tax credit: A guaranteed net income for working families of NZ$17,680 a year.

Parental tax credit: The credit is paid to working families for the first 8 weeks after the birth or adoption of a child. The parental tax credit is available to families who qualify for family support, the child tax credit, or both. The parental tax credit is NZ$150 (net) a week per qualifying child, and the maximum parental tax credit is NZ$1,200 per child per year.

Benefit adjustment: Benefits, except the in-work payment, are adjusted according to changes in the consumer price index for the previous year. The in-work payment is subject to periodic review and adjusted at the discretion of the government.

Administrative Organization

Ministry of Social Development (Work and Income) (http://www.msd.govt.nz) administers allowances through its branch and district offices. It also administers family support payments to people with gross annual income below NZ$35,000 who receive a benefit.

Inland Revenue Department (http://www.ird.govt.nz) administers the in-work payment, family tax credit, and parental tax credit, as well as family support for families whose gross annual income is greater than NZ$35,000 or who do not receive a benefit.

Oman

Exchange rate: US$1.00 equals 0.38 rials.

Old Age, Disability, and Survivors

Regulatory Framework

First and current law: 1991 (social insurance), implemented in 1992.

Type of program: Social insurance system.

Coverage

Citizens of Oman between ages 15 and 59 employed in the private sector under a permanent work contract.

Exclusions: Foreign workers, domestic servants, and artisans.

Source of Funds

Insured person: 6.5% of monthly basic salary.

The minimum monthly earnings for contribution purposes are 100 rials for citizens working in Oman; 200 rials for citizens working abroad.

The maximum monthly earnings for contribution purposes for citizens working in Oman are 3,000 rials; 800 rials for citizens working abroad.

Self-employed person: Not applicable.

Employer: 9.5% of monthly basic salary.

The minimum monthly earnings for contribution purposes are 100 rials for citizens working in Oman; 200 rials for citizens working abroad.

The maximum monthly earnings for contribution purposes for citizens working in Oman are 3,000 rials; 800 rials for citizens working abroad.

Government: 2% of monthly basic salary.

The minimum monthly earnings for contribution purposes are 100 rials for citizens working in Oman; 200 rials for citizens working abroad.

The maximum monthly earnings for contribution purposes for citizens working in Oman are 3,000 rials; 800 rials for citizens working abroad.

Qualifying Conditions

Old-age pension: Age 60 with at least 180 months of paid contributions (men) or age 55 with at least 120 months of paid contributions (women).

Early pension: A reduced pension is paid before retirement age with 240 months (men) or 180 months (women) of contributions. The minimum age for early retirement is age 45.

Deferred pension: The insured must have 180 months of contributions including at least 36 months in the last 5 years before retirement. There is no maximum age for deferral.

Disability pension: Must have 6 months of contributions before the onset of disability or 12 months of contributions including the 3 months immediately before the onset of disability.

Survivor pension: The deceased had at least 6 months of contributions or 12 months of contributions including the 3 months immediately before death.

Eligible survivors are the widow(s) or widower or the eldest son or, in their absence, the authorized person.

Marriage grant: Paid to an orphaned daughter when she marries. The daughter's orphan pension ceases on marriage.

Funeral grant: A lump sum is paid toward the cost of the insured's funeral.

Death grant: A lump sum is paid on the death of the insured.

Eligible survivors are the widow(s) or widower or the eldest son or, in their absence, the authorized person.

Old-Age Benefits

Old-age pension: The pension is calculated on the basis of 1/40 of the insured's average wage in the last 5 years of employment times the number of full years of contributions.

The minimum pension is 80 rials.

The maximum pension is equal to 80% of the pensionable salary.

Early pension: The pension is reduced according to age and gender: for men, the reduction is from 6% at age 59 to 30% at age 45; for women, the reduction is from 7% at age 54 to 25% at age 45.

Deferred pension: Calculated in the same way as the old-age pension.

Permanent Disability Benefits

Disability pension: The pension is equal to 40% of the insured's earnings at the onset of disability or based on the old-age pension formula, whichever is greater.

Survivor Benefits

Survivor pension: 25% of the deceased's pension is paid to a widow(er). If there is more than one widow, the pension is split equally among the widows.

The widow's pension ceases on remarriage.

Orphan's pension: 50% of the deceased's pension is paid to sons up to age 22 (age 26 if a full-time student, no limit if disabled) and unmarried daughters.

Other eligible survivors: 25% of the deceased's pension is split equally among other dependents, including the father, mother, brothers (up to age 22), and unmarried sisters.

In the absence of any of the above groups of eligible survivors, that portion of the survivor pension is split among the other groups, up to a maximum of 100% of the deceased's pension.

Marriage grant: A lump sum is paid equal to 15 times the orphan's pension.

Funeral grant: A lump sum is paid equal to 3 months of the deceased's earnings or pension, up to a maximum of 1,000 rials.

Death grant: A lump sum is paid equal to 3 months of the deceased's earnings or pension.

Administrative Organization

Minister of Manpower provides general supervision.

Managed by a nine-member board of directors chaired by the Minister of Manpower, the Public Authority for Social Insurance (http://www.taminat.com) administers the program.

Work Injury

Regulatory Framework

First law: 1977.

Current law: 1991 (social insurance), implemented in 1997.

Type of program: Social insurance system.

Coverage

Citizens of Oman between ages 15 and 59 employed in the private sector under a permanent work contract.

Exclusions: Foreign workers, domestic servants, and artisans.

Source of Funds

Insured person: None.

Self-employed person: Not applicable.

Employer: 1% of payroll.

Government: None.

Qualifying Conditions

Work injury benefits: There is no minimum qualifying period to receive benefits for a work injury or an occupational disease.

Temporary Disability Benefits

Daily allowances equal to 75% of the insured's current monthly earnings divided by 30 are paid for as long as the insured is unable to work.

Permanent Disability Benefits

Permanent disability pension: If the insured is totally disabled, the pension is equal to 75% of the insured's monthly basic earnings or old-age pension, whichever is greater.

The minimum pension is 80 rials.

Partial disability: If assessed as at least 30% disabled, a percentage of the full pension is paid according to the assessed degree of disability; if assessed as less than 30% disabled, a lump sum equal to 36 times the monthly pension is paid according to the assessed degree of disability.

Survivor Benefits

Survivor pension: 25% of the deceased's pension is paid to a widow(er). If there is more than one widow, the pension is split equally among the widows.

The widow's pension ceases on remarriage.

Orphan's pension: 50% of the deceased's pension is paid to sons up to age 22 (age 26 if a full-time student, no limit if disabled) and unmarried daughters.

Other eligible survivors: 25% of the deceased's pension is split equally among other dependents, including the father, mother, brothers (up to age 22), and unmarried sisters.

In the absence of any of the above groups of eligible survivors, that portion of the survivor pension is split among the other groups, up to a maximum of 100% of the deceased's pension.

Administrative Organization

Minister of Manpower provides general supervision.

Managed by a nine-member board of directors chaired by the Minister of Manpower, the Public Authority for Social Insurance (http://www.taminat.com) administers the program.

Pakistan

Exchange rate: US$1.00 equals 60.10 rupees.

Old Age, Disability, and Survivors

Regulatory Framework

First law: 1972, never implemented.

Current law: 1976 (old-age benefits).

Type of program: Social insurance system.

Note: There are two social assistance programs: one provides benefits to needy Pakistani Muslim citizens, the other to needy Pakistani citizens.

Coverage

Employees in firms with 10 or more workers; 20 workers for firms established on or after July 1, 2006.

Voluntary coverage for employees of firms with less than 20 workers.

Exclusions: Family labor and self-employed persons.

Special systems for public-sector employees; members of the armed forces; police officers; and employees of statutory bodies, local authorities, banks, and railways.

Source of Funds

Insured person: 1% of earnings.

The maximum monthly earnings for contribution and benefit purposes are 4,000 rupees.

Self-employed person: Not applicable.

Employer: 6% of payroll.

The maximum monthly earnings for contribution and benefit purposes are 4,000 rupees.

Government: Subsidies as needed.

Qualifying Conditions

Old-age pension: Age 60 (men) or age 55 (women) with at least 15 years of contributions. Retirement from covered employment is not necessary.

Age 55 for miners with 10 years of service in mining and 15 years of contributions.

Early pension: A reduced pension is paid from ages 55 to 59 (men) or ages 50 to 54 (women).

Old-age grant: Age 60 (men) or age 55 (women). The insured is ineligible for the old-age pension but has at least 2 years of covered employment.

Disability pension: Assessed with a 2/3 loss in earning capacity. Must have at least 15 years of contributions or 5 years of contributions including 3 out of the last 5 years.

Survivor pension: The deceased had at least 36 months of covered employment or was a pensioner at the time of death.

In order of priority, eligible survivors are the spouse, sons younger than age 18, daughters younger than age 18 or unmarried, the deceased's parents, and other dependents. The surviving spouse must have been married to the deceased before the deceased reached the minimum pensionable age for the old-age pension.

Old-Age Benefits

Old-age pension: The pension is calculated on the basis of 2% of average monthly earnings (based on the last 12 months' earnings) times the number of years of covered employment.

The minimum old-age pension is 1,300 rupees.

Early pension: The full old-age pension is reduced by 0.5% for each month that the pension is taken before age 60 (men) or age 55 (women). The minimum pension is reduced similarly.

Old-age grant: A lump sum is paid equal to 1 month's earnings for each year of covered employment.

Permanent Disability Benefits

Disability pension: The pension is calculated on the basis of 2% of average monthly earnings (based on the last 12 months' earnings) times the number of years of covered employment.

The minimum disability pension is 1,300 rupees.

Survivor Benefits

Survivor pension: 100% of the deceased's minimum pension is paid to the surviving spouse. In the absence of a surviving spouse, the pension is split equally among eligible orphans. In the absence of eligible orphans and if the surviving spouse dies within 5 years of first receiving the survivor pension, the survivor pension is paid to the deceased's surviving parents for up to 5 years after the death of the insured's spouse; in the absence of surviving parents, the remaining balance of the first 5 years' survivor pension may be paid to a dependent.

The minimum pension is 1,300 rupees.

Administrative Organization

Ministry of Labor, Manpower, and Overseas Pakistanis (http://www.pakistan.gov.pk) provides general supervision.

Employees' Old-Age Benefits Institution (http://www.eobi.gov.pk) administers the program.

Sickness and Maternity

Regulatory Framework

First law: 1962 (national law), never implemented.

Current law: 1965 (provincial social security).

Type of program: Social insurance system. Cash and medical benefits.

Coverage

Employees in industrial, commercial, and other establishments with five or more workers earning up to 5,000 rupees a month or 200 rupees a day.

Eligibility for benefits does not cease on leaving covered employment.

Special systems for public-sector employees, members of the armed forces, police officers, local authority employees, and railway employees.

Source of Funds

Insured person: 20 rupees a month.

The maximum earnings for contribution and benefit purposes are 5,000 rupees a month or 200 rupees a day.

Self-employed person: Not applicable.

Employer: 7% of monthly payroll or 210 rupees a month per covered employee.

The employer's contributions also finance work injury benefits.

The maximum earnings for contribution and benefit purposes are 5,000 rupees a month or 200 rupees a day.

Government: None.

Qualifying Conditions

Cash sickness benefits: Must have 90 days of contributions in the last 6 months.

Cash maternity benefits: Must have 180 days of contributions in the last 12 months.

Medical benefits: Must be currently covered.

Sickness and Maternity Benefits

Sickness benefit: The benefit is equal to 75% of the insured's earnings; 100% in cases of tuberculosis and cancer (50% in North-West Frontier Province and Balochistan). The benefit is payable after a 2-day waiting period in Sindh, North-West Frontier Province, and Balochistan (no waiting period in Punjab) for up to 121 days (365 days for tuberculosis and cancer) in a 1-year period.

Maternity benefit: 100% of the insured's earnings is paid for 12 weeks, including up to 6 weeks before the expected date of childbirth.

Death grant: 1,500 rupees is paid.

Workers' Medical Benefits

Medical services are provided mainly through social security facilities. Benefits include general medical care, specialist care, medicines, hospitalization, maternity care, and transportation.

Benefits are awarded for as long as it is considered necessary or for 6 months after the patient has exhausted entitlement to sickness benefits, whichever period is shorter.

Dependents' Medical Benefits

Medical services are provided mainly through social security facilities. Benefits include general medical care, specialist care, medicines, maternity care, and transportation. Hospitalization for dependents is provided only in cases of maternity, surgery, and cancer.

Administrative Organization

Provincial Labor Department provides general supervision.

Provincial Employees' Social Security Institutions in Punjab, Sindh, North-West Frontier Province, and Balochistan administer the program in each province. The institutions are managed by a tripartite governing body and a commissioner and are authorized to establish their own dispensaries and hospitals or to contract with public and private agencies for provision of medical services.

Work Injury

Regulatory Framework

First law: 1923 (workmen's compensation; remains in force for employees not covered by the current law), implemented in 1924.

Current law: 1965 (provincial social security).

Type of program: Social insurance system.

Coverage

Social security: Employees of industrial, commercial, and other establishments earning up to 5,000 rupees a month or 200 rupees a day.

Exclusions: Family labor, self-employed persons, and persons earning more than 5,000 rupees a month.

Workmen's compensation: Employees of industrial establishments with 10 or more workers earning up to 6,000 rupees a month.

Exclusions: Family labor, self-employed persons, and persons earning more than 6,000 rupees a month.

Special systems for public-sector employees, members of the armed forces, police officers, local authority employees, and railway employees.

Commercial and industrial establishments with 50 or more employees must provide group insurance for temporary and permanent disability and death benefits for employees earning less than 9,000 rupees a month.

Source of Funds

Insured person

Social security: 20 rupees a month for employees covered by the current law on June 30, 2001.

Workmen's compensation: None.

Self-employed person

Social security: Not applicable.

Workmen's compensation: Not applicable.

Employer

Social security: See source of funds under Sickness and Maternity, above.

Workmen's compensation: The total cost, including the cost of medical examinations.

Government

Social security: None.

Workmen's compensation: None.

Qualifying Conditions

Work injury benefits: There is no minimum qualifying period.

Temporary Disability Benefits

Social security: The benefit is equal to 60% of earnings (100% in Punjab and Sindh). The benefit is payable after a 3-day waiting period for up to 180 days (the waiting period is waived in Punjab).

Workmen's compensation: None.

Permanent Disability Benefits

Permanent disability pension

Social security: For a loss of earning capacity of 67% or more (total disability), the benefit is equal to 75% of earnings (100% in Punjab).

Partial disability: Up to 66% of the total disability benefit is paid, according to the schedule in law.

Workmen's compensation: For a permanent total disability, a lump sum is paid equal to 200,000 rupees. The cost of any medical examination is paid by the employer.

Workers' Medical Benefits

Medical services are provided mainly through social security facilities. Benefits include general medical care, specialist care, medicines, hospitalization, maternity care, dental care, and transportation.

Benefits are awarded for as long as it is considered necessary or for 6 months after the patient has exhausted entitlement to sickness benefits, whichever period is shorter.

Survivor Benefits

Survivor pension (social security): 60% of the deceased's total disability pension is paid to a widow or a needy disabled widower.

Orphan's pension (social security): Each orphan younger than age 16 receives 20% of the deceased's total disability pension; 40% for a full orphan.

Dependent parent's pension (social security): In the absence of a widow(er) and orphans, each dependent parent receives 20% of the deceased's total disability pension.

The maximum survivor pension is 100% of the deceased's total disability pension.

Death grant (social security): 1,500 rupees is paid.

Survivor grant (workmen's compensation): A lump sum of 100,000 rupees is paid.

Administrative Organization

Social security: Provincial Labor Department provides general supervision.

Provincial Employees' Social Security Institution administers contributions and benefits.

Workmen's compensation: Workmen's compensation commissioners in provinces provide general supervision.

Unemployment

Regulatory Framework

No statutory unemployment benefits are provided.

The labor code requires employers with 20 employees or more to pay a severance payment equal to the last 30 days' wages for each year of employment.

Palau

Exchange rate: Currency is the US dollar (US$).

Old Age, Disability, and Survivors

Regulatory Framework

First law: 1967.

Current law: 1987, implemented in 1991.

Type of program: Social insurance system.

Coverage

Gainfully occupied persons, including some categories of self-employed persons.

Voluntary coverage for self-employed persons with no employees and gross earnings less than US$10,000 a year but more than US$300 per quarter.

Exclusions: Casual labor and self-employed persons with no employees and annual gross income of less than US$300 per quarter.

Source of Funds

Insured person: 6% of earnings.

The maximum earnings for contribution and benefit purposes are US$3,000 per quarter.

Self-employed person: 12% of twice the salary of their highest-paid employee (12% of 1/4 of gross annual earnings, if no employees and declared annual earnings greater than US$10,000).

The maximum earnings for contribution and benefit purposes are US$3,000 per quarter.

Employer: 6% of payroll.

The maximum earnings for contribution and benefit purposes are US$3,000 per quarter.

Government: None; contributes as an employer.

Qualifying Conditions

Old-age pension: Age 60 with 1 quarter of coverage for each year after June 1968 (or since age 21, if later) up to age 60.

The old-age pension is payable to a pensioner who begins a new job after retirement.

Disability pension: Incapacity for substantial gainful activity due to a physical or mental disability that is likely to last at least a year or result in death. One quarter of coverage for each year after June 1968 (or since age 21, if later) with at least 12 quarters of coverage or at least 8 quarters of coverage during the last 13 quarters.

Survivor pension: The deceased had 1 quarter of coverage for each year after June 1968 (or since age 21, if later) or had at least 8 quarters of coverage in the 13 quarters preceding death.

The survivor pension is payable abroad under reciprocal agreement.

Lump-sum survivor benefit: Paid for the death of a worker with less than the minimum number of required quarters of coverage for a pension.

Eligible survivors are (in order of priority) the spouse, children, parents, legal representative, or persons who lived with the deceased.

Old-Age Benefits

Old-age pension: The pension is equal to 16.5% of the first US$11,000 of the insured's cumulative covered earnings, plus 2.7% of earnings between US$11,000 and US$44,000, plus 1.35% of earnings over US$44,000.

The minimum monthly old-age pension is US$47.50.

Permanent Disability Benefits

Disability pension: The pension is equal to 16.5% of the first US$11,000 of the insured's cumulative covered earnings, plus 2.7% of earnings between US$11,000 and US$44,000, plus 1.35% of earnings over US$44,000.

The minimum monthly disability pension is US$47.50.

Survivor Benefits

Survivor pension: 60% of the deceased's pension is paid to a widow(er) at any age.

Orphan's pension: Each orphan younger than age 18 (age 22 if a student; no limit if disabled before age 22) receives 15% of the deceased's pension.

Earnings test: The survivor pension is reduced by US$1 for each US$3 of earnings above US$500 a quarter if aged 50 or younger.

The minimum monthly survivor pension is US$47.50.

The maximum survivor pension is equal to 100% of the deceased's pension.

Lump-sum survivor benefit: A cash payment is paid and split equally among eligible survivors.

Administrative Organization

Palau Social Security System (http://www.ropssa.org) administers the program at the local level.

Papua New Guinea

Exchange rate: US$1.00 equals 2.94 kina (K).

Old Age, Disability, and Survivors

Regulatory Framework

First law: 1980 (provident fund).

Current law: 2000 (superannuation), implemented in 2002, with 2002 amendment.

Type of program: Mandatory occupational retirement system.

Coverage

Employed persons in firms with 20 or more workers.

Exclusions: Casual workers with employment contracts of less than 3 months, domestic servants, and self-employed persons.

Voluntary coverage for noncitizens.

Source of Funds

Insured person: 5.5% of earnings.

Self-employed person: Not applicable.

Employer: 7.7% of payroll.

Government: None.

To equalize contribution rates with those of the public sector, private-sector employee and employer contributions are to be increased to 6% and 8.4%, respectively, in 2008.

Qualifying Conditions

Old-age benefit: Age 55 and retired from covered employment; unemployed for 12 months.

A lump sum is paid at any age after a 1-year waiting period if emigrating permanently.

Drawdown payment: Permitted for the purpose of providing housing. Limited periodic drawdown payments are also permitted after 3 months of unemployment.

Disability benefit: Must be assessed with a total permanent incapacity.

Survivor benefit: Payable for the death of the insured before retirement.

Old-Age Benefits

A lump sum is paid equal to total employee and employer contributions plus accumulated interest.

Drawdown payment: Up to 60% of the member's accumulated contributions may be used for housing. The payment is treated as an advance on benefits. Members must make an additional 2% contribution until the full value of the advance is repaid. If an unemployed fund member has less than K1,000 in the account, the total amount can be withdrawn after 3 months.

Permanent Disability Benefits

A lump sum is paid equal to total employee and employer contributions plus accumulated interest.

Survivor Benefits

A lump sum is paid equal to total employee and employer contributions plus accumulated interest. The benefit is paid to a named survivor.

Administrative Organization

Public Employees Association Superannuation Fund Board manages the program.

Bank of Papua New Guinea (http://www.bankpng.gov. pg) regulates the superannuation funds and sets prudential standards.

Trustees of authorized superannuation funds appoint licensed investment managers and administrators.

Directors, investment managers, and fund administrators are responsible for ensuring that the routine management, investment, and administration of superannuation funds comply with the law.

Sickness and Maternity

Regulatory Framework

Limited medical services are available free of charge or at nominal cost in government clinics and hospitals.

The 1981 Employment Act requires employers to provide sick leave and maternity leave to employees.

Work Injury

Regulatory Framework

First law: 1958.

Current law: 1978 (workers' compensation).

Type of program: Employer-liability system, involving compulsory insurance with a private carrier.

Coverage

All employees, including domestic servants. (Workers are covered while traveling to and from work.)

Exclusions: Self-employed persons and casual workers.

Source of Funds

Insured person: None.

Self-employed person: Not applicable.

Employer: The total cost is met through the direct provision of benefits or insurance premiums.

Government: None.

Qualifying Conditions

Work injury benefits: There is no minimum qualifying period.

Temporary Disability Benefits

Information is not available.

Permanent Disability Benefits

Permanent disability pension: The pension is equal to 80% of average weekly earnings.

The minimum and maximum annual earnings for benefit calculation purposes are K625 and K1,875, respectively.

The minimum weekly pension is K18.

The maximum weekly pension is K75, plus K10 for each dependent child if the insured has a fully or partially dependent spouse; K65 a week for a single person. The maximum pension is 100% of the insured's earnings.

The maximum employer liability for total disability is K22,000.

Partial disability: A percentage of the full pension is paid according to the assessed loss of earnings.

The maximum employer liability for partial disability is K25,000.

Workers' Medical Benefits

Medical benefits include the reasonable cost of treatment, medicines, hospitalization, surgery, transportation, appliances, and specialist treatment, up to a maximum.

Survivor Benefits

Survivor grant: A lump sum is paid equal to eight times the annual earnings of the deceased at the time of the injury, plus K4.60 a week for each dependent child.

The minimum grant is K8,750, plus K10 a week for each dependent child.

The maximum grant is K25,000, plus K10 a week for each dependent child.

Eligible survivors include all family members (children younger than age 16) who were totally or partially dependent on the deceased's earnings and any person who by custom has a right to share compensation.

The insured's spouse and children must receive at least 50% of the survivor grant. A tribunal may decide eligibility and the amount payable to each other survivor.

Funeral grant: The cost of funeral expenses is paid, up to K750.

Administrative Organization

Department of Labor and Industry administers the program.

Philippines

Exchange rate: US$1.00 equals 52.81 pesos.

Old Age, Disability, and Survivors

Regulatory Framework

First and current law: 1954 (old age, disability, and survivors), with 1997 amendment.

Type of program: Social insurance system.

Coverage

Private-sector employees up to age 60 earning at least 1,000 pesos a month; domestic employees up to age 60 earning at least 1,000 pesos a month; and all self-employed persons up to age 60 with at least 1,000 pesos of monthly income.

Voluntary coverage for Filipinos recruited by a foreign-based employer for employment abroad; insured persons who are no longer eligible for compulsory coverage; and nonworking spouses of insured persons.

Special systems for government employees and military personnel.

Source of Funds

Insured person: 3.33% of gross monthly earnings, according to 29 income classes.

Voluntarily insured persons pay the combined insured person and employer contributions of 9.4% of gross monthly earnings, according to 29 income classes. The contributions for a voluntarily insured nonworking spouse are based on 50% of the gross monthly earnings of the working spouse.

The minimum monthly earnings for contribution and benefit purposes are 1,000 pesos (5,000 pesos for voluntarily insured overseas workers).

The maximum monthly earnings for contribution and benefit purposes are 15,000 pesos.

The above contributions also finance cash sickness and maternity benefits and funeral benefits.

Self-employed person: 9.4% of gross monthly earnings, according to 29 income classes.

The minimum monthly earnings for contribution and benefit purposes are 1,000 pesos.

The maximum monthly earnings for contribution and benefit purposes are 15,000 pesos.

The above contributions also finance cash sickness and maternity benefits and funeral benefits.

Employer: 6.07% (7.07% from January 2007) of the employee's monthly earnings.

The minimum monthly earnings for contribution and benefit purposes are 1,000 pesos.

The maximum monthly earnings for contribution and benefit purposes are 15,000 pesos.

The above contributions also finance cash sickness and maternity benefits and funeral benefits.

Government: Meets any deficit.

The minimum and maximum monthly earnings for contribution purposes are adjusted periodically by the Social Security Commission, subject to the approval of the President of the Philippines.

Qualifying Conditions

Old-age pension: Age 60 with at least 120 months of contributions before the 6-month period (January–June or July–December) in which the pension is first paid. Employment or self-employment must cease. Age 65, regardless of employment, with 120 months of contributions.

Age 55 for mine workers who worked underground for at least 5 years and who are involuntarily unemployed or have ceased self-employment.

The pension is suspended if an old-age pensioner resumes employment or self-employment before age 65. There is no employment test after age 65.

Old-age grant: Age 60 with less than 120 months of contributions.

Disability pension: Must be assessed with a permanent total or partial disability of at least 20% and have at least 36 months of contributions before the 6-month period (January–June or July–December) in which the disability began.

A Social Security System doctor assesses the degree of disability annually.

The pension is suspended if the disability pensioner recovers, resumes employment (in the case of a total disability), or fails to report for the annual physical examination.

Disability grant: Must be assessed with a permanent total or partial disability but have less than 36 months of contributions.

Survivor pension: Paid for the death of the insured. The insured had at least 36 months of contributions before the 6-month period (January–June or July–December) in which his or her death occurred; the death of an old-age or disability pensioner.

Eligible survivors are the surviving spouse and up to five dependent children younger than age 21; no limit if disabled (employed or married children are not eligible). The spouse's benefit ceases on remarriage, with the spouse's part transferred to the eligible surviving children.

Survivor grant: Paid if the deceased had less than 36 months of contributions.

Eligible survivors are the surviving spouse and up to five dependent children younger than age 21; no limit if disabled (employed or married children are not eligible). In the absence of spouse and dependent children, the benefit is paid to dependent parents or to the person named by the deceased.

Funeral grant: Paid to the person who paid for the funeral.

Old-Age Benefits

Old-age pension: The monthly pension is equal to 300 pesos, plus 20% of the insured's average monthly covered earnings, plus 2% of the insured's average monthly covered earnings for each year of service exceeding 10 years or 40% of the insured's average monthly covered earnings, whichever is greater.

Average monthly covered earnings are equal to the sum of the last 60 months of covered earnings immediately before the 6-month period (January–June or July–December) in which the pension is first paid divided by 60 or the sum of all monthly covered earnings paid before the 6-month period (January–June or July–December) in which the pension is first paid divided by the number of monthly contributions paid in the same period, whichever is greater.

The minimum monthly pension is 1,200 pesos if the insured contributed for at least 10 years but for less than 20 years; 2,400 pesos with at least 20 years of contributions.

There is no maximum monthly pension.

Partial lump sum: The insured may choose to receive the first 18 months' pension (not including dependent supplements and the 13th pension payment in the first year) as a lump sum.

Dependent's supplement: 10% of the old-age pension or 250 pesos, whichever is greater, is paid for each of the five youngest children younger than age 21 (no limit if disabled) conceived on or before the insured's date of retirement. The supplement ceases before age 21 if a child marries or starts work.

Schedule of payments: Thirteen payments a year (except for newly retired pensioners who choose a partial lump sum. In such cases, the periodic pension is payable from the 19th month.)

Benefit adjustment: Benefits are adjusted on an ad hoc basis according to changes in prices and wages and the financial health of the fund, subject to approval by the Social Security Commission.

Old-age grant: A lump sum is paid equal to employee and employer contributions plus 6% interest.

Permanent Disability Benefits

Disability pension: The monthly pension is equal to 300 pesos, plus 20% of the insured's average monthly covered earnings, plus 2% of the insured's average monthly covered earnings for each year of service exceeding 10 years or 40% of the insured's average monthly covered earnings, whichever is greater.

Average monthly covered earnings are equal to the sum of the last 60 months of covered earnings immediately before the 6-month period (January–June or July–December) in which the disability began divided by 60, or the sum of all monthly covered earnings paid before the 6-month period (January–June or July–December) in which the disability began divided by the number of monthly contributions paid in the same period, whichever is greater.

The minimum pension is 1,000 pesos a month if the insured has less than 10 years of contributions; 1,200 pesos with at least 10 years but less than 20 years; or 2,400 pesos with at least 20 years of contributions.

There is no maximum disability pension.

Dependent's supplement (permanent total disability): 10% of the disability pension or 250 pesos, whichever is greater, is paid for each of the five youngest children younger than age 21 (no limit if disabled) conceived on or before the onset of disability. The supplement ceases before age 21 if a child marries or starts work.

Partial disability: A percentage of the full pension is paid according to the assessed degree of disability. The total pension benefit is paid as a lump sum if the payment period is less than 12 months.

Supplementary allowance (permanent total and partial disability): 500 pesos a month.

Schedule of payments: Thirteen payments a year.

Benefit adjustment: Benefits are adjusted on an ad hoc basis according to changes in prices and wages and the financial health of the fund, subject to approval by the Social Security Commission.

Disability grant: For a permanent total disability, a lump sum is paid equal to the insured's monthly pension times the number of monthly contributions or 12 times the monthly pension, whichever is greater.

For a permanent partial disability, a lump sum is paid equal to the insured's monthly pension times the number of monthly contributions times the assessed degree of disability, or 12 monthly pensions times the assessed degree of disability, whichever is greater.

Survivor Benefits

Survivor pension: The pension is equal to 100% of the monthly old-age pension that would have been payable to the deceased.

The minimum monthly pension is 1,000 pesos if the deceased contributed for at least 10 years; 1,200 pesos with at least 10 but less than 20 years; 2,400 pesos with at least 20 years of contributions.

There is no maximum survivor pension.

Dependent's supplement: 10% of the deceased's pension or 250 pesos, whichever is greater, is paid for each of the five youngest children younger than age 21 (no limit if disabled) conceived on or before the date of death. The supplement ceases before age 21 if a child marries or starts work.

Survivors of an old-age or a permanent total disability pensioner receive 100% of the deceased's pension plus dependent supplements. In the absence of a surviving spouse and dependent children and if the insured died within 60 months after first receiving a pension, a lump sum equal to 60 months' pension minus the value of the pension already paid is payable to dependent parents. In the absence of dependent parents, the benefit is payable to the person named by the deceased.

Schedule of payments: Thirteen payments a year.

Benefit adjustment: Benefits are adjusted on an ad hoc basis according to changes in prices and wages and the financial health of the fund, subject to approval by the Social Security Commission.

Survivor grant: A lump sum equal to the deceased's monthly old-age pension times the number of monthly contributions or 12 times the monthly pension, whichever is greater.

Funeral grant: A lump sum of 20,000 pesos.

Benefit adjustment: Benefits are adjusted on an ad hoc basis according to changes in prices and wages and the financial health of the fund, subject to approval by the Social Security Commission.

Administrative Organization

A tripartite Social Security Commission is responsible for the general management, supervision, and regulation of the program.

Social Security System (http://www.sss.gov.ph) collects contributions and pays benefits under the direction and control of the Social Security Commission.

Sickness and Maternity

Regulatory Framework

First and current laws: 1954 (sickness), with 1997 amendment; 1969 (medical benefits), with 1995 amendment; and 1977 (maternity), with 1997 amendment.

Type of program: Social insurance system. Cash and medical benefits.

Coverage

Cash sickness and maternity benefits: Private-sector employees up to age 60; domestic employees earning at least 1,000 pesos a month; and all self-employed persons with at least 1,000 pesos of monthly income.

Voluntary coverage for Filipinos recruited by a foreign-based employer for employment abroad, insured persons who are no longer eligible for compulsory coverage, and nonworking spouses of insured persons.

Special system for government employees (sickness benefits only).

Medical benefits: Private- and public-sector employees up to age 60; domestic employees earning at least 1,000 pesos a month; and all self-employed persons with at least 1,000 pesos of monthly income.

Full coverage is provided to pensioners and retired persons, and limited coverage is provided to certain categories of people with low or no income.

Voluntary coverage for Filipinos recruited by a foreign-based employer for employment abroad and certain other groups of persons.

Source of Funds

Insured person

Cash sickness and maternity benefits: See source of funds under Old Age, Disability, and Survivors, above.

Medical benefits: Employed persons contribute 1.25% of gross monthly earnings, according to 22 income classes; none for pensioners and their dependents or for certain categories of people with low or no income; voluntary contributors pay 100 pesos a month.

For insured persons with monthly earnings of less than 5,000 pesos, the minimum monthly earnings for contribution purposes for medical benefits are 4,000 pesos.

For insured persons with monthly earnings of at least 25,000 pesos, the maximum monthly earnings for contribution purposes for medical benefits are 25,000 pesos.

Contribution are payable monthly, except for voluntary contributors who may pay contributions monthly, quarterly, semiannually, or annually.

Self-employed person

Cash sickness and maternity benefits: See source of funds under Old Age, Disability, and Survivors, above.

Medical benefits: 100 pesos a month.

Self-employed persons may pay contributions monthly, quarterly, semiannually, or annually.

Employer

Cash sickness and maternity benefits: See source of funds under Old Age, Disability, and Survivors, above.

Medical benefits: 1.25% of the employee's monthly earnings.

For employees with monthly earnings of less than 5,000 pesos, the minimum monthly earnings for contribution purposes for medical benefits are 4,000 pesos.

For employees with monthly earnings of at least 25,000 pesos, the maximum monthly earnings for contribution purposes for medical benefits are 25,000 pesos.

Government: Pays the cost of medical benefits for certain categories of people with low or no income; meets any deficit.

The minimum and maximum monthly earnings for contribution purposes for cash sickness and maternity benefits are adjusted periodically by the Social Security Commission, subject to the approval of the President of the Philippines.

The minimum and maximum monthly earnings for contribution purposes for medical benefits are adjusted periodically by the Philippine Health Insurance Corporation Board.

Qualifying Conditions

Cash sickness benefits: Must have at least 3 months of contributions in the 12 months immediately before the 6-month period (January–June or July–December) in which the incapacity began. The insured must be hospitalized or incapacitated at home for at least 4 days. Medical certification must be provided.

Cash maternity benefits: Must have at least 3 months of contributions in the 12 months immediately before the 6-month period (January–June or July–December) in which the birth or miscarriage occurred. Benefits are paid for up to four births, including miscarriages. Medical certification of the pregnancy and a birth certificate are necessary.

Medical benefits: Must have at least 3 months of contributions in the 6 months before the incapacity began; contribution conditions are waived for pensioners, retired persons, and certain categories of people with low or no income.

Sickness and Maternity Benefits

Sickness benefit: A daily allowance is paid equal to 90% of the insured's average daily covered earnings. The benefit is payable after a 3-day waiting period (except for an injury or an acute disease) for up to 120 days in a calendar year. The benefit payment period must not exceed 240 days for the same illness.

Daily covered earnings are equal to the sum of the 6 highest months of covered earnings in the 12 months before the 6-month period (January–June or July–December) in which the incapacity began divided by 180.

Maternity benefit: The benefit is equal to 100% of the insured's average daily covered earnings. The benefit is payable for 60 days for a miscarriage or a noncaesarian childbirth; 78 days for a caesarian childbirth.

Daily covered earnings are equal to the sum of the 6 highest months of covered earnings in the 12 months before the 6-month period (January–June or July–December) in which the birth or miscarriage occurred divided by 180.

Workers' Medical Benefits

Services are delivered by accredited health care providers who are paid directly by the health fund according to a fixed schedule.

Cost sharing: There is some cost sharing for general and specialist care, hospital care, laboratory and X-ray fees, surgery, and medicines.

Inpatient treatment is limited to 45 days a year.

Dependents' Medical Benefits

Services are delivered by accredited health care providers who are paid directly by the health fund according to a fixed schedule.

Cost sharing: There is some cost sharing for general and specialist care, hospital care, laboratory and X-ray fees, surgery, and medicines.

Inpatient treatment for all eligible dependents is limited to a total of 45 days a year.

Eligible dependents are the spouse; unmarried and nonemployed legitimate, acknowledged, or illegitimate children and legally adopted or stepchildren younger than age 21 (no limit if disabled); and parents aged 60 or older with income below a specified amount who are not covered through other means.

Administrative Organization

Cash sickness and maternity benefits: A tripartite Social Security Commission is responsible for the general management, supervision, and regulation of the program.

Employers pay sickness and maternity benefits directly to their employees and are reimbursed by the Social Security System. The Social Security System pays benefits to self-employed and voluntary members.

Social Security System (http://www.sss.gov.ph) collects contributions and administers benefits under the direction and control of the Social Security Commission.

Medical benefits: Department of Health (http://www.doh.gov.ph) provides policy coordination and guidance.

Philippine Health Insurance Corporation (http://www.philhealth.gov.ph) collects contributions for the medical care program and administers the provision of benefits. Medical care is provided by accredited providers.

Work Injury

Regulatory Framework

First and current law: 1974 (work injury), implemented in 1975, with 1996 amendment.

Type of program: Social insurance system.

Coverage

Employers and employed persons up to age 60, including domestic employees and Filipinos recruited by a foreign-based employer for employment abroad.

There is no voluntary coverage.

Exclusions: Self-employed persons.

Special systems for government employees and military personnel.

Source of Funds

Insured person: None.

Self-employed person: Not applicable.

Employer: 1% of insured's monthly earnings. The contribution does not vary according to the assessed risk level of the employer or the accident rate.

The maximum monthly earnings for contribution purposes are 1,000 pesos. The maximum monthly earnings for contribution purposes are adjusted periodically by the Employees' Compensation Commission.

Government: Meets any deficit.

Qualifying Conditions

Work injury benefits: Must have at least 1 month of contributions.

Temporary Disability Benefits

The benefit is equal to 90% of the insured's average daily covered earnings. The benefit is paid from the first day of disability for a work-related injury or sickness for up to 120 days; may be extended up to 240 days if further treatment is required.

Daily covered earnings are equal to the sum of the 6 highest months of covered earnings during the last 12 months divided by 180.

The minimum daily benefit is 10 pesos.

The maximum daily benefit is 200 pesos.

The benefit is suspended if the beneficiary does not provide a doctor's monthly medical report.

Permanent Disability Benefits

Permanent disability pension: The monthly pension equals 115% of the insured's old-age pension (115% of the sum of 300 pesos, plus 20% of the insured's average monthly covered earnings, plus 2% of the insured's average monthly covered earnings for each year of service exceeding 10 years or 115% of 40% of the insured's average monthly covered earnings, whichever is greater).

Average monthly covered earnings are equal to the sum of the last 60 months of covered earnings immediately before the 6-month period (January–June or July–December) in which the disability began divided by 60, or the sum of all monthly covered earnings paid before the 6-month period (January–June or July–December) in which the disability began divided by the number of monthly contributions paid in the same period, whichever is greater.

The minimum monthly pension is 2,000 pesos.

There is no maximum monthly pension.

Dependent's supplement (permanent total disability): 10% of the disability pension or 250 pesos, whichever is greater, is paid for each of the five youngest children younger than age 21 (no limit if disabled). The supplement ceases before age 21 if a child marries or starts work.

Partial disability: The pension is the same as the permanent total disability pension but is paid for a limited period according to the schedule in law for each specified disability. If the awarded duration of the pension is less than a year, the pension is paid as a lump sum.

Supplementary pension (permanent total and partial disability): 575 pesos a month.

The insured must have an assessed degree of disability of at least 20%. The degree of disability is assessed annually by a Social Security System doctor. The pension is suspended if the beneficiary is gainfully employed (in the case of a total disability), fails to undergo an annual physical examination, does not provide a doctor's quarterly medical report, or is fully rehabilitated.

Workers' Medical Benefits

Benefits include medical, surgical, and hospital services; appliances; and rehabilitation.

Survivor Benefits

Survivor pension: The pension is equal to 100% of the monthly permanent total disability pension that would have been payable to the deceased.

Dependent's supplement: 10% of the deceased's monthly pension is paid for each of the five youngest children younger than age 21 (no limit if disabled). The supplement ceases before age 21 if a child marries or starts work.

In the absence of an eligible spouse or dependent children, the pension (excluding dependent supplements) is paid to dependent parents for up to 60 months.

The minimum monthly pension is 2,000 pesos.

There is no maximum monthly pension.

Survivors of a permanent total disability pensioner: The pension is equal to 100% of the insured's monthly permanent disability pension, plus dependent supplements.

The pension is shared between the spouse and dependent children younger than age 21 (no limit if disabled) who are not married or earning 300 or more pesos a month from employment.

In the absence of an eligible spouse or dependent children, the insured's monthly pension (excluding dependent supplements) is payable to dependent parents for a maximum of 60 months, minus the number of months the pension was paid to the deceased before his or her death.

Funeral grant: 10,000 pesos is paid to the person who paid for the funeral.

Administrative Organization

Department of Labor and Employment (http://www.dole.gov.ph) provides general supervision.

Employees' Compensation Commission (http://www.dole.gov.ph/ecc), part of the Department of Labor, initiates and coordinates program policies and determines contribution rates.

Employers pay temporary disability benefits directly to their employees and are reimbursed by the Social Security System.

Social Security System (http://www.sss.gov.ph) collects contributions and pays permanent disability benefits.

Saudi Arabia

Exchange rate: US$1.00 equals 3.74 riyals.

Old Age, Disability, and Survivors

Regulatory Framework

First law: 1962 (social insurance), implemented in 1973.

Current law: 2000 (social insurance), implemented in 2001.

Type of program: Social insurance system.

Coverage

Saudi employees in the public and private sectors.

Voluntary coverage for self-employed persons, those working abroad, and those who no longer satisfy the conditions for compulsory coverage.

Exclusions: Agricultural workers, fishermen, domestic servants, family labor, and foreign workers. (Subject to certain conditions, excluded workers may receive coverage.)

Special system for civil servants and military personnel.

Source of Funds

Insured person: 9% of gross earnings.

The minimum monthly earnings for contribution and benefit purposes are 1,500 riyals.

The maximum monthly earnings for contribution and benefit purposes are 45,000 riyals.

Self-employed person: 9% of declared income.

The minimum monthly earnings for contribution and benefit purposes are 1,500 riyals.

The maximum monthly earnings for contribution and benefit purposes are 45,000 riyals.

Employer: 9% of payroll.

The minimum monthly earnings for contribution and benefit purposes are 1,500 riyals.

The maximum monthly earnings for contribution and benefit purposes are 45,000 riyals.

Government: The cost of administration during the initial phase, an annual subsidy, and any operating deficit.

Qualifying Conditions

Old-age pension: Age 60 (men) or age 55 (women) with at least 120 months of paid or credited contributions (credited contributions must not exceed 60 months).

Age 55 (men) with at least 120 months of contributions if engaged in arduous or unhealthy work.

Early pension: At any age with at least 300 months of contributions and if no longer covered by the program; at least 120 months of contribution if sentenced to prison for 1 or more years.

Retirement from covered employment is necessary.

Old-age pensions are not payable abroad.

Old-age settlement: Paid if the insured does not satisfy the qualifying conditions for an old-age pension.

Disability pension: Assessed with an incapacity for any work before age 60. Must have 12 consecutive months of contributions or 18 nonconsecutive months of contributions (24 consecutive months of contributions or 36 nonconsecutive months of contributions for voluntarily insured persons who first joined the scheme when aged 50 or older and who have lost more than 2/3 of their earning capacity). The disability must begin while the insured is in covered employment.

If the insured is no longer in covered employment when the disability begins, the pension is paid with at least 120 months of paid or credited contributions (credited contributions must not exceed 60 months).

Disability settlement: Paid if the insured does not satisfy the qualifying conditions for a disability pension.

Survivor pension: The deceased was in covered employment at the time of death and had 3 consecutive months of contributions or 6 nonconsecutive months of contributions (12 consecutive months of contributions or 18 nonconsecutive months of contributions for voluntarily insured persons who first joined the scheme when aged 50 or older); or was a pensioner.

If the deceased was no longer in covered employment at the time of death and was not a pensioner, the pension is paid with at least 120 months of paid or credited contributions (credited contributions must not exceed 60 months).

Eligible survivors include the widow(er); a dependent son younger than age 20 (age 25 if a full-time student); a dependent unmarried daughter; and brothers, sisters, parents, grandparents, and grandchildren in certain circumstances.

The survivor pension is not payable abroad.

Survivor settlement: Paid to eligible survivors if the deceased did not satisfy the qualifying conditions for a pension.

The survivor settlement is payable abroad.

Old-Age Benefits

Old-age pension: The pension is based on 2.5% of the insured's average monthly earnings during the last 2 years for each year of contributions, up to 100%.

The average monthly earnings for benefit calculation purposes must not exceed 150% of the insured's monthly earnings at the beginning of the last 5-year contribution period.

If the insured's monthly earnings decrease during the last 2 years before retirement, special provisions apply to adjust the average monthly earnings used for benefit calculation purposes.

Early pension: Calculated in the same way as the old-age pension.

The minimum pension is 1,725 riyals.

Old-age settlement: A lump sum is paid equal to 10% of the insured's average monthly earnings during the last 2 years before retirement for each month of the first 5 years of contributions plus 12% for each additional month.

Permanent Disability Benefits

Disability pension: If the insured was in covered employment when the disability began and the assessed degree of disability is at least 50%, the pension is equal to 2.5% of the insured's average monthly earnings during the last 2 years for each year of contributions, up to 100%.

The average monthly earnings for benefit calculation purposes must not exceed 150% of the insured's monthly earnings at the beginning of the last 5-year contribution period.

If the insured's monthly earnings decrease during the last 2 years before the disability began, special provisions apply to adjust the average monthly earnings used for benefit calculation purposes.

The minimum pension is equal to the insured's average monthly earnings or 1,725 riyals, whichever is greater.

Constant-attendance supplement: 50% of the disability pension is paid if the insured requires the help of others to complete daily tasks. The need for constant attendance is assessed by a General Organization for Social Insurance medical board.

Partial disability: A lump sum is paid for an assessed degree of disability of less than 50%.

Disability settlement: A lump sum is paid equal to 10% of the insured's average monthly earnings during the last 2 years before the disability began for each month of the first 5 years of contribution plus 12% for each additional month.

Survivor Benefits

Survivor pension: If there are three or more survivors, the pension is equal to 100% of the pension paid or payable to the deceased; 75% for two dependents; 50% for one dependent. The pension is split equally among all eligible survivors.

The minimum individual survivor pension is 345 riyals.

The minimum combined survivor pension is 1,725 riyals or the deceased's average monthly earnings used for pension calculation purposes, whichever is greater.

The pension for a female survivor ceases on marriage but may be reinstated if she is subsequently divorced or widowed.

Survivor settlement: A lump sum equal to 10% of the insured's average monthly earnings during the last 2 years before death for each month of the first 5 years of contributions plus 12% for each additional month.

Marriage grant: The survivor pension for a widow or an eligible daughter, sister, or granddaughter ceases on marriage and a grant is paid equal to 18 times her monthly survivor pension.

Death grant: A lump sum equal to 3 months' pension is split equally among eligible survivors.

The maximum death grant is 10,000 riyals.

Administrative Organization

Ministry of Labor (http://www.mol.gov.sa) provides general supervision.

Managed by a tripartite board, the Annuities Branch of the General Organization for Social Insurance (http://www.gosi.gov.sa) administers the program through district offices.

Sickness and Maternity

Regulatory Framework

No statutory social security benefits are provided for sickness and maternity.

The 1969 Social Insurance Law requires employers with more than 20 employees to pay 100% of wages for the first 30 days of sick leave and 75% of wages for the next 60 days.

Employers are also required to pay between 50% and 100% of wages (depending on the period of employment) to female employees for a maternity leave period of up to 10 weeks.

Work Injury

Regulatory Framework

First law: 1947.

Current law: 2000 (social insurance), implemented in 2001.

Type of program: Social insurance system.

Coverage

Saudi and non-Saudi employees in the private sector.

Source of Funds

Insured person: None.

Self-employed person: Not applicable.

Employer: 2% of payroll.

The minimum monthly earnings for contribution and benefit purposes are 400 riyals.

The maximum monthly earnings for contribution and benefit purposes are 45,000 riyals.

Government: An annual subsidy and any operating deficit.

Qualifying Conditions

Work injury benefits: There is no minimum qualifying period for a work injury or an occupational disease. Accidents that occur while commuting to and from work are covered.

Temporary Disability Benefits

The benefit is equal to 100% of the insured's daily wage; 75% if receiving inpatient treatment in a medical center at the expense of the General Organization for Social Insurance. The benefit is paid for each day until the insured is able to resume work.

Permanent Disability Benefits

Permanent disability pension: If assessed as totally disabled, Saudi insured persons receive 100% of average monthly earnings.

Average monthly earnings are based on the 3-month period immediately before the onset of disability.

The minimum monthly pension is 1,725 riyals.

If assessed as totally disabled, non-Saudi insured persons receive a lump sum equal to 84 months' permanent disability pension, up to a maximum of 330,000 riyals.

Constant-attendance supplement: 50% of the disability pension is paid (up to a maximum of 3,500 riyals) if the insured requires the help of others to complete daily tasks. The need for constant attendance is assessed by a General Organization for Social Insurance medical board.

Partial disability: Saudi insured persons receive a lump sum calculated on the basis of a percentage of the full pension according to the assessed degree of disability. For an assessed degree of disability of less than 50% that began when the insured was aged 40 or younger, the lump sum is equal to 60 months' pension times the assessed degree of disability; if the disability began when the insured was older than age 40, the lump sum is reduced by 1 month's pension for each year older than age 40.

The minimum partial disability lump sum is based on 36 months' pension.

The maximum partial disability lump sum is 165,000 riyals.

If assessed as partially disabled, non-Saudi insured persons receive a lump-sum equal to 60 months' pension times the assessed degree of disability, up to a maximum of 165,000 riyals.

The degree of disability is assessed by a General Organization for Social Insurance medical board.

Workers' Medical Benefits

All necessary medical, dental, and diagnostic treatment; hospitalization; medicines; appliances; transportation; and rehabilitation.

Survivor Benefits

Survivor pension: If there are three or more survivors, the pension is equal to 100% of the pension paid or payable to the deceased; 75% for two dependents; 50% for one dependent. The pension is split equally among all eligible survivors.

The minimum combined survivor pension is 1,725 riyals.

The pension for a female survivor ceases on marriage but may be reinstated if she is subsequently divorced or widowed.

Eligible survivors include dependent sons, brothers, and grandsons of the deceased younger than age 21 (age 26 if a full-time student); a widow, unmarried daughters, sisters, and granddaughters; parents; and grandparents.

Marriage grant: The survivor pension for a widow or an eligible daughter, sister, or granddaughter ceases on marriage and a grant is paid equal to 18 times her monthly survivor pension.

Death grant: A lump sum equal to 3 months' pension is split equally among eligible survivors.

The maximum death grant is 10,000 riyals.

Administrative Organization

Ministry of Labor and Social Affairs (http://www.mol.gov.sa) provides general supervision.

Managed by a tripartite board, the Occupational Hazards Branch of the General Organization for Social Insurance (http://www.gosi.com.sa) administers the program through district offices.

Singapore

Exchange rate: US$1.00 equals
1.57 Singapore dollars (S$).

Old Age, Disability, and Survivors

Regulatory Framework

First law: 1953 (provident fund), implemented in 1955.

Current law: 2001 (provident fund), with 2002, 2003, 2004, 2005, and 2006 amendments.

Type of program: Provident fund system.

Note: Central Provident Fund (CPF) operates four types of individual accounts: an ordinary account to finance the purchase of a home, approved investments, CPF insurance, and education; a special account, principally for old-age provisions; a medisave account to pay for hospital treatment, medical benefits, and approved medical insurance; and, from age 55, a retirement account to finance periodic payments from age 62.

Coverage

Employed persons, including most categories of public-sector employees, earning more than S$50 a month.

Self-employed persons earning an annual net trade income greater than S$6,000 are covered for hospitalization expenses and approved medical insurance.

Special system for certain categories of public-sector employees, including administrative service staff.

Source of Funds

Insured person: None if monthly earnings are less than S$500; 60% of the amount over S$500 if monthly earnings are between S$500 and S$750; 20% of monthly earnings up to S$900 if monthly earnings are over S$750.

Depending on the fund member's age, between 0% and 22% of the total insured person and employer contributions are placed in the ordinary account, between 0% and 7% are placed in the special account, and between 6% and 8.5% are placed in the medisave account. The medisave account covers the cost of hospitalization and medical expenses (see Sickness and Maternity, below). The maximum monthly contributions to the medisave account (depending on age) are between S$270 and S$382.50.

Fund members aged 50 or older contribute at lower rates.

The maximum monthly earnings for contribution purposes are S$4,500.

Insured persons may make additional voluntary contributions. The total insured person and employer voluntary and mandatory contributions must not exceed S$25,245 a year.

Mandatory contributions are tax-deductible, up to a specified limit.

Self-employed person: Between 6% and 8% (depending on age) of annual income to the medisave account only. Additional voluntary contributions are possible, up to a maximum.

The maximum monthly contribution to the medisave account (depending on age) is between S$270 and S$382.50.

Mandatory contributions are tax-deductible, up to a specified limit.

Employer: None on behalf of employees with monthly earnings less than S$50; 13% of monthly wages for employees with earnings greater than S$50 but no more than S$750; 13% of monthly wages up to S$585 for employees with monthly earnings greater than S$750.

Contributions on behalf of all employed fund members aged 50 or older are paid at lower rates.

The maximum monthly earnings for contribution purposes are S$4,500.

Employers may make additional voluntary contributions on behalf of employees. The total employer and insured person voluntary and mandatory contributions must not exceed S$25,245 a year.

Government: None.

Qualifying Conditions

Old-age benefit: Contributions are allocated to three separate accounts, and individual savings can be accessed under certain conditions.

Ordinary account: Funds can be withdrawn at age 55 subject to certain conditions.

Drawdown payment: Funds can be drawn down before age 55 to purchase a home or insurance (term-life insurance scheme and a mortgage-reducing insurance scheme operated by the Central Provident Fund), invest in approved instruments, and pay for education at approved local institutions for the member or his or her children.

Special account: Funds can be withdrawn at age 55 subject to certain conditions.

Drawdown payment: Funds can be drawn down before age 55 to make investments in approved instruments.

Medisave account: Funds in excess of S$28,500 (the medisave minimum sum) can first be withdrawn at age 55. The cessation of employment is not necessary.

Drawdown payment: Funds can be drawn down before age 55 to purchase medical insurance for the member and dependents from the Central Provident Fund or approved private providers.

Retirement account: At age 55, a retirement account is established in which fund members must place a maximum of S$94,600 (up to 50% of which can be pledged property). The cash proportion ensures monthly income from age 62 (age 60 for certain occupations), until the account is empty.

All funds may be withdrawn at any age if a member permanently emigrates from Singapore.

Disability benefit: Must be assessed with a permanent total incapacity for any work. The disability is assessed either by a registered doctor in any government hospital or by the Central Provident Fund Board's panel of doctors.

Survivor benefit: Paid to the survivor(s) named by the fund member.

Old-Age Benefits

Ordinary and special accounts: A lump sum is paid equal to total employee and employer contributions, plus at least 2.5% (ordinary account) and 4% (special account) compound interest, minus drawdown payments and the cash proportion of the retirement account.

Medisave account: At age 55, fund members must leave at least S$28,000 in the medisave account to meet the cost of future hospitalization. Savings in excess of S$28,000 (the medisave minimum sum) can be withdrawn subject to certain conditions. The account earns compound interest of at least 4%.

Drawdown payment: Up to S$800 (S$660 for medical insurance bought from the Central Provident Fund Board) per insured person per policy year can be used to purchase medical insurance. Fund members can purchase medical insurance for their dependents.

Retirement account: At age 55, a retirement account is established in which fund members must place a maximum of S$94,600 (up to 50% of which can be pledged property). The cash proportion ensures monthly income of S$750 from age 62 (age 60 for certain occupations), until the account is empty. The account earns compound interest of at least 4%. Funds can be deposited with a bank, left in the Central Provident Fund retirement account, or used to buy a life annuity from an insurance company. Annuities are first payable at age 62 or older.

Interest rate: Members receive a market-related interest rate (based on the 12-month fixed deposit and month-end savings rates of the major local banks) on their savings. Savings in the medisave, special, and retirement accounts earn additional interest of 1.5 percentage points above the annually credited interest rate. The Central Provident Fund Board guarantees a minimum rate of interest of 2.5% per year. Interest is computed monthly and compounded and credited annually.

Permanent Disability Benefits

Ordinary, medisave, and special accounts: A lump sum is paid equal to total employee and employer contributions, plus at least 2.5% (ordinary account) and 4% (medisave and special accounts) compound interest, minus drawdown payments; and after setting aside S$33,110 to provide monthly payments for 7 years and at least S$28,000 (the medisave minimum sum) in the medisave account to meet the cost of future hospitalization. If the insured is unable to set aside S$33,110 and at least S$28,000 (the medisave minimum sum) in the medisave account, monthly payments funded by ordinary and special account balances are provided instead of a lump sum.

Medisave account: Disabled fund members must leave at least S$28,000 (the medisave minimum sum) in the medisave account to meet the cost of future hospitalization. The account earns compound interest of at least 4%.

Drawdown payment: Up to S$800 (S$660 for medical insurance bought from the Central Provident Fund Board) per insured person per policy year can be used to purchase medical insurance. Fund members can purchase medical insurance for their dependents.

Interest rate: Members receive a market-related interest rate (based on the 12-month fixed deposit and month-end savings rates of the major local banks) on their savings. Savings in the medisave, special, and retirement accounts earn additional interest of 1.5 percentage points above the annually credited interest rate. The Central Provident Fund Board guarantees a minimum rate of interest of 2.5% per year. Interest is computed monthly and compounded and credited annually.

Survivor Benefits

Survivor benefit (all accounts): The benefit is equal to the remaining balances in the deceased's accounts and any term-life insurance payouts.

The fund member determines the proportion of benefit that different survivors receive. In the absence of named survivors, the benefit is distributed by the Public Trustee in accordance with the law.

Administrative Organization

Ministry of Manpower (http://www.mom.gov.sg) provides general supervision through its Income Security Policy Department.

Managed by a tripartite board and a chairman, the Central Provident Fund (http://www.cpf.gov.sg) is responsible for the administration of the program, including the custody of the fund, collection of contributions, and payment of benefits.

Members' funds are invested in Singapore government bonds and placed in advance deposits with the Monetary Authority of Singapore pending the issue of such bonds. The insurance fund is managed by institutional fund members and the Central Provident Fund Board.

Sickness and Maternity

Regulatory Framework

First laws: 1953 (provident fund), implemented in 1955; and 1968 (employment).

Current laws: 1996 (employment); and 2001 (provident fund), with 2002, 2003, 2004, 2005, and 2006 amendments.

Type of program: Employer-liability (cash sickness and maternity benefits), provident fund (medical benefits), and social assistance (medical benefits) system.

Coverage

Cash benefits (employer liability): All employed persons.

Medical benefits (provident fund): Employed and self-employed persons with annual net income greater than S$6,000.

Special system for certain categories of public-sector employees, including administrative service staff.

Medical benefits (social assistance): Singapore citizens unable to pay for medical treatment in approved hospitals and medical institutions can apply for financial aid from the medifund program. The amount of financial aid provided depends on individual circumstances. Under the separate public assistance program, individuals without employment or any source of income may be given free medical treatment at government hospitals and clinics.

Source of Funds

Insured person

Cash benefits (employer liability): None.

Medical benefits (provident fund): See source of funds under Old Age, Disability, and Survivors, above.

Medical benefits (social assistance): None.

Self-employed person

Cash benefits (employer liability): Not applicable.

Medical benefits (provident fund): See source of funds under Old Age, Disability, and Survivors, above.

Medical benefits (social assistance): None.

Employer

Cash benefits (employer liability): The total cost.

Medical benefits (provident fund): See source of funds under Old Age, Disability, and Survivors, above.

Medical benefits (social assistance): None.

Government

Cash benefits (employer liability): None.

Medical benefits (provident fund): Fund members are subsidized when using certain classes of hospital wards.

Medical benefits (social assistance): The total cost.

Qualifying Conditions

Cash sickness benefit (employer liability): Must have at least 6 months' employment. Medical certification is necessary.

Cash maternity benefit (employer liability): Must have at least 180 days' employment immediately before childbirth.

Medical benefits (provident fund): Must be a member of the medisave program. (Members can access savings in their medisave account.)

Medical benefits (social assistance): Provided to citizens satisfying tests of means and income.

Sickness and Maternity Benefits

Cash sickness benefit (employer liability): Up to 14 days of paid sick leave are provided a year (up to 60 days if hospitalized).

Cash maternity benefit (employer liability): The benefit is equal to 100% of the female employee's gross wages.

Working mothers are provided with up to 12 weeks of maternity leave. Employers pay for the first 8 weeks of leave for the first two births. Government reimburses employers for the additional 4-week leave period for the first two births and pays for the entire 12-week leave period for the third and fourth births, if the qualifying conditions are met. Government reimbursement is capped at S$10,000 each for the first two births and S$30,000 each for the 3rd and 4th births.

Workers' Medical Benefits

Outpatient treatment and inpatient hospital care are provided through government hospitals and approved private hospitals and medical institutions. Benefits include day-surgery treatment and prescribed medicines. The cost of medical treatment is deducted from the fund member's balance in the medisave account for approved treatments.

Medical consultation fees are paid by the employer.

The medisave account can be used to pay for the childbirth and prenatal expenses incurred for the first four live childbirths; also for the birth of the fifth and subsequent children if both parents have a combined medisave account balance of at least S$15,000 at the time of the childbirth.

Patients in hospital wards receive subsidies ranging from 20% to 80% of costs.

Maximum limits apply to costs deducted from the medisave account for different types of services (such as a maximum of S$300 for daily hospital charges, including a maximum of S$50 for a doctor's daily attendance fees).

Dependents' Medical Benefits

Members can use savings in their medisave account to help pay for the medical expenses of their spouse, children, parents, and grandparents. Grandparents must be Singapore citizens or reside permanently in Singapore.

The medical benefits, subsidies, and maximum limits on cost are the same as for the insured person.

Administrative Organization

Employer liability: Ministry of Manpower (http://www.mom.gov.sg) provides general supervision and enforces the law through its labor relations department.

Provident fund: Ministry of Manpower (http://www.mom.gov.sg) provides general supervision and enforces the law through its Income Security Policy Department.

Managed by a tripartite board and a chairman, the Central Provident Fund (http://www.cpf.gov.sg) is responsible for the administration of the program, including custody of the fund, collection of contributions, and payment of benefits.

Medical benefits: Ministry of Health (http://www.moh.gov.sg) provides medical services through government hospitals and private providers.

Work Injury

Regulatory Framework

First law: 1933 (workmen's compensation).

Current law: 1975 (workmen's compensation), with 1980 and 1990 amendments.

Type of program: Employer-liability system, involving compulsory insurance with a private carrier (unless exempted).

Coverage

All manual labor; nonmanual labor earning S$1,600 a month or less.

Exclusions: Self-employed persons, nonmanual labor with earnings greater than S$1,600 a month, domestic and casual workers, home workers, and family labor.

Special system for the police.

Source of Funds

Insured person: None.

Self-employed person: Not applicable.

Employer: The total cost, through the direct provision of benefits or insurance premiums.

Government: None.

Qualifying Conditions

Work injury benefits: There is no minimum qualifying period, but claims must be made within 1 year of the date of the accident.

Temporary Disability Benefits

The benefit is equal to 100% of the insured's average monthly earnings in the 12 months before the onset of disability and is paid for up to 14 days if not hospitalized (up to 60 days if hospitalized); thereafter, the benefit is equal to 2/3 of the insured's average monthly earnings in the 12 months before the onset of disability.

The benefit is payable from the first day of incapacity for a maximum of 1 year.

Permanent Disability Benefits

If the insured has an assessed degree of permanent disability of 100% (total disability), a lump sum is paid that varies according to the insured's age at the onset of disability and average monthly earnings.

The lump sum varies from 6 years of the insured's average monthly earnings in the 12 months before the onset of disability (if aged 66 or older) to 12 years of the insured's average monthly earnings in the 12 months before the onset of disability (if aged 40 or younger).

The minimum lump sum is S$49,000.

The maximum lump sum is S$147,000.

Constant-attendance supplement: If the insured has an assessed degree of permanent disability of 100% (total disability) and requires the constant attendance of another person, an additional grant equal to 25% of the lump sum is paid. Medical certification must be provided by a registered doctor.

Partial disability: A lump sum is paid equal to the lesser of the assessed degree of disability times S$147,000 or the assessed degree of disability times the insured's average monthly earnings in the 12 months before the onset of disability times a multiplying factor according to the schedule in law.

Survivor Benefits

A lump sum is paid that varies according to the insured's age at the time of death and average monthly earnings.

The lump sum varies from 4 years of the deceased's average monthly earnings in the 12 months before death (if the deceased was aged 66 or older) to 9 years of the deceased's average monthly earnings in the 12 months before death (if the deceased was aged 40 or younger).

Eligible survivors are a spouse, parents, grandparents, step-parents, children, grandchildren, stepchildren, and brothers and sisters. Survivors need not have been dependent. The Commissioner for Labor splits the lump sum among eligible survivors.

The minimum lump sum is S$37,000.

The maximum lump sum is S$111,000.

Administrative Organization

Ministry of Manpower (http://www.mom.gov.sg) provides general supervision through its Work Injury Compensation Branch, Occupational Safety and Health Division.

Commissioner for Labor, part of the Ministry of Manpower, enforces the law, approves agreements between employers and claimants, and distributes survivor benefits.

Employers must insure against liability with private insurance companies. The Ministry of Manpower may exempt any employer or class of employers from compulsory insurance. Exempted classes of employers include the government, statutory boards, financial companies, retail shops, and hotels.

Solomon Islands

Exchange rate: US$1.00 equals
6.96 Solomon Islands dollars (SI$).

Old Age, Disability, and Survivors

Regulatory Framework

First and current law: 1973 (provident fund), implemented in 1976, with amendments.

Type of program: Provident fund system.

Coverage

All employed workers aged 14 or older, including domestic servants and cooperative members, and casual workers earning at least SI$20 a month and working regularly at least 6 days a month.

Exclusions: Prisoners and persons detained in a mental hospital or leper institution.

Employees covered by equivalent private plans may contract out.

Voluntary coverage for unemployed and self-employed persons aged 16 to 25 as well as former employees who have previously contributed for at least 12 consecutive months, regardless of age.

Special system for public-sector employees.

Source of Funds

Insured person: 5% of wages.

Voluntary additional contributions by the insured person are permitted up to a combined monthly maximum of SI$100.

SI$5 is deducted annually from the member's provident fund account to finance death benefits.

Self-employed person: Not applicable.

Employer: 7.5% of monthly payroll.

Government: None.

Qualifying Conditions

Old-age benefit: Age 50, regardless of employment status; at any age if emigrating permanently.

Contributions must be paid after age 50 if the member continues to be an employee or starts a new job after retirement that is covered by the provident fund. If the member has withdrawn any of the amount in his or her account at age 50 and makes further contributions from employment, no further withdrawal can be made for 5 years.

Early withdrawal: Age 40 if permanently retired from covered employment.

Drawdown payment: Unemployed fund members may withdraw funds from their individual account after 3 months of continuous unemployment.

Disability benefit: Must be assessed with a permanent physical or mental incapacity to work.

Survivor benefit: The death of the fund member before retirement. The benefit is paid to the next-of-kin or to one or more named survivors.

Old-Age Benefits

A lump sum is paid equal to total employee and employer contributions plus accumulated interest.

Drawdown payment: The value of drawdown payments depends on the value of employee and employer contributions, plus accumulated interest, in the individual account and at the discretion of the individual fund member. (See also Unemployment, below.)

Interest rate adjustment: The interest rate is set by the National Provident Fund Board at the end of each fiscal year.

Permanent Disability Benefits

A lump sum is paid equal to total employee and employer contributions plus accumulated interest.

Interest rate adjustment: The interest rate is set by the National Provident Fund Board at the end of each fiscal year.

Survivor Benefits

Survivor benefit: A lump sum is paid equal to total employee and employer contributions plus accumulated interest.

Interest rate adjustment: The interest rate is set by the National Provident Fund Board at the end of each fiscal year.

Death benefit: The maximum benefit is SI$2,500.

Administrative Organization

National Provident Fund Board administers the program.

An independent tripartite body appointed by the Minister of Finance, the National Provident Fund Board comprises two representatives each of government, employers, and employees.

Sickness and Maternity

Regulatory Framework

No statutory sickness and maternity benefits are provided.

The Labor Act requires employers to provide up to 12 weeks' maternity leave to women employees (including up to at least 6 weeks after childbirth).

Work Injury

Regulatory Framework

First and current laws: 1952 (workmen's compensation), with 1969, 1979, and 1982 amendments; and 1981 (employment).

Type of program: Employer-liability system, involving compulsory insurance with a private carrier.

Coverage

Employed persons, including public employees, earning SI$4,000 a year or less; casual workers are covered under certain circumstances.

Source of Funds

Insured person: None.

Self-employed person: Not applicable.

Employer: The total cost.

Government: None.

Qualifying Conditions

Work injury benefits: There is no minimum qualifying period. All 3-day absences from work must be reported. Entitlement is based on an assessment of the injury and the resulting disability. No benefit is paid if the incapacity or death occurs more than a year after the worker has ceased to be employed.

Temporary Disability Benefits

The benefit ranges from 50% to 100% of earnings, according to the insured's monthly wage and the assessed degree of disability. If the incapacity lasts for more than 3 days, the benefit is paid from the first day until recovery, certification of permanent disability, or death.

The maximum monthly benefit is SI$160.

Workers with a temporary disability may undergo periodic medical examination by a doctor named and paid for by the employer.

Permanent Disability Benefits

A lump sum is paid equal to 48 months' earnings.

The maximum lump sum is SI$9,000.

Partial disability: A lump sum is paid based on 48 months' earnings, according to the assessed degree of disability. In cases of multiple injuries, individual benefit awards may be aggregated but must not exceed the permanent disability benefit.

Workers' Medical Benefits

Medical benefits include care, medicines, and appliances.

Appliances, including artificial limbs, dental appliances, and artificial eyes, that benefit the earning capacity of an injured worker are provided at the employer's expense. In such cases, the benefit will be subject to an earnings test.

Survivor Benefits

Survivor benefit: A lump sum is paid based on 36 months' earnings minus any permanent disability benefits paid to the deceased.

The maximum lump sum in cases in which the disability benefit has been paid is SI$9,000.

The maximum lump sum for a fatal work injury is SI$80,000.

Eligible survivors include members of the family living with the deceased at the time of his or her death who were totally or mainly dependent on the deceased's earnings. The courts determine how the survivor benefit is split among survivors.

Funeral grant: If there are no dependents, the grant covers reasonable burial expenses. Each case is treated separately, and receipts must be provided.

The maximum funeral grant is SI$30.

Administrative Organization

Labor Division administers the program.

Unemployment

Regulatory Framework

A statutory office assists the unemployed in seeking alternative employment by providing individual counseling and identifying suitable job vacancies.

Under the National Provident Fund Act, unemployed fund members may drawdown up to 1/3 of savings in case of unfair dismissal or if laid off, provided that the member's savings in the fund are greater than SI$10,000 and he or she is not reemployed within 3 months after dismissal. The amount left in the account can also be withdrawn later under certain provisions.

Employers are required to pay a dismissal benefit of 2 weeks' wages for each year of employment, provided that the employee has been in continuous employment with the same employer for 26 weeks or more and is younger than age 50.

Sri Lanka

Exchange rate: US$1.00 equals 102.90 rupees.

Note: This information dates from 1999.

Old Age, Disability, and Survivors

Regulatory Framework

First and current law: 1958 (provident fund), with amendments.

Type of program: Provident fund system.

Coverage

All employed persons up to age 55 (men) or age 50 (women).

Voluntary coverage for employees older than age 55 (men) or age 50 (women).

Exclusions: Family labor, civil servants, self-employed persons, farmers, and fishermen.

Employees covered by equivalent schemes may contract out.

Special systems for public-sector and local government employees, self-employed persons, farmers, and fishermen.

Source of Funds

Insured person: 8% of monthly earnings; additional voluntary contributions are permitted.

Self-employed person: Not applicable.

Employer: 12% of monthly payroll; additional voluntary contributions are permitted.

Government: None. (If the investment income of the fund is inadequate to pay any part of the interest payable on contributions, the deficit is met by Parliament but repaid by the fund.)

Qualifying Conditions

Old-age benefit: Age 55 (men) or age 50 (women) and retired from covered employment; at any age if the government closes the place of employment, if emigrating permanently, or for employed women who marry.

Drawdown payment: Drawdown payments are possible.

Disability benefit: Must be assessed with a permanent and total incapacity for work.

Survivor benefit: Paid if the fund member dies before retirement. The grant is paid to legal heirs or named beneficiaries.

Old-Age Benefits

Old-age benefit: A lump sum is paid equal to total employee and employer contributions, plus interest.

Drawdown payment: Fund members may withdraw funds from their individual account once every 5 years.

Interest rate adjustment: Set periodically by the Monetary Board of the Employees' Provident Fund, the annual interest rate must not be less than 2.5%.

Permanent Disability Benefits

A lump sum is paid equal to total employee and employer contributions, plus interest.

Interest rate adjustment: Set periodically by the Monetary Board of the Employees' Provident Fund, the annual interest rate must not be less than 2.5%.

Survivor Benefits

A lump sum equal to total employee and employer contributions, plus interest, is paid to one or more legal heirs or named beneficiaries.

Interest rate adjustment: Set periodically by the Monetary Board of the Employees' Provident Fund, the annual interest rate must not be less than 2.5%.

Administrative Organization

Ministry of Employment and Labor provides general supervision.

Employees' Provident Fund (http://www.epf.lk), under the Ministry of Employment and Labor, administers the program through district offices.

Central Bank of Sri Lanka (http://www.centralbanklanka.org) is responsible for the custody and investment of the financial assets of the Employees' Provident Fund (http://www.epf.lk) and for the payment of grants certified by the Commissioner of Labor.

Sickness and Maternity

Regulatory Framework

Medical care is available free of charge in government health centers and hospitals.

No statutory sickness and maternity benefits are provided.

Plantations have their own dispensaries and maternity wards and must provide medical care for their employees.

Employees in the plantation sector and certain wage and salary earners are entitled to 84 days of maternity leave before or after childbirth for the first two childbirths and 42 days for subsequent childbirths. The Maternity Benefits Ordinance requires employers to pay maternity benefits at the prescribed rate for 12 weeks for the first two childbirths

(6 weeks for subsequent childbirths), comprising 2 weeks before childbirth and 10 weeks after (2 weeks before and 4 weeks after childbirth for subsequent childbirths). Employed women covered under the Shop and Office Employees' Act get 84 days' paid maternity leave for the first two childbirths and 42 days' paid leave for subsequent childbirths.

Work Injury

Regulatory Framework

First and current law: 1934 (workmen's compensation), with 1946 and 1990 amendments.

Type of program: Employer-liability system. (Voluntary supplementary insurance is possible.)

Coverage

All workers, including contract workers.

Exclusions: Police and armed forces personnel.

Source of Funds

Insured person: None.

Self-employed person: Not applicable.

Employer: The total cost is met through the direct provision of benefits or insurance premiums. Premiums range from 1% to 7.5% of payroll, according to the assessed degree of risk.

Government: The total cost of medical benefits.

Qualifying Conditions

Work injury benefits: A minimum 3-day qualifying period for temporary disability; a continuous employment period of 6 months for an occupational disease.

In cases in which the employer voluntarily provides work injury insurance or compensation to workers, the amount of any such benefits paid are deducted from benefits payable under the work injury program.

Temporary Disability Benefits

50% of wages are paid after a 3-day waiting period, for up to 5 years. After 6 months' entitlement, the benefit may be paid as a lump sum. The benefit is payable abroad under certain conditions if emigrating permanently.

A worker entitled to a temporary disability benefit may be required to be examined by a registered doctor once a month.

The maximum monthly benefit is 5,000 rupees.

Permanent Disability Benefits

A lump sum is paid that varies according to wage class.

The minimum benefit is 21,168 rupees.

The maximum benefit is 250,000 rupees.

Partial disability: A lump sum ranging between 30% and 100% of compensation.

Workers' Medical Benefits

Provided in government hospitals free of charge.

Survivor Benefits

Survivor benefit: A lump sum of between 2 and 5 years of the insured's wages, according to wage class, is paid for the death of the insured.

Eligible survivors are the wife, legitimate dependent children, unmarried daughters, and a widowed mother. Other family members may be eligible if totally or partially dependent on the deceased.

The benefit is split among dependent relatives according to the decision of the Commissioner of Workmen's Compensation.

The minimum survivor benefit is 19,404 rupees.

The maximum survivor benefit is 250,000 rupees.

Funeral grant: The actual cost of the funeral, deducted from the survivor benefit, subject to a maximum in proportion to the value of the survivor grant (up to 10,000 rupees if survivor grant exceeds 40,000 rupees). The grant is paid to the person who paid for the funeral.

Administrative Organization

Ministry of Employment and Labor provides general supervision.

Department of Workmen's Compensation administers the program.

Family Allowances

Regulatory Framework

First law: 1990.

Current law: 1995 (low-income families).

Type of program: Social assistance system.

Coverage

Low-income families.

Source of Funds

Insured person: 25 rupees per month per family member.

Self-employed person: 25 rupees per month per family member.

Employer: None.

Government: The majority of the costs of the program.

Qualifying Conditions

Family allowances: Family earnings must be below 1,000 rupees a month.

Family Allowance Benefits

Family allowances: Between 100 rupees and 1,000 rupees is paid monthly, depending on family income and size.

Administrative Organization

Ministry of Agriculture, Livestock, and Samurdhi (Commissioner of Poor Relief) administers the program.

Syria

Exchange rate: US$1.00 equals 50.70 pounds.

Old Age, Disability, and Survivors

Regulatory Framework

First and current law: 1959 (social insurance), with 1976 and 2001 amendments.

Type of program: Social insurance system.

Coverage

Employees in industry, commerce, and agriculture; domestic workers; freelance workers; self-employed persons; and employers.

Voluntary coverage for Syrians working abroad.

Exclusions: Family labor.

Special system for civil servants.

Source of Funds

Insured person: 7% of earnings (plus an optional 1% of earnings for voluntary supplementary disability and death benefits).

Self-employed person: Information is not available.

Employer: 14% of payroll.

Government: None.

Qualifying Conditions

Old-age pension: Age 60 (men) or age 55 (women); at any age (men and women) in physically demanding or dangerous work, with 180 months of contributions.

Age 55 (men) or age 50 (women) with 240 months of contributions. At any age (men and women) with 360 months of contributions.

Early pension: At any age with 300 months of contributions.

Payments abroad are made at the discretion of the Institution of Social Insurance.

Old-age settlement: Age 60 (men) or age 55 (women) and does not satisfy the qualifying conditions for the old-age pension.

Disability pension: Paid for the loss of at least 80% of working capacity. The disability began during employment or within 6 months after leaving employment but is not due only to an occupational injury. The insured must have made contributions throughout the last 12 months or for a total of 24 months including the last 3 months.

Disability benefit (voluntary insurance): The assessed degree of disability must exceed 35%. The disability may be due to an occupational injury.

Survivor pension: The deceased met the contribution conditions for the disability pension or was a pensioner at the time of death. The death was not the result of an occupational injury.

Eligible survivors include an unemployed widow of any age or a disabled widower, orphans younger than age 21 (age 24 if disabled), and dependent parents.

Death benefit (voluntary insurance): Paid to eligible survivors for the death of the insured.

Funeral grant: Paid to help meet the cost of the funeral.

Old-Age Benefits

Old-age pension: The pension is equal to 2.5% of the insured's base earnings times the number of years of contributions, up to a maximum of 75% of the base earnings. The base earnings are equal to the previous year's average monthly earnings.

Early pension: The pension is equal to 2.5% of the insured's base earnings times the number of years of contributions, up to a maximum of 75% of the base earnings. The base earnings are equal to the previous year's average monthly earnings.

The minimum pension is equal to the legal minimum wage.

The maximum monthly pension is 3,450 pounds or 75% of base earnings if less.

Old-age increment: A lump sum is paid equal to 1 month's pension for every complete covered year beyond 30 years of coverage, up to a maximum of 5 month's pension.

Old-age settlement: A lump sum of between 11% and 15% of total covered earnings is paid.

Permanent Disability Benefits

Disability pension: The pension is equal to 40% of the insured's base earnings plus 2% for each year of covered employment. The base earnings are equal to the previous year's average monthly earnings.

The minimum pension is equal to the legal minimum wage.

The maximum pension is equal to 80% of base earnings.

Temporary disability pension: The minimum monthly pension is 343 pounds, plus 25 pounds for each dependent.

Disability benefit (voluntary insurance): A lump sum is paid equal to 50% of the insured's insurable earnings in the previous year. The benefit is increased by an additional 50% if the insured is totally disabled as a result of an accident at work.

Survivor Benefits

Survivor pension: The pension is equal to 37.5% of the deceased's disability pension.

Orphan's pension: The pension is equal to 25% of the deceased's disability pension for the first orphan (37.5% for a full orphan); 12.5% for the second orphan.

Dependent parent's pension: Each parent receives 12.5% of the deceased's disability pension.

The minimum survivor pension is 400 pounds a month for a widow; 96 pounds each for other survivors.

The maximum total survivor pension is equal to 75% of the deceased's disability pension.

Death benefit (voluntary insurance): A lump sum equal to 100% of the deceased's earnings in the previous year is paid to a survivor. The lump sum is increased by 50% if the insured's death was caused by an accident at work.

Funeral grant: A lump sum of 1 month's earnings is paid.

The maximum funeral grant is 100 pounds.

Administrative Organization

Ministry of Social Affairs and Labor provides general supervision.

Institution of Social Insurance, managed by a tripartite board of directors and a director general, administers the program through regional and district offices.

Work Injury

Regulatory Framework

Current law: 1959 (social insurance), with 1976 and 2001 amendments.

Type of program: Social insurance system.

Coverage

Employees in industry, commerce, and agriculture; municipal workers; and public employees.

Exclusions: Domestic servants and self-employed persons.

Source of Funds

Insured person: None.

Self-employed person: Not applicable.

Employer: 3% of payroll.

Government: None.

Qualifying Conditions

Work injury benefits: There is no minimum qualifying period.

Temporary Disability Benefits

The benefit for the first month is equal to 80% of the insured's earnings; thereafter, 100%.

The minimum monthly benefit is 2,000 pounds and is paid from the day after the injury occurred for up to 12 months.

Work injury benefits can be combined with other pension entitlements.

Permanent Disability Benefits

Permanent disability pension: If assessed with a degree of disability of at least 80%, the benefit is equal to 75% of the insured's average monthly earnings in the previous year.

The minimum monthly pension is 458 pounds.

Work injury benefits can be combined with other pension entitlements.

Partial disability: For an assessed degree of disability of 35% to 79%, a percentage of the full pension is paid according to the assessed degree of disability. For an assessed degree of disability of less than 35%, a lump sum of 1 year's partial pension is paid.

Workers' Medical Benefits

General and specialist care, surgery, hospitalization, drugs, X-rays, appliances, and rehabilitation.

Survivor Benefits

Survivor pension: 75% of the deceased's average monthly earnings in the previous year is split among eligible survivors as follows: 50% for the widow and 50% for orphans; if there is a dependent parent, 20% to the parent, 40% to the widow, and 40% to orphans.

The minimum monthly pension is 400 pounds for a widow; 96 pounds each for other survivors.

Funeral grant: A lump sum is paid equal to 1 month's earnings.

The minimum funeral grant is 80 pounds.

Administrative Organization

Ministry of Social Affairs and Labor provides general supervision.

Institution of Social Insurance, managed by a tripartite board of directors and a director general, administers the program through regional and district offices.

Taiwan

Exchange rate: US$1.00 equals
31.99 Taiwan dollars (NT$).

Old Age, Disability, and Survivors

Regulatory Framework

First law: 1950.

Current law: 1958 (labor insurance), implemented in 1960, with 1988, 1994, 2000, 2001, and 2003 amendments.

Type of program: Social insurance system. Lump-sum benefits only.

Coverage

Employees between ages 15 and 60 in firms in industry and commerce, mines, and plantations with five or more workers; wage-earning public-sector employees; public-utility employees; fishermen; and some self-employed persons in service occupations.

Voluntary coverage for employees in firms with fewer than five workers, the self-employed (except for those in service occupations with compulsory coverage), employees older than age 60 working in covered employment, and persons involuntarily unemployed with 15 years of coverage.

Special systems for civil servants, farmers, salaried public-sector employees, and the staff of private schools.

Source of Funds

Insured person: 1.1% of gross monthly earnings.

The maximum monthly earnings for contribution and benefit purposes are NT$43,900. (The monthly earnings for contribution purposes are adjusted according to changes in the minimum wage.)

The insured's contributions also finance cash sickness and maternity benefits.

Self-employed person: 3.3% of gross monthly income.

The maximum monthly earnings for contribution and benefit purposes are NT$43,900. (The monthly earnings for contribution purposes are adjusted according to changes in the minimum wage.)

The self-employed person's contributions also finance cash sickness and maternity benefits.

Employer: 3.85% of monthly payroll.

The maximum monthly earnings for contribution and benefit purposes are NT$43,900. (The monthly earnings for contribution purposes are adjusted according to changes in the minimum wage.)

The employer's contributions also finance cash sickness and maternity benefits.

Government: 0.55% of employee wages (self-employed, 2.2% of income) and the cost of administration.

The maximum monthly earnings for contribution and benefit purposes are NT$43,900. (The monthly earnings for contribution purposes are adjusted according to changes in the minimum wage.)

Government contributions also finance cash sickness and maternity benefits.

Qualifying Conditions

Old-age grant: Age 60 (men) or age 55 (women) with at least 1 year of coverage. Retirement from covered employment or self-employment is necessary.

Age 55 for miners with at least 5 years of coverage.

Early old-age grant: Age 55 (men) with 15 years of coverage; age 50 with 25 years of coverage (men and women); at any age with 25 years of coverage working for the same company (men and women).

Deferred old-age grant: The grant may be deferred until age 65.

Disability grant: Must be assessed with a permanent total or partial incapacity for work and have paid at least one contribution. The insured must be assessed as permanently disabled by a hospital designated by the Bureau of National Health Insurance.

Survivor grant: The deceased must have paid at least one contribution.

Eligible survivors (in order of priority) are the spouse and children, parents, grandparents, dependent grandchildren, and brothers and sisters.

Funeral grant: Paid to survivors eligible for the survivor grant. If there are no eligible survivors, the grant is paid to the person who organizes the funeral.

Old-Age Benefits

Old-age grant: A lump sum is paid equal to 1 month of the insured's average covered earnings in the 36 months before retirement for each year of contributions for the first 15 years, plus 2 months of the insured's average covered earnings in the 36 months before retirement for each year of contributions exceeding 15 years.

The maximum grant is equal to 45 months of the insured's average covered earnings in the 36 months before retirement.

Early old-age grant: A lump sum is paid equal to 1 month of the insured's average covered earnings in the 36 months before retirement for each year of contributions for the first 15 years, plus 2 months of the insured's average covered earnings in the 36 months before retirement for each year of contributions exceeding 15 years.

Deferred old-age grant: An increment of 1 month of the insured's average covered earnings in the 36 months before retirement is paid for each year of continued work and contributions after age 60, up to a maximum of 5 months' earnings.

Permanent Disability Benefits

Disability grant: If the insured is assessed as totally disabled, a lump sum is paid equal to 40 months of the insured's average covered earnings in the 6 months before the disability began.

Partial disability: A lump sum is paid from 1 to 33.3 months of the insured's average covered earnings in the 6 months before the onset of disability, according to the assessed degree of disability.

Survivor Benefits

Survivor grant: A lump sum is paid equal to 30 months of the deceased's average covered earnings in the 6 months before death; 20 months' average earnings is paid if the deceased had less than 2 years but more than 1 year of contributions; 10 months' average earnings if less than a year of contributions.

Funeral grant: A lump sum is paid equal to 5 months of the deceased's average covered earnings in the 6 months before death.

Administrative Organization

Labor Insurance Department of the Council of Labor Affairs (http://www.cla.gov.tw) provides general supervision.

Under the direction of the tripartite Labor Insurance Commission and its director general, the Bureau of Labor Insurance (http://www.bli.gov.tw) collects contributions and pays benefits.

Sickness and Maternity

Regulatory Framework

First law: 1950.

Current laws: 1958 (labor insurance), implemented in 1960, with 1988 amendment; and 1994 (national health insurance), implemented in 1995.

Type of program: Social insurance system.

Coverage

Cash sickness and maternity benefits: Employees between ages 15 and 60 in firms in industry and commerce, mines, and plantations with five or more workers; wage-earning public-sector employees; public-utility employees;

fishermen; and some self-employed persons in service occupations.

Voluntary coverage for employees in firms with fewer than five workers, the self-employed (except for those in service occupations with compulsory coverage), employees older than age 60 in covered employment, and persons involuntarily unemployed with 15 years of coverage.

Special systems for cash benefits for civil servants, farmers, salaried public-sector employees, and the staff of private schools.

Medical benefits: Must have resided in Taiwan for at least 4 months, including foreign nationals with a resident permit.

Source of Funds

Insured person

Cash sickness and maternity benefits: See source of funds under Old Age, Disability, and Survivors, above.

Medical benefits: Contribution rates vary according to 47 wage classes. Employees of public or private companies contribute 1.365% of gross monthly earnings, plus an additional 1.365% of gross monthly earnings for each dependent up to 4.095% of monthly earnings for three or more dependents.

The minimum monthly earnings for contribution purposes for medical benefits are NT$15,840 (equal to the minimum monthly wage).

The maximum monthly earnings for contribution purposes for medical benefits are NT$131,700.

The monthly earnings for contribution purposes are adjusted according to changes in the minimum wage.

Self-employed person

Cash sickness and maternity benefits: See source of funds under Old Age, Disability, and Survivors, above.

Medical benefits: Contribution rates vary according to 47 wage classes: 4.55% of gross monthly income for higher earners or 2.73% of income for lower earners, plus an additional 2.73% of gross monthly income for each dependent up to a maximum of 8.19% of monthly income for three or more dependents.

The minimum monthly earnings for contribution purposes for medical benefits are NT$15,840 (equal to the minimum monthly wage).

The maximum monthly earnings for contribution purposes for medical benefits are NT$131,700.

The monthly earnings for contribution purposes are adjusted according to changes in the minimum wage.

Employer

Cash benefits for sickness and maternity: See source of funds under Old Age, Disability, and Survivors, above.

Medical benefits: Contribution rates vary according to 47 wage classes: 3.185% of monthly payroll for employees of public or private firms, plus an additional 2.482% of monthly payroll for dependents, regardless of number.

The employer's contributions also finance work injury medical benefits.

The minimum monthly earnings for contribution purposes for medical benefits are NT$15,840 (equal to the minimum monthly wage).

The maximum monthly earnings for contribution purposes for medical benefits are NT$131,700.

The monthly earnings for contribution purposes are adjusted according to changes in the minimum wage.

Government

Cash benefits for sickness and maternity: See source of funds under Old Age, Disability, and Survivors, above.

Medical benefits: Contribution rates vary according to 47 wage classes: 0.455% of employee wages for employees of public and private firms, none for higher-earning self-employed, 1.82% of income for lower-earning self-employed. The average contribution of all insured persons for the dependents of military personnel and the heads of low-income families, plus any deficit. Contributes for the dependents of insured persons. Pays for the cost of administration.

Government contributions also finance work injury medical benefits.

The minimum monthly earnings for contribution purposes for medical benefits are NT$15,840 (equal to the minimum monthly wage).

The maximum monthly earnings for contribution purposes for medical benefits are NT$131,700.

The monthly earnings for contribution purposes are adjusted according to changes in the minimum wage.

Qualifying Conditions

Cash sickness benefit: The incapacity must be due to a nonwork-related injury or illness. There is no specified minimum qualifying period. The insured must provide medical certification.

Cash maternity grant: Must have 280 days of contributions before childbirth (181 days of contributions for a premature childbirth; 84 days of contributions in the event of a miscarriage).

Lump-sum supplement: Payable to an insured woman or an insured man for his spouse to help meet the costs associated with childbirth.

Medical benefits: Provided for a nonwork-related injury or illness.

Sickness and Maternity Benefits

Sickness benefit: The benefit is equal to 50% of the insured's average covered earnings in the 6 months before the incapacity began. The benefit is payable after a 3-day waiting period for up to 12 months; 6 months with less than 1 year of contributions.

Maternity grant: A lump sum is paid equal to 1 month of the insured's average covered earnings in the last 6 months before maternity leave for a normal or premature childbirth. Benefits are increased for multiple births.

Lump-sum supplement: A supplement is paid equal to 1 month of the insured's average covered earnings in the last 6 months for a normal or premature childbirth; 50% of this amount in the case of a miscarriage. Benefits are increased for multiple births.

Workers' Medical Benefits

Medical care is provided by private and public clinics and hospitals under contract with, and paid directly by, the Bureau of National Health Insurance. Benefits include preventive and prenatal care, inpatient and outpatient hospital treatment, surgery, and medicines.

There is no limit to duration.

The government provides free maternity medical care.

Cost sharing: For ambulatory and emergency care at clinics, 20% of scheduled fees; between 30% and 50% for hospital visits (according to the type of hospital and if without a doctor's referral); for inpatient care for short-term illnesses, from 10% of the cost for the first 30 days up to 30% from the 61st day and thereafter, depending on the duration of hospitalization; for inpatient care for chronic long-term illnesses, from 5% for the first 30 days up to 30% from the 181st day.

Exemption from cost sharing: Preventive health care, certain specific catastrophic illnesses, ambulatory services in mountainous areas and remote islands, and for all care for members of veteran or low-income households.

Dependents' Medical Benefits

Medical care is provided by private and public clinics and hospitals under contract with, and paid directly by, the Bureau of National Health Insurance. Benefits include preventive and prenatal care, inpatient and outpatient hospital treatment, surgery, and medicines.

There is no limit to duration.

The government provides free maternity medical care.

Cost sharing: For ambulatory and emergency care at clinics, 20% of scheduled fees; between 30% and 50% for hospital visits (according to the type of hospital and if without a doctor's referral); for inpatient care for short-term illnesses, from 10% of the cost for the first 30 days up to 30% from the 61st day and thereafter, depending on the duration of hospitalization; for inpatient care for chronic long-term illnesses, from 5% for the first 30 days up to 30% from the 181st day.

Exemption from cost sharing: Preventive health care, certain specific catastrophic illnesses, ambulatory services in mountainous areas and remote islands, and for all care for members of veteran or low-income households.

Eligible dependents include a nonemployed spouse, nonemployed parents or grandparents, and nonemployed children and grandchildren younger than age 20 (no limit if disabled). For low-income households, all relatives living with the insured.

Administrative Organization

Cash sickness and maternity benefits: Labor Insurance Department of the Council of Labor Affairs (http://www.cla.gov.tw) provides general supervision.

Under the direction of the tripartite Labor Insurance Commission and its director general, the Bureau of Labor Insurance (http://www.bli.gov.tw) collects contributions and pays benefits.

Medical benefits: Under the direction of a Supervisory Board, the Bureau of National Health Insurance (http://www.nhi.gov.tw) collects contributions and contracts with private and public clinics and hospitals to provide medical care.

Work Injury

Regulatory Framework

First laws: 1929 and 1950.

Current laws: 1958 (labor insurance), implemented in 1960, with 1988, 1994, 2000, and 2001 amendments; and 2001 (work injury), implemented in 2002.

Type of program: Social insurance system.

Coverage

Employees between ages 15 and 60 in firms in industry and commerce, mines, and plantations with five or more workers; wage-earning public-sector employees; public-utility employees; fishermen; and some self-employed persons in service occupations.

Special systems for civil servants, salaried public-sector employees, and the staff of private schools.

Source of Funds

Insured person: None.

Self-employed person: None.

Employer

Cash benefits: 0.06% to 3% of monthly payroll, according to the assessed risk of the industry. The average rate is 0.27%. The contribution rate for employers with more than 70 employees is adjusted annually according to the claims rate of the company.

Medical benefits: See source of funds under Sickness and Maternity, above.

Government

Cash benefits: The cost of administration.

Medical benefits: See source of funds under Sickness and Maternity, above.

Qualifying Conditions

Work injury benefits: There is no minimum qualifying period.

Temporary Disability Benefits

70% of the insured's average covered earnings in the last 6 months before the disability began is paid for the first 12 months; thereafter, 50% of earnings. The benefit is payable after a 3-day waiting period for up to 24 months.

Permanent Disability Benefits

Permanent disability benefit: The worker must be assessed as permanently disabled by a hospital designated by the Bureau of National Health Insurance.

If totally disabled (Group 1), a lump sum is paid equal to 60 months of the insured's average covered earnings in the last 6 months before the disability began.

Constant-attendance allowance: NT$8,000 is paid a month if assessed as totally disabled and in need of constant medical care, supervision, or help to complete daily tasks.

Partial disability: A lump sum is paid equal to between 1.5 and 50 months of the insured's average covered earnings in the last 6 months before the disability began, according to the assessed degree of disability (Groups 2 to 15).

Living allowance: After receiving the lump-sum benefit, a monthly allowance of between NT$1,000 and NT$6,000 is paid to insured persons with a partial or total permanent disability, according to the assessed degree of disability (Groups 1 to 15).

Workers' Medical Benefits

Medical care is provided by private and public clinics and hospitals under contract with, and paid directly by, the National Health Insurance Bureau. Benefits include inpatient and outpatient hospital treatment, surgery, and medicines.

There is no limit to duration.

Survivor Benefits

Survivor benefit: A lump sum is paid equal to 40 months of the deceased's average covered earnings in the 6 months before death.

Eligible survivors (in order of priority) are the spouse and children, parents, grandparents, dependent grandchildren, and brothers and sisters.

Survivor grant (income-tested): A lump sum of NT$10,000 may be paid to the dependent spouse, children, and parents.

Funeral grant: A lump sum equal to 5 months of the deceased's average covered earnings in the 6 months before death is paid to eligible survivors. If there are no eligible survivors, the grant is paid to the person who organizes the funeral.

Administrative Organization

Labor Insurance Department of the Council of Labor Affairs (http://www.cla.gov.tw) provides general supervision.

Under the direction of the tripartite Labor Insurance Commission and its director general, the Bureau of Labor Insurance (http://www.bli.gov.tw) collects contributions and pays cash benefits.

Under the direction of a supervisory board, the Bureau of National Health Insurance (http://www.nhi.gov.tw) contracts with private and public clinics and hospitals to provide medical care.

Unemployment

Regulatory Framework

First law: 1968, implemented in 1999, with 2000 and 2001 amendments.

Current law: 2002 (employment insurance), implemented in 2003.

Type of program: Social insurance system.

Coverage

Private- and public-sector employees between ages 15 and 60.

Exclusions: Self-employed persons, civil servants, teachers, and military personnel.

Source of Funds

Insured person: 0.2% of gross monthly earnings.

Self-employed person: Not applicable.

Employer: 0.7% of monthly payroll.

Government: 0.1% of employee wages and the cost of administration.

Qualifying Conditions

Unemployment benefit: The insured must have at least 1 year of coverage; unemployment must be involuntary; must be currently registered at a public employment office as being capable of, and willing to, work; must not have declined a suitable job offer; and must not be in occupational training.

The benefit is suspended if a suitable job offer, counseling, or vocational training is refused or the beneficiary fails to report to a public employment office once a month.

Early reemployment award: Payable if the unemployed person starts work before the maximum unemployment benefit payment period has expired.

Unemployment Benefits

Unemployment benefit: The benefit is equal to 60% of average monthly earnings in the 6 months before unemployment. The benefit is payable after a 14-day waiting period for up to 6 months; for up to 3 months for a new claim within 2 years of last receiving unemployment benefits for 6 months.

Early reemployment award: A lump sum is paid equal to 50% of the total unpaid benefit that would have been payable for the maximum duration of benefit.

Administrative Organization

Labor Insurance Department of the Council of Labor Affairs (http://www.cla.gov.tw) provides general supervision.

Under the direction of the tripartite Labor Insurance Commission and its director general, the Bureau of Labor Insurance (http://www.bli.gov.tw) collects contributions and pays benefits.

Thailand

Exchange rate: US$1.00 equals 38.15 baht.

Old Age, Disability, and Survivors

Regulatory Framework

First and current law: 1990 (social security), implemented in 1991 and 1998, with 1994 and 1999 amendments.

Type of program: Social insurance system.

Coverage

Employees aged 15 to 60.

Voluntary coverage for self-employed persons and for persons who cease to be covered after having compulsory coverage for at least 12 months.

Exclusions: Judges; employees of foreign governments or international organizations; employees of state enterprises; agricultural, forestry, and fishery employees; temporary and seasonal workers; and Thais working abroad.

Special systems for judges, civil servants, employees of state enterprises, and employees of private schools.

Source of Funds

Insured person: 3% of gross monthly earnings for old-age and family benefits. Disability and survivor benefits are financed under Sickness and Maternity, below.

Voluntary contributions are paid on the first 4,800 baht of earnings. Voluntary contributions finance old-age, disability, and survivor benefits; sickness and maternity benefits; and family benefits.

The minimum monthly earnings for contribution and benefit purposes are 1,650 baht.

The maximum monthly earnings for contribution and benefit purposes are 15,000 baht.

Self-employed person: A voluntary flat-rate annual contribution of 3,360 baht.

The self-employed person's contributions finance disability, survivor, and maternity benefits.

Employer: 3% of monthly payroll for old-age and family benefits. Disability and survivor benefits are financed under Sickness and Maternity, below.

The minimum monthly earnings for contribution and benefit purposes are 1,650 baht.

The maximum monthly earnings for contribution and benefit purposes are 15,000 baht.

Government: 1% of gross monthly earnings for old-age and family benefits only. Disability and survivor benefits are financed under Sickness and Maternity, below.

The minimum monthly earnings for contribution and benefit purposes are 1,650 baht.

The maximum monthly earnings for contribution and benefit purposes are 15,000 baht.

Qualifying Conditions

Old-age pension: Age 55 with 180 months of contributions. Employment must cease. If a pensioner starts a new job, the pension is suspended until the end of employment.

Deferred pension: A deferred pension is possible.

Old-age settlement: Age 55 with at least 1 month but less than 180 months of contributions. Employment must cease.

Disability pension: Must have at least 3 months of contributions in the 15 months before the onset of a total physical or mental disability and be incapable of work. The benefit is paid after entitlement to the cash sickness benefit ceases.

Medical officers assigned by the Social Security Office assess the degree of disability annually. The benefit may be suspended if the medical committee of the Social Security Office determines that the disability pensioner is rehabilitated.

Survivor benefit: A lump sum is paid if a pensioner dies within 60 months after becoming entitled to the old-age pension.

The lump sum is split among the surviving spouse, legitimate children, and a surviving father or mother, according to the number and category of survivor.

Death benefit: Paid if the deceased had at least 1 month of contributions in the 6 months before death or was a disability pensioner. The death must be the result of a nonoccupational injury or illness.

The eligible survivor is the deceased's named beneficiary; in the absence of a named beneficiary, the benefit is split equally among the surviving spouse, children, and parents.

Funeral grant: Paid if the deceased had at least 1 month of contributions in the 6 months before death or was a disability pensioner. The death must be the result of a nonoccupational injury or illness.

Old-Age Benefits

Old-age pension: The pension is equal to 15% of the insured's average monthly wage in the last 60 months before retirement.

Old-age pension increment: If the insured has paid contributions exceeding 180 months when reaching the pensionable age, the benefit is increased by 1% of the insured's average monthly wage in the last 60 months for each 12-month period of contributions exceeding 180 months.

There is no minimum pension.

Deferred pension: If the insured has paid contributions exceeding 180 months at the time the pension is first received, the benefit is increased by 1% of the insured's average monthly wage in the last 60 months for each 12-month period of contributions exceeding 180 months.

Permanent Disability Benefits

Disability pension: 50% of the insured's average daily wage in the highest paid 3 months during the 9 months before the onset of disability is paid until death.

There is no minimum pension.

Benefit adjustment: Benefits are adjusted on an ad hoc basis according to changes in the cost of living.

Survivor Benefits

Survivor benefit: A lump sum is paid equal to 10 times the deceased's monthly old-age pension.

Death benefit: If the deceased paid contributions for more than 36 months but less than 10 years, a lump sum is paid equal to 50% of the insured's average monthly wage in the highest paid 3 months during the 9 months before death multiplied by 3. If the deceased paid contributions for 10 or more years, a lump sum is paid equal to 50% of the insured's average monthly wage in the highest paid 3 months during the 9 months before death multiplied by 10.

Funeral grant: 30,000 baht is paid to the person who paid for the funeral.

Administrative Organization

Ministry of Labor (http://www.mol.go.th) provides general supervision.

Social Security Office collects contributions and pays benefits.

Sickness and Maternity

Regulatory Framework

First and current laws: 1990 (social security), implemented in 1991 and 1998, with 1994 and 1999 amendments; and 1990 (sickness and medical benefits).

Type of program: Social insurance system.

Coverage

Employees aged 15 to 60.

Voluntary coverage for self-employed persons and for persons who cease to be covered after having compulsory coverage for at least 12 months.

Exclusions: Judges; employees of foreign governments or international organizations; employees of state enterprises; agricultural, forestry, and fishery employees; temporary and seasonal workers; and Thais working abroad.

Special systems for judges, civil servants, employees of state enterprises, and employees of private schools.

Source of Funds

Insured person: 1.5% of gross monthly earnings (1.06% finances sickness and maternity benefits; 0.44% finances disability and survivor benefits). For voluntary contributors, see source of funds under Old Age, Disability, and Survivors, above.

The minimum monthly earnings for contribution and benefit purposes are 1,650 baht.

The maximum monthly earnings for contribution and benefit purposes are 15,000 baht.

Self-employed person: See source of funds under Old Age, Disability, and Survivors, above.

Employer: 1.5% of monthly payroll (1.06% finances sickness and maternity benefits; 0.44% finances disability and survivor benefits).

The minimum monthly earnings for contribution and benefit purposes are 1,650 baht.

The maximum monthly earnings for contribution and benefit purposes are 15,000 baht.

Government: 1.5% of gross monthly earnings (1.06% finances sickness and maternity benefits; 0.44% finances disability and survivor benefits).

The minimum monthly earnings for contribution and benefit purposes are 1,650 baht.

The maximum monthly earnings for contribution and benefit purposes are 15,000 baht.

Qualifying Conditions

Cash sickness and medical benefits: Must have at least 3 months of contributions in the 15 months before the onset of incapacity or the date of treatment.

The insured must provide medical certification.

Cash maternity, childbirth grant, and medical benefits: Must have at least 7 months of contributions in the 15 months before the expected date of childbirth.

Cash maternity benefits are paid to an insured woman. The childbirth grant is paid to an insured woman or to the wife of, or a woman who cohabits with, an insured man. The childbirth grant is paid to cover the cost of medical expenses related to childbirth.

Maternity benefits are paid for two childbirths only.

Sickness and Maternity Benefits

Sickness benefit: The benefit is equal to 50% of the insured's average daily wage in the highest paid 3 months during the 9 months before the incapacity began. The benefit is paid from the first day of certified absence from work (after the end of entitlement to statutory sick pay, usually 30 days, under the labor law) for up to 90 days for each illness and for up to 180 days in any calendar year; may be extended up to 365 days for a chronic condition.

There is no minimum benefit.

Maternity benefit: The benefit is equal to 50% of the insured's average daily wage in the highest paid 3 months during the 9 months before maternity leave and is paid for up to 90 days for each childbirth.

There is no minimum benefit.

Childbirth grant: A lump sum of 6,000 baht is paid.

Workers' Medical Benefits

Medical examination and treatment, hospitalization, medicines, ambulance fees, rehabilitation, and other necessary expenses are provided under the capitation system.

The insured must register with a hospital that is under contract, and benefits are delivered by the hospital with which the insured is registered. Medical care outside this hospital can be sought in case of emergency and accident only, in which case costs are reimbursed according to fixed rates.

There are no provisions for cost sharing.

Disability pensioners are entitled to receive subsidized medical care and rehabilitation.

Dependents' Medical Benefits

Necessary medical care related to childbirth for the wife of, or a woman who cohabits with, an insured man.

Administrative Organization

Ministry of Labor (http://www.mol.go.th) provides general supervision.

Social Security Office collects contributions and pays cash benefits.

Medical benefits are delivered by hospitals under contract to the Social Security Office.

Work Injury

Regulatory Framework

First law: 1972 (announcement of the revolutionary party), implemented in 1974.

Current law: 1994 (workmen's compensation).

Type of program: Employer-liability system, involving compulsory insurance with a public carrier.

Coverage

Employees of industrial and commercial firms.

Exclusions: Agricultural, forestry, and fishery employees; employees of state enterprises; employees of private schools; and government employees.

Special systems for government employees, employees of state enterprises, and employees of private schools.

Source of Funds

Insured person: None.

Self-employed person: Not applicable.

Employer: 0.2% to 1% of annual payroll, according to the degree of risk.

The contribution is made annually. Beginning with the 5th year of contributions, the company's accident rate is taken into account when assessing the degree of risk.

There are no minimum earnings for contribution and benefit purposes.

The maximum annual earnings for contribution and benefit purposes are 240,000 baht.

Government: None.

Qualifying Conditions

Work injury benefits: There is no minimum qualifying period.

Temporary Disability Benefits

The benefit is equal to 60% of the insured's monthly wage before the onset of disability, according to the schedule in law. The benefit is payable after a 3-day waiting period for a maximum of 1 year; the benefit is paid retroactively if the incapacity lasts more than 3 days. The insured must be unable to work.

The minimum monthly benefit is 60% of minimum daily wage multiplied by 26 and must not exceed 60% of monthly average wage. In 2006, the minimum monthly benefit is 2,184 baht.

The maximum monthly benefit is 12,000 baht.

Permanent Disability Benefits

For a total disability, the pension is equal to 60% of the insured's monthly wage before the onset of disability and is payable for a maximum of 15 years. Permanent disability benefits are paid according to the schedule in law.

The minimum monthly benefit is 60% of the minimum daily wage multiplied by 26 and must not exceed 60% of the average monthly wage. In 2006, the minimum monthly benefit is 2,184 baht.

The maximum monthly benefit is 12,000 baht.

Permanent partial disability benefit: The pension is equal to 60% of the insured's monthly wage before the onset of disability. The benefit is payable for a minimum of 2 months up to a maximum of 10 years, according to the schedule in law. In certain cases, the benefit may be paid as a lump sum.

The minimum monthly benefit is 60% of the minimum daily wage multiplied by 26 and must not exceed 60% of the average monthly wage. In 2006, the minimum monthly benefit is 2,184 baht.

The maximum monthly benefit is 12,000 baht.

The degree of disability is assessed annually by medical officers assigned by the Social Security Office.

Benefit adjustment: Benefits are adjusted on an ad hoc basis.

Workers' Medical Benefits

All necessary medical, surgical, and hospital services.

A maximum limit on the cost of medical benefits is set at 35,000 baht for each incident of work injury or occupational disease; up to 200,000 baht in certain specified cases, depending on the decision of the medical committee of the Office of Workmen's Compensation Fund.

Rehabilitation services are provided up to a maximum cost of 20,000 baht.

Survivor Benefits

Survivor benefit: The pension is equal to 60% of the deceased's last monthly wage and is payable for up to 8 years. (A reduced benefit may be paid as a lump sum.)

Eligible survivors include parents, the spouse, and children younger than age 18 (no limit if a student or disabled). The pension is split equally among all eligible survivors. In the absence of eligible survivors, any other dependent persons may be entitled.

The minimum monthly benefit is 60% of the minimum daily wage multiplied by 26 and must not exceed 60% of the average monthly wage. In 2006, the minimum monthly benefit is 2,184 baht.

The maximum monthly benefit is 12,000 baht.

Benefit adjustment: Benefits are adjusted on an ad hoc basis.

Funeral grant: A lump sum is paid equal to 100 times the highest minimum daily wage. The benefit is paid to the person who paid for the funeral.

Administrative Organization

Ministry of Labor (http://www.mol.go.th) provides general supervision.

Social Security Office administers the program through the Office of Workmen's Compensation Fund, which collects contributions and pays cash benefits.

Medical benefits are provided by hospitals under contract to the Social Security Office and meeting the standards of the Office of Workmen's Compensation Fund.

Unemployment

Regulatory Framework

First and current law: 1990 (social security), implemented in 2004.

Type of program: Social insurance system.

Coverage

Employees aged 15 to 60.

There is no voluntary coverage.

Exclusions: Judges; employees of foreign governments or international organizations; employees of state enterprises; agricultural, forestry, and fishery employees; temporary and seasonal workers; and Thais working abroad.

Source of Funds

Insured person: 0.5% of gross monthly earnings.

The minimum monthly earnings for contribution and benefit purposes are 1,650 baht.

The maximum monthly earnings for contribution and benefit purposes are 15,000 baht.

Self-employed person: Not applicable.

Employer: 0.5% of monthly payroll.

The minimum monthly earnings for contribution and benefit purposes are 1,650 baht.

The maximum monthly earnings for contribution and benefit purposes are 15,000 baht.

Government: 0.25% of gross monthly earnings.

The minimum monthly earnings for contribution and benefit purposes are 1,650 baht.

The maximum monthly earnings for contribution and benefit purposes are 15,000 baht.

Qualifying Conditions

Unemployment benefit: Must have at least 6 months of contributions in the 15 months before unemployment.

Must be registered with the Government Employment Service Office, be ready and able to accept any suitable job offer, and report not less than once a month to the Government Employment Service. Unemployment must not be due to performing duties dishonestly; intentionally committing a criminal offense against the employer; seriously violating work regulations, rules, or lawful order of the employer; neglecting duty for 7 consecutive days without reasonable cause; or causing serious damage to the workplace as a result of personal negligence.

The Social Security Office may suspend benefit payments for failure to comply with conditions.

Unemployment Benefits

If involuntarily unemployed, the benefit is equal to 50% of the insured's average daily wage in the highest paid 3 months during the 9 months before unemployment and is paid for up to 180 days in any 1 year; if voluntarily unemployed, the benefit is equal to 30% of the insured's average daily wage and is paid for up to 90 days in any 1 year.

The benefit is payable from the 8th day of unemployment.

The maximum daily benefit is 250 baht.

Administrative Organization

Ministry of Labor (http://www.mol.go.th) provides general supervision.

Social Security Office collects contributions and pays benefits.

Department of Employment (http://www.doe.go.th), subordinate to the Ministry of Labor (http://www.mol.go.th), registers the unemployed insured person for job placement and training through the Government Employment Service Office.

Family Allowances

Regulatory Framework

First and current law: 1990 (social security), implemented in 1998, with 1994 and 1999 amendments.

Type of program: Social insurance system.

Coverage

Employees aged 15 to 60.

Voluntary coverage for persons who cease to be covered after having compulsory coverage for at least 12 months.

Exclusions: Judges; employees of foreign governments or international organizations; employees of state enterprises; agricultural, forestry, and fishery employees; temporary and seasonal workers; and Thais working abroad.

Special systems for judges, civil servants, employees of state enterprises, and employees of private schools.

Source of Funds

Insured person: See source of funds under Old Age, Disability, and Survivors, above.

Self-employed person: Not applicable.

Employer: See source of funds under Old Age, Disability, and Survivors, above.

Government: See source of funds under Old Age, Disability, and Survivors, above.

Qualifying Conditions

Child allowance: Must have at least 12 months of contributions in the 36 months before the month of entitlement.

The benefit is payable for legitimate children younger than age 6 but for no more than two children at a time. If the insured becomes disabled or dies while the child is younger than age 6, the allowance is paid until the child is age 6.

Family Allowance Benefits

Child allowance: A monthly allowance of 350 baht is paid for each child.

Administrative Organization

Ministry of Labor (http://www.mol.go.th) provides general supervision.

Social Security Office collects contributions and pays benefits.

Turkey

Exchange rate: US$1.00 equals 1,345,000 liras.

Old Age, Disability, and Survivors

Regulatory Framework

First laws: 1949 (old age) and 1957 (old age, disability, and survivors).

Current laws: 1964 (social insurance), implemented in 1965, with 1999 amendment; and 1983 (agricultural employee social insurance), implemented in 1984, with 1999 amendment.

Type of program: Social insurance system.

Coverage

Employees (including foreign nationals) aged 18 or older working under a service contract in the public or private sector.

Special systems for civil servants; self-employed persons; farmers; some categories of agricultural worker; and bank, insurance company, and stock exchange employees.

Source of Funds

Insured person: 9% of monthly earnings.

The minimum monthly earnings for contribution and benefit purposes are 444,150,000 liras.

The maximum monthly earnings for contribution and benefit purposes are 2,886,975,000 liras (6.5 times minimum earnings).

Self-employed person: Not applicable.

Employer: 11% of monthly payroll; 13% on behalf of employees in arduous employment.

The minimum monthly earnings for contribution and benefit purposes are 444,150,000 liras.

The maximum monthly earnings for contribution and benefit purposes are 2,886,975,000 liras (6.5 times minimum earnings).

Government: None.

Qualifying Conditions

Old-age pension: If first insured on or after September 8, 1999, age 60 (men) or age 58 (women) with 7,000 days of contributions or 25 years of insurance coverage with 4,500 days of contributions.

If first insured before September 8, 1999, special conditions apply.

Miners younger than age 50 who have worked underground on a full-time basis for at least 20 years and who have at least 5,000 days of paid contributions (worked underground on a part-time basis for at least 25 years and have at least 4,000 days of contributions) can ask to receive the old-age pension; miners aged 50 or older who have a minimum of 1,800 days of insured employment are subject to other conditions.

Aged 50 or older and prematurely aged (and therefore unable to work until the full pensionable age), subject to other conditions.

An insured person of any age whose disability began before starting insured employment and who has at least 15 years of insurance coverage including at least 3,600 days of paid contributions, subject to the assessed degree of disability.

Gainful employment must cease on retirement. (In certain cases, employment may be permitted while receiving the old-age pension. In such cases, a social security support contribution of 30% of earnings must be paid.)

Deferred pension: There is no maximum age for deferral.

Old-age settlement: Age 60 (men) or age 58 (women); age 50 (men and women), prematurely aged, and not eligible for a pension.

The old-age pension and the old-age settlement may be partially payable abroad under reciprocal agreement.

Disability pension: The loss of 2/3 of working capacity with at least 1,800 days of contributions or insured for at least 5 years with an average of 180 days of paid contributions for each year of insurance.

The disability pension may be partially payable abroad under reciprocal agreement.

Survivor pension: The deceased met the contribution requirements for a disability pension or an old-age pension or was a pensioner at the time of death; was insured for at least 5 years and had paid contributions for an average of at least 180 days each year or for a total of 1,800 days.

Eligible dependents include a spouse (the spouse's pension ceases on remarriage); children younger than age 18 (age 20 if in pre-university education, age 25 if in university); a son aged 18 or older who is disabled and unemployed; an unmarried, widowed, or divorced daughter of any age who is without insured employment and is not receiving any social security benefits in her own right; and dependent parents.

Survivor settlement: The insured person was not eligible for a pension.

The survivor pension and survivor settlement may be partially payable abroad under bilateral agreement.

Funeral grant: Paid to the family on the death of an old-age pensioner or disability pensioner.

Old-Age Benefits

Old-age pension: If first insured on or after January 1, 2000, the pension is calculated on the basis of 3.5% of the insured's average annual earnings for each 360-day period of contributions up to 3,600 days, 2% for each 360-day period of the next 5,400 days, and 1.5% for each additional 360-day period.

If first insured before January 1, 2000, special conditions apply.

The maximum monthly pension is 878,682,251 liras.

Deferred pension: Calculated in the same was as the old-age pension.

Benefit adjustment: Benefits are adjusted periodically according to changes in the monthly consumer price index.

Old-age settlement: If the insured is not eligible for a pension, a lump sum is paid equal to total employee and employer contributions.

Permanent Disability Benefits

Disability pension: If first insured on or after January 1, 2000, the pension is equal to 60% of the insured's average annual earnings during the years before the disability began.

If first insured before January 1, 2000, special conditions apply.

Constant-attendance allowance: The pension is increased to 70% of average annual earnings.

Benefit adjustment: Benefits are adjusted periodically according to changes in the monthly consumer price index.

Survivor Benefits

Survivor pension: If the deceased was first insured on or after January 1, 2000, the pension is calculated as 60% of the insured's average monthly earnings, plus 2% for each 360-day period of contributions beyond 8,100 days but not more than 9,000 days, plus 1.5% for each 360-day period of contributions beyond 9,000 days.

If the deceased was first insured before January 1, 2000, special conditions apply.

Eligible survivors include the spouse, orphans, and the deceased's parents.

The minimum pension for one survivor is 335,035,956 liras; 365,571,678 liras for two survivors.

Survivor settlement: If the deceased was not eligible for a pension, a lump sum equal to total employee and employer contributions is split among survivors according to prescribed ratios.

Eligible survivors include the spouse, orphans, and the deceased's parents.

Funeral grant: A lump sum of 182,100,000 liras is paid.

Benefit adjustment: Benefits are adjusted periodically according to changes in the monthly consumer price index.

Administrative Organization

Ministry of Labor and Social Security (http://www.calisma.gov.tr) provides general supervision.

Social Insurance Institution (http://www.ssk.gov.tr), managed by a general assembly, board of directors, and president, administers the program.

Sickness and Maternity

Regulatory Framework

First laws: 1945 (maternity) and 1950 (sickness).

Current laws: 1964 (social insurance), implemented in 1965, with 1999 amendment; and 1983 (agricultural employee social insurance), implemented in 1984, with 1999 amendment.

Type of program: Social insurance system. Cash and medical benefits.

Coverage

Cash and medical benefits: Employees working under a service contract in the public and private sectors and their dependent family members. (Cash maternity benefits are provided only to an insured woman.)

Medical benefits only: Pensioners and their dependents are covered for medical benefits.

Special systems for civil servants, self-employed persons, and some categories of agricultural worker.

Source of Funds

Insured person: 5% of monthly earnings (sickness).

The minimum monthly earnings for contribution and benefit purposes are 444,150,000 liras.

The maximum monthly earnings for contribution and benefit purposes are 2,886,975,000 liras (6.5 times minimum earnings).

Self-employed person: Not applicable.

Employer: 1% of payroll (maternity).

The minimum monthly earnings for contribution and benefit purposes are 444,150,000 liras.

The maximum monthly earnings for contribution and benefit purposes are 2,886,975,000 liras (6.5 times minimum earnings).

Government: None; except contributions for sickness benefits for applicants for apprenticeships, apprentices, and students in technical schools.

Qualifying Conditions

Cash sickness benefits: Must have 120 days of contributions in the year before the diagnosis of illness.

Cash maternity benefits: Must have 120 days of contributions.

Medical benefits: For the insured person, 90 days of contributions in the year before the date of the first diagnosis of illness. For the insured's dependents, the insured must have 120 days of contributions in the year before the date of the first diagnosis of illness.

Eligible dependents include a spouse who does not work or receive any social security benefits; children younger than age 18 (age 20 if in pre-university education, age 25 if in university); a son aged 18 or older who is disabled and unemployed; an unmarried, widowed, or divorced daughter of any age who is without insured employment and is not receiving any social security benefits in her own right; and dependent parents.

Sickness and Maternity Benefits

Sickness benefit: The benefit for inpatient treatment is equal to 1/2 of daily earnings. The benefit for outpatient treatment is equal to 2/3 of daily earnings. The benefit is paid after a 2-day waiting period.

Benefit adjustment: The minimum and maximum daily insurable earnings for sickness benefit calculation purposes are adjusted according to changes in the minimum wage.

Maternity benefits

Incapacity for work: The benefit is equal to 2/3 of earnings and is paid for up to 8 weeks before and 8 weeks after the expected date of childbirth.

Pregnancy benefit: A lump sum of 50,000,000 liras is paid (subject to the certification of pregnancy before the date of birth).

Childbirth benefit: A lump sum of 56,000,000 liras is paid for a birth without complications, 116,000,000 liras for a birth by forceps, or 220,000,000 liras for a birth by caesarian section. In all cases, the Social Insurance Institution must receive certification of the birth within 3 months after the childbirth.

In cases in which medical services for pregnancy and childbirth cannot be provided directly through health facilities under contract to the Social Insurance Institution or government hospital, a fixed amount of money is provided according to the schedule in law. The fixed amount is increased for multiple births.

Nursing grant: A lump sum of 50,000,000 liras is paid for a live birth.

Benefit adjustment: The minimum and maximum daily insurable earnings for maternity benefit calculation purposes are adjusted according to changes in the minimum wage.

The Ministry of Labor and Social Security may make ad hoc adjustments to the pregnancy benefit, childbirth benefit, and nursing grant.

Workers' Medical Benefits

Medical services are usually provided directly to patients through the facilities of the Social Insurance Institution. Benefits include general and specialist care, hospitalization, laboratory services, medicines, maternity care, appliances, and transportation. Benefits are usually limited to 6 months; may be extended in special cases.

Cost sharing: The insured person pays 20% (10% for pensioners) of the cost of medicines and prostheses in outpatient treatment.

Dependents' Medical Benefits

Medical services are usually provided directly to patients through the facilities of the Social Insurance Institution. Benefits include general and specialist care, hospitalization, laboratory services, medicines, maternity care, appliances, and transportation. Benefits are usually limited to 6 months; may be extended in special cases.

Cost sharing: 20% (10% for a pensioner or the dependent of a pensioner) of the cost of medicines and prostheses in outpatient treatment.

Administrative Organization

Ministry of Labor and Social Security (http://www.calisma.gov.tr) provides general supervision.

Social Insurance Institution (http://www.ssk.gov.tr) administers the program through its branch offices. It operates its own dispensaries, hospitals, sanatoria, and pharmacies and contracts with private-sector service providers in localities where it has no facilities.

Work Injury

Regulatory Framework

First law: 1945 (industrial accidents).

Current laws: 1964 (social insurance), implemented in 1965, with 1999 amendment; and 1983 (agricultural employee social insurance), implemented in 1984, with 1999 amendment.

Type of program: Social insurance system.

Note: Work injury and occupational illness benefits are paid under Old Age, Disability, and Survivors.

Coverage

Employees working under a service contract in the public or private sector; applicants for apprenticeships, apprentices, and students; and convicted persons working in prison workshops.

Exclusions: Part-time domestic employees.

Special systems for civil servants, self-employed persons, and some categories of agricultural worker.

Source of Funds

Insured person: None.

Self-employed person: Not applicable.

Employer: Between 1.5% and 7% of payroll, according to the assessed degree of risk. The average contribution rate is 2.5% of payroll.

The minimum monthly earnings for contribution and benefit purposes are 444,150,000 liras.

The maximum monthly earnings for contribution and benefit purposes are 2,886,975,000 liras (6.5 times minimum earnings).

Government: None; except the cost of applicants for apprenticeships, apprentices, and students in technical schools.

Qualifying Conditions

Work injury benefits: There is no minimum qualifying period.

Temporary Disability Benefits

The benefit is equal to 2/3 of daily earnings; 1/2 of daily earnings if hospitalized. The benefit is paid from the first day of incapacity.

Benefit adjustment: The minimum and maximum daily insurable earnings for benefit calculation purposes are adjusted according to changes in the minimum wage.

Permanent Disability Benefits

Permanent disability pension: The pension is calculated on the basis of the insured's annual insurable earnings.

Total disability is assessed as the loss of earning capacity as a result of a work accident or an occupational disease.

Partial disability: For an assessed degree of disability of at least 10%, a percentage of the full pension is paid according to the assessed degree of disability. For an assessed degree of disability of at least 10% but less than 25%, the pension may be paid as a lump sum.

For an assessed degree of disability of at least 25%, the minimum pension must be equal to at least 70% of the lower limit of monthly earnings for contribution and benefit purposes.

There is no maximum pension.

Constant-attendance allowance: Equal to 50% of the pension.

Benefit adjustment: Benefits are adjusted according to changes in the monthly consumer price index.

Workers' Medical Benefits

Benefits include medical treatment, surgery, hospitalization, medicines, appliances, and transportation.

There is no limit to duration.

Survivor Benefits

Survivor pension: The minimum monthly pension for one survivor is at least 80% (90% for two survivors) of 35% of the lower limit of monthly earnings for contribution and benefit purposes.

There is no maximum pension.

Eligible dependents include a spouse (the spouse pension ceases on remarriage); children younger than age 18 (age 20 if in pre-university education, age 25 if in university); a son aged 18 or older who is disabled and unemployed; an unmarried, widowed, or divorced daughter of any age who is without insured employment and is not receiving any social security benefits in her own right; and dependent parents.

Dependent parents: If the total survivor pension awarded to the spouse and children is less than 70% of the insured's annual earnings, the difference is paid to a dependent father and mother; if the total survivor pension awarded to the spouse and children is 70% or more of the insured's annual earnings, no pension is paid for a dependent father and mother.

Funeral grant: A lump sum of 182,100,000 liras is paid to the family on the death of the insured worker.

Benefit adjustment: Survivor benefits are adjusted according to changes in the monthly consumer price index.

Administrative Organization

Ministry of Labor and Social Security (http://www.calisma.gov.tr) provides general supervision.

Social Insurance Institution (http://www.ssk.gov.tr) administers the program through its branch offices and health facilities.

Unemployment

Regulatory Framework

First and current law: 1999 (unemployment insurance), implemented in 2000.

Type of program: Social insurance system.

Coverage

Employees (including foreign nationals) aged 18 or older working under a service contract in the public or private sector and certain other specified groups.

Exclusions: Civil servants, workers in agriculture and forestry, domestic workers, military personnel, students, and self-employed persons.

Source of Funds

Insured person: 1% of monthly earnings.

The minimum monthly earnings for contribution and benefit purposes are 444,150,000 liras.

The maximum monthly earnings for contribution and benefit purposes are 2,886,975,000 liras (6.5 times minimum earnings).

Self-employed person: Not applicable.

Employer: 2% of monthly payroll.

Government: 1% of monthly earnings.

The minimum monthly earnings for contribution and benefit purposes are 444,150,000 liras.

The maximum monthly earnings for contribution and benefit purposes are 2,886,975,000 liras (6.5 times minimum earnings).

Qualifying Conditions

Unemployment benefit: Must have 600 days of contributions in the 3 years before unemployment, including the last 120 days of employment.

Unemployment Benefits

The minimum daily benefit is equal to 50% of average daily earnings, based on the last 4 months' earnings. The benefit is paid for 180 days to an insured worker with 600 days of contributions; for 240 days with 900 days of contributions; and 300 days with 1,080 days of contributions.

The monthly benefit must not be higher than the minimum wage for the industry in which the insured worked.

The maximum monthly benefit is 318,223,475 liras.

Unemployment benefits can be received in full at the same time as sickness and maternity benefits.

Benefit adjustment: Benefits are not adjusted but are calculated according to the insured's monthly earnings.

Administrative Organization

Ministry of Labor and Social Security (http://www.calisma. gov.tr) provides general supervision.

Social Insurance Institution (http://www.ssk.gov.tr) is responsible for collecting contributions.

Employment Agency (http://www.iskur.gov.tr) is responsible for any additional services and procedures.

Turkmenistan

Exchange rate: US$1.00 equals
5,200 manat (TM).

Old Age, Disability, and Survivors

Regulatory Framework

First law: 1956.

Current laws: 1998 (pensions) and 1998 (state allowances).

Type of program: Social insurance and social assistance system.

Local governments and employers may provide supplementary benefits out of their own budgets.

Coverage

Social insurance: All employed and self-employed persons.

Social pension: Persons not eligible for benefits under the 1998 pension law.

Source of Funds

Insured person: 1% of all earnings (plus a voluntary contribution of at least 4% of earnings made to a special personal bank account to supplement income in old age).

The insured's contributions also finance sickness and maternity benefits, work injury benefits, and family allowances.

Self-employed person: 1% of all earnings (plus a voluntary contribution of at least 4% of earnings to a special personal bank account to supplement income in old age).

Employer: 30% of payroll for urban employers; 20% of payroll for agricultural employers. For certain employers, the contribution varies according to sector.

The employer's contributions also finance sickness, maternity, and work injury benefits.

Government: Subsidies as needed and the total cost of social allowances.

The government also subsidizes cash benefits for sickness, maternity, and work injury.

Qualifying Conditions

Old-age pension: Age 62 with 25 years of covered employment (men) or age 57 with 20 years of covered employment (women); the qualifying conditions are reduced for mothers with three or more children or disabled children.

Age 58 (men) or age 55 (women) for military personnel; age 50 (men) or age 48 (women) for pilots and flight crew; or age 52 (men) or age 47 (women) for military personnel under contract.

Social pension (old-age): Age 67 or older (men) or age 62 or older (women) and not eligible for the old-age pension.

Disability pension: The pension is paid according to three groups of assessed disability: totally disabled, incapable of any work, and requiring care provided by another person at all times (Group I); disabled persons with reduced working capacity and requiring care provided by another person sometimes (Group II); disabled persons with reduced working capacity (Group III).

Eligible persons include persons disabled while in military service, disabled children younger than age 16, or persons disabled since childhood.

A territorial or state medical commission under the Ministry of Social Security assesses the degree of disability.

Social pension (disability): Paid to disabled persons not eligible for the disability pension.

Survivor pension: The pension is paid to surviving dependent family members regardless of whether the deceased was insured.

Old-Age Benefits

Old-age pension: The monthly pension is calculated on the basis of a state-set percentage amount (2.5%) for each year of covered employment, multiplied by monthly national average earnings in the last quarter before retirement, multiplied by a personal pension coefficient, multiplied by the number of years of covered employment.

The personal pension coefficient is the ratio of assessed earnings to gross national average earnings. Assessed earnings are equal to the insured's gross average earnings based on the best 5 consecutive years in all the years of covered employment. Gross national average earnings are calculated on the basis of the years of covered employment used to calculate assessed earnings.

The minimum pension is equal to 40% of the national minimum wage.

Benefit adjustment: Benefits are adjusted periodically according to changes in the national average wage.

Social pension (old-age): 100% of the minimum old-age pension is paid a month.

Permanent Disability Benefits

Disability pension: For a Group I disability (totally disabled, incapable of any work, and requiring care provided by another person at all times), the monthly pension is equal to 60% of the personal coefficient multiplied by gross national average earnings; for a Group II disability (disabled with reduced working capacity and requiring care provided by another person sometimes), 50% of the personal coefficient multiplied by gross national average earnings; for a Group III disability (disabled with reduced working capacity), 40% of the personal coefficient multiplied by gross national average earnings.

The personal coefficient is the ratio of assessed earnings to gross national average earnings. Assessed earnings are equal to the insured's gross average earnings based on the best 5 consecutive years in all the years of covered employment. Gross national average earnings are calculated on the basis of the years of covered employment used to calculate assessed earnings.

The minimum pension is equal to 40% of the national minimum wage.

The maximum pension is equal to 75% of the national minimum wage.

Eligibility for one benefit (sickness benefit, maternity benefit, child care allowance, survivor pension, or social pension) does not prevent eligibility for another benefit, but eligible persons must opt to receive one benefit only.

Constant-attendance allowance: 30% of the minimum old-age pension is paid a month (Groups I and II); 50% for a disabled war veteran or blind person (Group I) or a single disabled person (Group II).

Dependent's supplement (Groups I and II): 50% of the minimum old-age pension is paid a month for each nonworking dependent.

Benefit adjustment: Benefits are adjusted periodically according to changes in the national average wage.

Social pension (disability): 150% of the minimum old-age pension is paid a month if the disability began after childhood (Groups I and II) or for disabled children younger than age 16; 120% of the minimum benefit a month if the disabled person (Groups I and II) does not satisfy the conditions for covered employment; 100% of the minimum benefit a month for a person with a Group III disability.

Survivor Benefits

Survivor pension: 100% of the minimum pension is paid for one eligible survivor; if more than one eligible survivor, each receives 30% of the deceased's personal coefficient (40% for military personnel) multiplied by gross national average earnings.

The minimum pension is equal to 40% of the national minimum wage.

The personal coefficient is the ratio of assessed earnings to gross national average earnings. Assessed earnings are equal to the deceased's gross average earnings based on the best 5 consecutive years in all the years of covered employment. Gross national average earnings are calculated on the basis of the years of covered employment used to calculate assessed earnings.

The maximum pension is equal to 100% of the national minimum wage.

Benefit adjustment: Benefits are adjusted periodically according to changes in the national average wage.

Administrative Organization

Ministry of Social Security provides general coordination and supervision.

Regional and local departments of social security administer the program.

Sickness and Maternity

Regulatory Framework

First law: 1955.

Current laws: 1994 and 1998 (state allowances).

Type of program: Social insurance (cash benefits) and universal (medical care) system.

Coverage

Cash benefits: Employed and nonworking citizens.

Medical benefits: All persons residing in Turkmenistan.

Source of Funds

Insured person

Cash benefits: See source of funds under Old Age, Disability, and Survivors, above.

Medical benefits: Voluntary supplementary contributions for medical benefits.

Self-employed person

Cash benefits: See source of funds under Old Age, Disability, and Survivors, above.

Medical benefits: Voluntary supplementary contributions for medical benefits.

Employer

Cash benefits: See source of funds under Old Age, Disability, and Survivors, above.

Medical benefits: None.

Government

Cash benefits: The total cost for nonworking citizens.

Medical benefits: The total cost.

Qualifying Conditions

Cash and medical benefits: There is no minimum qualifying period.

Sickness and Maternity Benefits

Sickness benefit: With less than 5 years of uninterrupted work, the benefit is equal to 60% of earnings; with between

5 and 8 years, 80%; or if more than 8 years (or if with three or more children younger than age 16; age 18 if a student), 100%.

Insured persons may receive 5 days of paid leave to care for a sick family member; 7 days in exceptional cases or 14 days if caring for child younger than age 14 (or for the duration if the sick child is hospitalized).

Fourteen days of unpaid leave is provided to women caring for children younger than age 3, to a woman or a single parent raising two or more children younger than age 14, or for a man whose wife is on maternity leave. Disabled workers are entitled to 30 days of unpaid leave.

Maternity benefit: The benefit is equal to 100% of earnings and is paid for 56 days before and 56 days after the expected date of childbirth (72 days after for a difficult childbirth; 96 days after for multiple births).

Child care allowance: 100% of the minimum old-age pension (40% of the national average wage) for nonurban areas or 125% of the minimum old-age pension for urban areas is paid for a child younger than age 3 whose parents are disabled. A relevant birth certificate must be provided. The allowance is paid monthly, beginning the month following the last day of receiving maternity benefits.

Benefit adjustment: Benefits are adjusted periodically according to changes in the national average wage.

Workers' Medical Benefits

Medical services are provided directly to patients by public health providers. Benefits include general and specialized care, hospitalization, laboratory services, dental care, maternity care, vaccination, and transportation. Medicines are free if provided with hospitalization.

Dependents' Medical Benefits

Medical services are provided directly to patients by public health providers. Benefits include general and specialized care, hospitalization, laboratory services, dental care, maternity care, vaccination, and transportation. Medicines are free if provided with hospitalization.

Administrative Organization

Cash benefits: Ministry of Social Security and regional social security departments administer the program. Regional and local departments of social security administer maternity benefits for the unemployed and other nonworking citizens.

Enterprises and employers pay benefits to their own employees using funds from the Social Insurance Fund.

Medical benefits: Ministry of Health and Medical Industry and regional health departments are responsible for implementing state health care policy and developing health care programs. Ministry of Health and Medical Industry and regional health departments are responsible for providing medical services through clinics, hospitals, maternity homes, and other medical facilities, including private health providers.

Work Injury

Regulatory Framework

First law: 1955.

Current law: 1998 (state allowances).

Type of program: Social insurance (cash benefits) and universal (medical care) system.

Local authorities and employers can provide supplementary pension benefits out of their own budgets.

Coverage

All employed persons.

Source of Funds

Insured person

Cash benefits: See source of funds under Old Age, Disability, and Survivors, above.

Medical benefits: None.

Self-employed person

Cash benefits: Not applicable.

Medical benefits: None.

Employer

Cash benefits: See source of funds under Old Age, Disability, and Survivors, above.

Medical benefits: None.

Government

Cash benefits: See source of funds under Old Age, Disability, and Survivors, above.

Medical benefits: The total cost.

Qualifying Conditions

Work injury benefits: There is no minimum qualifying period.

Temporary Disability Benefits

The benefit is equal to 100% of earnings and is paid from the first day of disability until recovery or the award of a permanent disability pension. On the award of a permanent disability pension, the employer pays compensation to the insured.

Work injuries must be assessed by the competent authority.

Permanent Disability Benefits

Permanent disability pension: For a Group I disability (totally disabled, incapable of any work, and requiring care provided by another person at all times), the monthly pension is equal to 60% of the personal coefficient multiplied by gross national average earnings; for a Group II disability (disabled with reduced working capacity and requiring care provided by another person sometimes), 50% of the personal coefficient multiplied by gross national average earnings; for a Group III disability (disabled with reduced working capacity), 40% of the personal coefficient multiplied by gross national average earnings.

The personal coefficient is the ratio of assessed earnings to gross national average earnings. Assessed earnings are equal to the insured's gross average earnings based on the best 5 consecutive years in all the years of covered employment. Gross national average earnings are calculated on the basis of the years of covered employment used to calculate assessed earnings.

The minimum pension is equal to 40% of the national minimum wage.

The maximum pension is equal to 75% of the national minimum wage.

Eligibility for one benefit (sickness benefit, maternity benefit, child care allowance, survivor pension, or social pension) does not prevent eligibility for another benefit, but eligible persons must opt to receive one benefit only.

Constant-attendance allowance: 30% of the minimum benefit is paid a month (Groups I and II); 50% for a disabled war veteran or blind person (Group I) or a single disabled person (Group II).

Dependent's supplement (Groups I and II): 50% of the minimum benefit is paid a month for each nonworking dependent.

Work injuries must be assessed by the competent authority.

Benefit adjustment: Benefits are adjusted periodically according to changes in the national average wage.

Workers' Medical Benefits

Medical services are provided directly to patients by government health providers. Benefits include general and specialist care, hospitalization, laboratory services, transportation, and the full cost of appliances and medicines.

Survivor Benefits

Survivor pension: 100% of the minimum pension is paid for one eligible survivor; if more than one eligible survivor, each receives 30% of the deceased's personal coefficient (40% for military personnel) multiplied by gross national average earnings.

The personal coefficient is the ratio of assessed earnings to gross national average earnings. Assessed earnings are equal to the deceased's gross average earnings based on the best 5 consecutive years in all the years of covered employment. Gross national average earnings are calculated on the basis of the years of covered employment used to calculate assessed earnings.

The minimum pension is equal to 40% of the national minimum wage.

The maximum pension is equal to 100% of the national minimum wage.

Benefit adjustment: Benefits are adjusted periodically according to changes in the national average wage.

Administrative Organization

Temporary disability benefits: Enterprises and employers pay benefits to their own employees using funds from the Social Insurance Fund.

Pensions: Ministry of Social Security provides general coordination and supervision.

Regional and local departments of social security administer pensions.

Medical benefits: Ministry of Health and Medical Industry and health departments of local governments provide general supervision and policy coordination. Ministry of Health and health departments of local governments administer the provision of medical services through clinics, hospitals, and other facilities.

Unemployment

Regulatory Framework

First and current law: 1991 (employment).

Type of program: Social insurance system.

Coverage

All persons of working age residing permanently in Turkmenistan.

Source of Funds

Insured person: None.

Self-employed person: None.

Employer: 2% of payroll.

Government: Subsidies as needed from central and local governments.

Qualifying Conditions

Unemployment benefits: Registered at an employment office, able and willing to work, and receiving no income from employment. The benefit may be reduced, suspended, or terminated if the insured is discharged for violating work discipline, leaving employment without good cause, violating the conditions for job placement or vocational training, or filing fraudulent claims.

Unemployment Benefits

The total benefit is equal to three times the worker's gross monthly average earnings.

Benefit adjustment: Benefits are adjusted periodically according to changes in the national average wage.

Administrative Organization

State Employment Service and local employment offices regulate and administer the program.

Employers pay cash benefits.

Family Allowances

Regulatory Framework

A child care allowance is provided under Sickness and Maternity.

Uzbekistan

Exchange rate: US$1.00 equals 1,232 soms.

Old Age, Disability, and Survivors

Regulatory Framework

First law: 1956.

Current law: 1993 (state pension), with 1995, 1997, 1998, 1999, 2001, 2002, and 2005 amendments.

Type of program: Social insurance and social assistance system.

Local authorities and employers may provide supplementary benefits out of their own budgets.

Coverage

Social insurance: All employed persons residing in Uzbekistan.

Social pension: Needy elderly and disabled pensioners and certain other categories of resident, including victims of the Chernobyl catastrophe.

Source of Funds

Insured person: 2.5% of wages.

The insured's contributions also finance cash sickness and maternity benefits, work injury benefits, and family allowances.

Self-employed person: A monthly contribution at least equal to the value of the national minimum wage; self-employed persons who are of retirement age and disabled self-employed persons contribute at least 50% of this amount.

The self-employed person's contributions also finance family allowances.

Employer: 31% of total payroll; plus 0.5% of the value of gross sales (goods and services) or gross revenue.

The employer's contributions also finance cash sickness and maternity benefits, work injury benefits, and family allowances.

Government: Subsidies as needed and the total cost of social pensions.

Government subsidies also finance cash sickness and maternity benefits, work injury benefits, and family allowances.

Qualifying Conditions

Old-age pension: Age 60 (men) or age 55 (women), with a complete service period. The complete service period is 25 years of covered employment (men) or 20 years of work (women). Retirement from employment is necessary.

The qualifying conditions are reduced for those working in hazardous or arduous employment or in ecologically damaged areas, for unemployed older workers, for teachers with at least 25 years of service, and for other categories of worker.

Pensions are not payable abroad; a lump sum equal to 6 months of benefits is paid to pensioners before they leave the country permanently.

Social pension (old-age): Paid to needy old-age pensioners.

Disability pension: Paid according to three categories of disability: totally disabled, incapable of any work, and requiring constant attendance (Group I); totally disabled, incapable of any work, and not requiring constant attendance (Group II); and partially disabled and incapable of usual work (Group III).

The insured must have a minimum of between 1 and 15 years of covered employment, depending on age at the onset of disability.

An expert medical commission assesses the degree of disability.

Pensions are not payable abroad; a lump sum equal to 6 months of benefits is paid to pensioners before they leave the country permanently.

Social pension (disability): Paid to needy disability pensioners.

Survivor pension: The deceased must have had between 1 and 15 years of work, depending on age at the time of death. The pension is paid to surviving children regardless of whether they were dependent on the deceased and to nonworking dependents (including the spouse; either parent, if disabled and not of pensionable age; and grandparents, if no other support is available).

Pensions are not payable abroad; a lump sum equal to 6 months of benefits is paid to pensioners before they leave the country permanently.

Social pension (survivors): Paid to needy orphans.

Old-Age Benefits

Old-age pension: The pension is paid according to two income categories.

First tier (high-waged): With a complete service period, insured persons receive 55% of average monthly earnings, but not less than 100% of the national minimum wage.

Average earnings are based on the average wage over any consecutive 5-year period.

The minimum pension for high-waged insured persons varies between 50% of the national minimum wage (for an incomplete service period) and 100% of the national minimum wage (for a complete service period).

The maximum pension for high-waged insured persons with a complete service period is 5.25 times the minimum wage.

The national minimum wage is 12,420 soms.

Second tier: Insured persons receive 1% of average earnings a month for every year of service.

Social pension (old-age): Special pensions are awarded to certain categories of older person, including war veterans and former military personnel.

Benefit adjustment: Periodic benefit adjustments according to changes in the cost of living.

Permanent Disability Benefits

Disability pension: The pension depends on the severity of the assessed disability: totally disabled, incapable of any work, and requiring constant attendance (Group I); totally disabled, incapable of any work, and not requiring constant attendance (Group II); and partially disabled and incapable of usual work (Group III).

For a Group I disability, the pension is equal to 55% of average earnings over any consecutive 5-year period; 100% of the high-waged old-age pension with 25 years of covered employment (men) or 20 years of covered employment (women), plus a constant-attendance supplement.

For a Group II disability, the pension is equal to 55% of average earnings; 100% of the high-waged old-age pension with 25 years of covered employment (men) or 20 years of covered employment (women).

For a Group III disability, the pension is equal to 30% of earnings.

The minimum pension for a Group I or II disability is 100% of the minimum high-waged old-age pension; for a Group III disability, 50% of the minimum high-waged old-age pension.

Partial pension: If the insured does not have the required number of years of covered employment, a percentage of the full pension is paid according to the number of years below the required number of years of covered employment.

Social pension (disability): A social pension is paid for a Group I disability if the disability began in childhood and for disabled children younger than age 16. The monthly pension is equal to 100% of the minimum high-waged old-age pension. The monthly pension for a Group II disability for adults is equal to 50% of the minimum high-waged old-age pension; for a Group III disability, 30% of the minimum high-waged old-age pension.

Benefit adjustment: Periodic benefit adjustments according to changes in the cost of living.

Survivor Benefits

Survivor pension: If the deceased had a complete service period, the monthly pension for each dependent survivor is equal to 30% of the deceased's average earnings over any consecutive 5-year period, but not less than 50% of the national minimum wage.

The minimum pension is equal to 30% of the average monthly wage, but not less than the national minimum wage for the death of both parents or for the death of a single mother.

The national minimum wage is 12,420 soms.

Social pension (survivors): A social pension is paid to orphans younger than age 16 (no limit if disabled since childhood). The monthly pension is equal to 50% of the national minimum wage for a half orphan whose parent is receiving government support; orphans without a parent receiving government support, 100% of the national minimum wage.

The national minimum wage is 12,420 soms.

Benefit adjustment: Periodic benefit adjustments according to changes in the cost of living.

Administrative Organization

Ministry of Labor and Social Protection (http://www.gov.uz) provides general supervision and coordination.

Regional Departments of Social Protection administer the program.

Sickness and Maternity

Regulatory Framework

First and current laws: 1955 (temporary disability), with 1984, 1990, and 1992 amendments; and 1996 (universal medical benefits).

Type of program: Social insurance (sickness and maternity benefits) and universal (medical benefits) system.

Coverage

Cash sickness and maternity benefits: Persons in covered employment; persons on leave from employment while pursuing secondary, technical, or advanced education; and registered unemployed persons.

Medical benefits: All persons residing in Uzbekistan.

Source of Funds

Insured person

Cash benefits: See source of funds under Old Age, Disability, and Survivors, above.

Medical benefits: None.

Self-employed person

Cash benefits: Not applicable.

Medical benefits: None.

Employer

Cash benefits: See source of funds under Old Age, Disability, and Survivors, above.

Medical benefits: None.

Government

Cash benefits: See source of funds under Old Age, Disability, and Survivors, above.

Medical benefits: The total cost.

Qualifying Conditions

Cash sickness benefits: Sickness benefits are paid according to the length of the coverage period.

Cash maternity benefits: There is no minimum qualifying period.

Medical benefits: There is no minimum qualifying period.

Sickness and Maternity Benefits

Sickness benefit: With less than 5 years of uninterrupted employment, the benefit is equal to 60% of the last month's wage; 80% with between 5 and 8 years; 100% with more than 8 years (or if the insured has three or more children).

Maternity benefit: The benefit is equal to 100% of wages and is paid monthly for 70 days before and 56 days after childbirth (may be extended to 70 days after childbirth in the event of complications or multiple births). Mothers caring for children younger than age 2 may receive monthly paid leave equal to 20% of the national minimum wage. Working mothers are entitled to unpaid leave for a child between ages 2 and 3.

The national minimum wage is 12,420 soms.

Workers' Medical Benefits

Medical services are provided directly by government health providers. Benefits include general and specialist care, hospitalization, prostheses, medication, and other medical care services.

Dependents' Medical Benefits

Medical services are provided directly by government health providers. Benefits include general and specialist care, hospitalization, prostheses, medication, and other medical care services.

Administrative Organization

Cash sickness and maternity benefits: Ministry of Labor and Social Protection (http://www.gov.uz) provides general supervision and coordination. Cash benefits are provided directly by the enterprises and by local Departments of Social Protection.

Medical benefits: Ministry of Health (http://www.gov.uz) and its regional health departments provide general supervision and coordination. Ministry of Health and its local health departments administer the provision of medical services through government clinics, hospitals, maternity homes, and other facilities.

Work Injury

Regulatory Framework

First and current laws: 1955 (temporary disability) and 1993 (state pension).

Type of program: Social insurance (cash benefits) and universal (medical benefits) system.

Local authorities and employers may provide supplementary pension benefits out of their own budgets.

Coverage

Employed persons.

Source of Funds

Insured person: See source of funds under Old Age, Disability, and Survivors, above.

Self-employed person: Not applicable.

Employer: See source of funds under Old Age, Disability, and Survivors, above.

Government: See source of funds under Old Age, Disability, and Survivors, above; and the cost of medical benefits.

Qualifying Conditions

Work injury benefits: There is no minimum qualifying period.

Temporary Disability Benefits

The benefit is equal to 100% of earnings, but not less than the national minimum wage, and is paid from the first day of incapacity until recovery or the award of a permanent disability pension.

The national minimum wage is 12,420 soms.

An expert medical commission assesses the degree of disability.

Permanent Disability Benefits

Permanent disability pension: The pension depends on the severity of the assessed disability: totally disabled, incapable of any work, and requiring constant attendance (Group I); totally disabled, incapable of any work, and not requiring constant attendance (Group II); and partially disabled and incapable of usual work (Group III). For a Group I disability, the pension is equal to 55% of average earnings over any consecutive 5-year period; 100% of the high-waged old-age pension with 25 years of covered employment (men) or 20 years (women) of covered employment, plus a constant-attendance supplement.

For a Group II disability, the pension is equal to 55% of average earnings; 100% of the high-waged old-age pension with 25 years of covered employment (men) or 20 years of covered employment (women).

For a Group III disability, the pension is equal to 30% of earnings.

The minimum pension for a Group I or II disability is equal to 100% of the minimum high-waged old-age pension; for a Group III disability, 50% of the minimum high-waged old-age pension.

An expert medical commission assesses the degree of disability.

Pensions are payable abroad for a work injury or an occupational disease.

Workers' Medical Benefits

Medical services are provided directly to patients by governmental health providers. Benefits include general and specialist care, hospitalization, laboratory services, transportation, and the full cost of appliances and medicines.

Survivor Benefits

Survivor pension: The monthly pension is equal to 30% of the deceased's earnings over any consecutive 5-year period for each dependent survivor.

The minimum pension is equal to 100% of the national minimum wage; 200% for a full orphan or the death of a single mother.

The national minimum wage is 12,420 soms.

Administrative Organization

Temporary disability benefits: Enterprises and employers pay benefits to their own employees.

Pensions: Ministry of Labor and Social Protection (http://www.gov.uz) provides general supervision and coordination. Regional Departments of Social Protection administer the program.

Medical benefits: Ministry of Health (http://www.gov.uz) and its regional health departments provide general supervision and coordination. Ministry of Health and its local health departments administer the provision of medical services through clinics, hospitals, and other facilities.

Unemployment

Regulatory Framework

First law: 1992 (employment), with amendments.

Current law: 1998 (employment), with 1999, 2000, 2001, and 2006 amendments.

Type of program: Social insurance system.

Coverage

Citizens from age 16 to the pensionable age.

Source of Funds

Employee: None.

Self-employed person: Not applicable.

Employer: 3% of payroll.

Government: Subsidies as needed from central and local governments.

Qualifying Conditions

Unemployment benefit: Must have worked for at least 12 weeks in the last 12 months; persons of working age who register as a job seeker for the first time.

Long-term unemployed: Reentrants to the workforce who have less than 12 weeks of employment in the last 12 months but have at least 1 year of total employment.

Registered at an employment office, able and willing to work, and receiving no income from employment. The benefit may be reduced, suspended, or terminated if the insured is discharged for violating work discipline, leaving employment without good cause, violating the conditions for a job placement or vocational training, or filing fraudulent claims.

Unemployment Benefits

The monthly benefit is equal to 50% of average earnings in the last 26 weeks.

The minimum benefit is equal to 100% of the national minimum wage.

The maximum benefit is based on average earnings that do not exceed the national average wage.

Long-term unemployed: Reentrants to the workforce with skills receive 100% of the national minimum wage for the first 13 weeks and 75% of the national minimum wage for the following 13 weeks; reentrants to the workforce without skills receive 75% of the national minimum wage (50% if without dependents) for 13 weeks.

First-time job seeker: 75% of the national minimum wage (50% if no dependents) is paid for 13 weeks.

Dependent's supplement: 10% of the unemployment benefit is paid monthly for each dependent younger than age 16.

The national minimum wage is 12,420 soms.

Early retirement pension: The old-age pension is paid to unemployed persons within 2 years of reaching pensionable age. (See old-age benefits under Old Age, Disability, and Survivors, above.)

Administrative Organization

Employment Service and local counterparts, together with the National Federation of Trade Unions, administer the program.

Family Allowances

Regulatory Framework

First law: 1944.

Current laws: 1994 (family assistance), 1999, and 2002 (family allowances).

Type of program: Social insurance and social assistance system.

Coverage

Social insurance: Insured employed and self-employed persons.

Social assistance: All persons residing in Uzbekistan.

Source of Funds

Insured person: For social insurance benefits, see source of funds under Old Age, Disability, and Survivors, above. For social assistance benefits, none.

Self-employed person: For social insurance benefits, see source of funds under Old Age, Disability, and Survivors, above. For social assistance benefits, none.

Employer: For social insurance benefits, see source of funds under Old Age, Disability, and Survivors, above. For social assistance benefits, none.

Government: For social insurance benefits, see source of funds under Old Age, Disability, and Survivors, above. The total cost of social assistance benefits from republic, regional, city, and district budgets as well as from various extra-budgetary sources.

Qualifying Conditions

Young child allowance (social insurance): Paid for children younger than age 2. The allowance is income-tested, except for single-parent families and families with at least one disabled child.

Family assistance (social assistance): Paid for needy families or single persons on the recommendation of local neighborhood (mahalla) committees.

Family allowance (social assistance): Children must be younger than age 16 (age 18 if a student).

Family Allowance Benefits

Young child allowance (social insurance): A fixed monthly amount is paid equal to 200% of the national minimum wage, regardless of the number of children. The national minimum wage is 12,420 soms.

Family assistance (social assistance): The monthly amount is awarded according to the number of family members and the assessed need. The allowances are normally paid monthly for a period of 3 months; may be extended in certain cases. The monthly financial assistance is between 1.5 and 3 months of the national minimum wage. The national minimum wage is 12,420 soms.

Family allowance (social assistance): For families with one child, the monthly allowance is equal to 50% of the national minimum wage; for families with two children, 100%; for families with three children, 140%; for families with four or more children, 175%. Family allowances may be paid for up to 6 months; may be extended if family income has not changed. The national minimum wage is 12,420 soms.

Administrative Organization

Social insurance: Ministry of Labor and Social Protection (http://www.gov.uz) provides general supervision and coordination.

Social assistance: Citizens' Commissions, on the recommendation of local neighborhood (mahalla) committees, administer the program locally, assess eligibility for entitlement, and determine the award of benefits.

Vanuatu

Exchange rate: US$1.00 equals 108.35 vatu.

Old Age, Disability, and Survivors

Regulatory Framework

First and current law: 1986 (provident fund), implemented in 1987, with 1989, 1998, 2000, 2001, and 2003 amendments.

Type of program: Provident fund system.

Coverage

All employees older than age 14 in regular employment, including members of cooperative societies.

Noncitizens may apply to the Provident Fund Board for exemption if covered by another country's social security scheme.

Exclusions: Persons covered under employer-provided retirement programs approved by the Provident Fund Board; persons detained in prison, approved school, mental hospital, or leper asylum; and temporary workers in agriculture and forestry with employment contracts of less than 2 months.

Voluntary coverage for ministers of religious organizations and for any person without mandatory coverage between ages 14 and 55.

Source of Funds

Insured person: A minimum of 4% of monthly earnings (additional voluntary contributions are permitted without a ceiling). Voluntary contributors pay between 1,000 vatu and 10,000 vatu a month.

The minimum monthly earnings for contribution purposes are 3,000 vatu.

Self-employed person: Not applicable.

Employer: 6% of monthly payroll.

The minimum monthly earnings for contribution purposes are 3,000 vatu.

Government: None.

Qualifying Conditions

Old-age benefit: Age 55; at any age if emigrating permanently. If the member has withdrawn any amount and makes further contributions after age 55, no withdrawal is allowed until 2 years after the date of the last withdrawal, unless the member retires or dies.

Disability benefit: Must be permanently incapable of any employment due to a physical or mental disability. The disability is assessed by two registered medical practitioners.

Survivor benefit: Paid on the death of the fund member before retirement.

Death benefit: Paid to named survivors.

Old-Age Benefits

Old-age benefit: A lump sum is paid equal to total employee and employer contributions, plus compound interest.

Interest rate adjustment: Set annually by the Provident Fund Board depending on the financial performance of the fund. The current rate is 4% a year.

Permanent Disability Benefits

A lump sum is paid equal to total employee and employer contributions, plus compound interest.

Interest rate adjustment: Set annually by the Provident Fund Board depending on the financial performance of the fund. The current rate is 4% a year.

Survivor Benefits

Survivor benefit: A lump sum is paid equal to total employee and employer contributions, plus compound interest.

Eligible survivors are the spouse, dependent parents of the deceased or of his or her spouse, and children. Survivors must be named by the deceased, and the benefit is split among survivors as specified by the deceased.

Interest rate adjustment: Set annually by the Provident Fund Board depending on the financial performance of the fund. The current rate is 4% a year.

Death benefit: A lump sum of 230,000 vatu is paid to named survivors.

Administrative Organization

Ministry of Finance provides general supervision.

Managed by a general manager, a six-member tripartite Provident Fund Board administers the program.

Provident Fund Board is responsible for appointing a commercial fund manager and for setting the investment criteria.

Sickness and Maternity

Regulatory Framework

No statutory benefits are provided for sickness and maternity.

The 1983 Employment Act requires employers to:

- provide 100% of wages for sick leave for up to 21 days a year, if the employee has been in continuous employment with the employer for 12 months or more.

- provide 50% of wages for maternity leave of up to 12 weeks (6 weeks before and 6 weeks after the expected date of childbirth). Employers are required to allow a mother to interrupt work twice a day for 30 minutes to feed a nursing child.

- provide medical care for workers and for their dependents when the dependents are living on the employer's property.

Vietnam

Exchange rate: US$1.00 equals 15,955 dong.

Old Age, Disability, and Survivors

Regulatory Framework

First law: 1961 (public-sector employees).

Current law: 2002 (pensions), with 2003 amendment.

Type of program: Social insurance system.

Coverage

Private- and public-sector employees with employment contracts of at least 3 months, including domestic workers; employees in agriculture, fishing, and salt production; civil servants; and officers of the armed forces.

Exclusions: Self-employed persons.

Source of Funds

Insured person: 5% of gross monthly wages.

The minimum earnings for contribution purposes are equal to the minimum wage. (The minimum monthly wage for public-sector employees is 350,000 dong; the minimum monthly wage for private-sector employees varies according to profession.)

The maximum earnings for contribution and benefit calculation purposes are 9 million dong (January 2007).

Self-employed person: Not applicable.

Employer: 10% of monthly payroll.

The minimum earnings for contribution purposes are equal to the minimum wage. (The minimum monthly wage for public-sector employees is 350,000 dong; the minimum monthly wage for private-sector employees varies according to profession.)

The maximum earnings for contribution and benefit calculation purposes are 9 million dong (January 2007).

Government: None; subsidies as necessary and the total cost of old-age pensions for workers who retired before 1995.

Qualifying Conditions

Old-age pension: Age 60 (men) or age 55 (women) with 20 years of contributions; age 55 (men) or age 50 (women) with 30 years of contributions; age 55 (men) or age 50 (women) with 20 years of contributions, including at least 15 years of employment in hazardous or arduous working conditions or in certain geographic regions or with 10 years

of work in South Vietnam or Laos before April 30, 1975, or Cambodia before August 31, 1989.

Age 50 (men) or age 45 (women) with 20 years of contributions and an assessed degree of disability of at least 61%; regardless of age with 20 years of contributions, including 15 years in extremely hazardous or arduous working conditions and an assessed degree of disability of at least 61%.

Partial pension: A reduced pension is paid at age 60 (men) or age 55 (women) with between 15 and 20 years of contributions.

Early pension: An early pension is possible.

Periods of employment in the public sector before 1995 are credited for the purpose of contributions.

A pensioner residing abroad may nominate a relative residing in Vietnam to receive the old-age pension on his or her behalf.

Retirement from employment is necessary.

Old-age grant: Age 60 (men) or age 55 (women) and not eligible for the old-age pension.

Disability grant: Paid for a permanent total or partial disability at any age with an assessed degree of disability of at least 61%. The insured must have been in covered employment before the disability began.

A Ministry of Health medical board assesses the degree of disability.

Survivor pension: The deceased had more than 15 years of contributions or was a pensioner. The benefit is paid to a maximum of four dependent survivors.

Eligible survivors include a husband (aged 60 or older) or a wife (aged 55 or older) with income less than the minimum wage, children younger than age 15 (age 18 if a student), and a father (aged 60 or older) or a mother (aged 55 or older).

Survivor grant: Paid if there are no eligible survivors. The deceased had less than 15 years of covered employment. In the absence of eligible dependent survivors, the grant is paid to the surviving family.

Funeral grant: Paid to the person who pays for the funeral.

Old-Age Benefits

Old-age pension: With at least 15 years of coverage, the pension is equal to 45% of the insured's average earnings plus 2% (men) or 3% (women) of the insured's covered earnings for each year of coverage exceeding 15 years.

The maximum pension is equal to 75% of the insured's average earnings in the last 5 years before the pension is first paid.

Insured persons with more than 30 years of contributions also receive a lump sum equal to 50% of their average monthly earnings in the last 5 years before the pension is first paid for each year of contributions exceeding 30 years, up to a maximum of five times the minimum monthly wage.

Early pension: The pension is reduced by 1% of the insured's average earnings in the last 5 years before the pension is first paid for each year the pension is taken before the insured's normal pensionable age.

The minimum benefit is equal to the minimum wage. (The minimum monthly wage for public-sector employees is 350,000 dong; the minimum monthly wage for private-sector employees varies according to profession.)

Benefit adjustment: Benefits are adjusted according to changes in the minimum wage.

Old-age grant: A lump sum is paid equal to 50% of the insured's average monthly earnings in the last 5 years before applying for the pension times the number of years of contributions.

Permanent Disability Benefits

Disability grant: A lump sum is paid (not yet defined by legislation). The old-age pension is paid to certain groups of insured persons with an assessed disability of at least 61% (see qualifying conditions, above).

Survivor Benefits

Survivor pension: 40% of the minimum wage is paid for each eligible dependent survivor; 70% of the minimum wage if the survivor has no other means of support.

Survivor grant: A lump sum is paid equal to 50% of the deceased's last wage times the number of years of contributions, up to a maximum of 12 times the deceased's last wage.

For the death of a pensioner, a lump sum is paid equal to 12 times the deceased's monthly pension. The lump sum is reduced by the value of the deceased's monthly pension for each year the deceased received his or her pension. The minimum lump sum is equal to three times the deceased's monthly pension.

Funeral grant: A lump sum is paid equal to 8 months' minimum wage in the public sector (the minimum monthly wage for public-sector employees is 350,000 dong).

Administrative Organization

Ministry of Labor, Invalids, and Social Affairs (http://www.molisa.gov.vn) provides general supervision.

Vietnam Social Security collects contributions and pays benefits.

Sickness and Maternity

Regulatory Framework

First law: 1961 (public-sector employees).

Current laws: 1995 (sickness and maternity benefits), with 2003 amendment; and 2005 (medical benefits).

Type of program: Social insurance system.

Coverage

Cash sickness and maternity benefits: Private- and public-sector employees with employment contracts of at least 3 months, including domestic workers; employees in agriculture, fishing, and salt production; and civil servants and officers of the armed forces.

Voluntary coverage for cash sickness and maternity benefits for self-employed persons, school children, and students.

Medical benefits: Private- and public-sector employees with employment contracts of at least 3 months, including domestic workers; employees in agriculture, fishing, forestry, and salt production; members of cooperatives; pensioners; war veterans affected by agent orange and receiving a pension; dependents of army officers; persons who have received the old-age grant; civil servants; and officers of the armed forces.

Voluntary coverage for medical benefits is possible, including for insured persons with compulsory coverage who wish to have supplementary coverage.

Medical benefits only: Pensioners and veterans of the revolution.

Source of Funds

Insured person

Cash sickness and maternity benefits: None.

Medical benefits: 1% of gross monthly earnings. (Voluntary contributors pay between 30,000 dong and 160,000 dong a month, according to geographic region and profession.) Pensioners contribute 3% of the monthly benefit.

Self-employed person

Cash sickness and maternity benefits: Voluntary contributions only.

The minimum earnings for contribution purposes are equal to the minimum wage. (The minimum monthly wage for public-sector employees is 350,000 dong; the minimum monthly wage for private-sector employees varies according to profession.)

The maximum earnings for contribution and benefit calculation purposes are 9 million dong (January 2007).

Medical benefits: Voluntary contributions of between 30,000 dong and 160,000 dong, according to geographic region and the type of self-employment.

Employer

Cash sickness and maternity benefits: 5% of monthly payroll.

The minimum earnings for contribution purposes are equal to the minimum wage. (The minimum monthly wage for public-sector employees is 350,000 dong; the minimum monthly wage for private-sector employees varies according to profession.)

The maximum earnings for contribution and benefit calculation purposes are 9 million dong (January 2007).

The employer contributions also finance work injury benefits.

Medical benefits: 2% of monthly payroll.

Government

Cash sickness and maternity benefits: None.

Medical benefits: Administrative costs; the cost of benefits for low-income persons.

Qualifying Conditions

Cash sickness benefits: There is no minimum qualifying period. The incapacity must not be work-related.

The sickness benefit is also payable to an insured woman caring for a sick child. The benefit is paid for care given to the insured's first two children younger than age 7; paid to the father only in special circumstances.

Cash maternity benefits: There is no minimum qualifying period. The benefit is paid for the first two childbirths only. If one of the first two children dies, the insured is entitled to benefits for a third child.

Medical benefits: Provided for a nonoccupational injury or illness. The insured must have a minimum of 45 days of contributions.

Sickness and Maternity Benefits

Sickness benefit: The benefit is equal to 75% of the insured's wage and is paid for up to 30 days in a calendar year if the insured has less than 15 years of covered employment; 40 days if more than 15 years; 50 days if more than 30 years. If the insured is engaged in hazardous or arduous work or working in certain regions, the benefit is paid for up to 40 days in a calendar year if the insured has less than 15 years in covered employment; 50 days with between 15 and 30 years; 60 days with more than 30 years. The benefit may be extended to up to 180 days in a calendar year for prolonged hospitalization due to a specified illness.

Female employees receive 75% of wages for up to 20 days in a calendar year to provide care for a sick child younger than age 3; 15 days for a sick child between ages 3 and 7.

Benefit adjustment: Benefits are reviewed annually and adjusted if the cost of living increases by 10%.

Maternity benefit: The benefit is equal to 100% of the insured's wage for prenatal care, an abortion, or childbirth. The benefit is paid for three 1-day leave periods (or 2-day leave periods in special cases) for prenatal care, including for a pregnancy test. The benefit is also paid during statutory maternity leave for a maximum of 120 days (150 days if the insured is engaged in hazardous or arduous work; 180 days if working in certain regions or occupations). In the case of multiple births, an extra 30-day leave period is awarded for the second and subsequent children. A 20-day leave period is paid for a miscarriage in the first 3 months of pregnancy; a 30-day leave period for a miscarriage after the 3rd month.

Maternity benefits are also paid to insured women who adopt a newborn child.

Unpaid maternity leave may be provided, at the employer's discretion, to female employees after the end of statutory maternity leave.

Benefit adjustment: Benefits are reviewed annually and adjusted if the cost of living increases by 10%.

Birth grant: Equal to the insured woman's monthly wage.

Workers' Medical Benefits

Medical services are provided by public or private providers under contract to Vietnam Social Security.

Medical benefits include outpatient and inpatient services; medical, diagnosis, treatment, and functional rehabilitation during the treatment period; approved medicines; blood transfusion; surgery; medical materials, equipment, and hospital beds; the cost of prenatal examination and childbirth; the cost of treatment for transportation-related accidents; and a transportation subsidy for privileged groups and indigent people referred for medical treatment.

Treatment for various infectious diseases is covered by the national health program.

The medical fund covers the total cost of medical treatment for insured patients, according to the hospital fee schedule set by government.

Cost sharing: When advanced medical services are required, the fund reimburses 100% of the cost up to 7 million dong; if the cost is higher, the fund reimburses 100% of the cost for certain groups (including Vietnamese heroic mothers, war invalids, and persons older than age 90); or 100% of the cost less than 20 million dong for covered people whose contributions are paid by the government and the Social Insurance Fund (including individuals affected by agent orange, elderly disabled persons, old-age and other pensioners, and the poor); or 60% of the cost but not exceeding 20 million dong. Insured members pay the remaining amount not covered by the fund.

There is no limit to duration.

Dependents' Medical Benefits

Coverage is provided on an individual basis under the national health program.

Administrative Organization

Ministry of Labor, Invalids, and Social Affairs (http://www.molisa.gov.vn) provides general supervision.

Vietnam Social Security collects contributions, pays cash benefits, administers medical benefits, and contracts with public and private providers of medical services.

Work Injury

Regulatory Framework

First laws: 1947 and 1950.

Current law: 1995 (work injury), with 2003 amendment.

Type of program: Social insurance system.

Coverage

Private- and public-sector employees with employment contracts of at least 3 months, including domestic workers; employees in agriculture, fishing, and salt production; civil servants; and officers of the armed forces.

Source of Funds

Insured person: None.

Self-employed person: Not applicable.

Employer: See source of funds under Sickness and Maternity, above.

Government: None.

Qualifying Conditions

Work injury benefits: There is no minimum qualifying period for a work injury or an occupational disease.

Temporary Disability Benefits

100% of the insured's wage is paid during treatment and until the determination of permanent disability. The benefit is paid by the employer from the first day.

A Ministry of Health medical board assesses the degree of disability.

Permanent Disability Benefits

Permanent disability benefit: The monthly benefit depends on the assessed degree of disability (Groups I–VII). For an assessed disability of between 91% and 100% (Group I), 160% of the government-set minimum monthly wage is paid; between 81% and 90% (Group II), 140%; between 71% and 80% (Group III), 120%; between 61% and 70% (Group IV), 100%; between 51% and 60% (Group V), 80%; between 41% and 50% (Group VI), 60%; or between 31% and 40% (Group VII), 40%.

Constant-attendance allowance: A monthly benefit equal to 80% of the minimum monthly wage is paid to disabled persons (Groups I and II) who are unable to live independently.

Disability grant: For an assessed disability of between 5% and 10%, 4 months' minimum wage is paid; between 11% and 20%, 8 months' minimum wage; or between 21% and 30%, 12 months' minimum wage.

A Ministry of Health medical board assesses the degree of disability.

Workers' Medical Benefits

Medical benefits include inpatient and outpatient treatment, surgery, medicines, and rehabilitation.

Survivor Benefits

Survivor benefit: A monthly pension equal to 40% of the minimum monthly wage is paid for each of the first four eligible dependent survivors (70% of the minimum monthly wage if the survivor has no other means of support). A single lump sum is also paid equal to 24 times the minimum monthly wage.

Eligible survivors include the spouse, children younger than age 15 (age 18 if a student), and a father (aged 60 or older) or mother (aged 55 or older).

Survivor grant: In the absence of eligible dependent survivors, a lump sum is paid to other surviving family members equal to 50% of the deceased's last monthly wage times the number of years of contributions. The maximum grant is equal to 12 times the deceased's last monthly wage.

In the case of the death of a permanent disability pensioner, a lump sum is paid equal to 12 times the deceased's monthly pension. The lump sum is reduced by the value of the deceased's monthly pension for each year the deceased received his or her pension. The minimum lump sum is three times the deceased's monthly pension.

Funeral grant: A lump sum equal to 8 months' minimum wage in the public sector (the minimum monthly wage for public-sector employees is 350,000 dong) is paid to the person who paid for the funeral.

Administrative Organization

Ministry of Labor, Invalids, and Social Affairs (http://www.molisa.gov.vn) provides general supervision.

Vietnam Social Security collects contributions, pays cash benefits, administers medical benefits, and contracts with public and private providers of medical services.

Western Samoa

Exchange rate: US$1.00 equals 2.67 tala.

Old Age, Disability, and Survivors

Regulatory Framework

First and current law: 1972 (national provident fund), with 1972 and 1990 amendments.

Type of program: Provident fund and universal old-age pension system.

Coverage

Provident fund: Employed persons, including domestic servants.

Senior citizen benefit scheme: Western Samoan citizens aged 65 or older residing in Western Samoa.

Source of Funds

Provident fund

Insured person: 5% of gross monthly earnings. (Additional voluntary contributions are permitted, without a ceiling.)

Self-employed person: None.

Employer: 5% of monthly payroll.

Government: None; contributes as an employer.

Senior citizen benefit scheme

Insured person: None.

Self-employed person: None.

Employer: None.

Government: The total cost.

Qualifying Conditions

Provident fund

Old-age pension: Age 55 and retired from covered employment; at any age if emigrating permanently or after 12 consecutive months of residence overseas. If covered employment continues after age 55, contributions must continue to the fund. If new employment begins after funds are withdrawn at age 55, the fund member must contribute for 12 months before next withdrawing funds.

Early withdrawal: Age 50 and unemployed for 5 or more years.

Drawdown payment: Must have a minimum balance of 500 tala.

Disability pension: Must be assessed with a total incapacity for work in covered employment. A general medical practitioner assesses the disability.

Survivor pension: Paid for the death of the fund member. Eligible survivors include the spouse, children, and siblings.

Death benefit: Paid for the death of the fund member before age 55. The fund member must have been an active contributor at the time of death.

Eligible survivors include the spouse, children, and siblings.

Senior citizen benefit scheme: Age 65. Must be a Western Samoan citizen and reside in Western Samoa.

Old-Age Benefits

Old-age pension (provident fund): A fund member can choose from three benefit options: a monthly pension based on total insured person and employer contributions, plus interest; a monthly pension based on 75% of total insured person and employer contributions, plus interest, with the remaining 25% paid as a lump sum; or at age 55 fund members can opt to take a lump sum equal to the full amount in their account instead of a monthly pension.

Interest rate adjustment: The interest rate is adjusted every 3 years according to an actuarial review.

Drawdown payment: Up to 50% of the total insured person and employer contributions may be drawn down. The payment is repaid as a loan at an annual interest rate of 11%. If used for building a house, the loan must be at least 50,000 tala.

Senior citizen benefit scheme: 100 tala a month is paid. (Senior citizens also receive subsidized health care in public hospitals and free interisland travel on public seagoing vessels.)

Benefit adjustment: The senior citizen benefit is reviewed periodically by the government.

Permanent Disability Benefits

Disability pension (provident fund): A fund member can choose from three benefit options: a monthly pension based on total employee and employer contributions, plus interest; a monthly pension based on 75% of total employee and employer contributions, plus interest, with the remaining 25% paid as a lump sum; or at age 55 fund members can opt to take a lump sum equal to the full amount in their account instead of a monthly pension.

Interest rate adjustment: The interest rate is adjusted every 3 years according to an actuarial review.

Survivor Benefits

Survivor pension (provident fund): 50% of the deceased's monthly pension is split among named survivors according to proportions stated by the deceased.

Death benefit (provident fund): A lump sum of 2,500 tala is paid.

Benefit adjustment: The death benefit is adjusted according to the financial health of the fund.

Administrative Organization

Samoa National Provident Fund (http://www.npf.ws), managed by a tripartite board, administers the scheme.

Senior Citizen Benefit Scheme Department of the Samoa National Provident Fund administers the senior citizen benefit scheme.

Sickness and Maternity

Regulatory Framework

No statutory cash benefits are provided. (Cash benefits for temporary and permanent disability are provided for nonwork-related injuries under Work Injury, below.)

Some medical services are provided free of charge to the population through government health centers.

Other hospital and medical services are provided under the senior citizen benefit scheme and the work injury program.

Work Injury

Regulatory Framework

First law: 1960.

Current laws: 1978 and 1989 (accident compensation), with 2003 amendment.

Type of program: Employer-liability system, involving compulsory insurance with a private carrier.

Coverage

Employed persons.

Exclusions: Self-employed persons.

The total population is covered under a separate scheme for nonwork-related injuries, including injuries resulting from an accident involving a motor vehicle or a boat traveling within Western Samoa.

Source of Funds

Insured person: None for work-related injuries; 1% of earnings for nonwork-related injuries.

Self-employed person: Not applicable.

Employer: 1% of payroll for work-related injuries.

Government: None.

An earmarked tax of 0.05 tala per gallon on motor fuel finances benefits for victims of motor vehicle and boat accidents.

Qualifying Conditions

Work injury benefits: There is no minimum qualifying period.

Temporary Disability Benefits

70% of the insured's earnings is paid for up to 5 years after a 5-day waiting period; may be extended. The benefit is paid for a temporary disability resulting from a work-related or a nonwork-related injury (or from motor vehicle or boat accidents).

The maximum weekly benefit is 400 tala.

Permanent Disability Benefits

If the assessed degree of disability is at least 80%, the weekly benefit is equal to 70% of the insured's last earnings times the assessed degree of disability. The benefit is paid until rehabilitation or death.

The maximum weekly benefit is 400 tala.

Partial permanent disability: If the assessed degree of permanent disability is less than 80% and the injured person returns to work before the period of entitlement to temporary disability benefit ceases, a lump sum is paid according to the assessed degree of disability, up to a maximum of 8,000 tala.

Workers' Medical Benefits

Benefits include reasonable medical expenses; 15,000 tala is provided for artificial limbs or treatment abroad.

Survivor Benefits

Survivor grant: A lump sum of 20,000 tala is paid to dependents. For the death of a worker, a weekly payment of up to 200 tala is also paid for a maximum of 4 years.

Funeral grant: 2,000 tala is paid for a death caused by a work-related accident (or motor vehicle or boat accidents).

Administrative Organization

Labor Department provides general supervision.

Accident Compensation Corporation administers the program.

Yemen

Exchange rate: US$1.00 equals 196 rials.

Old Age, Disability, and Survivors

Regulatory Framework

First law: 1980.

Current law: 1991 (pensions), with 2000 amendment.

Type of program: Social insurance system.

Coverage

Public-sector system: Permanent employees of government agencies and all public-sector or quasi-public entities.

Special system for military and police personnel.

Private-sector system: Private-sector employees (nationals and foreigners), including Yemeni workers abroad.

Exclusions: Casual workers, agricultural workers, domestic workers, seamen, and fishermen.

Source of Funds

Public-sector system

Insured person: 6% of earnings.

The earnings used for contribution purposes include the basic salary plus all allowances paid to an employee but exclude bonuses and overtime wages.

Self-employed person: Not applicable.

Employer: 6% of payroll.

Government: None; contributes 6% of payroll as an employer.

Private-sector system

Insured person: 6% of earnings.

The earnings used for contribution purposes include the basic salary plus all allowances paid to an employee but exclude bonuses and overtime wages.

Self-employed person: Not applicable.

Employer: 9% of payroll for the old-age pension. (An additional contribution of 4% of payroll for the disability pension has yet to be implemented.)

Government: None.

Qualifying Conditions

Public-sector system

Old-age pension: Age 60 with at least 15 years of contributions (men) or age 55 with at least 10 years of contributions (women).

Early pension: Aged 50 to 59 (men) with more than 25 years of contributions or aged 46 to 54 (women) with 20 years of contributions; at any age with 30 years of contributions (men) or 25 years of contributions (women).

Early retirement is possible regardless of age (men and women) with 25 years of contributions if the insured becomes involuntarily unemployed.

Disability pension: Paid for a permanent total or partial disability.

Survivor pension: Paid for the death of an insured person before retirement.

Private-sector system

Old-age pension: Age 60 (men) or age 55 (women) with at least 15 years of contributions.

Early pension: Aged 50 to 59 (men) with more than 25 years of contributions or aged 46 to 54 (women) with 20 years of contributions; at any age with 30 years of contributions (men) or 25 years of contributions (women).

Reduced pension: Paid for retirement from normal employment at age 45 or age 50 with 20 years of contributions.

Disability pension: Paid for a permanent disability.

Disability grant: Ineligible for the nonwork-related or work-related disability pension but with at least a year of contributions.

Survivor pension: Paid for the death of an insured person before retirement.

Old-Age Benefits

Public-sector system

Old-age pension: The pension is equal to the insured's last gross monthly salary multiplied by the number of months of contributions, divided by 420.

The minimum monthly pension is 20,000 rials.

The maximum pension (100% of the insured's last gross monthly salary) is based on 35 years of contributions; 43% with 15 years.

Early pension: The pension is calculated in the same way as the old-age pension.

Benefit adjustment: Benefits are adjusted by 50% of the value of any salary increases paid to active civil servants.

Private-sector system

Old-age pension: The pension is equal to the insured's last gross monthly salary multiplied by the number of months of contributions, divided by 420.

The minimum pension is equal to 50% of the insured's last gross monthly salary.

Early pension: The pension is calculated in the same way as the old-age pension.

Reduced pension: If the insured retires from normal employment at age 45 with 20 years of contributions, the pension is reduced by 10%; at age 50 with 20 years of contributions, by 5%.

Benefit adjustment: Benefits are adjusted by 50% of the value of any salary increases paid to active civil servants.

Permanent Disability Benefits

Public-sector system

Work-related disability pension: The pension is equal to 100% of the insured's last gross monthly salary, plus a cash lump sum of 39,000 rials.

Permanent partial disability: A reduced pension and a reduced lump sum calculated in proportion to the assessed degree of disability are paid, according to the schedule in law.

Nonwork-related disability pension: For a total disability, the pension is equal to 50% of the insured's last gross monthly salary or the value of the old-age pension (but no less than the minimum pension), whichever is greater.

End-of-service payment: A lump sum is paid equal to 9% of the insured's last gross monthly salary times the number of months of contributions.

Benefit adjustment: Benefits are adjusted by 50% of the value of any salary increases paid to active civil servants.

Private-sector system

Work-related disability pension: For a total disability, the pension is equal to 100% of the covered monthly salary in the last year.

Nonwork-related disability pension: For a total disability, the pension is equal to 50% of the average monthly salary in the last year.

Disability grant: A lump sum is paid equal to 12% of the average monthly salary in the last year times the number of years of contributions.

Benefit adjustment: Benefits are adjusted by 50% of the value of any salary increases paid to active civil servants.

Survivor Benefits

Survivor pension (public- and private-sector systems): The pension is based on the deceased's entitlement to either the old-age or disability pension. The pension is split equally among named survivors.

Eligible survivors are the spouse(s), sons, daughters, parents, brothers, sisters, and dependent nephews and nieces.

Benefit adjustment: Benefits are adjusted by 50% of the value of any salary increases paid to active civil servants.

Administrative Organization

Public-sector system: Supervised by a board of directors, the General Authority for Insurances and Pensions administers the program.

Private-sector system: Supervised by a tripartite board of directors, the General Corporation for Social Security administers the program.

Sickness and Maternity

Regulatory Framework

A health insurance program for public-sector employees only.

Work Injury

Regulatory Framework

First and current law: 1991 (work injury).

Type of program: Social insurance system.

Coverage

Cash benefits: Permanent employees of government agencies and all public-sector or quasi-public entities; private-sector employees.

Medical benefits: Public-sector employees.

Source of Funds

Insured person: None.

Self-employed person: Not applicable.

Employer: 4% of total payroll (private-sector entities).

Government: None; contributes 1% of payroll as an employer (public-sector and quasi-public entities).

Qualifying Conditions

Work injury benefits: Permanent disability as a result of a work injury.

Temporary Disability Benefits

No benefits are provided.

Permanent Disability Benefits

Work-related disability benefits are provided under Old Age, Disability, and Survivors, above.

Workers' Medical Benefits

Medical benefits are provided only for public-sector employees under the health insurance program.

Survivor Benefits

Survivor pension: Survivor benefits are provided under Old Age, Disability, and Survivors, above.

Administrative Organization

Public-sector system: Supervised by a board of directors, the General Authority for Insurances and Pensions administers the program.

Private-sector system: Supervised by a tripartite board of directors, the General Corporation for Social Security administers the program.